Writing for Freedom

Studies in Contemporary Women's Writing

Series Editor

GILL RYE
Emerita Professor,
Centre for the Study of Contemporary Women's Writing,
Institute of Modern Languages Research, University of London

VOLUME 7

PETER LANG

Oxford • Bern • Berlin • Bruxelles • Frankfurt am Main • New York • Wien

Writing for Freedom

Body, Identity and Power
in Goliarda Sapienza's Narrative

Alberica Bazzoni

PETER LANG
Oxford • Bern • Berlin • Bruxelles • Frankfurt am Main • New York • Wien

Bibliographic information published by Die Deutsche Nationalbibliothek
Die Deutsche Nationalbibliothek lists this publication in the Deutsche
Nationalbibliografie; detailed bibliographic data is available on the Internet at
http://dnb.d-nb.de.

A catalogue record for this book is available from the British Library.

Library of Congress Cataloging-in-Publication Data

Names: Bazzoni, Alberica, 1986- author.
Title: Writing for freedom : body, identity and power in Goliarda Sapienza's
   narrative / Alberica Bazzoni.
Description: Oxford ; New York : Peter Lang, 2018. | Series: Studies in
   contemporary women's writing ; 7 | Includes bibliographical references
   and index.
Identifiers: LCCN 2017027724 | ISBN 9783034322423 (alk. paper)
Subjects: LCSH: Sapienza, Goliarda--Criticism and interpretation. | Identity
   (Psychology) in literature. | Power (Social sciences) in literature. |
   Women in literature.
Classification: LCC PQ4879.A675 Z54 2017 | DDC 853/.914--dc23 LC record
available at https://lccn.loc.gov/2017027724

Cover picture: 'Effe' © Eddi Milkovitsch.

Cover design by Peter Lang Ltd.

ISSN 2235-4123
ISBN 978-3-0343-2242-3 (print) • ISBN 978-1-78707-784-3 (ePDF)
ISBN 978-1-78707-785-0 (ePub) • ISBN 978-1-78707-786-7 (mobi)

© Peter Lang AG, International Academic Publishers, Bern 2018
Wabernstrasse 40, CH-3007 Bern, Switzerland
info@peterlang.com, www.peterlang.com, www.peterlang.net

This publication has been peer reviewed.

Printed in Germany

Contents

Acknowledgements

I am grateful to the Arts and Humanities Research Council, UK, and Oriel College, UK, which funded my doctoral studies at the University of Oxford. I also wish to thank the Isaiah Berlin Fund, the Christina Drake Fund, the Fiedler Memorial Fund and the Faculty of Medieval and Modern Languages, University of Oxford, for awarding me the Scholarships that enabled me to travel to Italy to carry out research interviews.

I give heartfelt thanks to Giuseppe Stellardi, for supporting me over the years with kindness, constancy and precision, stimulating discussions which helped me find the right direction for my research. I also wish to thank several people who contributed to this project: Sharon Wood and Emmanuela Tandello Cooper, who examined my PhD thesis and provided valuable advice as to how to structure this book; Michael Subialka, David Bowe, Riccardo Liberatore and Matthew Reza, whose thorough editing greatly improved the final shape of this book; Vilma de Gasperin, whose feedback and bibliographical suggestions had a substantial impact on my approach to Sapienza; Charlotte Ross, for her generous and detailed feedback on Chapter 3 on *Io, Jean Gabin*, which urged me to dig deeper into the theoretical aspects of the research; Katrin Wehling-Giorgi and Emma Bond, for the exciting collaboration on the conference *Goliarda Sapienza in Context* and the related volume; Giovanna Providenti, for providing me with relevant information about Sapienza, including a copy of the typescript of *Lettera aperta*; Ruth Glynn, Florian Mussgnug, Daniela La Penna and Ann Hallamore Caesar, for their interest in my project in its initial stages, which helped me believe I was going in the right direction; Angelo Pellegrino and Paola Pace, for welcoming me several times in their house in Rome, and for our precious conversations about Sapienza. Adele Cambria, who shared with me her memories of Sapienza, and allowed me to see her copy of the typescript of *Io, Jean Gabin*. Paola Blasi, who was so kind to talk to me about her life-long friendship with Sapienza. I also offer very sincere thanks to the editorial board of the 2015 Peter Lang

Young Scholars Competition in Women's Studies, for awarding me the prize that enabled me to publish this book; the two anonymous readers, who provided very helpful comments on the draft of the manuscript; and to Laurel Plapp at Peter Lang, who assisted me throughout the realization of this book project.

Lastly, my wholehearted gratitude goes to Tecla Castella, my family and my friends, without whose unfailing love and support this project would not have been possible.

Permission to quote from the translation Goliarda Sapienza, *The Art of Joy*, translated by Anne Milano Appel (2013), has been granted by Penguin and by Farrar, Straus & Giroux.

Angelo Pellegrino, for the Estate of Goliarda Sapienza through Piergiorgio Nicolazzini Literary Agency, has generously granted permission to quote from Goliarda Sapienza, *Lettera aperta* (1997), *Il filo di mezzogiorno* (2003), *L'arte della gioia* (2008), *L'università di Rebibbia* (2006), *Le certezze del dubbio* (2007) and *Io, Jean Gabin* (2010).

Earlier versions of parts of Chapters 1, 2 and 3, are published in the article 'The Performative Power of Narrative in Goliarda Sapienza's *Lettera aperta*, *L'arte della gioia* and *Io, Jean Gabin*', *Italian Studies*, 72, 1 (2017), 71–87.

Abbreviations

AG: *L'arte della gioia* (Turin: Einaudi, 2008)
AJ: *The Art of Joy*, trans. Anne Milano Appel (London: Penguin Books, 2013)
CD: *Le certezze del dubbio* (Milan: Rizzoli, 2007)
FM: *Il filo di mezzogiorno* (Milan: La Tartaruga, 2003)
JG: *Io, Jean Gabin* (Turin: Einaudi, 2010)
LA: *Lettera aperta* (Palermo: Sellerio, 1997)
UR: *L'università di Rebibbia* (Milan: Rizzoli, 2006)

Figure 1: Goliarda Sapienza with her mother, Maria Giudice, and her father, Peppino Sapienza. © Archivio Sapienza Pellegrino.

Figure 2: Goliarda Sapienza in the 1950s. © Archivio Sapienza Pellegrino.

Figure 3: Goliarda Sapienza in 1976. © Archivio Sapienza Pellegrino.

Introduction

Sapienza: Life and Works

After a long period in oblivion, Sicilian writer Goliarda Sapienza is rapidly coming to be regarded as a major figure in modern Italian literature. Her literary production is characterized by a subversive and eccentric attitude towards norms and institutions, together with an aspiration to achieve individual and social transformation, in which writing and literary communication are granted a fundamental role. This book explores the representation of freedom in Sapienza's narrative, by looking at the interplay between body, identity and power. The main aspects of this interplay taken into consideration here are gender, sexuality and political ideology.

Sapienza was born on 10 May 1924 in Catania, Sicily.[1] Her mother, Maria Giudice (1880–1953), originally from Lombardy, was one of the most prominent members of the Italian Socialist Party, as well as a feminist activist.[2] Giudice collaborated with national and international left-wing intellectuals, including such names as Antonio Gramsci, Umberto Terracini, Angelica Balabanoff and Lenin, and was on the front line fighting for women's and workers' rights both through demonstrations and journalism, activities for which she was repeatedly imprisoned. In 1919 Giudice moved to Sicily to help organize the local socialist divisions and trade unions. Her

---

1   See Giovanna Providenti, *La porta è aperta. Vita di Goliarda Sapienza* (Catania: Villaggio Maori Edizioni, 2010).

2   For a more detailed account of Maria Giudice's biography, see Providenti, *La porta è aperta*; Vittorio Poma, *Una maestra tra i socialisti. L'itinerario politico di Maria Giudice* (Milan and Bari: Cariplo-Laterza, 1991); Jole Calapso, *Una donna intransigente. Vita di Maria Giudice* (Palermo: Sellerio, 1996); and Umberto Santino, 'Maria Giudice', *Enciclopedia delle donne* <http://www.enciclopediadelledonne.it/biografie/maria-giudice/> [Accessed 6 September 2016].

former partner, Carlo Civardi, had died fighting as a soldier in World War I, leaving her with seven children. In Catania, she met Peppino Sapienza (1880–1949), a socialist comrade himself, who came from a working-class family but succeeded in becoming a lawyer.

Maria and Peppino started a new family. Goliarda was their only child, while many step-siblings from her parents' previous families lived in the same house in Via Pistone, Catania. During her childhood, she was surrounded by a nonconformist environment, characterized by loose boundaries between family and non-family members, a mix of different class backgrounds and an active political involvement, oriented towards feminism, anti-fascism and anti-clericalism. Since her father did not want her to be indoctrinated by fascist propaganda, at the age of fourteen he took her off formal schooling. She taught herself drama and piano, and at the age of sixteen she won a scholarship from the *Accademia d'arte drammatica* in Rome, where she moved with her mother. In 1943, after the armistice, she fought as a partisan with her father, who was involved in Pertini and Saragat's jailbreak. After the war, Sapienza went back to acting in theatres and started to work in the film industry. In 1947 she met Neorealist film director Francesco Maselli, who was her partner for twenty years and with whom she frequented Roman intellectual circles, comprising prominent figures such as Alberto Moravia, Pier Paolo Pasolini, Luchino Visconti, Attilio Bertolucci, Cesare Zavattini and Elsa Morante. In 1953, Maria Giudice died, after a long period of psychological decline. Her death coincided with Sapienza's first steps in writing, initially with a preference for poetry.[3]

In the late 1950s Sapienza started suffering from serious depression and, after a failed suicide attempt, was subjected to electroconvulsive therapy, which caused her to partially lose her memory. She recovered thanks to psychoanalytic therapy and through writing, publishing two semi-autobiographical novels: *Lettera aperta* [Open Letter], a journey into her childhood, and *Il filo di mezzogiorno* [Midday Thread], where she recounts her

---

3   On the night of Maria Giudice's death, Sapienza wrote the poem 'A mia madre' [To My Mother], now in *Ancestrale* [Ancestral] (Milan: La vita felice, 2013), 20–2.

own therapeutic experience.⁴ Sapienza then dedicated herself completely to writing, spending approximately ten years on her major novel, *L'arte della gioia* [*The Art of Joy*].⁵ She descended into poverty and spent a few days in prison after being convicted of theft. Her prison experience is recounted in *L'università di Rebibbia* [Rebibbia University], while in *Le certezze del dubbio* [The Certainties of Doubt] she tells the story of her transition from prison to freedom and her relationship with a woman she met in Rebibbia.⁶ In the last years of her life she taught acting at the *Centro Sperimentale di Cinematografia* in Rome and wrote more works, some of which were published posthumously. She died in Gaeta in August 1996.

Overall, Sapienza's narrative is closely informed by the experiences that characterized her life – her atypical upbringing, her early encounter with socialist and feminist political commitment, her work in theatre and cinema, depression, her experience with psychoanalysis, poverty and prison. From a position of marginality and eccentricity, Sapienza expresses a radical desire for freedom and for new, creative ways to conceive personal identity and human relationships, addressing a subversive criticism to the very core of Western thought and society, and representing an alternative and original voice in twentieth-century Italian literature.

During her life, Sapienza published four works: *Lettera aperta*; *Il filo di mezzogiorno*; *L'università di Rebibbia* and *Le certezze del dubbio*. To these should be added the publication in 1970 in *Nuovi Argomenti* of *Destino coatto* [Compulsory Destiny], a collection of short monologues

4   *Lettera aperta* [1967] (Palermo: Sellerio, 1997). The editing for the first edition by Garzanti was carried out by Enzo Siciliano. *Il filo di mezzogiorno* [1969] (Milan: La Tartaruga, 2003). *Lettera aperta* and *Il filo di mezzogiorno* were translated into French and published in a single volume: *Le fil d'une vie: Lettre ouverte, Le fil de midi*, trans. Nathalie Castagné (Paris: Viviane Hamy, 2008).
5   *L'arte della gioia* [1998] (Turin: Einaudi, 2008).
6   *L'università di Rebibbia* [1983] (Milan: Rizzoli, 2006). It was translated into French: *L'Université de Rebibbia*, trans. Nathalie Castagné (Paris: Attila-Le Tripode, 2013); *Le certezze del dubbio* [1987] (Milan: Rizzoli, 2007). It won the 'Premio Casalotti' in 1994.

recounting hallucinations and obsessions;[7] *Vengo da lontano* [I Come From Far Away], a short text on the theme of peace, published in 1991 in a collection of articles by a group of women writers on the occasion of the Gulf war;[8] and the first part of *L'arte della gioia*, in 1994.[9]

Sapienza's major novel, *L'arte della gioia*, written between 1967 and 1976, was rejected by several publishers in the course of over twenty years; it was published in full only after Sapienza's death in 1998, and its popular success came thanks to the French, German and Spanish editions.[10] This eventual success led to the Einaudi edition in 2008, which launched her work in Italy, and to the posthumous publication of a number of other works: a short semi-autobiographical novel, *Io, Jean Gabin* [I, Jean Gabin];[11] two collections of poems, *Ancestrale* [Ancestral] and *Siciliane* [Sicilian Poems] (the latter in Sicilian dialect);[12] two volumes of diaries;[13] a collection of plays and cinema subjects, *Tre pièces e soggetti cinematografici* [Three Plays and

7   'Destino coatto', in *Nuovi Argomenti*, 19 (July–September 1970); *Destino coatto* (Rome: Empiria, 2002).

8   'Vengo da lontano', in *Il cuore, la guerra e la parola* (Siracuse: Ombra editrice, 1991), 128–32.

9   *L'arte della gioia* (Rome: Stampa Alternativa, 1994). The 1994 partial edition corresponds to the section 'Parte prima' (5–126) in the 2008 Einaudi edition. According to Marcello Baraghini, director of Stampa Alternativa, the large success of the 1994 partial edition encouraged him to publish the whole work. In 1998, two years after Sapienza's death, Stampa Alternativa published the first complete edition of the novel, with the title *L'arte della gioia: romanzo anticlericale* (Rome: Stampa Alternativa, 1998). The subtitle *romanzo anticlericale* was chosen by Pellegrino jointly with the publisher (this information was provided to me in a private email exchange with Marcello Baraghini, 17 March 2014); it disappears in the 2003 reprint of the same edition, and in the 2008 Einaudi edition.

10   Further details of the history of publication of *L'arte della gioia* and its foreign editions are given in Chapter 2.

11   *Io, Jean Gabin* (Turin: Einaudi, 2010). It was translated into French: *Moi, Jean Gabin*, trans. Nathalie Castagné (Paris: Attila-Le Tripode, 2012).

12   *Siciliane* (Catania: Il Girasole Edizioni, 2012).

13   *Il vizio di parlare a me stessa. Taccuini 1976–1989* [The Bad Habit of Talking to Myself. Diaries 1976–1989] (Turin: Einaudi, 2011); *La mia parte di gioia. Taccuini 1989–1992* [My Part of Joy. Diaries 1989 – 1992] (Turin: Einaudi, 2013).

Film Synopses];[14] the short story *Elogio del bar* [In Praise of the Café];[15] and the novel *Appuntamento a Positano* [Meeting in Positano].[16] There is some uncertainty concerning the editing undergone by the posthumous works, since none of them contains a critical apparatus. In particular, the poems collected in *Ancestrale* and *Siciliane*, and the two volumes of diaries, lack information that would clarify the selection and editing criteria.[17] Only a careful investigation into the manuscripts will shed light on the editorial processes and choices involved in the publication of these works.[18]

Readership and Criticism

Since Sapienza's success is very recent and her work not yet established in the Italian literary canon, the choice to make this author the object of a monographic study already contains an implicit argument in favour of her relevance and significance. Two types of considerations support this choice. First, Sapienza is an author of substance, who deserves a place in the panorama of Italian and European literature, and through the exploration of her texts I endeavour to point out the elements of interest and originality that render them worthy of critical attention and appreciation. Second, after a long period of oblivion Sapienza's works, and especially *L'arte della gioia*, are now finding popular success and achieving critical

14 *Tre pièces e soggetti cinematografici* (Milan: La vita felice, 2014).
15 *Elogio del bar* (Rome: Elliot Edizioni, 2014).
16 *Appuntamento a Positano* (Turin: Einaudi, 2015).
17 Fabio Michieli raises some philological issues about *Ancestrale* in '"Ancestrale" di Goliarda Sapienza. Appunti di lettura, con una nota impropriamente filologica', *Poetarum Silva*, 7 November 2013 <http://poetarumsilva.com/2013/11/07/ancestrale-di-goliarda-sapienza-appunti-di-lettura-con-una-nota-impropriamente-filologica/> [Accessed 6 September 2016].
18 The archive of Sapienza's works is kept in Pellegrino's house in Rome. It has been made partially and intermittently available to individual researchers, but is currently closed to public consultation.

recognition, on a national as well as international level. Against the resistance of major publishers, the success of Sapienza's works has been enabled by readers and independent publishers, who allowed *L'arte della gioia* to circulate and find in France, Germany and Spain its way to a wider readership.[19] Since the Einaudi edition of *L'arte della gioia* in 2008, literary reviews, blogs, cultural events, readings and talks are multiplying in and outside of Italy. Moreover, Sapienza's life and works have become a source of inspiration to other artists, generating plays, performances, life writing and music.[20] Sapienza's success in finding this wider readership qualifies her work as half-way between experimentalism and legibility, as she blurs genre boundaries, intensely manipulates linguistic and narrative structures, and expresses radical social criticism, but nevertheless maintains an affable attitude towards her readers, who are invited to participate in her search for identity and freedom.[21] Whereas for a long time the ideal reader implicitly postulated by Sapienza's texts did not mesh well with her actual readers, contemporary readers seem to correspond to that ideal more fully, and they are thus more receptive to her works. If Sartre described the work of art as 'a spinning top which exists only in movement', implying that the text becomes communication only through a reader, Sapienza's texts, ignored for decades, are now undoubtedly spinning fast.[22]

Participating in the rising interest in Sapienza's works, in the past few years critics have begun to explore her texts. The core academic literature thus far comprises Sapienza's biography, *La porta è aperta*, by Giovanna Providenti; the critical introductions and afterwords that accompany

19   See Adele Cambria, 'Goliarda Sapienza e la terribile Arte della gioia', *L'Unità*, 26 September 2006.

20   For a list of artistic works inspired by Sapienza's life and writings, see the website 'Goliarda Sapienza in Context' <http://goliardasapienza2013.weebly.com/inspired-by.html> [Accessed 6 September 2016].

21   For an analysis of the relationship between experimentalism and readership in Italy, see Giovanna Rosa, *Il patto narrativo* (Milan: Il Saggiatore, 2008); Vittorio Spinazzola, 'Le articolazioni del pubblico', in Alberto Asor Rosa, ed., *Letteratura italiana del Novecento: bilancio di un secolo* (Turin: Einaudi, 2000), 180–202.

22   Jean-Paul Sartre, *What is Literature?*, trans. Bernard Frechtman (New York: Harper and Row, 1965), 34.

most editions of Sapienza's works; two essay collections in Italian, *Quel sogno d'essere*, edited by Providenti, and *Appassionata Sapienza*, edited by Monica Farnetti,[23] and one in English, *Goliarda Sapienza in Context*, edited by Emma Bond, Katrin Wehling-Giorgi and myself;[24] and a number of journal articles in Italian, English, Spanish and French. Among these, this study dialogues extensively with Charlotte Ross's articles, which are focused on the representation of gender and sexuality in Sapienza's narrative.[25] Furthermore, Sapienza's works are discussed alongside those of Elena Ferrante and Julie Otsuka in an edited volume on the notion of 'ambivalence' freshly published in Italian.[26] This critical bibliography is augmented by the growing number of literary reviews in several languages, which were boosted by the publication in the UK and the US of the English translation of *L'arte della gioia* in 2013.[27]

Critical work so far has endeavoured to reconstruct Sapienza's life and artistic activity and to identify the main themes and characteristics of her works. It has revealed the centrality of autobiography in her production, the relationship between selfhood and writing, her nonconformist representation of gender identity, motherhood and sexuality, her work's conflicted relationship with psychoanalysis and her original depiction of women's prison. In addition, the edited volumes *Goliarda Sapienza in Context* and

---

23 Monica Farnetti, ed., *Appassionata Sapienza* (Milan: La Tartaruga, 2012).

24 Alberica Bazzoni, Emma Bond and Katrin Wehling-Giorgi, eds, *Goliarda Sapienza in Context. Intertextual Relationships with Italian and European Culture* (Rutherford, NJ: Fairleigh Dickinson University Press, 2016). The volume comprises the proceedings of the conference *Goliarda Sapienza in Context*, which took place in London in 2013, and invited contributions.

25 Charlotte Ross, 'Identità di genere e sessualità nelle opere di Goliarda Sapienza: finzioni necessariamente *queer*', in Providenti, *Quel sogno d'essere*, 223–42; 'Goliarda Sapienza's Eccentric Interruptions: Multiple Selves, Gender Ambiguities and Disrupted Desires', in *altrelettere* (2012) <http://www.altrelettere.uzh.ch/article/view/al_uzh-2> [Accessed 19 July 2016].

26 Anna Maria Crispino and Marina Vitale, eds, *Dell'ambivalenza. Dinamiche della narrazione in Elena Ferrante, Julie Otsuka e Goliarda Sapienza* (Rome: Iacobelli, 2016).

27 *The Art of Joy*, trans. Anne Milano Appel (London: Penguin Books, 2013; New York: Farrar, Straus & Giroux, 2013).

Dell'ambivalenza begin to trace a map of intertextual relationships and affinities with Italian and international literature and thought. Sapienza studies are thus a new, fast-growing field, characterized by an initial effort to explore the author's work in several directions. Consequently, the body of research is still very fragmented, consisting of several survey-like critical interventions, and a few more detailed, specifically focused analyses, which nonetheless do not yet provide an organic picture of the whole.

This book is the first full-length monographic analysis of Sapienza's literary production and seeks to delineate its central poetics, which, I argue, has its pivotal tension in the ideal of freedom. Freedom is characterized as the firm opposition to any form of oppression, and as the possibility of accessing and enjoying bodily pleasures and empathetic relationships of care. Sapienza's works trace out a strenuous deconstruction of oppressive norms and structures, and they aim at retrieving a space of powerful bodily desire, which constitutes the foundation of the process of becoming a subject and an agent of social transformation. A distinctively original aspect of this research in this sense is the importance it attributes to the political dimension of Sapienza's works, in terms of their attention to ideology and literary engagement, and the close relationship they establish between the individual and political spheres. The processes of identity formation and the political domain are closely interconnected in Sapienza's works, and it is in the material presence of a body with desires that they find their main common ground.

Aims, Methodology and Theoretical Framework

This book comprises four chapters, each one developing a close textual analysis of one or more works: *Lettera aperta* and *Il filo di mezzogiorno* in Chapter 1; *L'arte della gioia* in Chapter 2; *Io, Jean Gabin* in Chapter 3; *L'università di Rebibbia* and *Le certezze del dubbio* in Chapter 4. Each chapter looks at the representation of identity formation and the characterization of freedom in the relevant work(s), progressing from the exploration of the internal composition of the self to the analysis of identity in its interpersonal and socio-political dimension. Moreover, each chapter includes the analysis of narrative structures and the narrating voice, investigating the central role of writing in the evolution of Sapienza's narrative. The separate analyses of individual works have been privileged over a thematic comparative approach in order to highlight the distinctiveness of each work and the evolving nature of her writing, avoiding the impression of Sapienza as an *auctor unius libri*. Since, with the exception of *L'arte della gioia*, Sapienza's works have not been translated into English, the extensive use of primary quotations, also provided in English translation, which serve primarily the purposes of close reading, will also enable non-Italian speakers to gain insight into Sapienza's production.

Sapienza's works first emerge as an effort to reconstruct her disrupted memory and identity, which dovetails with a criticism of social norms and oppressive power relationships. They can fruitfully be ascribed to the category of 'autofiction' – a combination and contamination of autobiography and fiction.[28] 'Autofiction' was used initially to designate the impossibility of truth and transparency of meaning in modern autobiographies; it is then used, especially in the Francophone context, to refer more broadly to autobiographical novels featuring an undecidable boundary between reality and fiction. Considerably ahead of their times, Sapienza's novels combine both meanings, as they explore the mechanisms of mediation, distortion and creation at work in autobiographical writing, and embrace a hybrid form of autobiography through which the author manipulates her own story. Chapter 1 analyses how the adult narrator of *Lettera aperta* and *Il filo di mezzogiorno* engages with the recollection of her childhood, her relationship with her extraordinary family and her troubled social integration, in order to retrieve a sense of self and the vitality with which she had progressively lost contact. Faced with the challenge of making sense

---

28   See Philippe Gasparini, 'Autofiction *vs* autobiographie', *Tangence*, 97 (2011), 11–24; Marie Darrieussecq, 'L'autofiction, un genre pas sérieux', *Poétique*, 107 (1996), 369–80. For a discussion of autofiction in the Italian context, see Carlo Mazza Galanti, 'Autofinzioni', *minima&moralia*, 8 July 2010 <http://www.minimaetmoralia.it/wp/autofinzioni/> [Accessed 28 March 2016].

of a series of contradictory models of gender, sexuality, class and political ideology, Goliarda, the child protagonist, struggles to orient herself
and master the position of radical diversity that is imposed on her. In the
midst of a whirl of incongruous messages, she becomes acutely aware of
the power underlying human relationships, where the need for love, also
expressed as the need to please others, gives rise to an excruciating conflict with her search for autonomy. In *Il filo di mezzogiorno*, the narrator
recounts her psychoanalytic therapy, internalizing but also negotiating
the therapist's interpretations of her past, especially as concerns gender
identity and sexuality. Through this double exploration of her childhood,
characterized by fragmentation, ellipses and analogical connections, the
narrator seeks to re-establish contact with her own living body as a source
of identity and agency.

Chapter 2 follows Modesta's long journey towards the realization of
a radical form of freedom, from the initial experience of sexual pleasure
to the exercise of violence and, finally, the acceptance of relationships of
dependence and care and of the impossibility of exerting full control. The
first part of the chapter explores the type of subject that, in *L'arte della gioia*,
takes on a struggle for freedom. It reflects on the centrality of the body
within the construction of the protagonist's self and her instrumental use
of rationality, which can be ascribed to Epicurean ethics. The novel features
the coexistence of different configurations of the self, which my analysis
relates to different positionalities with respect to power. Specifically, the
adoption of a strong and oppositional attitude is rendered necessary in
order for a subaltern subject to reject oppression, but the protagonist's
ultimate aim is to escape the replication of a binary logic of domination
and to enjoy a weak and fluid identity, centred on the pleasure of the senses,
queer desires and empathetic relationships of care. From a political perspective, *L'arte della gioia* continues and expands the deconstructive stance
put forward in the autobiographical works. It addresses several centres of
power and domination, among which Sapienza includes the PCI's agenda
and its militants' attitudes, and realizes a form of veritably anarchist literary engagement. This political stance entrusts the novel with the task of
promoting a yearning for freedom among the readers.

Io, Jean Gabin, analysed in Chapter 3, reconnects to *Lettera aperta* and *Il filo di mezzogiorno* as it focuses again on Sapienza's autobiographical recollection of her childhood, although this is intensely contaminated with fiction. This work, characterized by an ironic and light tone, plays with the protagonists' identification with the French actor Jean Gabin, who is assumed to be a model of a male identity, in contrast to women's submission, an anarchist hero, distinguished from mass conformism, and an example of how dream and imagination are situated against the constraints of reality and ideology. The child protagonist's and adult narrator's search for identity reaches fruition here in the position of an anarchist artist. The shortest and lightest narrative amongst Sapienza's works here considered, *Io, Jean Gabin* is possibly also the most ambiguous, for it plays with the protagonist's staged identities, at the same time pointing to the existence of a more authentic dimension of the self and interpersonal relationships, rooted in the body and empathetic communication. Similarly, the book exhibits a detachment from the core troubles of the narrator's past, whilst the protagonist's blithe and joyful attitude is openly fictional. The ambiguity of the text reflects the double position of the narrator: thanks to her endeavour to reconstruct herself, she has liberated herself from an oppressive past, but her narrative nonetheless does not have the power to change the reality of that past. Likewise, she lacks the power to change the material conditions that led the child protagonist of *Io, Jean Gabin* to adopt a male identity in order to escape the limitations of women's condition.

Chapter 4 examines Sapienza's 'prison diptych', formed by *L'università di Rebibbia* and *Le certezze del dubbio*. These works conclude Sapienza's autofictional journey, shifting the narrative focus from the recollection of childhood to the narrator's present, and from the investigation of the self to the portrait of a marginal reality. Prison is here an ambivalent space, which induces regression and degradation but also fosters empathetic relationships of care. In *Le certezze del dubbio*, Sapienza narrates her 'queer' relationship of friendship, love and care with the young terrorist Roberta. This unfolds against the backdrop of urban degradation and alienation in the Rome of the 1980s. After her long journey of self-reconstruction and identity formation, Sapienza represents herself as an anarchist artist who has chosen the margins of society as her elective space and who attributes to writing a fundamental role of care and social transformation.

Overall, this book postulates an evolution, from a performative and deeply unstable narrating 'I', prevailing in *Lettera aperta* and *Il filo di mezzogiorno*, to a reinforced narrating voice, which achieves a certain degree of detachment from her past, in *Io, Jean Gabin*, and opens to the representation of contemporary reality in *L'università di Rebibbia* and *Le certezze del dubbio*. The structure of the texts changes accordingly, from the loose assemblage of episodes and thoughts characterizing *Lettera aperta*, to the – minimal – plot developed in *Io, Jean Gabin* and then the linear narrative of the prison novels, passing through the fictional representation of a present *in fieri* and the plot without teleology of *L'arte della goia*. This corpus was selected from among Sapienza's works because each text here engages with the process of identity formation and the criticism of social norms, and because they are all narrative texts. Despite the differences in length and genre – *L'arte della gioia* is a long fictional novel, whilst the others are all short, semi-autobiographical works – and each work having its own distinctive features, themes and style, they form a rather compact group, which traces a clear development. The novel *Appuntamento a Positano*, written in 1984 straight after *Le certezze del dubbio*,[29] shares with the works here selected the narrative form and the autofictional genre, as well as specific themes and patterns such as female friendship, suicide, and the dialogic structure. However, its first-person tale of an aristocratic woman's life, for which Sapienza's narrating 'I' is little more than a sympathetic recipient, does not add significant elements to the investigation of this author's narrative journey towards freedom.

The aims of this study can be summarized as follows: first, it argues in favour of the significance and originality of Sapienza's works; second, it proposes the theme of freedom as an interpretative key, using that key to articulate the first full-length investigation of her narrative; third, it defines her works as being Epicurean and anarchist – two characteristics that place them at the intersection of psychoanalytic, post-structuralist and

---

29   See Angelo Pellegrino, 'I luoghi, la felicità, i personaggi', in Sapienza, *Appuntamento a Positano*, 177–81, 180.

Marxist-feminist discourses. While Sapienza's writing displays an eccentric and subversive attitude, it also gives voice to a yearning for becoming a subject and retrieving a space for personal agency, ultimately aspiring to individual and collective transformation. Finally, although an extensive intertextual analysis of Sapienza's works is beyond the scope of this book, it suggests similarities and points of contact with other Italian and international writers and thinkers, thus opening a number of comparative perspectives. Overall, it points out an affinity between Sapienza and the literary legacy of Luigi Pirandello and Italo Svevo, as well as specific tenets of postmodern fiction, but also a significant difference, concerning the struggle to acquire agency and subjectivity, which is extraneous to the trajectory of the modern and postmodern subject

In analysing the interplay between body, identity and power as the main grounds or territories where Sapienza's representation of a search for freedom takes place, this study adopts a composite theoretical frame. A plurality of approaches is necessary in order to account for the coexistence of different perspectives and tensions in Sapienza's works. Overall, my methodological approach tends to evidence how her narrative is influenced by and dialogues with a series of cultural, political, philosophical and artistic perspectives. In addition, I employ theoretical notions, such as Rosi Braidotti's concept of 'nomadic subjectivity,'[30] which are not part of Sapienza's own cultural background but prove useful to illuminate certain aspects of her works, especially those which anticipate questions and approaches that were developed by other thinkers only later. In particular, her narrative combines the theoretical anti-metaphysical and anti-logocentric perspective of post-structuralism, deconstruction and queer theory, with the ethical and political struggle for freedom and social transformation proper to Marxism and first- and second-wave feminism.

The specific challenge of this critical operation, which is also its distinctive value, consists in keeping together the analysis of different levels implicated in the world represented by Sapienza, from the articulation of body and identity to interpersonal relationships and the properly political

30   Rosi Braidotti, *Nuovi soggetti nomadi* (Rome: Luca Sossella editore, 2002).

dimension of the texts, and the analysis of different aspects of this world, namely gender, sexuality, class and ideology. The key interpretative focus on the notion of freedom links these different levels and aspects, providing structure and cohesiveness to the analysis. While each chapter sets out its specific theoretical frame, here I introduce the key notions informing this work as a whole. In particular, I focus on the elements highlighted in the title: the body, identity and power.

In Sapienza's works, the body represents a source of primary, vital impulses with which the self can only re-establish contact after overcoming layers of oppression. A perspective of this sort is productively established by means of Donald Winnicott's psychoanalytic approach, which focuses on reconnecting with a living and perceptive body.[31] The body is also the onto-logical dimension of the self, a being that precedes qualification, a perceiving and perceived unit in action, which recalls Edmund Husserl's phenomeno-logical perspective as well as Adriana Cavarero's reflections on the subject, in continuity with Hannah Arendt's existentialism.[32] It is the material condition of existence, particular and contingent, expelled by Cartesian rationality. The body is, finally, a sexed body, on which patriarchal norms exert control and violence, forcing it into the limits of the reproductive function and

---

31   I refer in particular to the notion of the True and False Self developed in: Donald W. Winnicott, *Collected Papers: Through Paediatrics to Psychoanalysis* (New York: Basic Books, 1958); *The Maturational Processes and the Facilitating Environment* (London: Hogarth Press and the Institute of Psychoanalysis, 1965).

32   On phenomenology, I refer in particular to: Rocco Donnicci, *Intenzioni d'amore, di scienza e d'anarchia. L'idea husserliana di filosofia e le sue implicazioni etico-politiche* (Naples: Bibliopolis, 1996); Jean-Claude Coquet, *Le istanze enuncianti. Fenomenologia e semiotica*, ed. Paolo Fabbri, trans. Elena Nicolini (Milan: Bruno Mondadori, 2008); Elio Franzini, *L'altra ragione. Sensibilità, immaginazione e forma artistica* (Milan: Il castoro, 2007); Hannah Arendt, *The Human Condition* (London: The University of Chicago Press, 1958). Within Adriana Cavarero's vast philosophical production, I refer to: *Tu che mi guardi, tu che mi racconti* (Milan: Feltrinelli, 1997) and *A più voci. Filosofia dell'espressione vocale* (Milan: Feltrinelli, 2003). Cavarero's works have been translated into English; see: *Relating Narratives: Storytelling and Selfhood*, trans. Paul A. Kottman (Stanford, CA: Stanford University Press, 2000) and *For More Than One Voice: Toward a Philosophy of Vocal Expression*, trans. Paul A. Kottman (Stanford, CA: Stanford University Press, 2005).

denying it the right to agency and sexual pleasure. Maria Giudice's Marxist-feminist teachings play a fundamental role in these novels as to this aspect, for Sapienza's reflection on the sexed body is never separated from a consideration of women as a social category, immersed in material conditions of exploitation and domination. Her narrative thus seeks to re-establish contact with a living body full of desires, seen as the primary site for the exercise of individual agency and a source of pleasures to be pursued.

The corporeal dimension of the self is not a self-contained and stable unity, but is rather always in interaction with the world, so that identity is defined in a situation of constant negotiation with social norms and human relationships. Sapienza's texts provide an insightful and articulated portrayal of the ways in which power intervenes in the process of identity formation, especially during childhood. First, she represents power in the form of explicitly oppressive social structures, institutions and legal systems, such as those of fascism and the Catholic Church, but also of patriarchy and heteronormativity. Marxist and feminist strands of thought play a central role in Sapienza's outlook and, accordingly, in my analysis. Her radical antagonism towards any hierarchy and her suspicion of all ideologies, including Marxism itself, is joined to a tradition of anarchist thought and political action. In addition to the political thinkers that directly influenced her world view, such as Michail Bakunin and Errico Malatesta, my analysis also employs Husserl's theory of anarchism, for it has important points of contact with Sapienza's narrative.

Second, through cultural stereotypes and social expectations, power becomes internalized and the struggle against it is brought inside the subject. Social norms and institutions exert a shaping force on individuals, conditioning and constraining their desires. This is the aspect of Sapienza's works that brings them closer to Freudian psychoanalysis, deconstruction and post-structuralism, and especially to Michel Foucault's reflections on the subject as always and unavoidably inhabited by power and Judith Butler's work on the construction of gender and sexual identities.[33] From

---

33   Michel Foucault, *The Will to Knowledge. Volume 1, The History of Sexuality*, trans. Robert Hurley (Harmondsworth: Penguin, 1990); Judith Butler, *Gender Trouble: Feminism and the Subversion of Identity* (London: Routledge, 1990).

the outset in *Lettera aperta*, identity is, in Sapienza's representation, socially constructed and internally divided. In this respect, she continues the line of modernist writers inaugurated – in the Italian context – by Pirandello and Svevo. As Pierpaolo Antonello and Giuseppe Fornari write, 'Heroes in modern novels constantly experience the "falseness" of their own desires, that is, the relational and "intersubjective" nature of their system of drives, the constant mediation of their "identity" and their desires'.[34] However, Sapienza also values a form of constant self-scrutiny that aims at distinguishing between different layers of desires, identifying those which are more heavily conditioned by socially oppressive power, and those which conversely come together with a liberating potential that qualifies them as being, if not 'authentic', at least 'less inauthentic'. In other words, she introduces a gradation in the constructiveness of desires, and bestows upon reason and self-knowledge an important role in re-establishing contact with more authentic parts of the self, which are located in bodily desires and pleasures. In this respect, her narrative closely recalls Epicurean philosophy, with its emphasis on knowing and understanding desires.[35]

Finally, Sapienza gives much attention – and it is a fairly original and anticipatory aspect of her works – to the power involved in the relationship between adults and children, which provides the pattern for power in the form of emotional dependence. In line with Winnicott's psychoanalytic approach, with which she possibly came into contact through her own therapy, Sapienza represents the effects of emotional neglect on a child's development of a sense of self. Power imbalances in human relationships are represented as having serious distortive and oppressive effects, which the narrator tries to undo and resist. Moreover, she does not reject the element of dependence involved in human relationships; instead, she first seeks to construct a sense of self that would not be crushed by those relationships.

---

34   Pierpaolo Antonello and Giuseppe Fornari, *Identità e desiderio. La teoria mimetica e la letteratura italiana* (Massa Carrara: Transeuropa, 2009), ix. Translation into English is mine, as always unless otherwise indicated.

35   See Epicuro, *Lettera sulla felicità* (Rome: Stampa Alternativa, 1990). It is worth pointing out that Epicurus' *Lettera sulla felicità* was translated into Italian by Sapienza's husband, Angelo Pellegrino.

In this way, she becomes capable of embracing dependence as a form of care rather than oppression.

Throughout her narrative, Sapienza seeks to deconstruct and oppose the conditions that affected her identity formation, at the same time proposing, in the centrality of bodily desire and anarchist relationships of care, possible ways to escape the limits of both the fragmented and the unitary subject. The body interacts with power but does not totally coincide with it, and it is connected to agency in a way that distinguishes Sapienza's narrative from post-structuralism. Whereas for example for Butler 'the body is not a "being", but a variable boundary, a surface whose permeability is politically regulated, a signifying practice within a cultural field',[36] Sapienza takes an approach more in line with thinkers such as Luisa Muraro, Adriana Cavarero, Rosi Braidotti and Stefano Ciccone.[37] Like them, she puts the materiality of personal and collective experience at the centre of her search for freedom. This form of experience is understood in its constructed historical features, but in her work it is nevertheless not dissolved through an unlimited theoretical deconstruction. In Muraro's words,

> the practice of starting from myself questions the subject without undoing it in a myriad of uncoordinated instances; it frees me from the relationships that make me what I am and makes me become what I want to be, while I can never claim the centre of this being and becoming. This is the narrow door, the step that marks my distance from postmodern thought.[38]

As Ciccone notes, desires are not superimposed by power onto subjects, but rather 'are founded on the conflicting relationship with corporeal experience'.[39] The body represents the 'point of connection of the physical,

---

36   Butler, *Gender Trouble*, 177.
37   Stefano Ciccone, *Essere maschi. Tra potere e libertà* (Turin: Rosenberg&Sellier, 2009). See also: Adriana Cavarero and Franco Reistano, *Le filosofie femministe* (Milan: Bruno Mondadori, 2002) and Paola Bono and Sandra Kemp, *Italian Feminist Thought: A Reader* (Oxford: Basil Blackwell, 1991).
38   Luisa Muraro, 'Il pensiero dell'esperienza', in *Per amore del mondo*, 2006 <http://www.diotimafilosofe.it/riv_wo.php?id=13> [Accessed 6 September 2016].
39   Ciccone, *Essere maschi*, 73.

the symbolic and the sociological',[40] which makes identity dynamic, at the same time anchoring its centrifugal fragmentation to a specific, irreducible individual position.

Sapienza, anticipating Luce Irigaray's point on women's need to become subjects, exposes the trajectory of the modern representation of identity as the product of a universalized male subject. Subjects in a subaltern position, historically devoid of autonomous identity, look at this trajectory from a rather different perspective.[41] The representation of identity, Sapienza's narrative shows, cannot be separated from the socio-historical position occupied by a subject. Through the representation of female characters who struggle to reconstruct their own identity, radically criticize any normative structure and look for personal freedom beyond and before power, Sapienza provides a compelling literary example of women's position with respect to the disruption of identity brought about by modernity and described by post-structuralism. She tells the story of a subject who fights to access a locus of agency in order to affirm the opening up of the self to multiplicity and weakness. In doing so, she recuperates the emancipatory aspirations of both the Enlightenment and Marxism, but she does so aiming at the creation of a new subject – one that is Epicurean and anarchist, embodied and relational. This is the meaning of the book's title, with its reference to the interplay between body, identity and power, as well as to the act of writing as informed by a yearning for freedom. The act of narrating is entrusted with a fundamental function, consisting in the possibility for the narrator to create her own story and transform the past, which has ended and involved great suffering, into a chosen, active, and joyful space for action.

40   Braidotti, *Nuovi soggetti nomadi*, 12.
41   See Luce Irigaray, *Speculum of the Other Woman*, trans. Gillian Gill (Ithaca, NY: Cornwell University Press, 1985); *This Sex Which is Not One*, trans. Catherine Porter (Ithaca, NY: Cornwell University Press, 1985).

Outside the Norm: The Re-construction of Identity in *Lettera aperta* and *Il filo di mezzogiorno*

Introduction

Lettera aperta, published by Garzanti in 1967, is Sapienza's first literary work. As the title suggests, it is addressed to an interlocutor, the reader, which is sometimes referred to in the singular and other times in the plural. Narrated in the first person, it recounts the story of a double formation, of a young girl in Sicily and a mature woman in her forties in Rome. The focus on the narrator's childhood alternates with the representation of her present, which is characterized by her struggle to survive by recollecting and reinterpreting her past, after her memory was ripped apart by electroconvulsive therapy. Episodes and figures from the narrator's childhood, with some additional minor scenes belonging to other significant periods of her life, compose a multifaceted and fragmented portrait of a young girl's troubled upbringing, and of an adult woman's endeavour to free herself from the weight of an oppressive past.

The double focus on the present and the past dovetails with an oscillation between the perspective of the adult narrator and that of the child protagonist. This manifold relationship entwining different narrative focuses and points of view shapes the text giving rise to a vertiginous manipulation of time, space and narrative identities, which are often impossible to untangle. Furthermore, the complexity of the text is enhanced by the simulation of the reconstructive work of an unstable and incomplete memory, so that the narration proceeds by fragments, analogical links, gaps and densely metaphorical passages, reproducing the struggle of a disrupted self.

The adult narrator presents herself as a woman experiencing serious existential difficulties, which have led her to two failed suicide attempts. Addressing the readers, she states in the opening lines of *Lettera aperta*:

> Non è per importunarvi con una nuova storia né per fare esercizio di calligrafia [...] che mi decido a parlarvi di quello che non avendo capito mi pesa da quarant'anni sulle spalle. Voi penserete: perché non se la sbroglia da sé? Infatti ho cercato, molto. Ma, visto che questa ricerca solitaria mi portava alla morte – sono stata due volte per morire 'di mia propria mano', come si dice – ho pensato che sfogarsi con qualcuno sarebbe stato meglio, se non per gli altri almeno per me. (LA 15)

> [It's not to bother you with a new story, nor to do a handwriting exercise [...] that I'm resolving to talk to you about that which I didn't understand and has been weighing on my shoulders for the past forty years. You'll probably think: why doesn't she sort it out herself? I tried, hard. But since this solitary search kept leading me to the point of death – twice I nearly 'died by my own hand', as they say – I thought that unburdening myself with someone would be better, if not for the others, at least for me.]

Lettera aperta is closely interlaced with the author's own life. From Sapienza's biography we know that in 1962 she was hospitalized in a psychiatric clinic after an overdose of sleeping pills and subjected to electroconvulsive therapy, which severely damaged her memory.[1] She spent the following four years trying to piece together her memories, at the same time struggling with depression and alcohol abuse, which led her to a second suicide attempt in 1964. During this period (1963–1965), she underwent an experimental psychoanalytic therapy with Dr Ignazio Majore, 'a wild therapy'[2] that bordered on an amorous relationship and that was closely followed by Majore's dramatic personal and professional crisis.[3]

---

1   See Providenti, *La porta è aperta*, 151.
2   Angelo Pellegrino, 'Un'analisi selvaggia', in FM 5–12.
3   On the relationship between Sapienza and Majore, central to FM, see Providenti, *La porta è aperta*, 156: 'Their relationship ended abruptly. Later, finding the whole thing funny, Goliarda would tell her friends that she drove her therapist crazy. What happened is that, in coincidence with (or because of) his relationship with Goliarda, Ignazio Majore went through a serious personal and professional crisis and quit his job and ended all therapeutic relationships'. Majore's account of those events can be found on his own website: 'In 1965, following theoretical and practical disagreement, he quit

Therapy helped her recover her memory and begin a process of deconstruction of the conditions that oppressed and devitalized her as she was growing up, but it did not completely cure her. Moreover, it burdened her with a new form of oppression, since the set of interpretations provided by the therapist are described by Sapienza as another strict and constraining pattern. *Lettera aperta* and *Il filo di mezzogiorno* were written during the period that followed those troubled events and both engage with the author's self-reconstruction by revisiting and reinterpreting her past. *Lettera aperta* ends on the narrator's demand to be left at liberty to enjoy her own body, newly reconquered thanks to writing: 'Vi lascio per un po': con questo poco di ordine che sono riuscita a fare intorno a me. Vorrei tacere per qualche tempo, e andarmene a giocare con la terra e con il mio corpo. Arrivederci' [I'll leave you for a while, with this little bit of order I've managed to create around me. I would like to stay silent for some time, and get out of here to play with the earth and my own body. Goodbye] (LA 159). Yet, in *Il filo di mezzogiorno* Sapienza feels the need to continue the exploration of her past to include an 'analysis of the analysis', recounting the therapeutic process by problematizing and challenging some of its aspects and tenets. In the concluding pages of the work, she refers explicitly to *Lettera aperta* and to the necessity of going beyond psychoanalysis:

> ... poi imbucai quella lettera che vi avevo scritto e fui convinta di avere ritrovato il mio corpo e il mio passato ... e andai al mare ... ma il mare era troppo freddo e salato per il mio corpo senza pelle. [...] No, non potevo giocare col mare né col mio corpo. [...] Quel medico, nello smontarmi pezzo per pezzo, aveva portato alla luce vecchie piaghe cicatrizzate da compensi, come lui avrebbe detto e le aveva riaperte frugandoci dentro con bisturi e pinze e che non aveva saputo guarire. (FM 178)

> [... then I sent that letter I had written to you and thought I had found my body and my past again ... and I went to the sea ... but the water was too cold and salty for my skinless body. [...] No, I couldn't play with the sea, nor with my body. [...] In dismantling me piece by piece, that doctor had exposed all the sores healed by compensation, as he would say, and rummaging with scalpel and pliers he reopened them, and didn't know how to heal them.]

---

his position as Associate Member and Teaching Psychoanalyst of the PSI' <http://www.psychomedia.it/neuro-snp/08-09/maiore.htm> [Accessed 6 September 2016].

Sapienza's relationship with psychoanalysis, specifically with a Freudian approach, which she appears to know well, would merit specific investigation.[4] In the course of this discussion, I will point out some aspects of this relationship, especially when conflicts or discordant interpretations emerge, and place it in the context of Sapienza's representation of her identity formation and search for freedom.

This chapter analyses the representation of the child protagonist's identity formation in *Lettera aperta* with some reference to *Il filo di mezzogiorno*, where connections appear between the two texts. It accounts for the forms in which power affects the child's formative path, such as the patriarchal and heteronormative structure of society, emotional neglect, ideological intransigence and discordant ethical models, which result in the protagonist's isolation and disorientation. The adult narrator seeks to undo these forms of oppression and retrieve or reconstruct contact with her own body, which is a source of desires and vitality. The first part of the chapter explores the representation of the interaction between the child's formative path and power as concerns gender and sexuality, in dialogue with Ross's rich analysis of this topic. Sapienza's frank exploration of sexuality includes a discussion of homosexuality, incest and sexual abuse of minors by adults as aspects of sexuality that were experienced personally by Goliarda or observed in her surrounding environment. The second part looks at power in the form of educational inconsistency and ideological

4   Sapienza also discusses Freud's theories in AG 350 and CD 61. Some critics have begun to explore this important aspect of Sapienza's work. See Emma Bond, 'Zeno's Unstable Legacy: Case-Writing and the Logic of Transference in Giuseppe Berto and Goliarda Sapienza', in Giuseppe Stellardi and Emmanuela Tandello Cooper, eds, *Italo Svevo and his Legacy for the Third Millenium: Contexts and Influences* (Leicester: Troubador Publishing Ltd, 2014), 101–13; Manuela Fraire, '*Il filo di mezzogiorno*. Goliarda paziente', in Farnetti, *Appassionata Sapienza*, 127–31; Maria Arena, '*Il filo di mezzogiorno*. Morte e rinascita attraverso la scrittura', in Providenti, *Quel sogno d'essere*, 149–56; Maria Teresa Maenza, 'Fuori dall'ordine simbolico della madre: Goliarda Sapienza e Luce Irigaray', in Providenti, *Quel sogno d'essere*, 243–60; Katrin Wehling-Giorgi, '"Ero separata da me": Memory, Selfhood and Mother-Tongue in Goliarda Sapienza and Elena Ferrante', in Bazzoni, Bond and Wehling-Giorgi, *Goliarda Sapienza in Context*, 215–29.

intransigence, which seal Goliarda's failed integration into her social context, and discusses the role of emotional neglect and its distorting effects on
desire.[5] Winnicott's notions of True and False Self, further developed by
Alice Miller, provide useful theoretical tools for understanding the mechanism of oppression deriving from emotional dependence and educational
inconsistencies.[6] Winnicott's and Miller's psychoanalytic approach, with
its emphasis on the body as a source of vitality and desire, also guides my
definition of what type of authenticity and freedom the narrator is looking for, beyond and before oppressive power. The last section approaches
the question of the interaction between the body, identity and power by
looking at the role played by narration in the narrator's re-construction of
her identity and in her attempt to bring the present and presence of the
body as an active force into the text. It examines the presence of a twofold narrating voice, the adult's and the child's, employing Mark Turner's
notion of 'blended space' to describe their often inextricable interaction.
The adult's perspective is itself in formation, and its relationship with the
story being narrated changes throughout the text, for the act of narrating
allows the narrator to reject normative identities and retrieve a space of
instinctual vitality.

Gender and Sexuality

The Mother's Feminist Model: Maria Giudice vs 'le donnette'

In *Lettera aperta* and *Il filo di mezzogiorno*, Sapienza narrates her process
of identity formation as a child. Within this process, questions related to
gender and sexuality occupy a prominent position, as the girl is exposed

---

5   For clarity, the name Goliarda will only be used to designate the child protagonist,
    never the adult narrator.
6   Alice Miller, *The Drama of Being a Child: The Search for the True Self* (London:
    Virago, 1985).

to, and negotiates, contradictory models of gender identity and sexual norms. Ross rightly points out that Goliarda's formation is influenced by dominant norms of gender and sexuality, but also by her mother's more progressive model.[7] In fact, Maria Giudice is the central female model for the young girl.[8] In *Lettera aperta*, set in a period – the early 1930s – when fascist power was well established and 'sembrò non dovesse cascare più' [looked like it would never fall] (LA 143), Maria has ceased any political activism. The only references to her previous political engagement in *Lettera aperta* are in her being defined as a 'sindacalista' [trade unionist] (31), and in a short anecdote, told to Goliarda by her uncle Nunzio, about a fascist attack against the office of the magazine that Maria and Peppino used to co-edit.[9] This information refers to the past, whereas, at the time when Goliarda is a child, Maria is a white-haired woman who spends her time in her room, studying, suffering from insomnia and headaches and waiting for fascism to fall.[10]

At bedtime, Maria tells Goliarda stories about the fight for social equality and about historical personalities such as Christopher Columbus, Galileo Galilei and Musolino the bandit, which trigger the child's dream to emulate them. However, the little girl's aspirations are immediately confronted with the gender difference that stands between her and her heroes:

> Anch'io dovevo diventare come loro. Ma cosa può diventare una donna? Tutte le donne che passavano per casa erano mogli di carcerati e cameriere: solo lei, mia madre, studiava, e allora dovevo studiare anch'io per diventare come lei, coi capelli bianchi e la voce forte quando discuteva con Ivanoe, con mio padre, con il professore Jsaya, con l'avvocato Castiglione. (LA 42)

7   See Ross, 'Identità di genere e sessualità', 227.
8   The mother-daughter relationship will become a central topic in several works by women writers especially since the 1980s; see, for example, Adalgisa Giorgio, ed., *Writing Mothers and Daughters* (New York and Oxford: Berghahn Books, 2002) and Patrizia Sambuco, *Corporeal Bonds: The Daughter-Mother Relationship in Twentieth Century Italian Women's Writing* (Toronto: University of Toronto Press, 2012).
9   See LA 143.
10   See LA 42, 145, 155.

[I, too, had to become like them. But what can a woman become? All the women who came into our house were prisoners' wives or maids. Only my mother studied, so I had to study too in order to become like her, with white hair and a strong voice when she conversed with Ivanoe, with my dad, with Professor Jsaya, with the lawyer Castiglione.]

Ho paura. Non è per me questo mestiere. 'Una femmina non può essere brigante'. No? Peccato. (LA 44)[11]

[I'm scared. This is not the job for me. 'A woman can't be a bandit'. No? What a pity.]

Through these stories, Maria teaches Goliarda to aspire to personal independence, a model that the child can see in practice only in her mother. Maria appears to be the only woman in possession of the means necessary to become like Columbus and Galileo, namely intelligence and education, thanks to which she gains men's respect and talks on a par with them. Moreover, Maria has also preserved her independence by rejecting the bond of marriage. Ross comments that Goliarda's 'distance from the normative models of gender derives from her desire to be the protagonist of her life, a desire that is encouraged by her mother's feminism.'[12] Maria's example instils in the little girl the aspiration to become strong and independent like her mother, thus marking the initiation of a troubled *dover essere* [duty to be], in contrast to social norms and in fulfilment of her mother's example. Goliarda prepares for this task through methodical training: 'Ma per farcela dovevo spiare (ed infatti spiavo) tutto quello che diceva agli altri, ed a mio padre specialmente. In un certo modo, ripensandoci, studiavo, mi preparavo a quel compito attraente e pauroso' [In order to succeed, I had to spy on (and indeed I did spy on) everything she said to others, especially to my father. In a way, now that I think about it, I was studying, I was preparing for that exciting and scary task] (LA 41).

11   Maria Rosa Cutrufelli takes a different line and chooses a female bandit as the protagonist of her Sicilian novel *La briganta* (1990); figures of female bandits are represented also, for example, in Carlo Levi, *Cristo si è fermato a Eboli* (1947), and, earlier, in Giovanni Verga's 'L'amante di Gramigna', in *Vita dei campi* (1880).
12   Ross, 'Identità di genere e sessualità', 227.

Goliarda also has three much older sisters, Olga, Licia and Musetta.[13] Licia studies at university, a choice that introduces a distance between the Sapienzas and their social context: 'Come seppi dopo, casa nostra era considerata un posto di perdizione: "Le donne studiano, e in scuole pubbliche, anche!"' [As I learnt later, our home was considered a place of perdition: 'Women study, and even in state schools!'] (LA 62). Although Goliarda calls one of her imaginary children 'Licia', she repeatedly marks a distance from her sister Licia and rather identifies with the other imaginary child of hers, called Goliardo.[14] About Musetta, Sapienza says that she was a 'donna autonoma e "di una disinvoltura più americana di quella americana"' [independent woman, and 'of a cheekiness that was more American than the American one'].[15] Yet in *Lettera aperta* such a 'disinvoltura' is represented mainly as frivolity and maliciousness, an example that the child does not seem to appreciate.[16] We know from Providenti's biography that Peppino, Musetta's stepfather, had a sexual relationship with her when she was still a minor, which is the reason why Olga and Licia moved to Lombardy when Goliarda was still a child.[17] Even though Goliarda's sisters are strong, independent female figures, their association with the protagonist's central anxiety represented by sexual abuse ultimately prevents them from becoming positive and viable role models for her.

The model of independent woman represented by Maria Giudice and partially by Olga, Licia and Musetta contrasts with the examples of power relationships between men and women that the young girl observes outside her family. The 'donnette' [silly women], who are weak and depend on men, constitute the negative counterpart to Maria's model and represent the female stereotype in a patriarchal society. Through the words of aunt Grazia, the narrator depicts women's condition as undesirable, since their dependence on men marks their submission and lack of autonomy:

13   Musetta (whose real name was Cosetta) was born in 1905, Licia in 1906 and Olga in 1913. See Providenti, *La porta è aperta*, 29–30.
14   Goliardo was also the name of Peppino's son who drowned in the sea when he was fourteen. See LA 38.
15   Providenti, *La porta è aperta*, 62.
16   See LA 56.
17   Providenti, *La porta è aperta*, 56.

Erano orribili quei grandi. Zia Grazia piangeva sempre e diceva: 'Che disgrazia nascere femmina: si ha sempre bisogno di loro.' Loro erano gli uomini grandi e forti [...]. Come il 'gigante', giù in cortile, che picchiava sempre Teresa, la mamma di Teresa, e Turi. E loro, era vero, avevano bisogno di lui: Teresa e la sua mamma gli volevano bene, avevano bisogno di lui, erano femmine. Turi invece quando il padre lo picchiò, come quella notte che svegliarono tutto il cortile, gli diede una coltellata al braccio e scappò. È sì, perché era grande anche lui e maschio. (LA 56)

[They were horrible, those grownups. Aunt Grazia used to weep all the time and say, 'what a misfortune, being born a woman, you always need them!' 'They' were the men, big and strong [...]. Like the 'giant', down in the courtyard, who always used to beat Teresa, Teresa's mother, and Turi. And, it's true, they needed him. Teresa and her mother loved him, needed him, they were female. Turi, on the other hand, when his father hit him, like that night when they woke up the whole courtyard, he stabbed him in the arm and ran away. Yes, because he was big too, and male.]

By looking at the sub-proletarian women who live in her neighbourhood, Goliarda notices their dependence on men, which exposes them to a situation of inescapable violence and subjugation. Maria achieved a status of independence thanks to education and by avoiding marriage; conversely, ignorance, poverty and marriage are the most relevant factors in determining female submission. Faced with this destiny of women's forced dependence on men, the little girl asks her teacher Jsaya for an explanation. When Jsaya replies that women need men like men need women, she asks herself: 'Cosa era questo bisogno, per quei brutti uomini grossi, come quello che alla Playa si era levato i pantaloni e si era mostrato?' [What was this need to those big ugly men, like the one at the Beach who pulled down his trousers and exposed himself?] (LA 57). Reflecting on the meaning of 'bisogno' [need], Goliarda concludes that, while for women it means lack of autonomy and subjection to men, men's need for women is located in sexuality, a need they fulfil through abuse and violence.

The story of Nica, Goliarda's best friend – and also her half-sister on her father's side, as she finds out later[18] – illustrates women's lack of autonomy and forced submissive destiny in a deeply patriarchal society. Nica is a creative and adventurous child, but, like most of Goliarda's friends,

18   Peppino Sapienza will recognize his paternity only when Nica is already an adult.

she comes from a sub-proletarian family. The only opportunity available to her as a poor and uneducated girl is to wait for a husband. In order to do so, she must preserve her virginity, otherwise she would risk ending up like the prostitutes she and Goliarda see in the streets of Catania: 'Anche noi possiamo finire così; basta uno sbaglio per una femmina' [We too can end up like that. One mistake is all it takes for a woman] (LA 126). Hence, as soon as she has her first menstrual cycle, which society interprets as the sign that she has become an adult woman, Nica faces a sudden restriction of her personal freedom: she is prevented from walking around in the streets, and her aspirations are reduced to 'aspettare un vero marito' [waiting for a real husband] (109). Nica is described as progressively losing her vitality, and Goliarda, using the conceptual instruments available to her as a child, interprets this change as a direct consequence of menstruation:

> Cosa erano quel sangue e quei dolori? Dovevano essere forti se Nica era diventata così magra e seria, e non giocava più nel cortile. Adesso che sapevo, vedevo che non usciva più, se non con la madre o il fratello, né alzava la testa a salutarmi quando stavo con Carlo e Arminio: solo se non c'erano uomini mi salutava, ma senza sorridere. Dovevano essere terribili quei dolori, se lei era cambiata così. (LA 110)

> [What were that blood and that pain? It must have been intense if Nica had grown so thin and serious, and no longer played in the courtyard. Now that I knew, I noticed that she no longer went out, except with her mother or her brother, nor did she raise her eyes to say hi to me when I was with Carlo and Arminio. Only when there were no men around would she say hi, but without smiling. That pain must have been terrible if she changed like that.]

Nica's development into an adult woman, sanctioned by the physical phenomenon of menstruation, seals her role in society, which is thus centred on her reproductive function. As soon as she becomes fertile, suddenly her condition changes from that of a child who is free to wander around and speak to anyone, to that of a woman who is restrained in her movements and actions. Nica dies young giving birth to a daughter, and in the narrator's powerful metaphorical connection, the blood that marked Nica's passage to the status of woman is the blood that was sucked out of her by the imposed role of wife and mother: 'Chi si era succhiato il sangue di Nica? Quella bambina che urlava nell'altra stanza? Quel marito che l'aveva sposata?' [Who had sucked Nica's blood? That baby who screamed in the next room? That husband who had married her?] (LA 116).[19]

Peppino, Patriarchal Power and the Threat of Sexual Violence

While Goliarda forms the idea of an imposed destiny of submission by observing the women she sees around her, male power and violence are also revealed abruptly and directly to her by Carmine, her father's colleague who sexually assaults her. The experience upsets the young girl and severely conditions her future perspective on the relationship between the sexes:

> [I maschi] ti fissavano tutti insieme ridendo, ridendo sempre, senza quasi aprire la bocca come l'avvocato e come quell'altro avvocato con la barba nera che veniva la sera da noi. Nell'anticamera mi aveva messo le mani dentro le mutandine, e poi se le odorò al naso. Io scappai. Si mise a ridere. 'Non scappare. Dovresti essere contenta, dall'odore si sente che sei quasi matura. Quando la mela è matura, è come la femmina; basta mettersi sotto l'albero, o sotto il balcone, e quella ti casca in bocca, dritta dritta.' No, non dovevo più alzarmi, né affacciarmi al balcone, come ieri. Carmine continuava a guardarmi da sotto. Aspettava. (LA 56)

> [[Men] would stare at you, all laughing together, laughing all the time, almost without opening their mouths, like the lawyer and that other lawyer with a black beard who used to come to our house in the evening. In the hall, he put his hands in my panties, and then smelled them. I ran away. He laughed. 'Don't run away. You should be happy, you can tell from the smell that you're almost ripe. When an apple is ripe, it's like a woman. You just stand under the tree, or under the balcony, and it falls straight into your mouth.' No, I mustn't get up, I mustn't look outside the window, like yesterday. Carmine kept looking at me from below. He was waiting.]

This episode is followed by the girl's inevitable physical development, represented in the text as a series of visionary and delirious images, after which the narrator informs the readers that she was in bed because she was seriously ill. Under the threat of sexual violence and of the restriction of freedom,

---

19   A different version of Nica's death is recounted by Sapienza in the poem 'A Nica, morta nel bombardamento di Catania dell'aprile 1942' [To Nica, Who Died in the Bombing of Catania in April 1942], in *Ancestrale*, 65–7.

growing up is thus compared to a disease. When Goliarda wakes up after a
long time, her perception of men has irremediably changed. She is scared of
her father – she notices the stiff, black hairs of his beard, his strong hands
that force her to open her eyes, his disgusting smile, and wonders whether
he, too, would take off his trousers like the man on the beach did.[20] While
in the passage on Carmine quoted above she associated her father with the
threatening attitude of 'i maschi', here for the second time Goliarda links
her father to sexual threat. She wishes that her mother or her sisters were
there, but at her bedside, together with her father, there is only the doctor,
who is also man. She concludes:

> Non avevo bisogno di loro, anche se ero una femmina. Finalmente la porta si richiuse.
> Non lo avrei più guardato in faccia. E se mi avesse costretto? Allora avrei dovuto
> ucciderlo. Non volevo sposare quell'avvocato come Licia e andare nel continente,
> non volevo nessuno. [...] Non uccisi mio padre, ma da quella notte lo chiamai sempre
> l'avvocato. Lo odiavo. (LA 61)

> [I didn't need them, even if I was a girl. Finally the door closed again. I wouldn't
> look at him in the eyes anymore. What if he forced me to? Then I would have to kill
> him. I didn't want to marry that lawyer, like Licia, and go to the continent, I didn't
> want anyone. [...] I didn't kill my father, but after that night I always called him the
> lawyer. I hated him.]

At this stage in the text, the reader does not have enough information
to understand this passage, but by the end some additional elements are
revealed that open up the possibility of an interpretation. Licia is Goliarda's
imaginary daughter, who at some point in the child's fantasies leaves Sicily
to marry a lawyer. But Licia is also Maria's real daughter, who in fact left
Sicily to escape from Peppino Sapienza, who posed a sexual threat to her
and to the other sister, Olga. The fact that in Goliarda's imagination Licia
marries a lawyer acquires meaning when put together with the reasons for
her departure – Peppino is, indeed, 'l'avvocato'. Through the dissemination
of narrative details, Sapienza is piecing together a negative image of her
father, who represents the threat of sexual abuse to her sisters.

20   See LA 60–1.

At this point it is fundamental to highlight that *Lettera aperta* reso-nates with a refrain, the cry of 'don't rape her!' that Maria keeps shouting in the mental hospital to which she has been admitted. With the exception of Castagné, who points out the figure of the rapist man, which obsesses *Lettera aperta*,[21] criticism has thus far overlooked the theme of rape, which conversely is central to the formation of Sapienza's view on the power rela-tionship between men and women in all her works:

> Quel grido 'Non la stuprare!' che mia madre ripeteva legata nel letto del manicomio, era rivolto a mio padre. Oggi riesco ad ascoltarlo ed a capire quello che non volevo accettare. Probabilmente l'avvocato si era innamorato di qualcuna delle figlie di mia madre, e per questo le due ragazze scapparono verso il continente. A me sembrò ter-ribile quel grido, tanto da seppellirlo nel fondo dello stomaco, intatto, senza averlo ascoltato. Ma è così, oggi lo vedo. Era così e piaccia o no, a te e a me che abbiamo le carni ammorbidite e pallide delle tante vergini Marie che ci hanno fatto fissare troppo a lungo. Sono riuscita a riascoltare quel grido e mi sono fatta coraggio, ma ho una paura terribile. (LA 133)

> [That cry 'Don't rape her!' that my mother used to repeat, tied in her bed in the mental hospital, was addressed to my father. Now I can listen to it, and understand what I didn't want to accept. The lawyer [my father] probably fell in love with one of my mother's daughters, and that's why the two girls ran away to the continent. That cry seemed so terrible to me that I buried it deep down in my stomach, intact, without listening to it. But that's what it is, now I see it. It was what it was, whether we like it or not – me and you, with our flesh softened and pale after the many Virgin Marys that we had to look at, for too long. I was able to listen to that cry again, I plucked up the courage, but I'm terribly frightened.]

In this passage, the adult narrator tries to come to terms with her father by setting his freedom against her (and the reader's) sexuality, described as weakened by moral and religious norms, but this attempt only results in a renewed fear. Goliarda's attitude towards her father is strikingly ambiguous, for she is attracted to his free, passionate and immoderate sexuality, but she also perceives it as threatening and abusive. Providenti points out the ambivalence of Sapienza's relationship with her father and the positive vital-ity represented by Peppino, his 'art of joy', yet she does not identify the fear

21 Natalie Castagné, 'Archeologia di Modesta', in Providenti, *Quel sogno d'essere*, 81–91, 87.

and hatred that characterize the other side of this relationship.[22] Peppino's sexuality is rooted in the same positive pole of passion and freedom that, as will be discussed later on, Maria lacks. At the same time, however, Goliarda is repulsed by the logic of power and prevarication that her father's freedom manifests. Such an ambivalence has a clear parallel in Modesta's attitude towards her (alleged) father at the beginning of *L'arte della gioia*, in which the girl is initially attracted to her father's physical strength and vitality, set against her mother's and sister's misery and submission, only to be raped by him immediately afterwards.

The connection between *Lettera aperta* and *L'arte della goia* as regards the relationship between the figure of the father and sexual violence is also established through the shared image of a blade. In *Lettera aperta*, this image of the blade recurs in connection with the father's intimidating gaze and laughter (as well as those of other male figures), which scare the little girl.[23] In *L'arte della gioia*, rape is described by Modesta as a blade cutting a lamb's flesh: 'Entrava la lama fra le cosce tremanti dell'agnello – la mano grande affondava nel sangue per dividere, separare – e lei sarebbe rimasta lì sulle tavole del letto, a pezzi' (AG 14) [The blade was entering the lamb's quivering thighs – the big hand sank into the blood to divide, split apart – and she would be left there on the planks of the bed, torn to pieces. AJ 17]. It is interesting to note that the same image is also used in *Il filo di mezzogiorno*, in this case to refer to the therapist's act of analysing Goliarda's past:

La sua voce [del terapista] [...] si faceva più tagliente, come lama affilata entrava nelle connetture più profonde dei miei nervi segando tendini, legamenti, vene ... [...] Ha smontato, ha scalzato col suo coltello le mie difese ... ma solo questo? Forse mi ha staccato anche la pelle, la prima carne, la seconda, col suo bisturi psicanalitico. (FM 93)

[His voice [...] became more cutting, like a sharp blade it penetrated into the deepest joints of my nerves, sawing tendons, ligaments, veins ... [...] He dismantled and got rid of my defences with his knife ... but is that all? Perhaps he took off my skin as well, the first layer of flesh, the second one, using his psychoanalytic scalpel.]

22   Providenti, *La porta è aperta*, 54.
23   The image of the blade is used with reference to Peppino, LA 117; Nunzio, LA 136; and Carlo, LA 118.

Here, as in *L'arte della gioia*, a blade cuts the woman's body into pieces, and leaves it suspended between life and death. Through the use of the same image, the narrator suggests a representation of psychoanalytic therapy as a relationship of power and even abuse, deeply implicated in patriarchal power, saying of the therapist: 'lui comanda qui' [He rules here] (FM 23); 'Lui è potente' [He is powerful] (24).

In *Lettera aperta*, Goliarda's father is a frightening male model for the girl, as he comprises the distinctive features of domination – he is a physically strong and sexually aggressive adult man. In the child's mind, men become inextricably associated with power and power is in turn associated with threat and violence. The narrator of *Lettera aperta* mentions a possible psychoanalytic interpretation of her fear and hatred of her father: 'sembra abbastanza comune che una bambina, a un certo punto, cominci ad odiare il proprio padre, e, se vi interessa, consultate qualche trattato di psicanalisi. Sarà stato sicuramente quando dicono loro: le sanno loro queste cose. Io so solo che da quella sera mio padre fu l'avvocato' [it seems quite common for a little girl to start hating her father at some point, and if you're interested you can consult some psychoanalytic treatise or other. Surely it will have been when they say it was, they know these things. All I know is that after that night my father was 'the lawyer'] (LA 61). The hatred of the father and its interpretation are then discussed extensively in *Il filo di mezzogiorno*. When the narrator talks about her relationship with her father, the therapist holds Maria responsible for teaching Goliarda to hate Peppino: "'Io gli volevo bene, ma lo odiavo anche". "Lo odiava? Era sua madre che la spingeva a questo?"' ['I loved him, but I also hated him.' 'You hated him? Did your mother encourage you to feel like this'?] (FM 47). As on many other occasions, he disregards her reply – 'Ma che dice? Mia madre non spingeva ad odiare nessuno, solo i fascisti' (47) [What are you on about?! My mother didn't encourage me to hate anyone, only the fascists] – and interprets Goliarda's negative feelings of hatred (which he also describes as fear and disgust, without distinguishing between them) as due primarily to Maria's example: 'sua madre le ha trasmesso la sua aggressività, il suo odio per gli uomini' [your mother imparted her aggressiveness and her hatred of men to you] (126). However, although the therapist is not able to recognize it, another possible reason behind Goliarda's negative feelings emerges from his own words. In discussing Goliarda's relationship with her partner Citto, Majore says that this is successful only because Citto has 'una personalità eccezionale; una dolcezza e una mancanza di volgarità' [an exceptional personality, gentleness and lack of vulgarity] (90), thus qualifying 'common' masculinity as the opposite of those qualities. He continues: 'Al primo uomo, con delle particolarità più maschili, più immerso nel collettivo maschile lei si è terrorizzata e per difesa si è irrigidita in quella che lei chiama frigidità' [With the first man who had more masculine characteristics, who was more implicated in the male collective, you were terrified, and as a defence you stiffened into what you call frigidity] (127). It is not difficult to read in the therapist's words a misrecognition of the fact that it is common masculinity itself, this 'collettivo maschile', that causes Goliarda's fear. Similarly, while insisting on Maria's responsibilities, the therapist describes Peppino's features that could have scared Goliarda as a child, his 'passionalità eccessiva' and 'sensualità scatenata' [excessive passionateness; wild sensuality] (126). Majore acknowledges that, in the environment where the little girl grew up, she was exposed to a situation in which 'le manifestazioni d'amore, d'erotismo intorno a lei si manifestavano in tinte brutali e tragiche' [the display of love and eroticism around you always had brutal and tragic connotations] (89). Nevertheless, he does not hesitate to define the adult woman's resulting perception of the relationship between the sexes as 'una visione distorta' [a distorted view] (89).

In light of the relationship with the therapist recounted in *Il filo di mezzogiorno*, the narrator's reference to a psychoanalytic interpretation of her hatred and fear towards her father in *Lettera aperta* can be read as subtle criticism, which to a certain extent anticipates the criticism of some tenets of Freudian psychoanalysis developed for example by Miller. According to Freud, most women have the – untrue – phantasy of having been seduced by their fathers when they were children. The phantasy, and not the real abuse, causes the neurosis.[24] Conversely, Miller shifts the focus

---

24   See Sigmund Freud, 'Femininity' [1933], in *The Standard Edition of the Complete Psychological Works of Sigmund Freud*, 24 vols, trans. and ed. James Strachey (London: Hogarth Press and the Institute of Psychoanalysis, 1953–1974), XXII. It is significant that Freud's early 'seduction theory', first presented in 'The Aetiology of Hysteria'

of her analysis from the phantasy of abuse to the environment of the child, stressing real child abuse as a cause of neuroses. Sapienza's representation of the material condition of women in a patriarchal context goes in the same direction, as she looks for the causes of her own neurosis outside of herself, in the actual oppression and abuse to which she was exposed. As the world portrayed in *Lettera aperta* suggests, the protagonist is scared of men not because of her mother's inculcation, but, quite directly, because Peppino sexually threatens his stepdaughters, because 'il gigante' beats up his wife and his daughter Teresina, and because Carmine sexually assaults the little Goliarda – in short, because the protagonist grows up in a patriarchal environment, where men's power over women constitutes the unavoidable context of the relationship between the sexes.

In this respect, *Lettera aperta* has connections to a number of literary works that unveil the reality of sexual abuse, or its constant threat, perpetrated by men – in particular but not exclusively – on girls and young girls.[25] Significant similarities are apparent for example with Dacia Maraini's *Bagheria* (1993), Fabrizia Ramondino's *Althénopis* (1981) and Lara Cardella's *Volevo i pantaloni* (1989). In all three works, an episode of sexual abuse or its threat is perpetrated on the authors themselves, by men who were close to their families: a friend of the child's father in *Bagheria*, a cousin in *Althénopis*, an uncle in *Volevo i pantaloni*. The topic is extensively present in Grazia Deledda's and Alberto Moravia's works, as highlighted by Luciano Parisi in two recent studies.[26] Furthermore, sexual abuse is also at the centre of Ferrante's *L'amore molesto* (1995), again at the expense of a little girl, and features prominently in the four volumes of the series

(1986), claimed that real sexual abuse during childhood was the cause of neurosis, but he later abandoned this view. The wisdom of and reasons for Freud's decision are a subject of unresolved controversy; see James B. McOmber, 'Silencing the Patient: Freud, Sexual Abuse, and "The Etiology of Hysteria"', *Quarterly Journal of Speech*, 82, 4 (1996), 343–63.

25   See Barbara Zecchi, 'Rape', in Rinaldina Russell, ed., *The Feminist Encyclopedia of Italian Literature* (Westport, CT: Greenwood Press, 1997), 280–3.

26   Luciano Parisi, 'Le adolescenti sole nella narrativa di Grazia Deledda', *Italian Studies*, 69, 2 (July 2014), 246–61; *Uno specchio infranto. Adolescenti e abuso sessuale nell'opera di Alberto Moravia* (Alessandria: Edizioni dell'Orso, 2013).

L'amica geniale (2011–2014). Morante's characters like Ida in *La storia* (1974) and Nunziatella in *L'isola di Arturo* (1957) are not spared their dose of sexual violence and abuse, and neither are Franca Rame, who recounts her traumatic experience in the play *Stupro* (1975), or Sibilla Aleramo in *Una donna* (1906), one of the first writers in Italy to overtly narrate and discuss her experience of sexual and domestic violence. As Maraini writes in *Bagheria*, in the 1970s and 1980s the practice of 'autocoscienza' [self-awareness] allowed this reality to emerge: 'I discovered that the so called "sexual abuse" perpetrated by adults against children was extremely common and it was well known to all or almost all little girls. Girls often don't say anything for the rest of their lives, because they are scared of the threats and warnings by the men who had taken them into some dark corners'.[27] Following Aleramo's example, in *Lettera aperta* Sapienza anticipates the social exposure of the problem of sexual and domestic abuse, which would be one of the achievements of the feminist movement in the 1970s and 1980s.

Resisting the Submissive Role: 'defemminilizzazione'

Thanks to Maria Giudice's counterexample, Goliarda is able to resist the assimilation of the dominant patriarchal culture to which she is exposed. Her rejection is resolute – she does not want to be a 'donnetta'. However, her resolution is represented as highly problematic, as it leads to her partial rejection of an identification with the female gender and to her refusal to grow up, ultimately resulting in a deep feeling of oppression.

Goliarda's resistance focuses in particular on menstruation, which marks the passage into adulthood and, at the same time, the acquisition of the status of 'woman', a situation in which patriarchal power exerts its control and domination much more strictly, as it happened to Nica. In her effort to negotiate her own gender identity, the little girl resorts to her mother's example. Since Maria is not submissive with men, Goliarda reflects, she surely does not have menstruation:

27   Maraini, *Bagheria*, 45–6. Maraini also includes representations of sexual and domestic violence in *La lunga vita di Marianna Ucria* (1990) and *Voci* (1994).

Cosa erano quel sangue e quei dolori? [...] Veniva a tutte le femmine? Anche mia madre l'aveva? No, lei non l'aveva, lei parlava con gli uomini come un uomo. Forse non veniva a tutte. Mia madre non aveva detto forse: 'Sono donnette che non sanno fare altro che aspettare un marito'? E anche aveva detto: 'Tu Goliarda, non sei una donnetta'. Infatti io non volevo un marito ma un compagno, come lei ... Certo, non veniva a tutte, ma solo alle donnette, e a me non sarebbe venuto. Sarei stata come mia madre. Avrei parlato come lei con gli uomini, e se non aspettavo un marito il sangue non sarebbe venuto. (LA 110)

[What were that blood and that pain? [...] Did all women have it? My mother too? No, she didn't have it, she talked to men like a man. Maybe not all women had it. Hadn't my mother said, 'they are silly women, who just wait for a husband'? And she had also said, 'You, Goliarda, are not like them'. Indeed, I didn't want a husband but a partner, like she did ... Sure, not all of them had it, only the silly ones, and I wouldn't have it. I would be like my mother. I would talk like her with men, and if I didn't wait for a husband, the blood wouldn't come.]

Goliarda, who identifies entering adulthood, and the sexed identity that comes with it, with being under the control of men, hopes it is possible for her to become a woman instead of a 'donnetta' by eliminating the marker of her sex, identified in menstruation. Hence, helped by her brother Carlo, she begins learning to box, in the hope of altering her sexed identity – 'per essere meno "bestiolina femmina"' [to be less of a 'girl cub'] (LA 110). In the world portrayed by Sapienza, there is no space yet for conceiving equality between the sexes without simply deleting the female element. To be an independent woman, for the little child, implies having to delete that element of women's physiology connected to their sexuality and reproductive potential, to set themselves apart from their own bodies. In a patriarchal context, like the one represented in *Lettera aperta*, a woman's achievement of agency and independence ultimately entails an assimilation to men.

Goliarda's reflection on her mother and menstruation is supported by the sexist perspective she absorbs from her social context. For example, according to the strongly misogynistic teacher Jsaya, being intelligent and well-spoken is a male characteristic: 'E sì, Goliarda: vedo che cominci ad esprimerti come un uomo, e non come un animaletto femmina. Sei come tua madre' [Well, Goliarda, I see that you're starting to talk like a man, and not like a girl cub. You're like your mother] (LA 63). Jsaya's words couple with uncle Nunzio's, who in praising Maria reaffirms the idea that intelligence and courage are intrinsically masculine virtues: 'Maria impareggiabile, intelligente più di un uomo e coraggiosa più di un uomo' [incomparable Maria, cleverer than a man and braver than a man] (153). In the end, the little girl cannot control her biological development and becomes, unavoidably, a woman. The process of growing up is described as a disease and is narrated as a long night of altered and delirious perceptions. When Goliarda wakes up, she does not identify with her own body, a decision that is marked by her refusal to look at her reflection in the mirror and that leads to self-annihilation: 'dovevo andare a letto senza guardarmi allo specchio, infilarmi nel letto e non muovermi più' [I had to go to sleep without looking at myself in the mirror, to go to bed and never move again] (59).

In *Il filo di mezzogiorno*, causes and meaning of the child's 'gender troubles' are the object of negotiation between the narrator and her therapist. In Majore's interpretation, once again Maria is responsible for the little girl's difficult development, as she would have forced Goliarda to act like a man, suppress her 'femininity' and undergo a process of 'defemminilizzazione' [de-feminization].[28] Femininity is characterized, in the therapist's view, as 'seni' [breasts], 'dolcezza' [gentleness] and, most importantly, as women's reproductive function, to the point that being sterile is equated with not being a woman: 'lei ha subito questo processo di defemminilizzazione [...]. Nel suo inconscio lei teme di essere stata sterilizzata e quindi di non essere una donna' [You underwent a process of de-feminization. [...] In your subconscious you are scared of having been sterilized and therefore of not being a woman] (FM 108). Majore applies Freud's views, who considers the healthy development of a woman as coinciding with a heterosexual orientation and the desire for a baby (especially male) as a substitute for the penis that she lacks.[29] Conversely, where penis envy and the Oedipus complex are not successfully resolved, possible reactions are the development of a powerful masculinity complex, neurosis and homosexuality. Internalizing the therapist's language, the narrator of *Il*

---

28   See FM 108.
29   Freud, 'Female Sexuality' [1931], in *The Standard Edition of the Complete Psychological Works of Sigmund Freud*, XXI; 'Femininity'.

filo di mezzogiorno partially acknowledges her own contempt for femininity, deriving from the identification of intelligence with masculinity, and blames early feminism (of which Maria was part) for this perception: 'vede, per me essere una donna intelligente si identificava come direbbe lei, comincio a copiarla vede? Sì, si identificava con l'essere mascolina, in tailleur, coi tacchi bassi, senza trucco, insomma il solito errore che imperversava a quell'epoca, eredità delle femministe del primo Novecento' [You see, I identified – as you would say, I'm starting to imitate you, see? – I identified being an intelligent woman with being masculine, in a suit, low heels, no make-up, that is, the usual mistake of that time, a legacy of the early twentieth-century feminists] (101).

Nevertheless, the adult narrator decidedly endorses some aspects of Maria's feminist model – which promotes women who are strong and autonomous, for example by rejecting marriage until divorce becomes legal – while the therapist considers these teachings to be the real negative cause of her 'defemminilizzazione' and pushes her towards a more traditional female role. For example, he insists on describing Citto as her 'husband', although she keeps contesting it and remarking that they are not married. He also affirms that being married would have given her 'un senso maggiore di sicurezza, di protezione' [a greater sense of safety and protection] (FM 31–2), and tries unsuccessfully to distance her from Maria's views. Likewise, he comments that she is 'troppo coraggiosa per una donna' [too brave for a woman] (85–6), in a context where an allegedly male characteristic is considered negatively when belonging to a woman. As ever, her response, which denies any such difference between men and women, goes unnoticed.

As Ross points out, Sapienza firmly criticizes normative discourses on gender and sexuality that pervade psychoanalytic thought, and particularly Freudian thought.[30] Ultimately, therapist and patient agree that there has

---

30   Ross, 'Identità di genere e sessualità', 234. Conversely, in *Le certezze del dubbio*, through Roberta's voice, Sapienza will drop all charges of 'misogyny' against Freud's thought: 'non è vero quello che le tue amiche femministe dicono di lui, non era misogino' [what your feminist friends say about him isn't true, he wasn't a misogynist], to which Sapienza replies: 'Anche io non sono d'accordo' [I disagree with them, too] (61).

40   CHAPTER I

been and there still is 'gender trouble' deriving from a clash with a normative
model of female gender identity. However, Majore interprets it as errone-
ous deviance from healthy femininity and attempts to push her back into
a normative female role. Conversely, the narrator addresses the material
conditions of women, who are controlled and undervalued, as her main
polemical objective, but she can only articulate the challenge for women
being intelligent and independent without simply being assimilated to men.
She refuses to be forced back into a normative gender role, but ultimately
cannot find a solution, for the solution is not in the individual response
of compliance, but in the negotiation with a material context: "'Ma deve
ammettere che lei è stata educata da sua madre troppo rigidamente. [...]."
"Sì, sì, lo so, ma che poteva fare? Lasciarmi in mano alle zie, ai fratelli che
tendevano, da buoni siciliani, a ridurmi una femminuccia? La storia esiste,
dottore'" ['You must concede that your mother raised you too rigidly [...].'
'Yes, yes, I know, but what else could she do? Should she have left me in the
hands of my aunts and brothers who, like typical Sicilians, were turning
me into a silly girl? History matters, doctor'] (FM 112). Here, Sapienza's
criticism of the normative aspects of psychoanalysis is radical, and voices
a Marxist-feminist approach to the problem of women's oppression. This
approach constitutes a fundamental interpretative frame and cultural reference for Sapienza, who since childhood was exposed to Maria Giudice's
example and, through her, to the thought and political action of figures
such as August Bebel, Anna Kuliscioff, Alexandra Kollontai, Angelica
Balabanoff, Karl Marx and Friedrich Engels.[31] In *Lettera aperta* and *Il filo
di mezzogiorno* Sapienza foregrounds the concrete power involved in the
constitution and enforcement of normative gender identities.

By deconstructing gender identities as normative, Sapienza combines
a Marxist-feminist critique, centred on power relationships, with a queer
perspective, which maintains that gender identities are socially constructed.[32] While in *L'arte della gioia* Sapienza will play on the disconnection
between sex and gender to explore queer identities and relationships, in

31 Particularly important is Bebel's *Women in the Past, Present and Future* (London:
    Reeves, 1885), cited and discussed in AG 91, 184, 243, 335.
32 Butler, *Undoing Gender* (New York: Routledge, 2004); *Gender Trouble*.

Lettera aperta and *Il filo di mezzogiorno* she focuses instead on the process through which social norms and gender identities are produced. Indeed, if sex and gender are not 'a set of biologically determined paths',[33] they are nonetheless imposed as compulsory identities in a highly regulated patriarchal society like the one portrayed by Sapienza. The narrator of *Lettera aperta* and *Il filo di mezzogiorno* seeks liberation from the imposition of social norms as necessary, metaphysical structures; she does so by retracing, in her narration, the process by which the norms themselves are formed and the material context of their imposition. The liberating 'queer' perspective of the novels belongs to the narrator's deconstructive operation, while the child undergoes a path of progressive oppression.

Maria's Betrayal

While Goliarda is able to resist a patriarchal model of gender thanks to her mother's feminist example, she also finds a crushing limit in Maria's trajectory, for the old woman descends into insanity and dies in a psychiatric hospital. Goliarda's gender formation in *Lettera aperta* and *Il filo di mezzogiorno* thus raises a central question, one that runs throughout all Sapienza's literary works and personal reflections: how is it possible for a woman to achieve independence and freedom without simply replicating the male model? Reformulated from a socio-political perspective, the same question would sound like this: if men have the power to shape and enforce structures, how can a woman, who does not have the same power, change such structures? How is it possible for a woman to change the balance of power between men and women, without adopting the same logic of power? In *Lettera aperta*, the young girl's struggle to make sense of her mother's nonconformist example and the completely different rules in force outside of her family provides an insightful representation of this challenge, which Goliarda Sapienza and Maria Giudice personally experienced in their lives as something overwhelmingly difficult. The child's consideration that since

33   Ross, 'Identità di genere e sessualità', 225–6.

42

CHAPTER I

her mother is independent she does not menstruate is a compelling representation of the real challenge women face in the material and symbolic
operation of achieving independence without a serious destabilization
of their identity. In Sapienza's representation, Maria is the victim of this
irreconcilable dichotomy. Whereas Modesta, the protagonist of *L'arte della
gioia*, will be able to transgress social norms and deconstruct all forms of
internal and external constraint without paying any price on the level of
personal identity or punitive social repercussions, Maria Giudice cannot
afford the same freedom. Instead, she faces what Anna Nozzoli defines as
the 'identity crisis that unavoidably hits the woman who does not adjust
to her subaltern position.'[34] Similarly, Michele Sovente notes: 'A woman's
realization of her difference from the female model leads to her loss of
identity.'[35] Diotima's project of a 'double-alterity', a difference both from
masculinity and normative femininity, which, in solidarity with Irigaray's
thought, suggests a possible way out of the impasse, was formulated over
twenty years later.[36]

In *Lettera aperta*, Maria pays a high personal price for her difference
from normative femininity. For Maria, being strong and independent
goes together with a rigidly ideological and uncompromising attitude:
'mia madre, così severa e inappellabile' [my mother, so stern and assertive]
(LA 141), 'mia madre non rideva mai' [my mother never laughed] (143),
'così schiva di tenerezze' [shying away from tenderness] (148). Similarly,
Sapienza remarks, 'a casa mia non si parlava mai di cose concrete' [at home
they never talked about concrete things] (131). In the narrator's interpretation, it is Maria's rigid attitude, resulting from her difficult position as a
woman, that is at the root of her mental illness. Voicing a highly dramatic
entanglement of love, imitation, frustration and rejection, Sapienza experiences Maria's insanity as a betrayal, because the path she indicated to her

34 Anna Nozzoli, *Tabù e coscienza: la condizione femminile nella letteratura italiana del
Novecento* (Florence: La Nuova Italia, 1978), 97.
35 Michele Sovente, *La donna nella letteratura oggi* (Fossano: Esperienze, 1979), 38.
36 See Diotima, *Il pensiero della differenza sessuale* (Milan: La Tartaruga, 1987).

daughter resulted in a painful failure.[37] Sapienza dedicates to her mother one of the most intense passages of the text, as well as one of the deepest understandings and most effective representations of the inner struggle suffered by women who, while contesting the patriarchal status quo, adopt an intransigent attitude:

> apro gli occhi e vedo la tua ossessione. Pazzia, come la chiamarono quegli uomini bianchi senza sguardo. Adesso vedo perché ti è scoppiata tra le mani proprio quando il tuo nemico cadde distrutto come tu pregavi. Cadendo lui, ti si ruppe la tensione d'acciaio per la quale hai vissuto estraniandoti da te stessa, dalla tua carne; cadendo il contraddittore, sei restata muta e sola, con i fatti della tua vita denudati della corazza che ti permetteva di non ascoltare i particolari, le virgole della tua vicenda. E nuda con te stessa, le passività femminili, le emozioni tenere delle tue spalle morbide, del tuo seno grande, si ruppero le dighe che la tua intelligenza aveva alzato fra te e te, spalancando una fiumana di paure, che avevi ignorato di avere. Come tutte le donne, essendo intelligente, dovevi esserlo più di un uomo; coraggiosa più di un uomo. Ma non si sfugge alla propria natura: puoi sì affamarla, costringerla al silenzio anche per molto tempo; ma prima o poi la sua fame la spinge fuori coi denti le unghie affilate e ti dilania le carni e le vene. (LA 147)

> [I open my eyes and see your obsession. Madness, as those gazeless white men called it. Now I see why it blew up in your hands just when your enemy fell down, destroyed as you prayed for. As he fell, the iron tension by which you had lived estranged from yourself, from your body, also broke down. As your antagonist fell, you remained mute and lonely, with the facts of your life stripped of the armour that allowed you to ignore the details of your life, its particulars. Naked before yourself, the female passivities, the tender emotions of your soft shoulders, of your big breasts, the dikes erected by your intelligence to separate you from yourself, broke, letting out a river of fears, which you didn't know you had. Like all women, being intelligent, you had to be more intelligent than a man. Braver than a man. But you can't escape your own nature. You can starve it, silence it, even for a long time, but eventually its hunger drags it out with teeth and sharp nails and it tears your flesh and veins apart.]

In Sapienza's view, Maria's insanity stands for the failure of a strategy that seeks to erase the bodily dimension in favour of abstract ideology. In the

---

37   See LA 148: 'Mi vendicavo di avermi tradito con la pazzia' [I took revenge because she betrayed me with her madness]. Maria's descent into insanity is also narrated in FM 37–9.

specific context of Sicily in the first half of the twentieth century, Maria's struggle for independence entails the adoption of an ideology and an inflexible attitude that overcomes individuality and represses the body. But the price she pays is too high, and at the end of her life her disregarded 'nature' floods back.

As an adult, Sapienza compares her mother with her friend Franca: 'quel suo parlare scandendo sicuramente i concetti, quella sua "crudeltà", mi riportarono alla "crudeltà" di mia madre, che è poi, oggi lo capisco, il tentativo, da donna, di essere più rigorose degli uomini. Rigore di idee, di ricerca, di vita' [the way she speaks, articulating notions with confidence, her 'cruelty', reminded me of my mother's 'cruelty', which – now I see it – is the attempt, as a woman, to be more rigorous than men. A rigour of ideas, research, life] (LA 143). Maria's rigour is compared, by contrast, with Franca's sensual smile, which expresses the person's corporeal and vital presence: 'Quando ridi – e tu ridi: mia madre non rideva mai – la tua fronte si distende luminosa, e le tue labbra si gonfiano di carne affamata e calda' [when you laugh – and you do laugh, my mother never did – your forehead relaxes, bright, and your lips swell with warm, hungry flesh] (143). While Franca can be both intelligent and sensual, rigorous and joyful, in a more deeply patriarchal society, such as in Sicily under fascism, Maria is trapped – she either accepts a submissive role, or has to pay a personal price that may lead her to insanity.

If Maria died insane, she clearly could not provide a viable example for Goliarda, and the narrator of *Il filo di mezzogiorno* is terrified at the prospect of replicating her mother's destiny: 'Mi dica la verità. Sono stata rinchiusa perché ero pazza? Pazza come mia madre?' [Please tell me the truth, did they lock me up because I was insane? Insane like my mother?] (FM 38); 'Io non volevo somigliare a mia madre, ma purtroppo era chiaro che le assomigliavo se ero stata pazza come lei' [I didn't want to be like my mother, but unfortunately it was clear that we were similar if I was insane like her] (47). In *Lettera aperta*, the adult narrator goes back to her mother's model and discovers what went wrong, namely the erasure of the corporeal dimension, where love and desires reside. Reinstating the body is thus the existential, epistemological, ethical and political endeavour that

Sapienza undertakes through *Lettera aperta*, *Il filo di mezzogiorno* and all her subsequent works.

At first glance, Sapienza appears to be replicating a binary model of gender difference here. Maria adopts a rigid ideology, associated with the male domain, and represses the particularity and concreteness of her body, associated with the female sphere. Using Cavarero's terminology, such a gender binary would belong to the 'patriarchal symbolic order, which as we know is dichotomous and associates man with the mind and woman with the body.'[38] Sapienza's interpretation of her mother's insanity would be entrenched in a tradition that links men to the *logos* (abstract and universal rationality), and women to the *aisthesis* (fleshy concreteness). As Butler puts it, 'this association of the body with the female works along magical relations of reciprocity whereby the female sex becomes restricted to its body, and the male body, fully disavowed, becomes, paradoxically, the incorporeal instrument of an ostensibly radical freedom.'[39] Nevertheless, in *Lettera aperta* the conceptualization of gender difference is more complex and actually rather different from the patriarchal dichotomy described above. Specifically, Sapienza does not suggest any necessary connection between abstract rationality and men. Men do not represent a *logos* separated from the *aisthesis*. Such a separation of *logos* and *aisthesis* pertains to those women who oppose their allegedly natural submissive position. It is Maria who has to put her fleshy concreteness aside in order to access the position of power that alone can guarantee her independence. Here Sapienza anticipates to some extent a point that is fundamental especially to Irigaray and that is well summarized by Burns: 'part of the project of creating a feminine subject is to dismantle the Cartesian and phallocentric separation of mind and body and push the woman's body, as part of her being, into the speaking subject.'[40] The patriarchal binary model – abstract rationality linked to men, body linked to women – does not take into

---

38   Cavarero, *A più voci*, 110.
39   Butler, *Gender Trouble*, 17.
40   Jennifer Burns, *Fragments of Impegno: Interpretations of Commitment in Contemporary Italian Narrative, 1980–2000* (Leeds: Northern Universities Press, 2002), 85. For a clear and articulate discussion of women's problematic position with respect to the

account the different perspectives from which men and women relate to *logos* and *aisthesis*. Sapienza's representation deconstructs this model by showing that the difference is a difference in power, which forces women into an impossible position whereby they have to choose between their independence and their body, for in order to gain power they have to renounce parts of themselves. Conversely, for those men, like Goliarda's father, who enjoy a position of power, the relationship between *logos* and *aesthesis* would be much less conflicting, because their sexed body does not stand in the way of their power. In fact, in *Lettera aperta* men are represented as closer to the *aisthesis*, a position that clearly overturns the patriarchal discourse. While Maria, in order to be independent, needs to delete and suppress her body, Peppino is represented as free to express his wild and passionate sexuality.

Norms and Sexuality

In addition to Maria's mental illness and Peppino's association with domination and sexual threat, *Lettera aperta* features two episodes that increase the girl's divergence from both her mother's and her father's models of gender identity and sexual mores. These episodes concern the parental repression of the young girl's sexuality. Maria slaps her when she finds out that she has a homosexual experience with Nica; Peppino and Goliarda's brothers Carlo and Arminio harshly reproach her when they catch her holding hands with a boy. Through these episodes, Sapienza expands her discourse to question the very legitimacy of imposing norms on sexuality, including a controversial interpretation of homosexuality and incest.

The episode involving Peppino and Goliarda's brothers takes place when she is about to move to Rome, at the age of seventeen. The exercise of authority by the male members of her family confirms, in the girl's eyes, the impossibility for her to access the same sexual freedom as men. The unmasking of male power is represented through the girl's changed

body, see Sidonie Smith, *Subjectivity, Identity and the Body* (Bloomington: Indiana University Press, 1993), 1–23.

perception of her brother Carlo's body, involving the recurring image of a blade: 'i baffi neri lucevano appuntiti come lama, non l'avevo mai guardato bene. O lui era cambiato? [...] Ma i baffi, lì alla luce, tagliavano più forte, e lo respinsi con tutte le mie forze' [the pointy black moustache shone like a blade, I had never observed him carefully before. Or had he changed? [...] But there in the light, his moustache was cutting deeper, and I pushed him away as hard as I could] (LA 118). After being reproached by her brothers, Goliarda faces her father, who threatens to slap her (the text does not make it clear whether he does it or not). Peppino's reaction reveals the deep inconsistency between the ideal of freedom he enjoys and professes, and the exclusion of women from it, between his personal example of sexual liberty and the prohibition to Goliarda to follow it.

Maria's repression of Goliarda's homosexual experimentation is particularly relevant for the narrator, who devotes a significant part of the text to the character of Nica and to the sense of a loss of natural vitality attached to the interruption of their relationship.[41] The story of the relationship between the two girls is told from the child's perspective, who experiences it as joyful and untroubled. When Maria finds out about it, she slaps Goliarda, thus imposing a prohibition on the girl's previously unproblematic desire. Giuliana Ortu notes that Maria's attitude is disorientating and incoherent, as she censored Goliarda's sexual experimentations, while at the same time authorizing her to pursue her own freedom in the world.[42] In remembering this episode, the adult narrator reflects on how her mother's ban deprived her of a possibility of understanding her own body and desires, obstructing her development. In *Il filo di mezzogiorno*, the therapist replicates the repression exerted by Maria's slaps:

'Deve finirla signora di fare all'amore con queste immagini di donna femminili che crede di amare e invece solo teme'. Le mani, ora, di ghisa, nel cerchio della luce, immobili sulle ginocchia mi schiaffeggiavano ... deve finirla di fare all'amore ... con ... Nica ... [...] avevo tanta voglia di abbracciarla ... ma non dovevo ... E quel pomeriggio

41 See LA 96. See also FM 16, 21, 30.
42 Giuliana Ortu, 'Cosa vedono gli occhi di quella bambina. *Lettera aperta*', in Farnetti, *Appassionata Sapienza*, 148–79, 173.

quei due schiaffi psicanalitici mi strapparono dalle braccia Nica ... Titina ... Haya ...
[...] Haya quale maleficio ci tiene lontane?... Nica, non ci vedremo più? (FM 109)

['You must stop making love with these female images of women that you think you
love but actually only fear'. His hands, now made of iron, in the circle of light, lying
still on his knees, were slapping me ... you must stop making love ... with ... Nica ....
[...] I desperately wanted to hug her, but I must not ... That afternoon, those psychoanalytic slaps tore Nica from my arms ... Titina ... Haya ... [...] Haya, what evil
spell keeps us apart?... Nica, will I never see you again?]

The therapist also argues that her need for female friends is excessive and
that 'l'amicizia fra donne è sempre un po' ambigua' [friendship between
women is always a little ambiguous] (FM 70).[43] Yet, the narrator does
not accept the therapist's heteronormative interpretation.[44] She calls him,
contemptuously, 'piccolo borghese' [petit bourgeois] (70), objects that his
perspective is blatantly sexist and ultimately loses control and slaps him,
thus replicating and overturning Maria's slaps. While in *Il filo di mezzogiorno* Sapienza questions the legitimacy of heteronormative discourses, in
Lettera aperta she appears to have partially internalized them:

Lo stadio di omosessualità o di masturbazione, se esaurito nel suo limite, non è necessario alla comprensione di se stessi, del proprio corpo? Se bloccato, come avviene
sempre, può provocare un arresto a dodici, quattordici anni: nel corpo e purtroppo
anche nella mente. C'è forse qualche omosessuale adulto fra voi che copre una simile
mancanza di crescita con 'estetismi', 'vocazione di natura', 'destino'? Dico solo quello
che si è fatto chiaro a me, solo per me, nelle mie emozioni. Non vi arrabbiate, anche
perché chi vi parla è stata bloccata a dodici, quattordici anni come voi. È una per-
sona costretta come voi che dice queste cose. Un'omosessuale come voi. (LA 97–8)

[Isn't a phase of homosexuality or masturbation, if it is kept within bounds, necessary to the knowledge of one's self and body? If it is repressed, as always happens, it
can cause a block at the age of twelve or fourteen, in the body and sadly also in the

43   On another occasion, he inquires about Goliarda's friend: 'Era un po' morbosa questa
     Jane? L'accarezzava?'[Was this Jane a bit sick? Did she touch you?], FM 138.
44   On the notion of heteronormativity, see Monique Wittig, *The Straight Mind and
     Other Essays*, trans. Louise Turcotte (Boston, MA: Beacon Press, 2002) and Adrienne
     Rich, 'Compulsory Heterosexuality and Lesbian Existence', *Signs*, 4, 5, *Women: Sex
     and Sexuality* (Summer 1980), 631–60.

mind. Is there perhaps some adult homosexual among you, who makes up for a similar lack of development with 'aestheticism', 'nature', 'destiny'? I'm only saying what has become clear to me, only for me, in my emotions. Please don't get angry, also because the person who is talking to you was blocked at the age of twelve or fourteen like you. It's a constrained person like you who says these things. A homosexual like you.]

In *Lettera aperta*, we have on the one hand the child, who never questions the legitimacy of her desires, does not feel guilty and simply suffers from being prevented from enjoying her relationship with Nica; on the other hand, the adult narrator considers homosexuality, alongside masturbation, as a form of self-knowledge, a natural passage towards a mature sexual orientation, but this is nonetheless supposed to be heterosexual. Early experimentation is presented as useful in order to fully enjoy heterosexuality, but not to question its limits. In her analysis of Sapienza's representation of sexuality, Ross highlights a tension between a 'queer' perspective and internalized social norms, as 'the narration of her gender identity and sexuality [...] oscillates between reproducing and contesting socio-cultural norms',[45] and notes that 'her comments are both transgressive for a text published in 1967, since she declares herself "homosexual", and rather homophobic, since this is cast as a problematic state of arrested development.'[46]

As an example of the oscillation between rejection and internalization of social norms, Ross points out the varied repetition of the act of slapping. In *Lettera aperta*, Maria slaps Goliarda to inhibit her homosexual desire. In *Il filo di mezzogiorno*, however, the narrator rebels against the therapist's homophobic and normative attitude by slapping him, and in doing so she 'repeats and resignifies her mother's gesture, potentially reversing the prohibition of homosexuality by accusing the accuser.'[47] In *Le certezze del dubbio*, the narrator and protagonist slaps her friend Roberta, after an intense confrontation charged with erotic desire.[48] Whereas it is true that Sapienza's works show a persistence of this oscillation between norm and rebellion, her conscious choice to represent and discuss such

45   Ross, 'Identità di genere e sessualità', 225.
46   Ross, 'Eccentric Interruptions', 17.
47   Ibid. 17.
48   See Chapter 4.

oscillation can also be interpreted as a detachment from heteronormative discourses, rather than their internalization. In these texts, Sapienza gives voice to frustration at her own internalization of norms, representing the difficulty of freeing herself from imposed constraints. The interpretation of such constraints as negative and oppressive is clear already at the stage of *Lettera aperta*, which represents the narrator's attempt to re-establish contact with her own desires beyond and before the imposition of social norms and categories. Her choice to include a pre-adolescent homosexual experience, in the absence of any reference to guilt, and her insistence on the negative consequences of her mother's prohibition of it, suggest that the author is knowingly using narration to denounce sexual repression and regain access to her own desires.

In the adult narrator's reconstruction, the loss of Nica deprived her of the freedom to discover and understand her own body, which explains the association of homosexuality and masturbation. The young girl's desire for Nica, on the contrary, has nothing to do with masturbation and much to do with homosexuality, as the narrator overtly indicates by representing the impossibility of the child hugging herself or replacing Nica's body with her own reflection in the mirror.[49] The adult narrator shifts her attention from homosexual desire to the repression of experimentation in general. In other words, the narrator's main focus is not homosexuality as deviance from heterosexuality, but sexual immaturity as opposed to free experimentation, as she is interested in addressing and overcoming the restrictions she underwent as a child by retrieving a sense of freedom that preceded them. What she will do with her reconquered freedom, whether the result will be a homosexual, heterosexual, bisexual or fluid identity, actually does not appear to interest the narrator as much.

The development of the theme of homosexuality and sexual experimentation throughout Sapienza's works provides a vivid representation of the difficulty to free desire from oppression and internalized norms. By voicing such a struggle, however, Sapienza's texts also work as a clear denunciation of the negativity of the repression she underwent, 'in line

49   See LA 97.

with Foucault's criticism of the disciplinary power that controls children's sexuality.[50] Modesta's example, with her symbolic liberation, shows where Sapienza's desire for free sexuality would lead – to a fluid, joyful sexuality that disrupts any rigid category of identity and sexual orientation.[51] In *L'arte della gioia*, too, homosexual experimentation (this time, however, not in childhood but in late adolescence) is described as functional to a full and mature heterosexual relationship. Nevertheless, this idea is contradicted immediately afterwards by Modesta's own behaviour as well as her explicit opinions, when she discusses and rejects the Freudian understanding of 'normal' sexual orientation as heterosexual.[52] Comparing the representation of sexual orientation in *Lettera aperta*, *Il filo di mezzogiorno* and *L'arte della gioia*, Ross remarks that Modesta's boundless queer energy is absent from the more autobiographical works.[53] However, if *Lettera aperta* and *Il filo di mezzogiorno* do not contain the same queer energy as *L'arte della gioia*, the difference is to be found more in the lack of energy than in the lack of 'queerness'. The literary operation of these novels consists precisely in reacquiring this lost energy, by deconstructing the norms that oppressed and interrupted the protagonist's own desires. What the adult narrator associates with the abrupt interruption of her relationship with Nica is the loss of direct contact with her own body, associated with a source of vitality and creativity. Indeed, Nica is also a storyteller with powerful creative imagination: 'Quante storie avrei ancora potuto ascoltare da lei, se quei due schiaffi che vennero dopo non mi avessero strappato dalle sue mani, dalla sua voce! [...] Non solo il suo corpo, ma la sua fantasia mi rubarono quei due schiaffi. E solo il suo corpo e la sua fantasia?' [How many more of her stories I could have listened to, if those two slaps that came after hadn't torn me from her hands, her voice! [...] Those slaps didn't just steal her body from me, but also her imagination. And was it only her body and imagination?] (LA 107).

50   Ross, 'Identità di genere e sessualità', 230–1.
51   For the notion of 'fluid sexuality', see Lisa Diamond, *Sexual Fluidity: Understanding Women's Love and Desire* (London: Harvard University Press, 2008).
52   See AG 347–9. Cf. the discussion of sexuality in AG in Chapter 2.
53   See Ross, 'Identità di genere e sessualità', 241.

The narrator's deconstruction of dominant social norms provides
the thread linking the theme of homosexuality and that of incest, which
is introduced by the narrator's discovery that Nica is her half-sister. She
recounts three cases of incest she witnesses around her: betweeen Musetta
and Arminio (Goliarda discovers only later that they are not siblings but
stepsiblings); between Teresa and her father, 'il Gigante'; and between
Ivanoe's friend and his mother.[54] It is in the context of these incest episodes that Sapienza claims sexual freedom beyond any category and social
constraint:

> L'attrazione carnale e della fantasia non sopporta limiti e non ne nascono mostri né
> sventure se non come in tutti gli accoppiamenti. Non userò più la parola 'incesto': o
> meglio, la userò per me quando per consuetudine, compassione continuerò a vivere
> con un uomo che non mi attrae più e che non è più attratto da me. [...] Questo è il
> vero incesto dal quale nascono sicuramente mostri, dolori, sventure umilianti. Ma
> quella signora, Teresa: – penserò ai vostri abbracci come a un terribile fatto di natura,
> come la nascita e la morte. (LA 131–2)

> [Sexual and mental attraction suffer no constraints nor do they generate monsters
> or misfortunes any more than any other type of intercourse. I will no longer use the
> word 'incest', or, better, I'll use it for me, when out of habit or pity I go on living
> with a man I'm no longer attracted to and who is no longer attracted to me. [...]
> This is the real incest, which certainly gives birth to monsters, sorrow, humiliating
> misfortunes. But that lady, and Teresa – I'll think about your embraces as a terrible
> fact of nature, like birth and death.]

Sapienza uses the theme of incest, arguably one of the deepest cross-
cultural taboos, to highlight the norms that give structure to society.[55] In
fact, she is deeply fascinated with the theme of incestuous relationships,
which she also explores in *L'arte della gioia*, *Le certezze del dubbio*, and
the plays *La grande bugia* and *La rivolta dei fratelli*. In this passage, she

54   See LA 123, 126, 128.
55   See Claude Lévi-Strauss, *The Elementary Structures of Kinship*, rev. edn, trans. James
     Harle Bell and John Richard von Sturmer (Boston, MA: Beacon Press, 1969); see
     also Arthur P. Wolf and William H. Durham, eds, *Inbreeding, Incest, and the Incest
     Taboo: The State of Knowledge at the Turn of the Century* (Stanford, CA: Stanford
     University Press, 2004).

overturns the meaning of the word 'incest' using it to designate not the infraction of a norm (which is presented as socially constructed), but the imposition of falsifying and de-naturalizing constraints on individual sexual freedom. However, it is significant to point out that Sapienza carries out a defence of sexual freedom beyond categories, not with regard to sexual orientation, but instead in relation to the culturally disturbing issue of incest, and in particular incest between parents and children. In the context of a narrative that is deeply concerned with power relationships and with male violence against women, a possible explanation of this peculiar approach to the issue of incest can be found in the disposition of the chapters. In the text, the discussion of incest is followed by the disclosure of the meaning of Maria's cry 'don't rape her'. Through the acceptance of incest as 'nature', the narrator tries to come to terms with her father's sexuality, to which she attaches both positive (liberating) and negative (violent) connotations. By introducing the issue of Peppino's violent sexuality through the defence of sexual freedom, Sapienza is possibly looking for a direction from which to approach this disquieting issue. Yet, overall her attempt to accept her father's sexual aggressiveness by framing it as sexual freedom beyond norms founders against the fear and hatred it inspires.

A Conflicting Education, a Failed Integration

Sapienza's Family: An Island within Fascist and Catholic Sicily

Intertwined with the young protagonist's search for identity in terms of gender and sexuality, we witness her attempt to orient herself amidst the whirl of contradictory examples to which she is exposed. The main challenge for the girl is the distance between the Sapienzas and the rest of society in terms of political ideology and religion, resulting in the absence of univocal and viable educative models for her. In addition, the Sapienzas' relative economic wealth clashes with the living conditions of the most disadvantaged social classes visible in her neighbourhood, a clash that she struggles to reconcile with socialist ideology. Finally, the child also feels isolated within her family, which expects her to act as an adult and emotionally neglects her, inducing in her a compliant attitude that will ultimately lead her to a deep sense of oppression and loss of self. Inheriting a critical attitude towards state and religious institutions from her family, as an adult Sapienza turns her criticism against all absolute structures, including her family's ideology and its focus on an excessively responsible and autonomous individual.

In *Lettera aperta*, the representation of the relationship between the Sapienzas, the rest of society and the protagonist's own personal position spans cultural, political, religious and class aspects. The Sapienza family, together with the tutor Jsaya, embrace an anti-fascist and anti-Catholic perspective, which in the context of a society whose official dominant culture is fascist and Catholic, entails the opposition to state institutions and norms. Such an anti-institutional position dovetails with contempt for the middle class, which, for example in the Brunos, is represented as the social basis of fascist and Catholic conformism and respectability. These are the years when fascism's power is strongest, and both Maria and Peppino have paid a high price for their opposition. Peppino's son, Goliardo, drowned in the sea at the age of fourteen, probably killed by the Mafia on behalf of fascists; both Peppino and Maria were repeatedly imprisoned, and Maria was constantly under the strict control of fascist police.

The regime leaves little space for political activism, which in Sapienza's recollection of her parents in the 1920s and 1930s is forcibly confined to the space of resistance against the dominant rhetoric. Goliarda's education is thus directly affected by her parents' effort to counteract the rhetoric of the regime. This contrast emerges clearly in connection with state school, addressed as the place where the regime imposes its mystifying and con- formist culture, which for the girl plays the role of 'counter-education'.[56] While Maria generically urges her to study, insisting on the importance of

56   Milagro Martín Clavijo, 'I luoghi della formazione di Goliarda Sapienza: *Io, Jean Gabin*', in Providenti, *Quel sogno d'essere*, 157–74, 165.

education for women's independence, Goliarda is instructed by her father and her tutor Jsaya to despise state schooling, repeatedly described as a 'buco marcio, dove insegnano solo bugie' [rotten hole, where they teach only lies] (LA 51). In order to counteract the mystifying role played by institutional education, Peppino exposes Goliarda to brutal reality:

> 'Dove vai così presto?'
> 'A scuola'.
> 'Ma che vai a fare in quel buco? Vieni con me: così, almeno per un giorno, non sentirai bugie. Aspetta, hanno ucciso un bambino a Sciacca e andremo di persona a vedere com'è andata'. (LA 51)

> ['Where are you going this early?'
> 'To school.'
> 'What are you going to that hole for? Come with me, so at least for a day you'll not listen to any lies. Wait, a child has been killed in Sciacca, and we'll go and see in person what happened.']

Similarly, Jsaya responds to the 'cazzate' [bullshit] (LA 140) taught at school by using crude language and behaviour. When he teaches Goliarda Giovanni Pascoli's poem *Romagna*, he insults the poet, described as sub-servient to power, and spits from the window on the soldiers in the street. The opposition between public and family spheres reaches its peak in the episode of Goliarda's candid criticism of religion, when she repeats in class the expression 'la droga della religione' [the drug of religion], which she heard from Jsaya. Harshly reprimanded, she feels painfully isolated from her schoolmates: 'E quel buco, già così orribile, divenne per me un posto di tortura' [and that hole, already so horrible, became a place of torture for me] (64). The episode reflects the difficulty that Goliarda inherits from her parents' position in relating to their social context while contesting its norms. When Goliarda is fourteen years old, Peppino interrupts any contact between her and state institutions by removing her from school and burning her uniform. Martín Clavijo highlights the personal reper-cussions for the protagonist of the radical separation from the dominant culture of her social context, as she will have to learn completely on her

own, combining different views without a guide and finding herself at the
margins of society once and for all.[57]

The contrast between family and dominant culture is clearly articulated
as a fight against the lies spread by official propaganda. Against falsifying
rhetoric, the little girl is expected to act as a fully formed, strong, autonomous subject, who is able to orient herself amidst conflicting messages
and take a position. The disproportion between expectations of mature
responsibility and the child's still fragile personality is evident, for example,
in the passage in which Ivanoe reproaches Goliarda as she is caught lying
about her name. Ivanoe tells her that she should not apologize, because 'a
casa mia scusarsi era ritenuto un gesto dolciastro, cattolico' [in my family,
apologizing was considered a sugary, Catholic gesture] (LA 46–7); Ivanoe's
intransigent perspective combines the criticism of the hypocrisy of the
Catholic practice of forgiveness with a call for individual responsibility
and coherence, rejecting even the simple habit of apologizing, when this is
not accompanied by an actual commitment to change: 'Sei un individuo, e
sei responsabile delle tue azioni. Non chiedere scusa, ma cerca di riparare'
[you're an individual, and you're responsible for your own actions. Don't
apologize, but try and fix it] (47). The opposition is straightforward: on the
one hand, there is a false rhetoric, linked to Catholicism and fascism; on
the other, false rhetoric has to be countered by authentic actions, founded
on individual freedom and responsibility.

The notions that Goliarda receives from her family about Catholicism
reflect the same contrast between authenticity and the falsifying rhetoric
of institutions. Maria appreciates Jesus' message, which she interprets as an
egalitarian call, as Jesus is 'il primo rivoluzionario, il primo ad aver detto
che sulla terra ricchi e poveri siamo tutti uguali' [the first revolutionary,
the first to say that we're equal in this world, rich and poor] (LA 78).
However, the girl's experience in a church shows a reality that contradicts
this egalitarian view of Jesus' message. Inspired by her mother's words and
the positive example of Sister Maria, Goliarda decides to worship Jesus;
brought to the local church for the first time, she notices the precious

57   Martín Clavijo, 'I luoghi della formazione di Goliarda Sapienza', 165.

furniture, the strong scent and people's smart clothes, and listens to the priest's unintelligible words:[58]

La chiesa era fresca e profumata, mentre fuori c'era il mercato, il caldo, la puzza di pesce. Ma dove era il Signor Gesù Cristo di suor Maria? Quello sull'altare d'oro era tutto pieno di gemme e di argento come un pupo, e non portava il cuore in mano. Aveva gli occhi duri e guardava soddisfatto tutti quei lampadari e quell'omaccio che parlava, parlava e non si capiva niente. (LA 79)

[The church was cool and smelled nice, while outside there was the market, the heat, the smell of fish. But where was Sister Maria's Lord Jesus Christ? The one on the golden altar was all covered in gems and silver like a puppet, and didn't carry his heart in his hand. He had severe eyes, and he looked with satisfaction at all those chandeliers and that man who talked, talked and you couldn't understand a word.]

Through the child's gaze, the narrator sets up a contrast between Jesus' egalitarian message and the Church. Sapienza's approach to religion is here played out on political ground, closely recalling Antonio Gramsci's arguments about the Church as a power institution, mainly developed in those years when he was collaborating with Maria Giudice in Turin.[59] Catholicism is criticized for realizing a disconnection between words and actions, which would betray Jesus' genuine call for equality and transform faith into mere external practices, which function to cover the Church's exercise of power.

Class, Political Commitment and the Rejection of Ideology

In addition to these conflicts, Goliarda also faces a difference between her family and its social context with respect to class position. The Sapienzas

---

58   Mass was celebrated in Latin until 1969.
59   See, for example, Gramsci's analysis of the types of action purposely used by the Church to influence believers, in Gramsci, 'Stregoneria', in *Avanti!*, 4 March 1916, and 'L'appello ai pargoli', in *Avanti!*, 31 July 1916. Gramsci later ironically criticized the use of Latin as a means to confuse uneducated people, see his 'Letter to Teresina', 16 November 1931, in Gramsci, *Lettere dal carcere*, ed. Sergio Caprioglio and Elsa Fubini (Turin: Einaudi, 1968), 525–6.

embrace the working-class cause, but as a relatively wealthy family they are at the same time distant from the indigent and uneducated people they support. The description of uncle Nunzio provides a vivid example of Goliarda's acute awareness of the hierarchical structure of society: 'L'avevo visto per tanti anni povero, solo, che veniva da noi con un bastone lunghissimo, e, dignitosamente, essendo lui calzolaio e mio padre avvocato e noi figli di avvocato, non entrava a parlare in cucina o nella stanza del pianoforte, ma aspettava fra i clienti, quietamente' [I saw him for many years, poor, lonely, coming to our place with a long stick, and with dignity, as he was a cobbler and we were a lawyer's children, he wouldn't come and talk in the kitchen or the piano room, but instead he would wait with the clients, quietly] (LA 39).

Similarly, the spatial disposition of the setting in the text features an apparent vertical opposition between the second floor, the 'piano nobile' [noble floor] (LA 66), and the courtyard, crowded with a varied population. Goliarda is allowed to wander around the courtyard and the neighbourhood and mix with their inhabitants, but the distance between the two environments cannot be erased, as marked by the path the girl has to follow to go back upstairs into her home. The hierarchical structure of society interferes with the free and playful dimension embodied by Nica:

Perché non ci lasciano giocare con la terra? Perché non mi hanno lasciata giù in cortile a costruire con la terra l'Etna? Avevamo cominciato a fabbricarlo con Nica subito, la sera che c'eravamo incontrate. Ma lei fu richiamata in casa per la preghiera e io tornai su al secondo piano a pensare di diventare un individuo utile alla società. (LA 89)

[Why don't they let us play with the earth? Why didn't they let me build an Etna of earth, down in the courtyard? We had started building it with Nica, immediately, the night we met. But they called her back home for prayers, and I went back up to the second floor thinking about how to become a socially useful individual.]

While themes related to gender and sexuality have already started to be explored by critics, the dimensions of class and political ideology in relation to identity have not yet raised specific interest, possibly because of Sapienza's conflicting, at times controversial and provocative, position on left-wing commitment. However, in *Lettera aperta*, as well as in subsequent works, the issue of left-wing commitment and ideology and Sapienza's positioning in society from the perspective of class and professional occupation play a central role. *Lettera aperta* articulates this theme in a series of interconnected points, with personal and political repercussions. First, the child experiences an excruciating conflict between political commitment and self-love, for she sees her parents' activism as resulting in the sacrifice of themselves and their own children. Feeling neglected by her parents, who are too 'impegnati' – here, both in the sense of 'committed' and 'busy' – to take care of her, she comes to experience her personal needs as egoistic drives that clash with the moral duty of political struggle. Second, because of this contrast between her own interests and political commitment, she feels oppressed by the perceived superiority of her mother's revolutionary commitment and therefore feels blocked for a long time in the expression of her own reality, which is not that of the subaltern classes. Finally, she identifies in her parents' mentality – and, later, in that of her left-wing friends – a form of ideological intransigence that she blames for being too similar, in its conceptual frame, to that of their antagonists – either religion or fascist power. These themes come to be portrayed in the text in a variety of ways.

The child's discovery of poverty and her privileged condition is highly dramatic and initiates an inner conflict that will torment her throughout her life. She asks her mother: 'Se c'è tanta gente che muore di fame, perché io ho questo piatto pieno?' [if there are so many people who starve to death, why do I have this plate full of food?], to which Maria replies, 'se domani venisse il momento di nutrire te a discapito degli altri, non esiterei a dare ugualmente a te come agli altri, a costo di vederti pallida e magra come loro. Una madre che leva agli altri per la propria creatura è una bestia criminale' [if some day I had to feed you to the detriment of others, I wouldn't hesitate to give to you and the others equally, even if this meant seeing you pale and thin like them. A mother who steals from others to feed her own creature is a criminal beast] (LA 71–2).[60] Feeling guilty for her privilege, Goliarda stops eating and falls seriously ill. The

---

60 Maria's words are reported also in FM 151, in the context of the child's feeling that she cannot count on her parents' love, and that she should not 'chiedere troppo' [ask for too much].

encounter with the reality of poverty gives rise to a conflict between personal and collective good, which is formulated by Maria in terms of a contrast between altruistic moral duty and egoistic natural instincts. Maria's choice is definite – a mother who favours her child over other children is a criminal beast, in which 'beast' evokes the idea of individualism as a natural instinct, which breaks egalitarian and altruistic moral norms and is therefore 'criminal'. In the context of stark social inequality, the condition of a wealthy left-wing person is represented to the little girl as intrinsically contradictory, as the options she has are either to transgress her individual needs or her moral principles. Altruism and self-love are perceived as antithetical, beginning a lacerating conflict in the little girl's search for identity, a theme to which Sapienza returns extensively in *Io, Jean Gabin*.

Speaking directly to the readers, Sapienza undertakes an uncompromising criticism of her parents' strict ideology, which she compares to fascism itself for its Manichean rhetoric:

> Per mio padre e mia madre [...] il sale della vita era l'odio e la ribellione. Peccato che di ironia non ne sapessero niente. Certo, quando sono vissuti e hanno lottato, l'ironia era un lusso troppo grande, ma è un peccato lo stesso, perché si sono trovati a lottare il fascismo con la stessa ottusità e rettorica del fascismo. Questo li faceva – l'ho scoperto con l'orrore che potete immaginare – un po' fascisti. Ma quello di combattere il nemico con le sue stesse armi mi pare sia un vizio che sarà molto difficile levarci. (LA 36)

> [For my father and my mother [...] hatred and rebellion were the spice of life. It's a pity that they knew nothing of irony. Surely, when they lived and fought, irony was too great a luxury, but it's a pity all the same, because they ended up fighting against fascism with the same narrow-mindedness and rhetoric as fascism. This made them – and I discovered this with horror, as you can imagine – a bit fascist. But it seems to me that this bad habit of fighting the enemy with its own weapons will be hard to eradicate.]

She addresses a similar criticism to her contemporary left-wing friends. Through a number of brief extra-diegetic remarks, Sapienza gives voice to her own argumentative relationship with the intelligentsia gravitating around the Italian Communist Party (PCI) she used to frequent in

Rome.[61] As Pellegrino notes, 'it is relevant to recall the problem of cultural hegemony: Alicata, Togliatti, Maselli, the Party. Goliarda was not politically aligned, and they repeatedly pointed it out to her, directly and indirectly.'[62] Sapienza, through her works, advocates against the structuring of reality into absolute and fixed categories that overcome concrete individual experience, so that her radically anti-ideological approach clashes with a rigidly communist agenda. Gian Franco Venè's description of the ideological conditioning of Italian writers in the 1960s and 1970s offers a productive insight into the reasons why Sapienza's position was considered subversive: 'Faced with a world that was split in two blocks, hence called to a peremptory choice that did not allow any free examination of reality as a whole, writers were, once again, a priori political [...] That is, they thought they could identify human salvation *tout court* within the ideological side they chose.'[63]

Sapienza also questions the possibility and appropriateness of pretending to understand and speak for the subaltern classes when not facing the same troubles. In other words, the difference between the social condition of the relatively wealthy intellectuals, among whom Sapienza places herself and her family, and the subaltern classes, introduces an element of structural incoherence. This is probably the most controversial part of Sapienza's political discourse, especially at the time, as she is painfully aware. Indeed, she accuses firstly her family and then her communist friends of supporting a mystifying and oppressive ideology, which would prevent her from giving voice to her own reality. Confronted with the imperative to relate to society from a rigidly communist perspective, Sapienza literally rebels against the oppressive imposition to limit her field of expression to communist political engagement. Interestingly, however, in the text the subject

61 I gathered information about Sapienza's relationship with the Roman left-wing intelligentsia from a series of interviews with Sapienza's friends Paola Blasi and Adele Cambria (Rome, September 2013).
62 Pellegrino, 'Un personaggio singolare, un romanzo nuovo, una donna da amare per sempre', in Farnetti, *Appassionata Sapienza*, 69–88, 81.
63 Gian Franco Venè, *Il capitale e il poeta* (Milan: Sugar, 1973), 417.

who carries out such an imposition shifts from her family and friends to sub-proletarian women, an emblem of the condition of victim:

> Queste donne, oggi lo vedo, mi hanno chiuso la bocca per tanti anni. Come? Vi spiego: essendo derelitte, vittime della società, io fui costretta ad amarle, a conoscere le loro storie, metterle in un altarino, accendere lumini e a pensare solo a loro, scrivere solo su di loro. Così quando incominciai a desiderare di esprimermi, incominciai anche a pensare storie macchinose su di loro, ad immedesimarmi nei loro travagli che solo mi sembravano degni di essere raccontati, e, essendo io e nata e vissuta al secondo piano, *piano nobile*, come si diceva, che potevo saperne? (LA 66).

> [For many years, these women – now I see it – prevented me from speaking. How? Let me explain. As they were the destitute victims of society, I was forced to love them, learn their stories, put them on an altar, light candles to them, and think only about them, write only about them. So when I started wanting to express myself, I also started to create laboured stories about them and to identify with their troubles, which seemed the only worth telling. And since I was born and raised on the second floor, *the noble floor*, as they used to say, what could I possibly know about them?]

Addressees of a moral duty to be put before personal freedom and accomplishment, in Sapienza's representation the victims turn into frightening and oppressive figures. The obligation to speak about the victims is perceived by the narrator as a source of deep falsehood, an ideological constriction from which no social emancipating development can arise.[64] Her sense of oppression is strictly related to the perceived pressure of political ideology on her freedom of expression. It is not surprising, then, that the trauma inflicted on communism in Italy by the XX Communist Congress in 1953, which revealed Stalin's crimes, is linked to the possibility it opens up for her to explore a personal way to artistic expression:

> E così venne il ventesimo congresso e allora tutto non fu così bloccato, così concluso, sicuro: allora, forse, potevo anche parlare di un figlio di avvocato, di quel *piano nobile* nel quale ero cresciuta e non dovevo per forza scendere in cortile e fingere di essere Nina la cagna, o Teresa la figlia del gigante. Potevo. E come potei, incominciai. Mi

---

64   Cf. Sapienza's discussion of the Communist Party in the film *Lettera aperta a un giornale della sera*, dir. Francesco Maselli (Italy, 1970) <https://www.youtube.com/watch?v=GtCNFMh1gzM> [Accessed 5 June 2016].

venivano poesie d'amore, storie di bambini borghesi tentati dalla religione. Io dovevo accusare. Poesie d'amore! Se mia madre mi avesse vista! (LA 67)

[Then came the Twentieth Congress, and things were no longer so blocked, so definite; then maybe I could even talk about a lawyer's son, about that *noble floor* where I grew up, and I didn't have to go down in the courtyard and pretend to be Nina the bitch, or Teresa, the giant's daughter. I was free. And I started as I could. I was writing love poems, and stories of bourgeois children who were tempted by religion. I had to accuse. Love poems! If my mother could see me!]

Here Sapienza recounts the path that led her to finally feel free to talk about what she really wanted, somehow transgressing her mother's example. Pellegrino describes Sapienza's maturation as 'a vocation that she long repressed due to a wrongly conceived scruple [...] towards her mother's superior political and revolutionary commitment.'[65] The impact of this historical event on Sapienza's personal and artistic path is discussed further in *Il filo di mezzogiorno*, where the relevance of history is used to contrast the therapists' idea that everything in the life of an individual is set out in the first years of life: 'il ventesimo congresso ... il mio tentativo di uscire da una costruzione ideologico-religiosa che, a casa mia, mi avevano imposto, e che si era strutturata nelle mie ossa diventando il mio scheletro stesso. Non per niente incominciai a scrivere dopo il ventesimo congresso' [the Twentieth Congress ... my struggle to go beyond an ideological-religious construction that my family had imposed on me, and that had grown in my bones to become my very skeleton. It's significant that I started writing after the Twentieth Congress] (FM 90–1).

Sapienza claims the right to enjoy her freedom, secured by her status of wealthy person, supported by her partner, and use it to talk about her real situation and personal interests, allegedly mainly concerned with love. Yet, she feels constantly under the poor women's observation and judgement: 'Lo sapevamo che ci avresti tradite. Tu parli di te, del tuo disordine di piccola borghese, delle tue camicette marcite: – e non vedi come siamo vestite di stracci?' [We knew you would betray us. You talk about yourself, your petit bourgeois mess, your rotten blouses – don't you see that we're

65 Pellegrino, 'Un'analisi selvaggia', 9.

wearing rags?] (LA 67). Ultimately, Sapienza ends up putting her moral dilemma at the very centre of narration. Despite her programmatic declaration that she would pursue indifference to moral duty, her inner conflict takes centre stage as an inescapable and irresolvable structural dilemma. As Venè points out, 'When poetic honesty clashes with dogmas, it gives rise to a tragic laceration that has the important advantage of representing the truth of a social or ethical situation.'[66] What can be read as the assertion of a bourgeois writer's nonchalant insensitivity towards the interests of the less privileged class, actually turns into the expression of a structural contradiction that the narrator is experiencing to the extreme of its consequences. When, as a child, Goliarda learns about poverty, she reacts very strongly, falling ill and stopping eating. She undergoes a similar physical reaction when she detects an analogy between fascism and her parents' political commitment. As an adult, she indicates the conflict between personal freedom and ideological intransigence as playing a central role in her depression. Far from being able to enjoy freely her privileged position, Sapienza gives voice to the repercussions of structural inequality and ideological distortions on her personal life. In doing so, she releases social and political issues such as class inequality from an ideological approach, and still succeeds in including them in her narrative discourse.

An Empty Task

Confronted with a contradictory environment and pressed by her family's intransigence, the young protagonist struggles to make sense of her position in the world. Martín Clavijo points out the different sources and directions of Sapienza's education as represented in her autobiographical works, and describes them as a bombardment of conflicting messages that undermine the little girl's ability to interpret them autonomously: 'Her upbringing at home is not regular, not planned and not gradual, and does not take into account the child's age. Goliarda receives small teachings, or, often,

66   Venè, *Il capitale e il poeta*, 254.

formative bombs from all directions.' 'At times, it looks as if Iuzza were in the middle of a battlefield, a war of conflicting ideas, different insights on the world, on life, on feelings, on love.'[67] Natalie Castagné also stresses the nonconformist features of Sapienza's upbringing, and relates them to the marginal, radical and eccentric position of her characters and narrative: 'An upbringing of this kind [...] could only produce an exceptional character [...]. We could also say, a character outside the norm.'[68] The result of this 'upbringing outside the norm'[69] is irreducible diversity and 'extreme singularity'.[70] This is initially represented as a sentence to solitude, expressed in Goliarda's painful discovery of the uniqueness of her name:

> E un pomeriggio, esasperata da questo nome che tutti, in cortile, al mare, notavano con meraviglia, cercai fino a notte sull'elenco telefonico di Catania, disperatamente, una sorella o un fratello che portasse questo nome. Piangendo dovetti accettare la realtà: non c'era nessuna Goliarda o Goliardo in tutta Catania, e per me in tutto il mondo. Ero sola. (LA 38)

> [One afternoon, exasperated by this name that everyone – in the courtyard, on the beach – marvelled at, I searched through the phonebook of Catania into the night, desperately looking for a sister or a brother with this name. Crying, I had to accept the fact that there was no Goliarda or Goliardo in the whole of Catania, and, for me, in the whole world. I was alone.]

The eccentric position resulting from Goliarda's upbringing appears to be extremely difficult for the child to master, for it entails both isolation and a lack of viable models with whom to empathize. The first problem, isolation, reflects the child's and subsequently the adult's difficulty in reconciling norm and singularity and put her emphasized diversity in communication with her social context. The second problem, the lack of viable models, entails for the child a struggle to elaborate autonomous strategies of identity construction outside a recognizable position in her social context. Devoid

67 Martín Clavijo, 'I luoghi della formazione di Goliarda Sapienza', 162, 172. Iuzza is Goliarda's nickname.
68 Castagné, 'Archeologia di Modesta', 84.
69 Pellegrino, 'Un personaggio singolare', 83.
70 Castagné, 'Archeologia di Modesta', 82.

even of a provisional orienting centre, she is constantly at the mercy of conflicting forces, threatened by her own emotions and dependent on the adults' contradictory judgements. As Martín Clavijo remarks, an education to rebellion is not an easy path to follow for a child.[71] Likewise, Castagné observes that it is precisely the imposition of autonomous responsibility on a child, who does not have the instruments to master it, that marks Goliarda's isolation also within her own family, composed of adults:

> In her autobiographical novels, Goliarda illustrates, uncompromisingly, the negative aspects of an otherwise commendable educational approach and the effects of rigorous dogmas on a very sensitive child, who was too young to reflect properly on those principles and who therefore took them literally, at the cost of falling ill. In other words, she represents her isolation within her own tribe, the family group that surrounded her [...].[72]

As Miller observes, the development of a strong sense of self, in contact with one's own instincts and desires, is an increasingly difficult task for a child when he or she is exposed to contradictory messages:

> Today it is hardly possible for any group to remain so isolated from others who had different values. Therefore it is necessary today for the individual to find his support within himself, if he is not to become the victim of various interests and ideologies. This strength within himself – through access to his own real needs and feelings and the possibility of expressing them – thus becomes crucially important for him on the one hand, and on the other is made enormously more difficult through living in contact with various different value systems.[73]

Goliarda, in *Lettera aperta*, is at the same time educated to freedom and not left free to discover, build and shape such a freedom by herself, for she is required to act as an already formed subject, whilst still a child. Her identity formation is thus portrayed as a burdensome training, a 'long toil [...] to understand what she could be in her life.'[74] Expressions such as 'dovere'

---

71   Martín Clavijo, 'I luoghi della formazione di Goliarda Sapienza', 165.
72   Castagné, 'Archeologia di Modesta', 84.
73   Miller, *The Drama of Being a Child*, 80.
74   Ortu, 'Cosa vedono gli occhi di quella bambina', 155.

[duty], 'allenarsi' [training], 'cercare' [searching], 'provare' [trying], and 'imparare' [learning], recur throughout the text, contributing to the communication of a sense of methodical application of energies to construct personal identity, departing from the awareness and expression of her own desires. The idea of training dovetails with that of task, *compito*, which the narrator herself identifies as the kernel of her endeavour: "'Compito" deve essere la parola-chiave, dato che mi torna tanto alle labbra' ['Task' must be the key word, since it keeps coming back to my lips] (LA 130). Nonetheless, the girl's task is precisely the identification of the task itself, the search for a personal aim, without which the training she undergoes would result in an empty effort, necessarily unsuccessful.

One episode in particular, in *Lettera aperta*, illustrates such a void in the girl's training, and her wish to be allowed to be a child, that is, to access a simple enjoyment of the present. Goliarda is playing with Nica and other girls in a courtyard. The game consists in pretending to be dead and resisting tickling. When thanks to prolonged practice Goliarda wins, she does not know what to ask for a reward. She has shown she is able to do something properly, 'la cosa fatta proprio bene' [the thing done very well] (LA 142), but the content of the training, the purpose beyond the demonstration of ability, is irrelevant. She starts asking for anything that comes into her mind, and feels relieved when finally someone in her family tells her that she cannot demand too much, as this gives her at least an indication of where to set the limit and how to behave. Miller observes that, in those subjects who go through a process of severe disconnection and repression of desires, 'in general, there is a complete absence of real emotional understanding [...] and no conception of their true needs – beyond the need for achievement', a description that provides a fitting commentary on Goliarda's confusion in this episode.[75]

In contrast to this type of search, when she wants to tell Nica about her discovery of the need to moderate requests, she changes her mind and prefers simply to enjoy her friend's company and play with her:

75 Miller, *The Drama of Being a Child*, 20–1.

Correndo mi immaginai di incontrare Nica, e di dirle: 'Non si può chiedere troppo,
non hai ragione, non si può chiedere troppo ...'. Nica era davanti al portone, le andai
vicina decisa, ma non so perché non le dissi niente: forse perché avevo corso ed ero
tutta sudata. Forse perché lei: 'Giochiamo a lassa e pigghia?'. Era un gioco bellissimo,
e a lassa e pigghia giocammo fino a che il lampione accese il suo cerchio intorno a
noi e in quel cerchio giocammo ancora ore e ore. (LA 115)

[As I was running, I imagined meeting Nica and telling her, 'You can't ask for too
much, you were wrong, you can't ask for too much ...'. Nica was by the door, I came
close to her, with determination, but I didn't say anything, I don't know why. Maybe
because I was sweaty from running. Or because she said 'shall we play "leave and
take"?' It was a wonderful game, and we played it until the street lamp lit its circle
around us, and in that circle we played for hours and hours.]

Here, the dimension of a tiresome task that troubles Goliarda and that she
wants to communicate to Nica is simply put aside in favour of the spontane-
ity of playing with her friend. Consistently with the role played as regards
sexuality, Nica is represented in connection with the positive pole of physical
instincts, before and beyond norms. The relationship between the two girls
can be described as a 'resonant' communication, which in Cavarero's terms
expresses the correspondence of pre-semantic vocalic exchange between
two interlocutors.[76] Resonance works as the recognition and enjoyment of
each other's physical presence without imposing an external reference and
scope to the mutual participation. It corresponds to a specific political perspective, which aims at reinstating physical singularity and co-presence of
the interlocutors into semantic language, with its generalizing and abstract
categories and norms. The expression of a harmonic and resonant communication between Nica and Goliarda is reinforced by the image of the circle
of light that encloses the two girls, as well as by the chiasmic structure of the
sentence 'giochiamo a lassa e pigghia – a lassa e pigghia giocammo'.

The enjoyment of free, simple play with Nica is set against the active
task to which Goliarda feels called by her family, that of finding her way to
become 'un individuo utile alla società' [a socially useful individual] (LA
89). Urged by her family's example, she looks for her identity in terms of a

76   See Cavarero, *A più voci*, 199.

social role, a profession that would define who she is. She initially gets inspiration from exceptional personalities (real and fictional) she sees around her or hears about, such as Musolino the bandit, Sister Maria and Norma (the protagonist of Bellini's opera). This modality of identity formation closely reflects the one described by Freud, according to whom identity is formed through the identification with other people and the internalization of their qualities and attributes.[77] In *Il filo di mezzogiorno*, the therapist applies precisely this interpretative approach when he discusses Goliarda's identification with Nica and Maria;[78] the same mechanism is central to *Io, Jean Gabin*, in which the protagonist strongly identifies with the French actor Jean Gabin. However, the protagonist of *Lettera aperta* gives up these attempted emulations one by one. The endeavour to achieve a personal position in society by imitating the actions of other characters results in an unsuccessful strategy for the child, for it requires a mature determination that she does not possess. As the narrator remarks, her limit is specifically a limit of will, of pursuing an objective at any cost, when she does not share the aim but only the external actions of the characters she wants to emulate. The whole text is inhabited by this painful tension between what the girl feels she should be, her moral call to social utility, and her need to pause from this active search for identity to simply enjoy a given state of things.

After a series of failures, Goliarda is initiated by her neighbour Anna into the artisan craft of manufacturing chairs. For the first time, her training has a specific goal, and she enjoys the secure feeling of having a place in the world, an activity commensurate with her ability. Moreover, unlike Musolino, Sister Maria or Norma, the job of artisan offers her the opposite of an exceptional social position, hence endowing her with a sense of belonging to her social context through manual work. Unfortunately, this break from her challenging and tiresome search is interrupted by Anna's sudden departure, which deeply upsets her. In the narrator's interpretation, this episode marks the failure of her attempt to accomplish social integration by exercising a common profession. With the loss of the artisanal work, she loses the possibility of being useful to society, which would guarantee

77   See Freud, *The Ego and the Id*, trans. Joan Riviere (London: Hogarth Press, 1927).
78   See FM 61–2, 69.

her a recognizable and legitimate place. Anna's departure corresponds to
the interruption of the narrator's recollection of her path towards matu-
rity, which stops on the threshold of Anna's house and never returns to it:

> È per questo che ancora aspetto piangendo Anna la sediara sulla sua soglia. La sua
> assenza mi strappò dalle mani un modo di 'essere utile all'umanità': mi ricacciò in
> quel secondo piano a vagare per le stanze con le mani in mano. E se sono ancora
> accasciata su quella soglia, non è per la stessa ragione? Non è Anna che piango ed
> aspetto, ma la Rivelazione. Di essere 'utile'. La rivelazione di essere una 'prescelta' da
> Dio o da Marx per redimere, è la parola, 'redimere l'umanità'. (LA 91)

> [That is why I am still waiting for Anna the artisan, crying on her doorstep. Her
> absence snatched a way of being 'useful to humanity' right out of my hands; it
> threw me back to that second floor, wandering from room to room with nothing
> to do. And isn't it for the same reason that I'm still lying by her doorstep? It isn't
> Anna that I cry and wait for, but the Revelation of being 'useful'. The revelation
> of having being 'chosen' by God or Marx to redeem – that's the right word – 'to
> redeem humanity'.]

Power and Human Relationships: The Child Entertainer

After these failed attempts to integrate into society, the protagonist is left
with unresolved contradictions: on the one hand, the imperative of social
usefulness and the tendency to think of her own identity in terms of a burdensome imitation of models; on the other, the need to simply enjoy the
pleasure of life and exercise her own personal freedom. At the root of this
failed identity formation lies a primary, fundamental form of power that
oppresses Goliarda and undermines her 'compito', her task. This consists
in the child's dependence on her family's approval and affection, which she
feels is never secured, and the distorting effect this has on the expression –
and ultimately even the awareness – of her own desires:

> Dunque, torniamo a me: non era di altro che vi volevo parlare; torniamo a me oggetto
> malleabile e alla mercé per fame. Il bambino è il primo operaio sfruttato, dipende
> dai grandi e sempre, per un tozzo di pane, si abbassa a divertire, leccare le mani dei
> padroni, si lascia accarezzare anche quando non ne ha voglia: così comincia la pro-
> stituzione. (LA 65)

[So let's get back to me – that's all I wanted to talk to you about. Let's get back to me, a malleable object, forced by hunger into a state of neediness. The child is the first exploited worker. He depends on grownups and always stoops to entertain his masters and lick their hands in exchange for a piece of bread. Thus prostitution begins.]

The child's dependence on the appreciation of adults is represented as a power relationship, not dissimilar from the one described between men and women. In these texts, women and children share a position of submission and dependence, which threatens the possibility for them to develop an autonomous sense of the self. The process of compliance with external expectations and the inner conflicts this generates are exemplified in *Il filo di mezzogiorno* by the figure of the 'child entertainer', who performs in front of an audience, progressively losing her vitality:

> Cominciai a marciare intorno intorno e tutti applaudivano e ridevano ... la recita andava bene, la memoria funzionava ma, man mano che dicevo le battute e marciavo sentii le mie gambe al ritmo della marcia diventare rigide, di legno, scricchiolavano e anche le braccia ... la carne stoppa ... le gambe scricchiolavano sempre più forte e caddi a terra rotta in pezzi. (FM 118)

> [I began marching all around and everybody clapped and laughed ... the show was going well, my memory was working, but, as I was saying the lines, marching, I felt my legs stiffen to the rhythm of the march, like wood, they creaked, and so did my arms ... flesh like coarse fabric ... my legs creaked more and more and I fell on the floor, broken into pieces.]

The therapist's interpretation of Goliarda's excessive dependence on others' approval and love, and the connection repeatedly established between neglect and depression, indicate that Sapienza possibly came in contact with Winnicott's psychoanalytic approach (or a correlated version of it) through her own therapeutic experience.[79] Winnicott's approach is centred on the role of a loving environment in fostering the child's sense of the self, which is linked to the experience of a 'spontaneous impulse' and the expression of a 'spontaneous gesture'.[80] This approach

---

79 See FM 43, 76, 118–19, 120–1.
80 Winnicott, *The Maturational Processes and the Facilitating Environment*, 145.

is further developed by Miller, who investigates children's adaptation
to parental expectations when a loving environment is not adequately
provided. Miller writes:

> Children who fulfil their parents' conscious or unconscious wishes are 'good', but if
> they ever refuse to do so or express wishes of their own that go against those of their
> parents, they are called egoistic and inconsiderate.
>   Accommodation to parental needs often (but not always) leads to the 'as-if per-
> sonality' (Winnicott has described it as the 'False Self'). This person develops in
> such a way that he reveals only what is expected of him, and fuses so completely with
> what he reveals that – until he comes to analysis – one could scarcely have guessed
> how much there is to him, behind this masked view of himself.[81]

In the representation of her role as a child entertainer, Goliarda's need to
accommodate herself to the fulfilment of others' expectations in order to
win their love exerts a distorting pressure on the development of her self.
Whenever a power inequality is involved, as in the relationship between
men and women and between adults and children, power relations seem to
erase the possibility of authentic expression and communication, leading
to what Miller describes as the 'tragedy of the loss of the self, or alienation
from the self.'[82]

A similar condition of 'alienation from the self' emerges from the
narrator's ironic recollection of the record kept by her family of all the
times she cried in a day. Beside the real reasons for crying, among which
the sight of a beggar stands out – 'Ore 19. G. ha pianto perché ha visto
un mendicante che dormiva contro il muro' [7pm. G. cried because she
saw a beggar sleeping against the wall] (LA 70) – Goliarda also stresses
her instrumental use of weeping as a way to gain love, for she even trains
to fake crying. Likewise, the narrator of *Il filo di mezzogiorno* recounts:
'i miei fratelli mi volevano far piangere per mostrare come ero sensibile

---

81   Miller, *The Drama of Being a Child*, 12–13, 27.
82   Ibid. 47. In this respect, Sapienza's representation of the child entertainer is also in line
      with a Marxist critique of alienation in a hierarchically structured society, explicitly
      evoked by Sapienza in the reference to the 'operaio sfruttato', the exploited worker.
      See, for example, Giulio Preti, 'Un concetto da chiarire: Alienazione', *Il filo rosso*, 1
      April 1963.

ai loro amici' [my brothers wanted to make me cry to show their friends
how sensistive I was] (FM 43), and an analogous scene is narrated in
Io, Jean Gabin.[83] One of the most communicative expressions of feelings, such as crying, becomes here the sign of the child's difficulty in
establishing a sincere communication when dependence and power are
involved: 'Quella sera che cercando con gli occhi il mio bollettino, risultò
composto di solo due righe, fui disperatissima. Possibile? Avevo pianto
solo due volte? E piansi tutta la notte ma nessuno mi sentì' [That night,
when, looking at my record, I saw only two lines, I was devastated. How
was it possible? Did I only cry twice? And I cried all night, but nobody
heard me] (LA 70). The true weeping finds vent in solitude, outside the
reach of a communication that is experienced as necessarily distorting,
thus signalling the protagonist's isolation from her family. Her crying is
true, as is her passion for performing, but when these expressive forms
are oriented towards the dependence on other people they prevent communication instead of enabling it.

As she grows up, Goliarda chooses the profession of dramatic actress,
in which she appears to be exceptionally talented, and moves to Rome. In
one of the very few occasions in which the narrator talks about what she
likes to do, rather than what she feels she ought to be training for, she
states: 'Mi piaceva cantare, ballare e si divertivano tutti quando lo facevo, anche in
cortile' [I liked singing, dancing, and they all enjoyed it when I did, even
down in the courtyard] (LA 89). The choice to be an actress ultimately
appears to be founded on her personal inclination rather than on the desire
to emulate her parents' or others' example. Nonetheless, the narrator refers
to her talent for acting and entertaining as a form of alienation, carried
out in order to attract love and attention. As such, acting shifts from the
expression of personal enjoyment and desire to its opposite, namely the
manipulation of the self to conform to other people's expectations. In the
end, she does not find in this career choice the affirmation of autonomy
she was trying to achieve as a child:

83   See JG 59.

A Roma, con la borsa di studio tra le mani, [...] entrai nel compromesso, mi rattrappii nel servaggio di avere successo ai loro occhi, di piacere. Credevo alla loro serietà e alla mia, e per venti anni rimasi anchilosata a servirli, a dire parole ambigue. A fare finta di non avere paura e a non dormire per paura dei loro atti, delle loro decisioni che, come una volta, subivo. (LA 158)

[In Rome, with the scholarship in my hands, [...] I entered a compromise, I was trapped in the need to be successful in their eyes, to be appreciated. I believed in their seriousness and in mine, and for twenty years I remained stiff, serving them, saying ambiguous words. I pretended I wasn't scared, while I couldn't sleep because of the fear of their actions and decisions, which, once again, they imposed on me.]

The representation of the child entertainer and the condition of inauthenticity have clear connections with the work of Pirandello, who is a fundamental artistic reference for Sapienza.[84] Of particular importance here is Pirandello's representation of identity as a 'mask'. In works such as *Il fu Mattia Pascal* (1904) and *Uno, nessuno, centomila* (1926), and in many among the plays collected in *Maschere nude* (1958), the mask is the necessary and unavoidable mediation between the self and others, so that identity is always, and inescapably, split. If socialization and inauthenticity are coextensive, for Pirandello rebellion is useless, for no emancipatory outcome can derive from it.[85] In Sapienza's works, on the other hand, the narrator rebels against the distortion and oppression deriving from the compliant mask, considering it, at least in part, as connected more to power imbalance than to communication itself. The deconstruction of social norms and the acknowledgement of one's own desires (in Winnicott's terms, the development of a True Self) help recognize the difference between adaptation and complete self-annihilation in the compliance with a role, which turns identity into the mask itself. This is a necessary step in order

84 On the relationship between Sapienza and Pirandello, see Bazzoni, 'Pirandello's Legacy in the Narrative Writings of Goliarda Sapienza', *Pirandello Studies*, 36 (2016), 111–26.
85 On the political dimension of Pirandello's understanding of identity, see Venè, 'È l'alienazione che condanna gli uomini alla loro classe sociale', in *Pirandello fascista: la condizione borghese tra ribellione e rivoluzione* (Venice: Marsilio Editori, 1981), 103–12.

to recuperate a sense of self that enables agency, precisely what, according to Sidonie Smith, women have historically been prevented from exercising: 'The unified self disperses, radiating outward until its fragments dissipate altogether into social and communal masks. Thus woman's destiny cannot be self-determined, and her agency cannot be exercised.'[86] Miller, too, attributes an empowering potential to the development of a sense of self that enables agency, something that power – both as institutional power and as the power of adults over children – contrasts and undermines. The access to agency by subjects in a subaltern position thus has an inherently political effect:

> 'Society' not only suppresses instinctual wishes but also (and above all) it suppresses particular feelings (for instance, anger) and narcissistic needs (for esteem, mirroring, respect), whose admissibility in adults and fulfillment in children would lead to individual autonomy and emotional strength, and thus would not be consonant with the interests of those in power. However, this oppression and this forcing of submission do not only begin in the office, factory or political party; they begin in the very first weeks of an infant's life.[87]

The path of self-reconstruction undertaken by Sapienza diverges from the inescapability of Pirandello's mask for it aspires to access agency where this has never been exercised before. Participating in women's struggle to become subjects, the representation of identity provided by Sapienza appears incommensurable with the trajectory of the modern subject, for there is no sense of a previously universal and rational subject falling apart, but rather the coming into being of a new subjectivity.

From this different perspective, although complete liberation from all forms of conditioning is not possible, some relationships, such as the one with Nica in *Lettera aperta* and the ones with the narrator's female friends in *Il filo di mezzogiorno*, are represented as less distorting than others, and actually have the potential of strengthening rather than undermining the construction of identity. In all her works Sapienza carves out the space for relationships of friendship, often with a strong component of homosexual

---

86   Smith, *Subjectivity, Identity and the Body*, 13.
87   Miller, *The Drama of Being a Child*, 127–8.

desire, which pierce the mask and allow the expression of the self and the achievement of true, empathetic communication. In *Lettera aperta* and *Il filo di mezzogiorno*, the narrator exposes and contests the conditions that, in her upbringing, led to the formation of an oppressive mask that drained her vitality, and aims at reconstructing a stronger sense of the self beyond social norms. Overall, the protagonists' process of growing up traces the parable of a failed social integration and an unresolved construction of personal identity. On the other hand, by recounting the story of her childhood, the adult narrator identifies and deconstructs the forms of oppression to which she was subjected, seeking to undo them and re-establish contact with her own desires and with her own living body. Writing becomes for Sapienza the space where she can turn imposition and oppression into active creation and self-creation.

Staging the Past, Voicing the Present

Fragmented Memories and Narrative Blends

Lettera aperta inaugurates Sapienza's literary endeavour. The coincidence of protagonist's and author's name ascribes the work to the autobiographical genre,[88] and the central theme of a young girl's upbringing recalls the structure of the *Bildungsroman* or, more specifically, the 'romanzo del divenire' [novel of becoming], the definition suggested by Laura Fortini and Paola Bono (along the lines of the Bakhtinian *novel of emergence*) to emphasize the openness of the formative process.[89] *Il filo di mezzogiorno*, also a first

---

88   See Philippe Lejeune, *On Autobiography*, ed. Paul John Eakin, trans. Katherine Leary (Minneapolis: University of Minnesota Press, 1989).

89   Paola Bono and Laura Fortini, 'Introduzione', in Bono and Fortini, eds, *Il romanzo del divenire. Un Bildungsroman delle donne?* (Rome: Iacobelli, 2007), 7–13. Mikhail Bakhtin, 'The *Bildungsroman* and its Significance in the History of Realism (Toward a Historical Typology of the Novel)', in *Speech Genres and Other Late Essays*, ed.

person autobiographical narrative, continues the journey started in *Lettera aperta*, exploring the narrator's past and present situation through the representation of her psychoanalytic therapy. Within the literary genres of autobiography and 'romanzo del divenire', however, these works present a number of features that enrich and destabilize their genre structure, realizing, in Anna Langiano's words, 'an open and impure novelistic form'.[90]

The first and most evident element of contamination in *Lettera aperta* and *Il filo di mezzogiorno* is the hybridism of themes and styles, which include, beside the recollection of childhood and the family saga, extra-diegetic political, social and artistic reflections, as well as anecdotes and portraits that depart from the narrator's childhood. Similarly, the narrator alternates a rationalistic and essayistic prose with a densely metaphorical, analogical and fragmented use of language. Significantly, the first version of *Lettera aperta*, prior to Enzo Siciliano's editing, featured a much more extensive presence of extra-diegetic remarks concerned with the narrator's present and her socio-cultural context, to the point that the form of pamphlet or critical essay competed with the autobiographical genre as overall structure of the work.[91]

Having survived two suicide attempts and partially lost her memory due to electroconvulsive therapy, Sapienza embarks on a journey of self-reconstruction, revisiting her childhood in the attempt to recompose her disrupted memory. Accordingly, the narrative discourse is subject to intense fragmentation: events are linked through analogical rather than chronological associations, and characters, voices and episodes are often confused or even obscure, as the narrator is caught in the middle of the process of recollecting her past. As Langiano points out, 'Goliarda Sapienza's writing pursues a systematic fragmentation of meaning. Temporal hierarchies are

---

Caryl Emerson and Michael Holquist, trans. Vern W. McGee (Austin: University of Texas Press, 1986), 10–59.

90 Anna Langiano, '*Lettera aperta*: il dovere di tornare', in Providenti, *Quel sogno d'essere*, 131–47, 143.

91 On the editing carried out by Siciliano, see Langiano, '*Lettera aperta*: il dovere di tornare'. I am grateful to Providenti and Ross for providing me with a copy of the original typescript.

destabilized, and the coherence of cause and effect is replaced with the co-presence of different temporal domains and seemingly unrelated events.'[92] The same fragmentation characterizes *Il filo di mezzogiorno*, where the narrator proceeds by freely associating, and often mixing, figures and episodes. In both texts, the narrative discourse reproduces the work of a disrupted memory, with its incoherencies, gaps and analogical associations.[93]

In addition to the fragmentation of the narrative discourse, due to the isomorphism between disrupted memory and narration, *Lettera aperta* and *Il filo di mezzogiorno* feature a doubling of the narrating voice. An adult narrator, a woman in her forties in Rome, alternates with a child's voice, that of the young Goliarda in the late 1920s and early 1930s in Catania. As Ortu points out, 'The *speaking voice* alternates. Clearly, it is always the adult Goliarda who is writing, but often it is as if the child's view emerged without mediation or analysis, and with the *direct recording* of the lights, the sounds and the words of her childhood.'[94] Similarly, both Anna Carta and Mariagiovanna Andrigo describe the narrator's participation in the episodes from her childhood as a 're-enactment', thus stressing the element of re-presentation of the child's perspective.[95] Not only is the perspective twofold, but also the focus, since the present of the narrator alternates with recollections from her childhood as the foregrounded topic of narration. The narrator of the story, with her own present troubles, her struggle to remember and survive, effectively constitutes the co-protagonist of the books. By telling the story of the progressive oppression she underwent as a child, the adult narrator seeks to undo it, retrieving an instinctive vitality and becoming the active subject of her own narrative.

92   Langiano, '*Lettera aperta*: il dovere di tornare', 138.
93   For an exploration of the mechanisms of analogy and fragmentation in *Lettera aperta*, see Mariagiovanna Andrigo, 'L'evoluzione autobiografica di Goliarda Sapienza. Stile e contenuti', in Providenti, *Quel sogno d'essere*, 117–30; Langiano, '*Lettera aperta*: il dovere di tornare'; and Ortu, 'Cosa vedono gli occhi di quella bambina.'
94   Ortu, 'Cosa vedono gli occhi di quella bambina', 151. My emphasis.
95   Andrigo, 'L'evoluzione autobiografica di Goliarda Sapienza', 124; Anna Carta, 'Finestre, porte, luoghi reali e spazi immaginari nell'opera di Goliarda Sapienza', in Providenti, *Quel sogno d'essere*, 261–76, 267.

The dynamic, pulsating connection established between the process of recollection and the narrator's search for identity in *Lettera aperta* and *Il filo di mezzogiorno* differs significantly from the stable relationship between present and past set in traditional forms of autobiography, such as in the works by Augustine, Rousseau, Goethe and Alfieri. In those works, the past is presented as concluded, detached from the present and exalted in its exemplarity. To borrow Cavarero's words, in traditional autobiographies 'the underlying notion is that there is in the first place a self-aware subject who, in writing his life, transposes the substantial reality of his self into words, and that his self is independent from the text.'[96] While according to Cavarero the traditional, rational subject uses narration to detach the present from the past, in *Lettera aperta* and *Il filo di mezzogiorno* the past is not concluded, but active on the present and actively interpreted by the present narrator who interacts with it. The act of remembering and narrating affects the past itself, as this is dismantled and explored repeatedly, according to the evolving meaning it assumes in the present.

Sapienza achieves such a mutual contamination of past and present through a variety of narrative techniques. For example, the narrator comments on the effects of re-evoking certain episodes, and interacts with figures from her past as if they were present in the same spatio-temporal domain as hers. Furthermore, she constantly manipulates tenses and temporal and spatial deictics so as to blur the distinction between the adult and the child perspective: '*dovevo* aver dormito molto [...] era domenica e *avevo* ancora il malditesta. Sicuramente *ho* anche i capelli bianchi. *Devo* andare a controllare' [*I must have slept* for a long time [...] it *was* Sunday and I still *had* a headache. *I'm* sure I also *have* white hair. I *have to* go and check]; '*La sera prima*, finalmente, avevo visto "La Regina Cristina". [...] *Ieri sera* pioveva quando siamo usciti dal cinema' [*The night before* I had finally seen 'Queen Christina'. [...] *Yesterday*, when we left the cinema, it was raining] (LA 57. My emphasis). *Il filo di mezzogiorno* features a similar oscillation between past and present: 'Ma *ora*, mi *guarda* come

96 Cavarero, *Tu che mi guardi*, 91.

guardava mia madre. Non *potevo* sopportare quello sguardo' [But *now* he *is looking* at me as my mother used to do. I *couldn't* stand that look] (FM 40. My emphasis). The changes in tenses and deictics disrupt the cohesion and linearity of the events, blurring the line between the spatio-temporal coordinates of the narrator and those of the child, between present and past.

A striking example of the interaction between present and past is the episode of Anna 'la sediara', when Goliarda is abandoned by the artisan and waits for her sitting outside the shut door of her house. Anna's sudden departure deprives Goliarda of the training in manufacturing chairs that had given her a sense of fulfilment. This episode, associated with a loss of identity, has its repercussions for the narrator as well, since she – the adult woman – is still in search of an identity she lost in front of Anna's shut door. Re-experiencing the child's own trouble – Sapienza uses the verb 'risillabare' [to pronounce again] – the narrator waits like the child and, like the child, seeks to find her place in society, her 'utilità', her identity. The child's act of waiting on Anna's threshold is paralleled by the narrator's own suspension of narration, which results in a blank space on the page:

> Ma Anna era andata via e non mi aveva neanche guardata. [...] Mi sedetti sulla soglia, sotto quella porta sbarrata, e aspettai fino a notte. Aspettai, ma sapevo che non sarebbe tornata. [...] Scusatemi, ma visto che aspetto debbo lasciarvi per un po'. Non posso costringervi ad aspettare con me. Quando uno aspetta e piange, non è divertente né utile per gli altri e così, abbiate pazienza, se resto su questo gradino muta per qualche tempo, debbo aspettare, ma da sola.
> *[Blank space on the page]*
> ... Devo tornare a quel gradino: solo tornando a quella soglia oggi, forse, potrò capire il senso di questa attesa, che, come tante altre cose, ci fanno subire i grandi.
> *[Blank space on the page]*
> Anche oggi, come ieri ho aspettato piangendo, seduta sulla soglia: stasera, ieri sera, tre sere fa, un anno? (LA 87–8)

[But Anna had left and hadn't even looked at me. [...] I sat on the doorstep, by that locked door, and waited until night. I waited, but I knew she wouldn't come back. [...] I'm sorry, but since I'm waiting, I must leave you for a while. I can't make you wait with me. When someone waits and cries, it's neither useful nor entertaining for others, so please be patient while I stay here on this doorstep, in silence. I must wait, but alone.

[*Blank space on the page*]

... I must go back to that doorstep, only by going back to that door, today, might I understand the meaning of this waiting that grownups impose on us, like so many other things.

[*Blank space on the page*]

Today, like yesterday, I waited, crying, sitting on the doorstep – tonight, yesterday, three nights ago, a year?]

The child's wait becomes a pause in the process of recollecting, and this hiatus in turn becomes a blank space on the page and invites the readers to share in the time of the story narrated as well as in that of narration. Through writing, the time of the pause translates into the material space on the page, generating a short-circuit between space of the story narrated, narrative discourse and material, extra-textual reality.

The visual technique of a blank space on the page is one of the numerous characteristics, together with the regular appeals to the readers and the non-linear, digressive structure of narration, that connect *Lettera aperta* with Laurence Sterne's *Tristram Shandy*.[97] Sterne's influence on *Lettera aperta* is indeed pervasive, and would merit specific enquiry, but it is sufficient to point out here that *Tristram Shandy* is mentioned twice in the novel, with explicit references to the materiality of the book – 'la mia stanza è un po' troppo umida, e così Tristram si è tutto appicciato a questo libraccio, e per staccarlo lo dovrei squarciare da capo a fondo' [my room is a bit too damp, and so Tristram got stuck to this other book, and if I wanted to separate it I should rip it apart from top to bottom] (LA 30), and to the meta-narrative dialogue with the readers:

---

97   Laurence Sterne, *The Life and Opinions of Tristram Shandy, Gentleman* (1760). In this respect, *Lettera aperta* (and the same is true of all Sapienza's autobiographical works) also reconnects with the nineteenth-century Italian tradition of anti-novelistic, autofictional writings, such as Carlo Dossi's *L'altrieri: nero su bianco* (1868) and *Vita di Alberto Pisani* (1870), and Ugo Foscolo's unfinished autobiographical novel *Sesto tomo dell'io* (1799–1800).

NOTA: [...] ho premesso un 'Si può non leggere' o, come avrebbe detto il nostro
caro fedele amico Tristram Shandy:
CHIUDETE LA PORTA[98]

NOTE: [...] I put a 'You can skip this' before, or, as our dear and loyal friend Tristram
Shandy would have said:
CLOSE THE DOOR

Mark Turner's concept of 'blended space' can provide a useful tool to
understand Sapienza's manipulation of narrative in the passage above, in
particular in her dialogue with the readers. In *The Literary Mind*, Turner
provides a cognitive analysis of the fundamental mechanisms of thought,
which he identifies as essentially narrative. According to Turner's cognitive theory, human thought relies on the centrality of stories, which bring
together and combine different conceptual spaces to produce a coherent
unit. Turner applies his theory to the analysis of literary texts, pointing out
the ability of stories to creatively 'blend' separate conceptual spaces. In particular, he analyses the interaction between story narrated and narration. He
proposes to situate this kind of interaction (typically in the case of a *mise
en abyme* of the narrative discourse) in what he defines a 'blended space', a
conceptual space separated from both that of the narrator and that of the
characters. In this third conceptual space, elements from the two domains
are blended, creating a contact and interaction that would be impossible in
either domain. In Turner's words, 'in the blend, the narrator, the readers,
and the characters can inhabit one world'.[99]

While the practice of blending story narrated and narration is widespread in literary texts, it is normally deployed in the direction of the
narrator's intervention into the story narrated, so that he or she acquires
'special powers' in the story narrated: the narrator can move freely in
time and space, read the characters' minds, etc.[100] Sapienza also effects

98   LA 36–7. The warning to the readers about a chapter that can be skipped has another
     important precedent in Alessandro Manzoni's introduction of the digression on
     Cardinal Federigo Borromeo in Chapter XII of *I promessi sposi* (1840).
99   Turner, *The Literary Mind*, 75–6.
100 Ibid. 76.

a conflation between narration and story narrated in a different, unexpected manner. In *Lettera aperta* and *Il filo di mezzogiorno*, the narrator not only affects the story narrated with her 'special powers' but also, and more importantly, the story narrated affects the narrator. It is the child's wait that causes the narrator to pause, and invites the readers to wait with her, lingering on the blank space on the page. Similarly, the narrator's remembrance of the poor women by which she felt oppressed as a child surfaces despite the narrator's will. Although she tries to resist – 'non vi voglio parlare di loro' [I don't want to talk to you about them] (LA 66) – these women invade the narrator's room and, at the same time, the page: 'queste donne – se vi devo dire la verità, ancora adesso, anzi proprio adesso che le ho accusate – sono entrate e si sono sedute sulle sedie, sul divano, in piedi contro il muro e mi guardano senza dire niente' [these women – to tell the truth, still now, now that I have accused them – walk in and sit on the chairs and the sofa, or stand against the wall, and stare at me without saying anything] (67) In the end, talking about those women, although painful, has a positive effect on the narrator – 'Ho fatto bene a parlare con voi di queste donne [...] non vedete che sono sparite' [I was right to talk about these women with you [...] don't you see that they disappeared] (69) – thus confirming the active role that narration of the past has on the narrator's own present.

The Readers as an Audience, the Text as an Oral Performance

Another 'blended space' in *Lettera aperta* is the one shared by the narrator with the readers, who are repeatedly evoked as interlocutors who are present in the same space as the narrator. The readers are called to perform an active role in the discourse, since the narrator relies on their reactions to orient her act of remembering and narrating. Let us see how this works in the text. At the beginning of *Lettera aperta*, Dina, the narrator's housekeeper, comments negatively on a decorative object on a shelf. Her comment, 'Quanto è brutto!' [So ugly!] (LA 16) triggers the narrator's journey into her past, configured as an act of 'tidying up' her memories and parallel to the physical act of tidying up the room – getting rid of ugly objects, keeping good memories. Dina represents the textual figure of the reader, whose judgement orients the narrator in her selecting and sorting endeavour. It is important to note, however, that the act of tidying up the room is not a metaphor for putting order on the memories, since the memories are, in fact, physically attached to the objects in the room. The sorting out of objects belongs to the space of the adult narrator, who is tidying up objects in her room, while the tidying up of memories belongs to the space of narration, where memories are being evoked and sorted out in the narrative discourse. Again, narration and the space of the narrator conflate.

While in the incipit Dina provides a textual figure for the reader, inhabiting the same space as the narrator's, straight after the episode of the 'ugly object' Sapienza leaves behind any textual mediation and directly addresses the readers, who are invited to participate actively in the process of tidying up: 'Scusate ancora, ma ho bisogno di voi per essere in grado di sbarazzarmi di tutte le cose brutte che ci sono qui dentro. Parlando, dalla reazione di chi ascolta, puoi capire cosa va tenuto e cosa buttato' [I'm sorry, but I need your help to be able to get rid of all the ugly things in here. As I'm talking, I can see what to keep and what to throw away based on the audience's reaction] (LA 16). In the text, the readers are represented as actually performing this role, since the narrator is able to perceive their reactions to the text as she narrates: 'Vedo dai vostri visi che questa morte vi ha affaticati' [I can see from your eyes that this death tired you] (36). Clearly, the space where such a communication between readers and narrator can take place, overcoming temporal and spatial impossibility, is properly a blended space.

As the whole setting of the text indicates, the blended space created by Sapienza, where story narrated, narration and readers can communicate and influence each other, is configured as a theatrical space. Indeed, Sapienza's experience as an actress, first in theatre and later in cinema, leaves a significant trace on her writing. Narration is an oral performance, which, memory after memory and through the dialogue with the readers, (re)creates the narrator's own identity. The act of narrating is qualified throughout the text as oral speech, pronounced in front of an audience, which Langiano defines 'reader-spectator'.[101] Narration is a 'sproloquio' [rambling speech] (LA 31), to think and remember is 'parlare, comunicare' [to talk, to communicate], to read is 'ascoltare' [to listen] (53) and to end the narration is 'tacere' [to fall silent] (159). *Il filo di mezzogiorno* also features an oral dialogical structure, with the therapist in the role of main interlocutor and active participant. In the last sections of the text, the role of interlocutor shifts from Majore to Giovanna, Sapienza's nurse, and from her to the readers themselves, thus reconnecting with the project of *Lettera aperta*: '[gli] occhi di Giovanna Jane ... dietro a quegli occhi [...] intravidi altri occhi, altri visi di amici [...] che avrebbero ascoltato e volli parlare, raccontare, essere confortata e guidata' [Giovanna-Jane's eyes ... and behind those eyes [...] I glimpsed other eyes, the faces of other friends [...] who would listen, so I wanted to talk, to recount, to be supported and guided] (FM 184).

To qualify narration as irreducibly vocal entails attributing to intersubjective communication a crucial role. Cavarero notes: 'Within the etymological field of the Latin *vox* [voice], the first meaning of *vocare* is "to call", "to invoke". Before being words, the voice is an invocation, addressed to the others and trusting in an ear that welcomes it.'[102] Through her voice, the narrator of *Lettera aperta* imitates a physical presence on a stage, shared with the audience. In doing so, she brings her physical existence into the text, refusing to dissociate language from the body and thought from communication. Sapienza's literary operation recalls Cavarero's argument in favour of the voice – physical and uniquely personal – as opposed to abstract, universal and disembodied representations of thought and language. As the philosopher puts it, 'unlike thought, which tends to inhabit the immaterial world of ideas, speech is always a matter of bodies, which are necessarily passionate, pulsating and full of unrestrained desires.'[103] Similarly, according to Jean-Claude Coquet, a French linguist of phenomenological orientation, the linguistic 'I' is always and primarily a body, and written language necessarily bears traces of the corporeal dimension of oral speech: 'The

101 Langiano, '*Lettera aperta*: il dovere di tornare', 133.
102 Cavarero, *A più voci*, 185.
103 Ibid. 149.

body takes part as much in reading as in writing. [...] Therefore writing is inseparable from the voice.'[104]

Sapienza's writing is performative in the sense that it affects the present of the narrator, but also in the sense that it is staged as a performance, in which the narrator, in place of remembering a concluded and detached past, through her speech enunciates herself in the present, mimicking her physical presence. As Cavarero notes, 'time and space of narration are *not* always and necessarily posthumous. In fact, by imitating direct speech, the *mimesis* situates the hero's tale in the time and space of its happening.'[105] In *Lettera aperta*, the text performs the present and presence of the body. Sapienza's work thus features a centrality of the body not only on a thematic level, but also in the very structures of the text, and in particular in the characterization of narrative as a performance. Her literary operation puts at the centre that primary relationship between thought, language and body evidenced by phenomenology. As Paolo Fabbri writes in his introduction to Coquet's work, 'it is not language that expresses the external state of things; instead, the state of things enunciates itself in language, through projective modalities that maintain, to different degrees, a relationship with the somatic experience of reality.'[106] If traditional autobiographies separate the past from the present, Sapienza conversely creates a performative space where the different temporal layers constituting the self can interact with each other and with the readers, because 'there is no discontinuity between the event, the experience of the event [...] and the expression of the event. They complement each other.'[107]

By subtracting her biography from the concluded and detached dimension of the past, 'what is done and cannot be undone',[108] and re-presenting it into her discourse, Sapienza can thus exert her agency on her own story and appropriate it. Narrative enables the narrator to undo the oppressive path she underwent as a child and liberate herself, marking her own

104   Coquet, *Le istanze enuncianti*, 68.
105   Cavarero, *Tu che mi guardi*, 163.
106   Paolo Fabbri, 'Tra *Physis* e *Logos*', in Coquet, *Le istanze enuncianti*, vii–xx, xi–xii.
107   Coquet, *Le istanze enuncianti*, 40.
108   Cavarero, *Tu che mi guardi*, 24.

biography as a chosen space and not an imposed destiny. She becomes, in other words, the actor of her own story and even suggests that theatre, 'quest'estratto di vita' [this distillation of life], was created by humans 'per tenerla in pugno almeno per un paio d'ore' [to have it under control at least for a couple of hours] (LA 31). Writing is thus, for Sapienza, a way to exert her own agency, to turn passivity into active construction and gain control of her life. Through writing, she accomplishes an autogenesis and creates herself as a narrator, just as Aleramo does in *Una donna*. Significantly, the appropriation of life through a performance of the self is thematized in the text with a specific reference to acting: 'Oggi, 10 maggio 1965, compio 41 anni ed ho quasi finito questo mio libro che se riuscirò ad impararlo a memoria – io non so improvvisare: ho fatto l'attrice e devo, per parlare, avere un copione – sarà il mio parlare a voi. Oggi rinasco o forse nasco per la prima volta. Ho un anno, solo un anno' [Today, 10 May 1965, I turn 41, and I've almost finished this book, which, if I can learn it by heart – I can't improvise, I was an actor and in order to speak I need a script – will be my speech to you. Today I'm born again, or perhaps I'm born for the first time. I'm just one year old] (146). Clearly, there lies a crucial contradiction here, for the operation of appropriating and re-presenting the past as a chosen story performed by the actor-narrator is and remains, after all, fictional: 'the mise-en-scene is obviously a fiction, a representation – in other words, a story'.[109] However, the fictional performance of the self participates in a deeper, non-fictional reality, since it expresses the very real constitution of identity through narration.

Carta, pointing out the affinity between the use of narration in *Lettera aperta* and Cavarero's philosophy of narrative, notes that 'Sapienza's auto-biographical writing contains a reflection on the nature, motivations and originary status of narration'.[110] In *Lettera aperta*, Sapienza exhibits the process through which the self constructs its own story, a process that, in Cavarero's perspective, is intrinsically narrative, for 'narrative memory is the home of the self'.[111] Similarly, Turner attributes a primary and fundamental

109 Cavarero, *Tu che mi guardi*, 163.
110 Carta, 'Finestre, porte, luoghi reali e spazi immaginari', 275.
111 Cavarero, *Tu che mi guardi*, 49.

cognitive role to the human faculty of organizing reality into stories, for narration is understood as the founding structure of thought and language.[112] From a sociological perspective, Margaret Somers finds in 'conceptual narrativity' and the 'ontological dimension of narrative' the key notions to understanding the processes of identity formation.[113] Where the characterization of the text as oral performance and the mimesis of a present *in fieri* have a component of fiction, the use of narration to recompose memories and reconstruct the self are an extremely powerful tool whose very real effects on the narrator herself are represented in *Lettera aperta*.

The notion of performative narrative, understood in the light of Cavarero's reflections on the voice and narration and of Coquet's notion of the permanence of the body in language, helps us make sense of the contradiction in Sapienza's narrative between the aspiration to establish a bodily foundation for identity and a self that is always the result of a linguistic, textual operation. Sapienza writes: 'Per me quella che chiamiamo vita, prende consistenza solo se riesco a tradurla in scrittura' [For me, what we call life assumes substance only if I can translate it into words];[114] On this twofold motor in Sapienza's writing, Ross observes that Sapienza's sense of the self is constructed and mediated through language: 'In order for her experiences to assume substance, they must paradoxically be channelled through the text, although she repeatedly insists on the corporeal character of our ontological condition.'[115] The contradiction between textual and bodily foundation of identity is overcome by the characterization of text as itself constituted and inhabited by the body, and the very process of identity formation as narrative. Configured as a performative speech in which the narrator, like an actor, performs her own story, the text coincides with the physical act of narrating, which has a very real, material effect on the narrator herself. Autobiographical narration in *Lettera aperta* thus retains a relationship with extra-textual reality, inasmuch as it enables the narrator

---

112   See Turner, *The Literary Mind*, 15.
113   Margaret Somers, 'The Narrative Constitution of Identity. A Relational and Network Approach', *Theory and Society*, 5, 23 (October 1994), 605–49, 606–7.
114   CD 139.
115   Ross, 'Identità di genere e sessualità', 224.

to survive and appropriate her own past. As Maria Arena puts it, 'writing becomes her cure, the place where her desire revives'.[116] After *Lettera aperta*, *Il filo di mezzogiorno* continues her autofictional journey by recounting her own psychoanalytic experience, thereby explicitly merging therapy, identity formation and writing. To use Sapienza's own words from *L'arte della gioia*, 'chi nasce con il talento di raccontare è anche uno che guarisce' (AG 489) [a person born with the talent to tell stories is also someone who heals. AJ 643]. Indeed, the conclusive chapter of *Lettera aperta* ends on the narrator's demand for the freedom to play with her own body, that source of vitality with which, thanks to the narration of her own story, she has regained contact. Narration does not only represent the formation of the self, but realizes it.

116   Maria Arena, '*Il filo di mezzogiorno*. Morte e rinascita attraverso la scrittura', 151.

'Gioiosa forza nomade': Epicureanism and Anarchism in *L'arte della gioia*

Introduction

L'arte della gioia is Sapienza's major work, in terms of its length, popularity and critical acclaim. However, it took a long time before its importance was recognized, and the troubled history of its publication is now well documented.[1] According to Pellegrino, and as stated in the 1998 edition by Stampa Alternativa, the novel was written between 1967 and 1976, a period during which Sapienza retired from working in the cinema industry to undertake her vast literary project. When she finished *L'arte della gioia*, she was already known in artistic and intellectual circles in Rome, but this did not help her get her novel published. The publication of *L'arte della gioia* by Einaudi in 2008, which launched Sapienza's success in Italy, came after a long series of rejections from several Italian publishers,[2] two limited editions by Stampa Alternativa, and the wide consensus achieved by the German, French, Spanish and Catalan translations. Since then, the novel has been translated also into Portuguese, Greek, English, Finnish and Turkish.[3] Over forty years after the first edition of *Lettera aperta* and

---

1   See Maria Belén Hernández, 'La fortuna literaria de Goliarda Sapienza', *Arena Romanística*, 5 (2009), 140–52; 'La fortuna letteraria de *L'arte della gioia* in Europa', in Providenti, *Quel sogno d'essere*, 99–113; Cambria, 'La terribile arte della gioia'; Pellegrino, 'Lunga marcia dell'*Arte della gioia*', in AG v–x, and 'Un personaggio singolare'; Domenico Scarpa, 'Senza alterare niente', in AG 515–38.

2   See Sapienza, *Cronistoria di alcuni rifiuti editoriali dell'*Arte della gioia, ed. Angelo Pellegrino (Rome: Edizioni Croce, 2016).

3   See the Bibliography for a complete list of foreign editions of Sapienza's works.

approximately thirty years after *L'arte della gioia* was brought to completion, finally Sapienza is beginning to be regarded internationally as a significant author worthy of critical attention.

Before proceeding to a detailed analysis, some elements of uncertainty concerning the editing of this novel must be mentioned. According to Pellegrino, the typescript of *L'arte della gioia* underwent a drastic reduction, from 800 to 500 pages.[4] He declares that he initially worked on the editing of the text together with Sapienza, straight after the completion of the novel, and then continued on his own in complete freedom.[5] On another occasion, he states that he continued the editing even after Sapienza's death, and that this second editing coincided with the idea of a complete edition for Stampa Alternativa: 'Goliarda died suddenly. [...] After careful consideration, I took the manuscript, *worked on it again*, and decided to publish it in a limited edition of a thousand copies with Stampa Alternativa.'[6] The final text of *L'arte della gioia* then would have undergone, by admission of Pellegrino, a substantial reduction and editing, even after the author's death. To this, another revision must be added, the one carried out jointly by Sapienza and Anna Maria Baraghini for the first, partial edition of *L'arte della gioia* in 1994, which concerned only the first part of the novel and which might explain the difference in concision and cohesiveness that is apparent between the first part and the rest of the book. A comparison between the manuscript, the typescript sent to the publishing houses before Sapienza's death and the published version of the novel could help understand motivations, directions and responsibilities of the substantial editing undergone by *L'arte della gioia*. Finally, Giovanna Providenti suggests that Sapienza began writing the novel in 1969 (instead of 1967) and finished it in 1978, when it was sent to a number of publishers.[7] Unfortunately, the

4   This information was provided to me by Angelo Pellegrino in a private conversation (Rome, November 2011).
5   See Pellegrino, 'Lunga marcia dell'*Arte della gioia*', viii – ix; 'Un personaggio singolare', 77–8.
6   Pellegrino, 'Un personaggio singolare', 83–4. My emphasis.
7   See Providenti, 'L'opera di Goliarda Sapienza tra ambivalenza e ambizione', in Providenti, *Quel sogno d'essere*, 289–302. The critic bases her hypothesis on the draft

manuscript of *L'arte della gioia* has not been made available to the public so far. Waiting for a proper philological research to be carried out, I use the 511-page text published by Einaudi in 2008.

L'arte della gioia, divided in four parts, recounts the story of Modesta, a fictional character born on 1 January 1900 in Sicily, in a valley near Catania.[8] As a child, Modesta lives in a state of extreme poverty with her mother and her sister Tina, who has Down's syndrome. One day, at the age of about nine, while Tina is shouting and crying, Modesta discovers the pleasure of masturbation. She immediately communicates her joyful discovery to Tuzzu, her playmate and first guide, who at first is shocked but then is seduced by the young girl. When Modesta arrives at home, she finds a man who claims to be her father. He shuts the mother and Tina in a storage room and rapes Modesta. When she wakes up, still in shock, she sets fire to the shack with an oil lamp. The mother and Tina die, while the police officers do not find the corpse of the father.

Modesta is rescued by Tuzzu and entrusted to madre Leonora, abbess of a nunnery. She grows up, committing herself to the study of piano and theological texts, surrounded by Leonora's love. At the same time, she suffers from the constrictions and self-privation characterizing life in the nunnery. She finds a true friend in Mimmo, the gardener. After discovering and saying overtly that Leonora secretly masturbates, Modesta loses the mother superior's protection and stages a suicide attempt. Madre Leonora, seriously ill, writes a will in which she leaves Modesta a small inheritance and orders her to experience worldly life before deciding whether to take her vows or not. Nonetheless, as Leonora appears to be likely to live long, Modesta secretly saws the hand rail of the astrological observatory of the mother superior, who falls and dies. In conformity to Leonora's will, Modesta, who is now around sixteen years old, leaves the nunnery and is brought to Villa Carmelo, property of Leonora's aristocratic family of

---

of a letter to Attilio Bertolucci, dated 21 August 1969, in which Sapienza mentions her project to write a novel and which Providenti interprets as referring to the initial idea of *L'arte della gioia*.

8   Valle del Bove, a desert basin covered by lava flows, close to the Etna volcano. In the novel it is called 'Chiana del Bove'.

origin, the Brandifortis. There she meets princess Gaia (Leonora's mother) and Beatrice (Leonora's secret daughter), with whom Modesta begins a love affair. The other inhabitants of the house are the maid Argentovivo, the servant Pietro, and Ippolito, Leonora's mentally ill brother. Modesta manages to make Ippolito grow fond of her and marries him, thus becoming part of the family and acquiring power in the administration of the patrimony. In the meantime, she falls in love with Carmine, administrator of the Brandifortis' landholdings, and becomes pregnant. She finds a trunk full of books by Voltaire, Diderot, Marx, Bebel and other philosophers, which initiate her into socialism and anti-clericalism.

In 1918 the Spanish Flu devastates Catania and Villa Carmelo, leaving Gaia half-paralysed. When Modesta learns that Gaia wants them to remain in Villa Carmelo until their death instead of moving to Catania, and that Beatrice intends to obey, she does not hesitate to let Gaia die by not helping her during a stroke, she burns Gaia's will and finally moves to Catania. The arrival in the city marks the transition to the second part of the novel. Modesta sells most of the family's properties to escape the burden of administrative work, and is abandoned by Carmine, who does not want to upset his sons. She gives birth to Eriprando, and spends her time studying and writing. She meets the young doctor Carlo Civardi, who teaches her to swim – an achievement that symbolizes her newly found freedom – and introduces her to a group of Sicilian socialists. Carlo and Modesta have a brief love affair, which fails because of their sexual and emotional incompatibility, but they start a close friendship. Carlo marries Beatrice, whose relationship with Modesta had in the meanwhile turned into close sisterhood. On the day of the wedding, Carmine goes to Modesta's house and reveals to her that he is going to die soon because of a heart disease, and they start a new relationship, which lasts until Carmine's death. At his funeral, Modesta meets his son, Mattia, and the two begin a passionate and conflicted love affair. When Carlo is killed in a fascist assault, Modesta is suspicious of Mattia and this causes a fight in which they shoot each other.

The third part is devoted to the romantic relationship between Modesta and Joyce, a communist political refugee who struggles with depression and has a passion for psychoanalysis. The house in Catania where they live is inhabited by a large and atypical community; in addition to Eriprando there are: Bambù, daughter of Carlo and Beatrice (who died insane after Carlo's assassination); Stella, a nursemaid, and her son 'Ntoni; Mela, a young orphan helped by Modesta, and Jacopo, son of Ippolito and his nurse. Against the background of rampant fascism, Modesta educates this exceptional community in anti-fascism, laicism and gender equality. Joyce, incapable of accepting her own homosexuality and disagreeing with Modesta's free lifestyle, decides to leave.

The fourth part is the most complex due to the number of characters on stage. Modesta, now short of money, reconciles with Mattia, who helps her sell some precious canvases. Stella, the nursemaid, dies giving birth to a son, Carluzzu, conceived with Eriprando, while Bambù and Mattia fall in love. When World War II breaks out, Modesta is arrested for having secretly helped the communist party, which at that time was illegal. In prison she meets Nina, an energetic anarchist woman from Rome. In 1942 the two women are confined to an island where they suffer from hunger and thirst. After the armistice, they are rescued by Jacopo, who brings them home and then leaves again to go and fight as a partisan. After two years of painful wait, Eriprando, Jacopo and 'Ntoni come back from the war, although the latter is psychologically devastated from his experience in a concentration camp. Modesta commits herself to the communist cause, giving public speeches and writing articles, but quits all political activities and rejects the offer of a seat in parliament as she disagrees with the conformist and rigid mentality of the PCI. Against the Party and her own son Eriprando, she defends her independence by opening a book store in Catania and beginning a new love relationship.

How is the theme of freedom developed in *L'arte della gioia*? In continuity with the previous chapter, this question is answered by putting the relationship between body, identity and power at the centre of the investigation. The first part of the chapter analyses the configuration of identity in the novel, with a predominant focus on the protagonist, Modesta. She emerges as a multifaceted and internally divided character who features different, often conflicting, instances of the self. She is capable of exercising self-determination and violence, firmly rejecting any form of oppression, but also experiences dependency on others and refuses to settle in any definite identity, pursuing an ethics of pleasure, fluidity and experimentation.

Self-control and overwhelming emotions, political commitment and the pursuit of individual pleasure, violence and care coexist and clash in the character of Modesta, requiring a combination of interpretative approaches. In defining what type of subject Sapienza places as the agent of a struggle for freedom, I employ different notions of identity, drawing in particular on Husserl's phenomenological subject and Braidotti's feminist nomadic subject. These notions of the subject account for a combination of strong and weak configurations of identity, which, I argue, is a crucial feature of Sapienza's narrative. The second part of the chapter engages with the collective dimension of the novel, exploring the interaction between personal identity and social structures. Gender, sexuality and politics are the main grounds of investigation. I propose here an interpretation of the libertarian ethics of the novel and the type of subject that is conceived as its protagonist. Overall, *L'arte della gioia* voices a powerfully transgressive aspiration to accomplish a radical form of freedom, pointing to a materialistic and Epicurean ethics. It is a novel that has at its core the ideal of individual and social liberation. Finally, I analyse the novel's narrative structures and the positioning of the narrating voice, focusing in particular on her empathetic relationship with the readers and on the role of the voice.

Whereas close textual analysis is predominant in the other chapters, the length of *L'arte della gioia* requires a more incisive and succinct critical discourse, and this necessarily turns into a reduced presence of textual data. However, tracing comprehensive interpretative lines is a particularly risky operation concerning this novel. In fact, *L'arte della gioia* is a deeply self-contradictory work – and clearly intended to be so. Centred on the 'contraddizione che è il perno della natura' (AG 264) [the contradiction that is at the core of nature. AJ 352], it intrinsically resists systematization. Sapienza's writing aims at 'capturing reality in its constant and contradictory becoming, seeking to "grasp" such a becoming without blocking it.'⁹ The analysis of this novel is therefore particularly challenging from a methodological point of view, for general interpretations cut through the living

9   Tullia Rodigari, 'La personalità culturale e storica di Goliarda Sapienza' (Unpublished Doctoral Thesis, Università degli Studi di Milano Bicocca, 2011), 169. I thank Rodigari for allowing me to see and cite her work prior to its publication.

body of contradictions that are one of its defining features. My aim is then to provide significant insights into this world of contradictions, balancing a systematic and analytical approach with the specificity of the work under analysis, with its fierce resistance to structure and univocal interpretations.

The Configuration of Identity: Epicureanism

The Centrality of the Body

In *L'arte della gioia*, and especially in the characterization of Modesta, the corporeal dimension plays a crucial role. The body is at the centre of an endeavour of redefinition of the subject, which is itself at the centre of a project of radical social transformation, but this process is richly problematic. I reflect here specifically on the position and role of the body within the configuration of identity of the protagonist Modesta, and its relationship with the overarching theme of the text, the struggle for freedom. From the powerful and abrupt opening to the novel, the body is exposed in its material existence and experienced in its physical perceptions:

> *Ed eccovi me* a quattro, cinque anni in uno spazio fangoso che trascino un pezzo di legno immenso. Non ci sono né alberi né case intorno, solo il *sudore* per lo *sforzo* di trascinare quel corpo duro e il *bruciore acuto delle palme ferite* dal legno. Affondo nel fango sino alle caviglie ma devo tirare, non so perché, ma lo devo fare. (AG 5. My emphasis)[10]

---

10 FM features a very similar description of a desert land, accompanied by the therapist's psychoanalytic interpretation: 'In quel campo sterminato di terra bruciata dal gelo... non c'era né ombra né alberi, non un filo d'erba solo il gelo della lampadina accesa, non c'erano case intorno...[...] "Lei percepisce sua madre come una terra sconfinata e brulla senza vita, senza alberi, gli alberi sono simbolo di vita, un campo sconfinato, brullo, impossibile a possedersi, ad abbracciarsi"' [In that immense field, burnt by the frost... there was no shade, no trees or leaves of grass, only the cold of the light bulb, and no houses around... [...] 'You perceive your mother as an immense and bare

[I'm four or five years old, in a muddy place, dragging a huge piece of wood. There
are no trees or houses around. Only me, *sweating*, as I *struggle* to drag that rough log,
my *palms burning, scraped raw* by the wood. I sink into the mud up to my ankles but
I have to keep tugging. I don't know why, but I have to.] (AJ 5)

It is a veritably existentialist incipit, which portrays a little child who has
been 'thrown into the world' (to quote Heidegger's concept of *Geworfenheit*,
'throwness') without mastering the conditions of her existence, nor its
meaning.[11] Giacomo Debenedetti's analysis of modern characters such as
Svevo's Zeno Cosini and Pirandello's Mattia Pascal provides here a fitting
description.[12] These characters find themselves caught in what Debenedetti
defines the 'epic of existence', which has neither internal coherence nor
external justification, and they suffer from the 'guilt of being present, without a reason, among things whose reason they ignore':[13] 'devo tirare, non so
perché, ma lo devo fare.' Modesta exposes herself to the readers' recognition,
first and foremost in the material, perceptive and perceived dimension of
the body. The identity of the protagonist is immediately presented through
its physical and relational presence in the world.[14]

The centrality of the body in *L'arte della gioia* is pointed out by a
number of critics. Modesta's passionate nature and powerful sexual drive
have been read in the direction of a re-evaluation of the material dimension
of existence, set against a universal and abstract rational subject, as well
as a re-appropriation of agency on women's part. For example, Trevisan
talks about the "'intensely perceptive" body of the protagonist' and argues
that Modesta's body is '*res cogitans* and *res extensa*, "living flesh" and "full

---

land without life, without trees. Trees are a symbol of life. An immense, bare land,
impossible to possess, to hug'] (111).

11   Martin Heidegger, *Being and Time*, trans. John Macquarrie and Edward Robinson
(Oxford: Blackwell, 1967).

12   See Giacomo Debenedetti, *Personaggi e destino: la metamorfosi del romanzo contemporaneo* (Milan: Il Saggiatore, 1977).

13   Ibid. 126.

14   The exposition of the body to external recognition, the impossibility to master one's
own origin and the concrete, individual presence in the world are all themes that
Sapienza has in common with existentialist thought, and in particular with Hannah
Arendt's theoretical elaboration.

identity", hence able to overcome the dualism that has long characterized the body."[15] Similarly, Rodigari describes Modesta as 'a woman whose body and intellect are merged',[16] a definition that again stresses the original and productive reconfiguration of the pair body-mind. The centrality of the body is also highlighted in several literary reviews and comments by common readers, which exalt Modesta's powerful instincts, together with the sensual and erotic dimension of the text.[17]

It is arguably appropriate to describe Modesta as sensual, and her body as perceptive, desiring and passionate. However, if we look at the role of the body in the overall configuration of the protagonist's identity and her relationship with power, we find that the overcoming of the body-mind dichotomy is not as straightforward and univocal as it may initially look. In fact, from these critical accounts an unresolved ambiguity emerges, which requires specific analysis: Modesta is described as a sensual character who acts in accordance with her passions, instincts and emotions; on the other hand, she is also described as driven by an intellectual and calculating determination. For example, Claude Imberty argues that the body, and in particular her sexual drive, is the real motor of Modesta's actions.[18] Modesta cultivates an acceptance of passions and an abandonment to the always renovated surprise of love. According to Imberty, her hedonistic approach is radically different from the ethics of the control of passions that traditionally marks the final maturation in coming-of-age novels. Yet, Imberty also notes a sharp contrast between the characterization of the

---

15   Alessandra Trevisan, '"La gioia è più che ogni voluttà": sessualità e maternità ne *L'arte della gioia*', in Providenti, *Quel sogno d'essere*, 53–60, 56.

16   Rodigari, 'La personalità culturale e storica di Goliarda Sapienza', 6.

17   See, for example: 'It is the sensual, corporeal and physical sphere that expresses the emotions, and desires are almost the only motor for decisions', *Centro donna Lilith di Latina* <http://www.centrodonnalilith.it/images/L%27arte%20della%20Gioia%20-%20G.Sapienza.pdf> [Accessed 10 September 2016]; 'It is an autobiographical narration in which there is no split between mind and body', review on Amazon, 5 December 2010 <http://www.amazon.it/Larte-della-gioia-Goliarda-Sapienza/dp/8806199609> [Accessed 10 September 2016].

18   Claude Imberty, 'Gender e generi letterari: il caso di Goliarda Sapienza', *Narrativa*, 30 (2008), 51–61.

protagonist in the first part and the rest of the novel: 'How can we reconcile the portrait of Modesta as an adult, and that of Modesta as a child and
teenager? The intellectual, adult woman is so different from the violent girl
that the reader has the impression of dealing with two characters, or one
character with two opposite personalities.'[19] Not only, in Imberty's view,
Modesta's personality dramatically changes throughout the text, to the
point of being unrecognizable. The critic also defines the adult woman as
'intellectual', thus pointing to a rather different characterization of identity
than the sensual and passionate one previously described. In fact, Modesta
is a multifaceted character featuring conflicting instances of the self. The
complexity of her character manifests in the discrepancy between her
thoughts and her words, her inner desires and her awareness of them, her
rationalist attitude and the eruption of her passionate emotionality. As
Maria Belén Hernández rightly points out, 'her personality is polymor-
phous, even monstrous at times [...]. Her motivations are ambivalent and
full of inner conflicts.'[20] Likewise, Rodigari discusses the 'Machiavellian'
use of rationality by Modesta, who 'is able to calculate and scheme, decide
and act; at the same time, she relies extensively on intuition.'[21]

   In an essay on Modesta's ethics, Andrée Bella stresses the constant
self-analysis practised by Modesta in order to understand and master her
own emotions and motivations, and relates it to the Cynics' practice of
parrhesia. This is 'a constant practice of self-awareness that [...] did not
coincide arbitrarily with one's own appetites and feelings, with the self
in its immediacy, but aimed toward the search for truth through critical
thinking as an indispensable condition to achieve freedom and therefore
a true happiness.'[22] In contrast to a character who is abandoned to uncontrolled passions, Modesta would be guided by strong rational will and
would exert strict self-control. In Bella's words, 'Modesta is very rigorous in

---

19   Imberty, 'Gender e generi letterari', 56.
20   Hernández, 'La fortuna letteraria de *L'arte della gioia*', 106.
21   Rodigari, 'Goliarda, Modesta e Machiavelli', in Providenti, *Quel sogno d'essere*, 93–8,
      96.
22   Andrée Bella, 'A Backbone Held Together by Joy', in Bazzoni, Bond and Wehling-
      Giorgi, *Goliarda Sapienza in Context*, 47–61, 49.

analysing her own fears, desires, and aspirations in her ceaseless exercise to improve herself and nourish "the joy of life"'.[23] The question then arises: is Modesta sensual or intellectual – or both? Are her actions driven primarily by corporeal instincts and passions, by an unproblematic bodily desire, or is there a nuanced relationship or even a conflict between different aspects of the protagonist's self? There seems to be an unresolved ambiguity in the character of Modesta, which criticism reflects, but does not fully articulate. The examination of the roles of the body in the representation of Modesta, and of the interaction between the character and power, provides relevant insights to interpret this ambiguity.

From the complexity of meanings attached to the body, a starting point is the body as the source of instincts. The body may be intended here, phenomenologically, as the individual biological organism, a kinaesthetic unit, the material ground of perception and a source of vital energy and physical pleasure. In Husserl's view – then re-elaborated for example by Winnicott's strand of psychoanalysis as well as Turner's cognitivism – thought is rooted in the physical interaction between the body and the world.[24] Between physical perceptions and abstract thought there is a continuum, not radical alterity. The connection between the different layers of experience is sustained by a primary desire: 'The totality of life is a process of being-driven, of yearning', Husserl writes.[25] At the very core of the subject, in other words, lies a drive, a desire, which guides the body's kinaesthetic interaction with the world, from the satisfaction of primary needs – such as hunger and sleep – to the search for knowledge and understanding. The same perspective is endorsed by Braidotti, whose combination of phenomenology and post-structuralism provides important insights into Sapienza's work. According to Braidotti, 'This *founding, primary, vital* desire to know is

23   Bella, 'A Backbone Held Together by Joy', 51.
24   See, for example, Antonio Damasio, *Descartes's Error: Emotion, Reason and the Human Brain* (New York: G. P. Putnam, 1994); Mark Johnson, *The Body in the Mind. The Bodily Basis of Meaning, Imagination and Reason* (London: University of Chicago Press, 1987); George Lakoff and Mark Johnson, *Metaphors We Live By* (London: University of Chicago Press, 1980); Turner, *The Literary Mind*.
25   Husserl, B.I 21, 6, cited in Donnicci, *Intenzioni d'amore, di scienza e d'anarchia*, 203.

necessary and therefore originary. It is what remains unthought at the heart of thought, because it is the essential condition for any form of thought to take place. Desire, as the a priori condition of thought, exceeds thought itself.'[26] This originary impulse, founded in the *aisthesis*, is an aspiration to establish a complete knowledge of an object, shaped in analogy with the originary impulse to fulfil a drive. Desire thus establishes a continuity between *aisthesis* and *logos*, but is never fully reducible to thought, inasmuch as it constitutes its condition of possibility.

For Modesta, 'the body is desire and appetite',[27] which from the very opening of the text constitutes the propelling force of her thoughts and actions. *L'arte della gioia* is framed by this primary desire, which takes the shape first and foremost of sexual pleasure, as the novel begins and ends on an orgasm – the first one experienced by Modesta as a child, and the last one when she is a mature woman. As Emily Cooke remarks, 'The discovery of pleasure initiates Modesta's appetite more generally – for knowledge, for experience, for autonomy. It turns her outward, toward nonsexual things, by inwardly sustaining her.'[28] In the first pages of the book, Modesta experiences sexual pleasure for the first time, and her discovery is represented as belonging to a sphere before and beyond norms and ethics, that is, a realm completely extraneous to social structures and their constituting power. Surprised by her new, wonderful experience, Modesta asks her friend Tuzzu about it: 'Non dovevo lasciarlo andare via, dovevo chiedergli perché – quando lo guardavo prima, e ora che tenevo il suo braccio – mi nasceva dentro quel desiderio di accarezzarmi là dove ...' (AG 9) [I couldn't let him get away, I had to ask him why – when I was watching him before, and now that I was holding his arm – why I felt that urge to touch myself in the spot where ... AJ 10]. When the boy expresses dismay and disapproval – 'Ma guarda se sono domande da fare! E alla tua età! Una peste sei! [...] Non ti vergogni?' [What kind of question is that to ask! At your age! You're a scourge! [...] Aren't you ashamed of yourself?] – she replies: 'se io

---

26   Braidotti, *Nuovi soggetti nomadi*, 77. My emphasis.
27   Rodigari, 'Goliarda, Modesta e Machiavelli', 179.
28   Emily Cooke, 'Disobedience is a Virtue: on Goliarda Sapienza's "Art of joy"', *The New Yorker*, 24 January 2014.

l'ho scoperto che nessuno me l'ha detto, vuol dire che tutti lo sanno' (9) [I discovered it myself. Nobody told me, so it must mean that everyone knows about it. 10]. In this dialogue, the child Modesta puts forward – and the point is crucial – the idea of the possibility of a desire that exceeds social regulation, norms and categories.

Although the representation of Modesta, as will be discussed in greater detail later on, has much in common with post-structuralist views of the subject, the prominent role of the body as the source of a primary desire also partially distances her from these positions, and brings her closer to phenomenological approaches to the body, instincts and desires. According to the post-structuralist theoretical reflections on the body and power developed in particular by Foucault and Butler, there is no desire before and beyond the constitutive power of social regulation, because 'the illusion of a sexuality before the law is itself a creation of that law'.[29] Identity is intrinsically constructed, desire is constituted and not just repressed by power. There is, in other words, no desire prior to social regulation that can be retrieved. In this absence of any 'core', 'material', 'authentic' or 'own' desire, even the 'I' dissolves, its unity being only a linguistic performance.[30] Conversely, in *L'arte della gioia* there seems to exist a material domain preceding or exceeding any constituting power, and this belongs to the realm of physical desires.

By opening her novel with the representation of a character, the young Modesta, in a direct and unproblematic relationship with her own powerfully vital drives, Sapienza marks a clear difference from previous autobiographical works. In *Lettera aperta* and *Il filo di mezzogiorno*, she focuses extensively on the circumstances and modalities of constitution of desire by power. Her autobiographical narratives investigate how identity is formed, and qualify this process as a series of 'disconnections' – or, in Ross's words, 'interruptions' – of desire.[31] Nonetheless, these texts also feature a path towards the reconstruction of a form of desire that is perceived as less extraneous, a dimension of the self potentially closer to

29   Butler, *Gender Trouble*, 94.
30   Ibid. 163.
31   Ross, 'Eccentric Interruptions'.

a living body, beyond alienating power relationships. In the conclusive
paragraph of *Lettera aperta*, the narrator asks precisely for the freedom to
frequent her own body: 'Vi lascio per un po': con questo poco di ordine
che sono riuscita a fare intorno a me. Vorrei tacere per qualche tempo,
e andarmene a giocare con la terra e con il mio corpo' [I'll leave you for
a while, with this little bit of order I've managed to create around me. I
would like to stay silent for some time, and get out of here to play with
the earth and my own body] (LA 159). Modesta's story begins from here,
from that 'terra' and that 'corpo' – a source of instincts, a site of desire
and vitality of the self.

Since the primary motor of sexual pleasure lies outside power, it provides Modesta with a solid ground from which to contest power itself,
whether in the form of socio-political institutions or conceptual categories,
enabling her struggle for freedom. In *L'arte della gioia*, the body is thus a
site of liberating pleasure, often exhibited in frontal opposition to oppressive power. This is evident for example in the passage, set in the nunnery,
in which Modesta cuts the bands that constrain her breasts:

> Strappandomi il grembiule e la camicia, le mie mani trovarono quelle fasce strette
> 'perché il seno non si mostrasse', che fino a quel momento erano state come una
> seconda pelle per me. Una pelle dall'apparenza morbida che mi legava col suo biancore
> rassicurante. Presi le forbici e le tagliai a pezzi. Dovevo respirare. E finalmente nuda
> [...] ritrovo la mia carne. Il seno libero esplode sotto le mie palme e mi accarezzo lì
> in terra. (AG 41–2)

> [Tearing off my smock and shirt, my hands found those tight strips 'so your breasts
> won't show', which until that moment had felt like a second skin to me. A seemingly
> compliant skin that bound me with its reassuring whiteness. I took the scissors and
> cut them to shreds. I had to breathe. And finally naked [...] I rediscover my flesh.
> My released breasts explode beneath my palms and I stroke myself there on the
> floor.] (AJ 57)

Sexual pleasure is the source of the protagonist's strength, and creating
the conditions for enjoying it is the objective of her actions. Pleasure provides the initial inspiration to struggle for freedom and a resource to resist
oppression, reflecting Husserl's statement that 'man must already be free in

order to be able to accomplish freedom.'[32] In other words, the discovery of
a pleasure beyond power is the ground on which the protagonist builds her
aspiration to be able to access that pleasure in the future, thus triggering her
struggle for freedom. Bodily desire is therefore at the same time a primary
condition and an objective, a potentiality that is already within oneself
and one that must be achieved, in accordance with Epicurean ethics: 'we
consider pleasure as the founding principle and aim of a happy life, because
we recognize it as our first and kindred good. It is the starting point of every
choice and of every aversion, inasmuch as we make the feeling of pleasure
or pain the rule by which to judge every good thing.'[33] Joy, the key word
of the title that signifies physical pleasure, fulfilled desire and freedom, is
a starting condition, but also the result of an 'art'. The circularity of the
novel, inaugurated and concluded with two joyful orgasms, manifests on
the level of narrative structure this circularity of pleasure and freedom.

A Weak / Strong Subject

So far, this analysis has approached the role of the body by taking into
consideration its function as source of a strong desire. However, the representation of Modesta presents us with a configuration of the self that is
highly self-conflicting. Similarly to *Io, Jean Gabin*, as will be discussed in
Chapter 3, in *L'arte della gioia* physical instincts are inscribed within a polarity between agency and passivity, as they are the locus of an authentic sense
of the self, but also disruptive forces that destabilize the subject. Modesta
constantly finds herself between being overwhelmed by the insurgence of
uncontrolled forces and an active self-analysis and self-regulation – quite
a different picture compared to the sensual and erotic character described
so far. The definition of 'intellectual' given by Imberty, and its coexistence with other critical definitions of Modesta that focus on the bodily
dimension, now become clearer. The combination of powerful desire and

32   Husserl, E III 4, 26, cited in Donnicci, *Intenzioni d'amore, di scienza e d'anarchia*,
      250.
33   Epicuro, *Lettera sulla felicità*, 13.

instrumental use of reason and self-control is particularly evident in the part of the novel set in the nunnery. Here, Modesta is able to channel her passionate ardour and use it to deceive the nuns:

> Ecco come uscirne. [...] Chiusi gli occhi per raggiungere Tuzzu e quel mare che dava terrore e affanno. E, con tutta la forza che il desiderio e il terrore mi davano, gridai forte, ma con una sola piccola variante. Invece del nome di Tuzzu, dicevo: – Madre, perdono, madre! –, e pensavo a Tuzzu dimenticato da tanto tempo: – Perdono, madre, perdono! (AG 29).

> [So that was how to get out of there. [...] I closed my eyes to rejoin Tuzzu and the sea that left me fearful and breathless. And with all the strength inspired by desire and terror, I cried out loudly, but with one small variation. Instead of Tuzzu's name, I said: 'Mother! Forgive me, Mother!' And I thought of Tuzzu, whom I had forgotten for so long: 'Forgive me, Mother, forgive me!'] (AJ 39)

In this passage, Modesta wants to regain contact with that material and libidinal core of the self that she had long neglected, represented by the image of the sea and the character of Tuzzu. However, in order to do so, she needs to escape the nuns' oppressive power, and therefore to exert self-control. In the action of asking emphatically for forgiveness, the authentic 'forza', 'desiderio', 'terrore' combine with an instrumental use of reason and self-control, in the deception of that 'piccola variante', a cunning lie. The control that the character exercises on her own instincts is clearly presented as an instrument to resist oppression and assert agency. This specific understanding of the potential danger posed by the body, and the importance of dominating the body as an empowering exercise of agency, is also evident in Modesta's ability to fake bodily symptoms. For example, Modesta's feigning of an epileptic fit, at the beginning of the novel, appears to be a direct response to the utter lack of agency that characterizes the protagonists of Morante's *La storia*, Ida and Useppe.[34] While Ida is being raped, she has a

---

34   For a detailed comparative analysis of the two novels, see Bazzoni, 'Agency and History in Sapienza's *L'arte della gioia* and Morante's *La storia*', in Bazzoni, Bond and Wehling-Giorgi, *Goliarda Sapienza in Context*, 147–61. For an analysis of Ida's lack of agency, see Wehling-Giorgi, '"Totetaco": The Mother-Child Dyad and the Pre-Conceptual Self in Elsa Morante's *La Storia* and *Aracoeli*', *Writing Childhood*

seizure that takes her away from the violence she is undergoing. Conversely, Modesta simulates a seizure when she is being questioned by a police officer straight after she was raped by her father and killed her mother and her sister. She uses the fit as an instrument to avoid questions and cover her murder. The same episode where Morante represents Ida's extreme passivity is overturned by Sapienza to represent Modesta's rebellious agency.

When the conditions of enjoyment of bodily desires are not granted, the instinctual dimension can become a counter-productive force, against which the character must resort to self-analysis and self-control. While Modesta's aim is to attain freedom and pleasure, she is not continuously immersed in an unproblematic enjoyment of the senses, because such a condition is not given in a continuum, nor is it given always in the same shape. The interruption of the enjoyment of freedom and pleasure, and the consequent use of calculating will, is evident when it comes from outside the character, in the form of patent oppression by other characters – the nuns, princess Gaia or Prando. But power can also take the shape of internalized norms, stereotypes, expectations and emotional dependence on others, thus leading to an internal split in the subject. As Modesta learns throughout her life, instinctual reactions can themselves be conditioned – that is, constructed by the shaping force of social and cultural structures and by interpersonal dependence. In these cases, instinctual reactions and emotions must be carefully deconstructed:

> Può tanta nostalgia assalirti alle spalle anche se non si vuole più bene come prima? Non avendo altro da fare, mi misi a cercare di capire cos'era quella nostalgia. Altro che pentirmi, dovevo studiare me stessa e gli altri come si studia la grammatica, la musica, e smetterla di abbandonarmi così alle emozioni, che bella parola, emozioni! Ma ormai non avevo più tempo per le parole, dovevo solo pensare a che cosa era quella nostalgia. (AG 30)

> [Can such longing weigh you down even if you no longer love her as you did before? Having nothing better to do, I began trying to understand what that longing was. Never mind repenting. What I had to do was study myself and others like you study

in Postwar Women's Writing, special issue of *Forum for Modern Language Studies*, 1, 49 (2013).

grammar and music, and stop indulging in my emotions. Such a beautiful word, 'emotions'! But I had no time for words now. I had to think about what that long-ing was.] (AJ 41)

While Modesta practises self-reflection and tries to master her own emo-tions, on many occasions she conversely loses control, is unable to interpret her own reactions, transposes every thought directly onto the body. In these moments, the line between control and acceptance, between guid-ing and following emotions, is blurred. For example, the expressions 'devo', 'dovevo' [I have to, I had to], recurring throughout the text, mark at the same time an active choice and the acceptance of a condition: 'Ma dovevo avere pazienza' (AG 169) [But I had to show patience. AJ 231]; 'E io non dovevo gridare, nè piangere, nè chiedere. Dovevo solo guidare' (170) [And I mustn't scream or cry or ask questions. I must simply drive. 232]; 'Dovevo essere cauta' (178) [I had to be careful. 242]; 'Doveva accettare quella paura' (193) [She had to accept that fear. 262]; 'Devo accettare il pericolo' (238) [I must accept the danger. 318].

The ambiguity between rational choice and the predominance of instincts is particularly noticeable in the episode of the staged suicide attempt in the nunnery. Here Sapienza plays with the topos of the well, which was discussed in a public exchange between Natalia Ginzburg and Alba de Céspedes in 1948.[35] The well is taken by the two writers to sym-bolize the deepest moments of depression in which women fall: 'Women have the bad habit of falling in a well, from time to time; they fall prey to a terrible sadness, and drown in it.'[36] Ginzburg considers this 'acquaint-ance with sorrow' from a negative perspective, while to de Céspedes it is a source of strength, for it provides a deeper understanding of 'weakness,

35   Natalia Ginzburg, 'Discorso sulle donne', in Maria Rosa Cutrufelli et al., eds, *Il pozzo segreto. Cinquanta scrittrici italiane* (Florence: Giunti, 1993), 27–32; Alba de Céspedes, 'Lettera a Natalia Ginzburg', in *Il pozzo segreto*, 32–6. Sapienza herself is present in the same volume with 'Gelosia', a short story from the collection *Destino coatto*, 201–3. Fortini discusses Sapienza's treatment of the topos of the well in 'Beyond the Canon: Goliarda Sapienza and Twentieth-Century Italian Literary Tradition', in Bazzoni, Bond and Wehling-Giorgi, *Goliarda Sapienza in Context*, 131–46, 141–2.

36   Ginzburg, 'Discorso sulle donne', 27.

dreams, sadness, aspirations, and all those feelings that form and improve the human soul.'[37] In *L'arte della gioia*, Modesta recounts that many girls have committed suicide by falling in the well in the nunnery garden. She too is descending into a state of depression, after Madre Leonora and the other nuns have withdrawn their affection for her and hold her in contempt. Unlike the other girls, however, Modesta plans to fall in the well ensuring that the gardener Mimmo would save her, using such a staged suicide attempt to regain the nuns' favour. Sapienza thus overturns the image of the well from a symbol of lowest depression into one of resurgence. Yet, the scene of Modesta's falling into the well is strikingly ambiguous. For days, Modesta looks for the strength to jump in the well, but when she finally resolves to do it, she is not fully in control of her actions:

> Le mani sudate scivolavano sulla pietra levigata. Due volte caddi in terra e mi rialzai, ma poi fui in piedi sull'orlo. Che Mimmo mi vedesse bene ... E, forse perché avevo corso tanto, o per la voce di suor Costanza che mi rintronava nella testa facendomi perdere l'equilibrio, o perché l'orlo del pozzo era levigato e viscido, scivolai giù senza nemmeno aver dovuto ricorrere a quel coraggio che tanto avevo invocato. (AG 39)

> [My sweaty hands slipped on the polished stone. Twice I fell to the ground and got back up, but eventually I was standing on the brink. So Mimmo could see me clearly ... And maybe because I had run so hard, or because Sister Costanza's voice echoing in my head made me lose my balance, or because the edge was smooth and slippery, I slid down without even having to summon the courage I had so anxiously sought for so long.] (AJ 53–4)

Surely, Modesta is making sure that Mimmo is there, ready to save her – there is no doubt about the staged nature of her gesture. And yet, there is a degree of truth in her desperation, and the insisted plurality of reasons that made her fall, together with the intense alteration of her perceptions, blur the line between a calculated, strategic decision, and an impulsive action beyond control.[38]

---

37   De Céspedes, 'Lettera a Natalia Ginzburg', 34.
38   This is particularly striking when related to Sapienza's own life. She attempted suicide twice, but on both occasions it is not clear whether she actually wanted to kill herself, or exceeded the dose of sleeping pills by accident, or was looking for a demonstrative

Despite her 'Nietzschean will',³⁹ Modesta is not always able to see
clearly through her own emotions and even her perceptions, which are
subject to the interference of imagination, analogies and hallucinations.
The text features frequent syntactical constructions in which a perception
is followed by a question about the nature of the perception itself, expressing Modesta's difficulty in interpreting what she is experiencing: 'il suo
pianto improvviso e disperato mi accecò. O era calato il sole?' (AG 65)
[her unexpected, desperate tears blinded me. Or had the sun gone down?
AJ 93]; 'Il silenzio della clinica mi urlò nel cervello [...] costringendomi
dietro una parete invalicabile d'attesa. O era ancora la parete scivolosa del
pozzo, da dove carponi cercavo di risalire alla luce?' (170) [the hospital's
silence screamed more loudly in my head [...], confining me behind an
insurmountable wall of waiting. Or was it the slippery wall of the well,
from which I was trying to crawl back up to the light on my hands and
knees? 232]. Likewise, Sapienza often uses syntactic structures in which
perceptions and emotions are physical forces acting upon the characters,
a feature that recurs in all her writings: 'la scoperta di non essere la sola a
dubitare di Dio m'aveva acceso una vampata nel sangue da essere costretta
a serrare la bocca per non gridare di gioia' (36) [discovering that I was not
alone in doubting God had brought on a heat flash, forcing me to clamp my
mouth shut to keep from screaming with joy. 49]. From the opening scene,
in which Modesta drags a trunk without knowing why, to the recurring
explosions of uncontrolled emotions – 'credevo di ridere e invece, con mia
sorpresa, mi trovai a piangere sul suo petto' (79) [I thought I was laughing
and instead, to my surprise, I found myself crying on her chest. 113] – there
is a structural ambiguity concerning the motor of the protagonist's actions
and her control of them, between active simulation and untamed instincts.
Such an ambiguity recurs throughout the novel alongside those situations

action. Similarly, it is not clear whether she went to prison intentionally, as she herself
stated, or the theft was due to other reasons, mainly her poverty (see Chapter 4).

39   Romaric Sangars, 'Goliarda Sapienza: l'art de la joie', *Chronicart.com*, 13 November
2005 <http://www.chronicart.com/livres/goliarda-sapienza-l-art-de-la-joie/>
[Accessed 19 August 2016].

in which, conversely, the components of instincts and rationality are clearly distinct and acting in solidarity, with a subject fully in control of her actions. While Modesta's determined will aims at conquering freedom and independence through self-control and simulation, her emotionality claims the right to inconsistency, fluidity, passivity, play and experimentation. The aim of such a 'bodily reason' is to annex as much experience as possible and not settle into any definitive identity. Hence, Modesta accumulates contradictory traits: she is intelligent, a talented piano player, a passionate lover with both men and women, a murderer; she writes tales and poems, manages the family's estate, speaks as an equal with lawyers and policemen and carries an undisputed authority over her and others' children. Sometimes she is cruel, aggressive and authoritative; on other occasions, she is fragile, naïve, childish and needy. She oscillates between her contradictory features, propelled forward by her will to appropriate multiple experiences, to experiment with a construction of the self not aimed at anything but the richness of the experience itself. This multifaceted representation is enabled by the very configuration of Modesta's self: a cold and calculating will unifies Modesta's identity by working towards a goal, but the goal is the freedom for identity to be manifold and dynamic. When the conditions of enjoyment of a free emotionality are secured, this is represented as a positive freedom; otherwise, uncontrolled perceptions, desires and emotions are a dangerous force to be carefully monitored.

In her struggle for freedom, Modesta needs to apply a strenuous deconstruction of her own emotions in order to re-access that primary, vital instinct that constitutes the core of her aspiration to be free. In this respect, the body becomes itself a multi-layered ground, where some instinctual manifestations lie at a greater distance than others from an authentic core, and the intervention of lucid self-reflection becomes a necessary tool to orient the subject towards the understanding of herself. The power to be opposed is brought inside the character, contributing to her internal conflicts. In fact, Modesta is characterized by continuous afterthoughts, oscillations and re-considerations. She is, in other words, almost constantly thinking, checking and controlling herself, because that freedom of the body that she seeks is not a stable condition, granted once and for all, but rather an objective that requires active fight, inside and outside herself.

Overall, no choice is made in the text between self-control and unreadable perceptions and desires, between a rational and strong-willed self, acting in solidarity with a powerfully desiring body, and multiple, centrifugal and uncontrolled impulses. The possibility of an authentic self is, in other words, continually evoked and subverted. Here lies the core contradiction of the character of Modesta, and of Sapienza's narrative at large. It constantly oscillates between different instances of the self, instincts and rational self-control, emotional outbursts and careful reflection. The relationship between body and mind, not at all pacified, is thus inscribed within the dimension of a continuous struggle for freedom from internal and external constraints.

A productive way to account for the contradictions and inner conflicts characterizing Modesta is to look at the dynamics of the interaction between the different configurations of the self and power. The theoretical elaboration by Braidotti in *Nuovi soggetti nomadi* provides a useful insight into these dynamics. Braidotti, in continuity with Foucault, Gilles Deleuze, Félix Guattari and, in the Italian context, Gianni Vattimo, argues for the dissolution of a metaphysical, strong understanding of the subject, to which she opposes the figure of the nomad:

> The figuration of the nomadic subject is clearly opposed to the stability and fixity of the humanistic subject, who manages the phallologocentric capital as a master and owner.
>
> A subject who is no longer one, no one, nor one hundred thousand, but pure becoming.
>
> The subject is a mosaic of fragments that are held together by a symbolic bond: the attachment to, and the identification with, the phallologocentric symbolic structures. A rabble, which thinks of itself as the centre of the universe; a jumble of flesh, full of desire and fears, who rises up to the peaks of an imperial consciousness.[40]

However, Braidotti, in line with the work of the group Diotima, notes how the notion of a weak subject – such as the post-structuralist, nomadic one – carries different values depending on the position of those who embrace it. For subjects in a subaltern position (such as, historically, women and

---

40   Braidotti, *Nuovi soggetti nomadi*, 16, 21, 28.

ethnic, sexual or religious minorities), discourses on fragmentation, fluidity, openness and weakness of the self carry quite a different meaning than they do for subjects in a dominant position. The idea of a weak subject indeed can be used by strong subjects to keep the weak subjects weak. In Cavarero's words:

> For man who has placed himself and who has understood himself for thousands of years as the strong subject – this recuperating of a weakness generously left in the custody of the 'more of the less' woman is indeed the flirting of a subject who does not uproot the foundations of his own representation (and why should he?) but replaces quite freely the categories of his logic ... The path of 'pensiero debole' is not the path by which a woman can arrive to speak herself, to think herself, to represent herself.[41]

A strong notion of identity is a tool of oppression and domination, when assumed by a subject in a dominant position, hence the deconstruction of dominant identities is inscribed in a process of making space for the emancipation of other identities, which is a 'welcome development for western philosophy'.[42] On the other hand, a strong sense of self is not a means of oppression but rather an instrument of liberation, when endorsed by a subject in a subaltern position. To say that the subject is necessarily weak and fragmented, before subaltern subjects can access a locus of agency and expression, serves the interests of those in a dominant position, for such a discourse keeps the dominated groups in the position of not being subjects. Weakness, in other words, needs to be the result of an autonomous opening up of the subject to change and plurality, not the heteronomous imposition by a strong subject. As Braidotti puts it, 'The truth is that you cannot deconstruct a subjectivity that has never been fully granted. [...] In order to herald the death of the subject, you must first have achieved the right to speak as a subject; in order to demystify the metadiscourse, you

41   Cavarero, 'Per una teoria della differenza sessuale', in Diotima, *Il pensiero della differenza sessuale*, 43–79, 48, cited in Renate Holub, 'Weak Thought and Strong Ethics. The "Postmodern" and Feminist Theory in Italy', *Annali d'italianistica*, 9 (1991), 124–43, 135.
42   Holub, 'Weak Thought and Strong Ethics', 135.

must first have gained access to a position where you can speak.'[43] Similarly, Monique Wittig remarks, 'I do not know who is going to profit from this abandonment of the oppressed to a trend that will make them more and more powerless, having lost the faculty of being subjects even before having gained it. I would say that we can renounce only what we have.'[44]

In their approach to deconstruction, thinkers such as Braidotti, Cavarero and Wittig take into consideration different positionalities with respect to power. They qualify theories and practices, including deconstruction itself, as endowed with different power-values, because descriptions of identities are themselves political. Their perspective allies with minorities' emancipatory struggles and instrumental identity politics, while nonetheless remaining radically anti-essentialist.[45] According for example to Michael Dyson, a distinction must be drawn between the violent and conservative pride of the dominant social group (in his discourse, white pride) and the potentially subversive pride of the oppressed.[46] The concept of pride here refers to a strong notion of identity, but it carries opposite values depending on who uses it and for what purposes, since 'not all identity politics are created equal.'[47] The same approach is applied by Braidotti to feminist struggles, since the position of women is not symmetrical to that of men in relation to the crisis of the modern subject, which is and remains in fact a dominant white male subject. Only after the subject has achieved a certain degree of agency and freedom from oppression it can open up to multiplicity and fluidity, otherwise, in Braidotti's words, 'we run the risk of

43   Braidotti, *Nuovi soggetti nomadi*, 136.
44   Wittig, *The Straight Mind*, 57.
45   The concept of a 'strategic essentialism' was first formulated by Gayatri Chakravorty Spivak. See Donna Landry and Gerald MacLean, eds, *The Spivak Reader* (London: Routledge, 1996), 214.
46   Michael Dyson, *Pride* (Oxford: Oxford University Press, 2006). When Modesta first meets her alleged father, she expresses her admiration for his strength using precisely the word 'pride': 'il sangue mi rideva *d'orgoglio* per la sua *forza*' (AG 12) [My blood rejoiced, proud of his strength. AJ 14]. My emphasis.
47   Dyson, *Pride*, 54.

a leap from the Neolithic age to the post-industrial era, skipping the most important stage – the process of modernization as our becoming subjects.'[48] This perspective integrates post-structuralism by taking into account different positionalities with respect to power as concerns the deconstruction of identity. As such, it helps capture the core of Sapienza's narrative representation of the relationship between body, identity and power, accounting for the combination of strong and weak notions of the self. Modesta's objective in the novel is to liberate identity from normative and conclusive structures. However, in order to undertake this deconstruction, she needs to resort to an instrumental use of those same categories she seeks to overcome. She is fighting on two front lines, against a strong, universal and abstract notion of identity, on the one hand, and against an oppressed, weak and voiceless subject on the other – that is, not to be one. The novel thus combines an antagonistic spirit, evident in Modesta's strong determination and even use of violence, with a much more nuanced and fluid representation of the character's identity and relationship with her context, for the various configurations of the character derive from her shifting positionality in the face of power. Through narrative, Sapienza links the configuration of identity to the dynamics of a changing context; specifically, in the evolution of the character, openness and disruption of the self change value, from a negative and painful condition to an affirmative and strong choice, that is, from oppression to agency. This map of Modesta's configuration of the self can now be put into the temporal dimension of the narrative, following the evolution of the protagonist throughout the sixty years of her life.

Modesta's Parable

At the beginning of the novel Modesta is presented as a rebellious child, whose discovery of pleasure provides her with the strength and vitality necessary to aspire to fight oppression. She begins where the protagonist

48   Braidotti, *Nuovi soggetti nomadi*, 160.

of *Lettera aperta* was left, having re-established contact with her bodily instincts. Straight after the presentation of the material conditions in which she lives, Modesta tells the readers that she does not feel loved by her mother, and that she responds to the absence of a loving environment with hatred. This hatred is better understood when linked to the autobiographical texts and the theme of power in the form of emotional dependence as it is developed there. Indeed, in *Lettera aperta* and *Il filo di mezzogiorno*, the child protagonist experiences her mother's love as something that she must win with great effort. The primary and unfulfilled need for love in the autobiographical texts puts the child into a state of painful dependency and is therefore represented as oppressive and distorting for her fragile self.

The homicide of Modesta's mother and sister in *L'arte della gioia* can be productively interpreted as the initiatory rejection of this dependence. The murders of the mother and Tina, together with that of Leonora and Gaia, have been read by critics as aimed against negative images of women. For example, Providenti argues that the three women who die in the first part of the novel are all maternal figures to the protagonist, and 'symbols of femininity – the victim, the mystic, the masculine woman – from which the author wants to distance herself.'[49] Similarly, according to Maria Teresa Maenza, Modesta kills 'the image of the mother who accepts and conforms to the patriarchal system.'[50] As criticism suggests, the mother is a negative example of victim, from which Modesta wants to distance herself. However, to the child she is also and mainly a source of emotional dependence, an aspect that has been generally overlooked by critics so far. By killing her mother, Modesta challenges one fundamental form of oppression that Sapienza exposed in her autobiographical works, namely the distorting dependence deriving from a – neglected – need for love. The problem of emotional dependence and of the power involved in interpersonal relationships is a major theme in Sapienza's narrative, which in the previous chapter I read in its psychological and social dimension through Winnicott's and Miller's reflections. In *L'arte della gioia*, there is an initiatory rejection of such a relationality within power, which determines the initial void of

49   Providenti, *La porta è aperta*, 43.
50   Maenza, 'Fuori dall'ordine simbolico della madre', 255.

communication between Modesta and the other characters as well as her search for radical independence.

Structured on parental dynamics, the relationships in the novel are invariably described through the lens of power imbalances. Sapienza maintains an acute sense of the power involved in human relationships, often embodying it in the characters' physical size: 'Era cresciuto, o era la sigaretta che lo faceva sembrare più grande? Come gli posso parlare ora che è diventato così grande?' (AG 7) [Had he gotten bigger, or was it the cigarette that made him look older? How can I talk to him now that he's so grown up? AJ 8]; 'O io ero diventata più alta, o lei era più piccola del normale' (68) [Either I had grown taller or she was smaller than normal. 98]; 'Come faceva a sembrare alta da lontano e così piccola fra le braccia?' (73) [How could she seem so tall from a distance, yet so small in my arms? 105]; 'Lei è strana Modesta, a volte sembra alta, forte, a volte come adesso piccola e fragile come una bambina' (292) [You're strange, Modesta. Sometimes you seem tall and strong; at other times, like now, you seem small and fragile, like a child. 388]. Joyce is a 'donna grande' [big woman], Gaia is a 'grande vecchia' [big old woman], and the father, Mimmo, Carmine, Prando and Jacopo are all described as having a 'grande corpo' [big body]. As Modesta grows up, power remains a fundamental component of human relations, but these do not threaten the very survival of the character, as she has developed a sense of self that allows her to accept emotional dependence while at the same time rejecting oppression. The murder of the mother thus can be read as the will to get rid from the very beginning of what, in Sapienza's narrative, is a primary form of distorting power, namely an unsatisfied need for maternal love.

In the first part of the novel, the characteristics of self-control, Machiavellian reason and strong determination prevail. Firstly in the convent, and then in Villa Carmelo, Modesta experiences serious difficulties in communicating with the other characters, she is calculating, distrustful and radically split between will and emotionality. She practises 'l'esercizio della prudenza' (AG 58) [the practice of prudence. AJ 83], a combination of suspicion, simulation and cunning, and the 'preghiera dell'odio' (76) [prayer of hatred. 109], the uncompromising rejection of oppression in any form. The turning point in the novel is Modesta's marriage with Ippolito and the acquisition of the status of 'princess'. A fifth of the way into the book, Modesta has already attained riches, love and independence, and she feels like 'un vecchio e saggio monarca' (99) [a wise old monarch. 140]. Yet, this position of strength is not the final objective of the protagonist but only the enabling condition of her freedom. It allows her to enter a completely different dimension of existence, characterized by the possibility of experimenting, changing and enjoying life in multiple forms. The passage thus marks a shift from an oppositional characterization of the self, where the exercise of self-control and instrumental use of rationality dominate, to a much more nuanced and joyful relationship with her body, powerfully and poetically represented in the scene of Modesta's first encounter with the sea:

Sbalordita da quella vicinanza, aprii gli occhi per richiuderli accecata da quell'immensità di tetti neri lucenti al sole, precipitanti verso un cielo blu che si stendeva all'infinito, là dove lo sguardo poteva arrivare: il mare! Il mare di Tuzzu, blu! [...] E, forse perché mi aspettavo di vederlo dall'alto come prima, dovetti alzare gli occhi per trovare quel cielo liquido rovesciato che fuggiva calmo verso una libertà sconfinata. Grandi uccelli bianchi scivolavano in quella vertigine di vento. I polmoni liberati s'aprivano e per la prima volta respiravo. Per la prima volta lagrime di riconoscenza mi scendevano sulle labbra. (AG 125–6)

[Stunned by its proximity, I opened my eyes and shut them again, dazzled by the expanse of dark rooftops shining in the sun, plunging into a blue sky that stretched to infinity, as far as the eye could see: the sea! Tuzzu's blue sea! [...] And maybe because I expected to see it from above like before, I had to look up to find that inverted liquid sky which flowed serenely toward boundless freedom. Great white birds glided in the dizzying wind. My lungs, released, opened up and I breathed for the first time. For the first time, tears of gratefulness rolled down my face.] (AJ 176)

When Modesta attempts to swim for the first time, her initial reaction is to try to grasp and contain the water: 'Lottavo per afferrare quel corpo liquido che mi sfuggiva sorprendendomi da tutte le parti' (AG 136–7) [I struggled to grasp that fluid body that eluded me, surprising me on all sides. AJ 190]. After several failed attempts, she succeeds thanks to Carlo, who teaches her to surrender herself to the force of the sea rather than trying to control it. It is significant that, in the novel, Carlo is represented as a character embodying limpid rationality – originally from Lombardy, he is a doctor with a solid positivist faith in socialism. Modesta resorts to the advice of her rationalistic friend in order to learn to swim, that is, on a straightforward metaphorical level, to accept the impossibility of full control and give in to fluidity. However, although Modesta admires Carlo, she cannot love him with passion. Rationality is deprived of its totalizing role and intrinsically relativized by being retrieved as a provisional and limited means, however useful and necessary.

Modesta's arrival in Catania is for her the moment of highest strength, but also of isolation and rigidity. From then onwards, she progressively relaxes the strict control she exerts on herself and timidly opens herself to the possibility of establishing equal and sympathetic relationships with other characters. This phase also coincides with a shift in the narrative focus from Modesta's inner reflection and identity formation towards outer reality. In the context of the advent of fascism, the text registers a growing presence of social and political issues, which goes together with an increase in the use of dialogues, although Modesta's self-reflection and subjective perspective still play an important role. In the second phase of her relationship with Carmine, for example, she has acquired that strength and self-knowledge that allows her to establish direct contact with her inner feelings, emotions and joyful instincts, without having to control or repress them. The emotional and desiring sphere, inner and authentic core of the self, is described by the word 'cuore' [heart], a term previously despised because it was obfuscated and encrusted with falsifying concepts and rhetoric, but now finally liberated: 'La parola cuore ripetuta dalla sua voce perde il significato ambiguo che me l'ha fatta odiare. E vedo il mio *cuore, occhio e centro, orologio e valvola del mio spazio carnale.* Nel buio con le palme ascolto il suo pulsare violento che dal seno alle tempie sudate grida di *gioia* e non si vuole quietare' (AG 203. My emphasis) [Spoken by his voice, the word 'heart' loses the ambiguity that had made me hate it. And I see my heart, the eye and nucleus, the chronometer and regulator of my carnal centre. In the dark, I listen with the palms of my hands to its violent throbbing, crying out with joy from my chest to my perspiring brow, unwilling to quiet down. AJ 275].

The effort to oppose and deconstruct oppressive structures allows Modesta to enjoy the pleasure of her body and accept love for and from other characters. However, whenever something or someone threatens her

freedom, she does not hesitate to resume her fierce and independent attitude. This happens for example with Mattia, whom she decidedly refuses
to marry, not acquiescing to his pressure.[51] Modesta survives a violent fight
with him, and the scar that runs on her forehead symbolizes precisely the
joint between opposed forces in Modesta's self – where the joint, the scar
incised in the flesh, is a simultaneous unification and separation, symbol
of the 'contradiction that is at the core of nature': 'Quella cicatrice che
divide la fronte sta ora a dimostrare la saldatura del suo essere prima diviso.
Rinasce Modesta partorita dal suo corpo, sradicata da quella di prima che
tutto voleva, e il dubbio di sé e degli altri non sapeva sostenere' (AG 264)
[The scar that bisects her forehead is now a sign of the healing of her being,
itself divided earlier. Modesta is reborn from her body, uprooted from that
earlier Modesta who wanted everything, and who couldn't tolerate doubts,
in herself or others. AJ 352]

    After Carlo's death, Beatrice's insanity and the advent of fascism,
Modesta mitigates her initial ferocity and progressively learns to accept
her own limits; she moves in the space of an accepted oscillation between
control and uncontrolled reactions, dependence and independence. For
example, she entrusts herself completely to Joyce:

> Per la prima volta in vita mia il desiderio di abbandonarmi a qualcuno che non fosse
> me stessa mi prese furioso. [...] Senza più esitare, riaprendo gli occhi, versai nel suo
> sguardo che come un vaso raccoglieva emozioni, lacrime, durezze e dolcezze senza
> incrinarsi, tutte le tappe gioiose e aspre di quella che allora mi appariva la mia lunga
> vita. (AG 303)

> [For the first time in my life I was seized by an intense desire to unburden myself
> with someone who wasn't me. [...] Without further hesitation, I opened my eyes
> again and poured into hers all the joy and bitterness of what then seemed to me my
> long life. And like a vase, her eyes took in emotion, tears, hardships and pleasures
> without cracking.] (AJ 401–2)

---

51   Later on she wards off Prando when he wants to force her to get married, and she is
     equally resolute in claiming her independence from the Communist Party.

In a game that recalls the one played by Goliarda with her mother in *Lettera aperta*, Modesta switches the role of care with her adopted son Jacopo and with Prando: 'Mamma, lo sai come ti chiamerò d'ora in poi [...]? La mia mamma bambina' (AG 452) [Mama, you know what I'll call you from now on? [...] My *mamma bambina*, my child Mama. AJ 593].[52] Likewise, with Nina Modesta reaches peaks of dependence and regression to infantilism, particularly in the episode in which Nina helps her defecate, and in general in the scenes set in prison and in confinement:

> Io mi liberavo e lei in piedi mi accarezzava i capelli sussurrando: – Brava di mamma, brava, falla tutta, tutta che ti salva!... – E, cosa che non avrei mai potuto immaginare, nel lasciarmi andare un godimento più dolce del rosolio e della lingua di Tuzzu mi fa ora piangere e sospirare non di vergogna ma di piacere, ripetendo: – Nina, Nina non mi lasciare ... (AG 426)

> [I let it all out and she stood there stroking my hair and whispering: 'There's a good girl, *brava*, let it all out, all of it, it will do you good!...' And, something I would never have imagined: as I let myself go, a pleasure sweeter that *rosolio* or Tuzzu's tongue now makes me sigh and weep, not from shame, but from joy, as I say over and over again: 'Nina, Nina, don't leave me ...'] (AJ 558)

The adult Modesta is thereby depicted as much more fragile and dependent than the strong-willed, hating, dissimulating girl and young woman of the first part of the novel. In remembering different figures from her past, in particular Beatrice, Gaia and Leonora, she softens her memories. Moreover, towards the end of the novel her perceptions are increasingly distorted, her imagination interacts more invasively with her senses and we witness a loosening of her control over herself and others. Nonetheless, her mature age also coincides with the culmination of her self-knowledge and her mastery of the art of joy:

> Ora solo una pace profonda invade il suo corpo maturo a ogni emozione della pelle, delle vene, delle giunture. Corpo padrone di se stesso, reso sapiente dall'intelligenza della carne. Intelligenza profonda della materia ... del tatto, dello sguardo, del palato.

52   See also AG 400, 459. The same pattern is found in the relationship between Sapienza and Roberta in *Le certezze del dubbio* (see Chapter 4).

Riversa sullo scoglio, Modesta osserva come i suoi sensi maturati possano contenere senza fragili paure d'infanzia tutto l'azzurro, il vento, la distanza. Stupita, scopre il significato dell'arte che il suo corpo s'è conquistato in quel lungo, breve tragitto dei suoi cinquant'anni. È come una seconda giovinezza, ma con in più la coscienza precisa d'essere giovani, la coscienza del come godere, toccare, guardare. (AG 482–3)

[Now, only a profound peace invades her mature body at each sensation of her skin, veins, joints. A body that is its own master, made wise by an understanding of the flesh. A profound awareness ... of touch, sight, taste. Lying on her back on the rocky ledge, Modesta observes how her developed senses can take in the entire blue expanse, the wind, the distance, without the fragile fears of childhood. Astonished, she discovers the meaning of the skill her body has acquired during the long, brief course of her fifty years. It's like a second childhood, but with a precise awareness of being young, an appreciation of how to touch, see, enjoy.] (AJ 634)

Abandoning herself to the pleasure of the senses and the enjoyment of her body constitutes Modesta's achievement in the novel, thus marking a space that is chosen and not endured by the character. This achieved freedom does not coincide with a final and crystallized form of identity; rather, it is the possibility of experimenting change and multiplicity. Nor does it seal the character's full independence. On the contrary, it involves allowing herself to establish sympathetic relations with others and enjoying emotional inter-dependence, as with Nina. Modesta's movement toward agency is thus constructed as a movement toward the freedom to experience the pleasure of the body and relationships of care.

What Sapienza contests through the character of Modesta is the abstract and metaphysical feature of the humanistic rational subject; conversely, the subject in *L'arte della gioia* is represented as internally divided and socially constructed, but also as the carrier of creative imagination and subversive desires, through a phenomenological reconsideration of the body as a site of power, perception and desire. Ultimately, the configuration of Modesta's identity presents several blurred, ambiguous and contradictory areas. While critics have rightly put much emphasis on the liberating energy and absolute will of the text and Modesta, this discussion has also pointed out a greater complexity, including the character's struggle, insecurity, oscillation between control and uncontrolled emotions, as well as her need for love, which her extraordinary strength cannot entirely efface. A multifaceted description is necessary to capture the tensions she embodies, her oppositional violence and her overwhelming emotions, her ability to kill in order to assert her independence and her regression to an infantile need for love and care. Most importantly, freedom is ultimately achieved by Modesta by frequenting the body, rather than controlling it, as she listens to its drives, impulses, desires and emotions, and elaborates the strategies for enjoying pleasure. The representation of Modesta reflects a properly Epicurean understanding of the relationship between body and rationality and the role of pleasure in orienting choices. The art of joy is 'a firm knowledge of desires',[53] the awareness of the material dimension of existence, of the flesh and its drives. It is from the contact with this dimension that the subject can exercise her freedom and open to complexity, multiplicity, contradiction and change. The words Maria Serena Palieri uses to describe Sapienza offer a fitting depiction on her main character: 'Frail? On the contrary, she seems strong enough to allow herself to be frail.'[54]

A Feminist and Anarchist Novel

Forms of Patriarchal Power

What do 'power' and 'freedom' mean in the socio-historical context represented in the novel, and what is the relationship established with it by the characters? In his afterword to *L'arte della gioia*, Scarpa remarks: 'In *L'arte della gioia*, history, despite its prominence, is an add-on.'[55] His interpretation is quite dismissive of Sapienza's philosophical and political perspective, and replicates the traditional bias that resists accepting women's participation and right to participate in the public sphere. Contrary to Scarpa's perspective, the historical and political dimension is a fundamental component

---

53   Epicuro, *Lettera sulla felicità*, 12–13.
54   Maria Serena Palieri, 'La Sapienza e lo scrivere', *L'Unità*, 26 July 2003.
55   Scarpa, 'Senza alterare niente', 522.

of *L'arte della gioia*, insofar as it constitutes the necessary context that
generates and frames Modesta's struggle for freedom. From a perspective
drawing attention to the ideological content of *L'arte della gioia*, the general
structures or centres of power that Sapienza deconstructs are patriarchy
and totalizing ideologies. More specifically, she takes a stand against the
oppression of women, heteronormativity, the traditional family, inequality
among social classes, fascism, the power of the Catholic Church and the
dogmatic attitude of the left. The ideology of the novel is thus configured
as a rebellion against the hierarchy implicit in the reduction of existence
to one dominating coordinate, and as a hymn to plurality and change.

The first and most evident form in which the socio-historical context
affects the character is patriarchal power. Although in no way limited to
opposition to patriarchal power, the representation of freedom in *L'arte
della gioia* and Modesta's trajectory cannot arguably be understood without
reference to that social context. Patriarchal power manifests itself in various
forms: as material oppression, such as sexual violence and legal constraint,
and as cultural conditioning, such as the inculcation of a sense of inferiority in women. At the beginning of the novel, Tuzzu questions Modesta's
intelligence, on the basis of her sex: 'Ma che vuoi capire! Locca sei e pure
se non fussi locca, le femmine, come dice mio padre, da quando mondo è
mondo non capiscono niente' [What more do you want to know! *Locca*,
a crazy fool, that's what you are! And even if you weren't *locca*, females, as
my father says, have never understood a thing, not since the world began].
Modesta's rejection of the role prepared for her by society as a female is
ready and determined: 'E invece capisco' (AG 8) [But I do understand.
AJ 9]. Similarly, the mother and Tina are described as victims, 'scimunite
che piangono' (13) [silly ninnies crying. 16], whose condition Modesta
aspires to escape. As a child, Modesta is confronted with two opposite roles:
women, who are stupid and subdued, and men, like Tuzzu and Modesta's
alleged father, who are strong and independent. The representation of
patriarchal power at this stage in the novel features a frontal opposition
between two social positions, with an elementary form of domination of
men over women.

Modesta's alleged father represents a better perspective to the girl
than the one offered by her mother and Tina; he is tall, smiley, vital and

strong, and he carries with him the promise of travels and adventures, which initially arouse Modesta's admiration. When he shuts the mother and Tina in the small room, she comments: 'il sangue mi rideva d'orgoglio per la sua forza' (AG 12) [My blood rejoiced, proud of his strength. AJ 14]. This expression closely recalls a similar statement in *Lettera aperta*, referred to Sapienza's own father: 'perché non so dire del suo abbraccio, dell'ammirazione per la sua forza fisica?' [Why can't I speak of his hug and of my admiration for his physical strength?] (LA 50). In *Lettera aperta*, too, the figure of the father is admired for his strength, which is connected to his independence, vitality and powerful sexuality. But such a position of power is also perceived as scary and threatening, and *Lettera aperta* reso-nates with the refrain 'don't rape her' shouted by Maria and addressed to Goliarda's father. The same ambiguity between admiration for strength and fear of violence is present in the opening pages of *L'arte della gioia*, but here the underlying violence inscribed in male power, partially concealed in *Lettera aperta*, comes to the surface and is made explicit from the very beginning, as Modesta's father rapes her. If in *Lettera aperta* male power was a partially denied threat, screaming in the background, in *L'arte della gioia* it is exposed openly and directly in its most evidently sexed form. As in Morante's *La storia* and Aleramo's *Una donna*, an 'initiatory' rape frames the story, showing how patriarchal power is the material context that can be endured, escaped or opposed, but is there, the unavoidable starting point of these writers' personal and historical discourse.

As Modesta grows up, she faces the oppression of women in the form of limitation of their intellectual and professional development. While Mimmo the gardener and doctor Milazzo tell Modesta about the world outside the convent walls, the perspectives offered to her as a woman are described through the nuns' words. They discourage her from nourishing intellectual ambitions and suggest to her the only social roles suitable for a woman: 'Sarta, ricamatrice, cuoca, sceglierai tu fra queste attività umili che sono le uniche che si confanno a una donna. Studiare è un lusso che corrompe' (AG 38) [seamstress, embroiderer, cook. You will choose among these humble skills that are the only suitable ones for a woman. Studying is a luxury that corrupts. AJ 52]. In the Brandifortis' house, princess Gaia is respected and obeyed insofar as she behaves and is perceived to behave in a manly manner, thus conveying the notion that ruling is a male prerogative. Later in the novel, Modesta manages to resist any form of patriarchal power, even though she is periodically threatened by external pressures. For example, Mattia wants to marry her at any cost, but she refuses; she does the same when her son Prando insists that she either gets married or goes to live with him. Carmine, too, threatens Modesta to tie her to him by getting her pregnant: 'Ma non scherzare con l'uomo perché, se voglio, t'inchiodo a me con un figlio' [But don't fool around with this man because, if I want to, I'll saddle you with a child], to which she responds by talking about the possibility for women to get an abortion: 'con una semplice operazione, di una maledizione mi sono liberata. E lo rifaccio se ti prende intenzione di inchiodarmi' (AG 209) [with a simple, painless operation, I rid myself of an inconvenience. And I'd do it again if you got the idea of trapping me. AJ 283]. Sapienza here addresses two major topics that were being debated in Italy in the early 1970s, namely divorce and abortion. She illustrates the material oppression that marriage and unwanted pregnancies can exert on women, and stands resolutely against them, voicing a position that is close to the core arguments and demands of second wave feminist movements.[56]

Patriarchal power pervades the novel, affecting not only Modesta but also and more deeply the other characters. For example, Madre Leonora, seduced and made pregnant by Carmine, takes refuge in a nunnery; Nina, who is arguably the most determined and independent female character, left school because of the 'antica autosvalutazione donnesca' (AG 441) [usual old female self deprecation. AJ 587], and in prison is raped by several fascist soldiers, as she tells Modesta: 'Fatti 'na ragione, parlando di scherzi da uomini in divisa che ponno fa d'altro per ridurti un colabrodo davanti e di dietro, eh?' (423) [Think about it: when it comes to games men in uniform play, what else can they do to reduce you to a colander, front and back, huh? 555]; Carmela, the poor woman who gives advice to Modesta, was forced to prostitute herself since she was a child – 'a

---

56   Divorce in Italy became legal in 1974, abortion in 1978.

dieci anni m'hanno messo un uomo tra le gambe' (102) [I was ten years old when they put a man between my legs. 143]; Beatrice 'è stata vittima della sua infanzia, o, come dite voi, del suo destino coatto' (315) [she was the victim of her childhood or, as you psychoanalysts say, of her unavoidable destiny. 417]; and Carmine's first wife dies after he tries to get her pregnant at any cost even though she is ill and exhausted: 'E scavavo, scavavo oro dalle sue labbra e dal suo abbraccio, ma senza riconoscenza e attenzione per lei. [...] Dovevo saperlo che troppo chiedevo perché sfinita e pallida era' (202) [So I mined her, I mined gold from her lips and her embrace, but without appreciating or paying attention to her. [...] I should have known I was asking too much, because she was worn out and pale. 273–4]. In the last part of the novel, where discussions about the current political situation multiply, Modesta accuses left-wing men, and in particular the PCI, of which Prando is a member, of perpetuating patriarchal oppression; communist militants, Modesta says, undervalue women, exploit their work and treat feminist discourses with patronizing condescension.[57] The polemics against left-wing men and their contiguity with patriarchal power is an important reference for understanding *L'arte della gioia*, which will be discussed further.

Women are not the only victims of patriarchal power. Quite uniquely for the novels of her time, Sapienza includes in her work a perspective on the male position with respect to power and the social construction of masculinity.[58] An interesting example is the failed relationship between Modesta and Carlo. In Carlo's attitude towards sex, Sapienza gives an insightful representation of the separation of sex (associated with prostitutes) and affection (associated with wives) that constrains men as well as women. Carlo, who is prudish and nervous, is convinced that a respectable woman should be reserved and completely passive: 'stai ferma ... così mi piaci, ferma con gli occhi chiusi' (AG 166) [Hold still ... that's how I like you, still, with your eyes closed. AJ 227]. Therefore, he cannot accept Modesta's passionate and disinhibited attitude, he gets angry and calls

---

57   See AG 479–80.
58   For a rich exploration of the construction of masculinity in Italian culture, see Ciccone, *Essere maschi*.

her 'volgare' (167) [vulgar. 228] when she tries to talk about it, thus spoil-
ing any possibility of harmony between them. Through Modesta's voice,
who firmly rejects the role of passive partner in which Carlo would want
to force her, Sapienza explicitly blames the literary representation of the
role of the sexes for forging Carlo's wrong expectations, thus attributing
a prominent function to social construction in the formation of gender
norms: 'ti eri fatta una tua santa un po' dantesca da amare. O preferisci
Petrarca, come credo? [...]. Poveri ragazzi! A noi *Madame Bovary*, a voi
Laura!' (165) [you had created for yourself a Dantesque saint to love.
Or would you prefer Petrarch, as I imagine you do? [...] You poor men!
For us, Madame Bovary, and for you, Laura. 226]. Finally, Carlo agrees
with Modesta on the necessity of breaking that 'solitudine fra uomo e
donna che dura da secoli' (169) [loneliness that for centuries has existed
between men and women. 231]. The construction of masculinity is, in
Modesta's words, a 'demolizione al contrario' (481) [reverse destruction.
631] that teaches young men to be strong and virile, that is, to distinguish
themselves from the weakness characterizing women: 'Sei un uomo, devi
dimostrare quanto sei virile, Carluzzu! Non una mezza donna come questi
giovani d'oggi!' (481) [You're a man. You have to prove how manly you
are, Carluzzu! Not womanish like today's young men! 631–2]. Whereas
some men, like Carmine and Prando, appear to fit conveniently into
a dominant role and benefit from their position of power, others are
rather limited by it, like Carlo and Mattia. Both men and women are
constrained and imprisoned by patriarchal structures, which regiment
the complexity of reality and identities into a fixed binary pattern, as
stated in a dialogue between Mattia and Modesta: '"A me hanno inse-
gnato che nell'anima di un uomo non c'è posto per dubitare." "Questo
vi insegnano per chiudervi, carusi, in una corazza di doveri e false certezze. Come a noi donne, Mattia: altri doveri, altre corazze di seta, ma
è lo stesso"' (343) ['I was taught that there's no place in a man's soul for
doubt.' 'They teach you that in order to imprison you *carusi* in a suit of
armour made up of obligations and false certainties. Like they do with
us women, Mattia: different obligations, different armours. Silken ties,
but it's the same thing.' 452].

From Gender Binarism to Coexistence of Differences and Sexual Fluidity

Within her criticism of patriarchal structures, Sapienza makes space for a multiplicity of approaches and responses to oppression. The only constant in Modesta's position is her utter and uncompromising rejection of the role of victim, together with her determination to pursue pleasure in diverse and changing forms; but the strategies towards the accomplishment of freedom vary depending on the context. This results in a multifaceted and at times self-contradictory representation of gender identities and sexual orientations, open to being read through different strands of feminist and queer theories. Overall, a binary opposition between men and women, which hints at an essentialist understanding of gender and sexual orientation, coexists with a much more fluid and post-structuralist perspective, and with a Marxist-feminist critique of gender hierarchies. Moreover, Sapienza's polemical objective shifts, consisting alternately in women who accept their submission, who perpetrate the submission of other women, who join men in positions of power, or in men who control, rape, exploit and devalue women, and the overall structure of patriarchal society.

The first part of the novel features a clear opposition between the condition of women and that of men, who play the role of subalterns and rulers respectively. Initially, as Ross points out, Modesta's rebellion finds a resource in the adoption of masculine behaviour – the only one practically available to her.[59] Her characteristics of strength, self-determination and intelligence are considered 'masculine' by the other characters and by Modesta herself: 'Io non sarei stata una donnetta. Come la principessa volevo diventare, quella sì che era una donna forte e volitiva come un uomo' (AG 61) [I would not be a silly woman. Like the Princess, that's how I wanted to be. Now there was a woman who was as strong and wilful as a man. AJ 86].[60] This statement at the same time expresses and undermines an essentialist perspective on gender. While some features appear to be distinctively masculine, they can be nonetheless appropriated by a woman,

---

59   See Ross, 'Eccentric Interruptions', 15–16.
60   The expression closely recalls *Lettera aperta*, where the protagonist rejects the role of
     'donnetta' and emulates her mother Maria, who is compared to a man. See Chapter 1.

although this constitutes a transgression of her gender characterization, which Ross, drawing from Halberstam's notion of 'female masculinity', appropriately terms 'donna-uomo'.[61]

Until Modesta's arrival in Catania, the adoption of a masculine attitude is the only way for her to gain respect, and she takes pride in being associated with men, for it means being attributed positive characteristics that stereotypically belong to the male gender. In a second phase, however, once she has attained independence and power and has escaped the condition of victim, she reconsiders the title of 'man', which was once esteemed, and distances herself from the characteristics of patriarchal domination attached to it: '"Voscenza principessa, se mi posso permettere, lei uomo doveva nascere." Un tempo quella frase mi sembrava il più alto riconoscimento che si potesse avere dagli altri, ma adesso il terrore di diventare come Gaia mi opprimeva il torace e mi levava il fiato' (AG 131) ['*If I may say so, Princess,* Voscenza *should have been born a man.'* At one time I had thought those words were the highest recognition one could receive from other people, but now the terror of becoming like Gaia tightened my chest so that I couldn't breathe. AJ 181]. It is useful for Modesta to appropriate those qualities from which women were excluded, but this appropriation must not turn into the exercise of domination. For Modesta, power must be pursued insofar as it enables her to access freedom, not at the expense of it; it is, in other words, an instrument of liberation, not oppression.[62]

Whilst in the first part of the novel Modesta is a 'donna-uomo', that is, in this context, a woman who adopts masculine behaviour in order to escape the limits imposed by society on her gender, as soon as she obtains power and freedom she opens herself to multiple and fluid gender identities. The necessary but limiting identity of the 'donna-uomo' becomes the free and joyful 'mezza maredda e mezzo carusu' (AG 201) [Half *carusu* and half *maredda*. AJ 272], a 'queer' mix of femininity and masculinity.[63] In addition, Modesta also adopts an emphatic femininity in other phases

---

61   Ross, 'Eccentric Interruptions', 15. See Judith Halberstam, *Female Masculinity* (London: Duke University Press, 1998).
62   See, for example, the dialogue about power between Mattia and Modesta, AG 404.
63   *Carusu* and *maredda* are Sicilian terms for *boy* and *girl*.

of her life and in the context of other relationships. Indeed, as she grows up, she stops associating strength and independence with the male gender, exposing the socially constructed feature of both masculinity and femininity. Liberated from the power that dictates the hierarchy of the genders and their binary distribution of traits, gender constructs lose any naturalness, leaving the subject free to experiment with multiple identities. Modesta thus recognizes the process through which gender division is constituted as intrinsically social, and tries to educate the children living in Villa Suvarita outside of gender binarism:

> 'Ma che c'è Stella, Elena, perché li dividete?'
> 'Ma correva come un maschiaccio, principessa! Si sporca il vestitino'.
> Ecco come comincia la divisione. Secondo loro Bambolina, a soli cinque anni, dovrebbe già muoversi diversamente, stare composta, gli occhi bassi, per coltivare in sé la signorina di domani. (AG 265)

> ['What is it, Stella, Elena? Why did you separate them?'
> 'But she was running like a tomboy, Princess! She'll dirty her little dress.'
> That's how the rift begins. According to them, Bambolina, only five years old, should already act differently, remain composed, eyes lowered, to cultivate the young lady of tomorrow.] (AJ 353–4)

This fluidity of gender categories is reflected in the representation of the secondary characters, as Sapienza distributes 'masculine' and 'feminine' traits regardless of the characters' sex. In doing so, she does not only disconnect sex from gender, as in the case of Gaia, but also destabilizes the gender constructs themselves. All the binaries of traits which traditionally distinguish masculinity and femininity (such as strength/weakness; rationality/emotions; mind/body; independence/dependence) are displaced from male and female characters as well as from one another, as they do not appear as a coherent system. In other words, male and female characters may have at the same time or at different times both 'feminine' and 'masculine' characteristics, thus disrupting the internal coherence of gender constructs. For example, Modesta is described as strong-willed, astute and able to fight against oppression, a representation that in the first part of the novel appears to belong to the male construct. However, some characters – both female and male – do not share the same characteristics of strength and are rather submissive and in need of protection, something which would stereotypically belong to the female construct. For example, as Modesta tells Carlo, 'anche Jacopo come Bambolina non ha astuzia e crudeltà. È per loro che bisogna lottare' (AG 466) [Jacopo, like Bambolina, lacks shrewdness and ruthlessness. It's for them that we must fight. AJ 611].

The blurring of gender constructs is particularly evident when gender interacts with other social categories, such as class and ethnicity.[64] In the dialogue between Modesta and Marco that concludes the book, Modesta appears to affirm an essentialist foundation of gender differences and a symmetrical complementarity between men and women: 'Tu sei uomo, Marco, e non sai nel tuo corpo, o sapevi e poi nella fretta di agire hai dimenticato, le metamorfosi della materia e tremi un po' a questa parola. Ma se ti stringi a me, io, donna, ti aiuterò a ricordare e a non temere quel che deve mutare per continuare a essere vivo' (AG 509) [You're a man, Marco, and you don't know – or you knew and then, in your haste to act, forgot – the material transformations in your body, so the world makes you tremble a little. But if you hold me close, I, a woman, will help you remember, and not be afraid of that which must change in order to continue living. AJ 668]. This passage evokes the stereotypical association of men with rationality and abstraction and women with a material, bodily and natural domain. However, the representation of the other male characters throughout the text does not support such a binary view. Indeed, most male characters are represented as in direct contact with the material dimension of the body and with nature. Tuzzu is associated with the landscape of the Chiana del Bove and the sea; Mimmo is described as being part of the wood: 'Il suo corpo fasciato di velluto marrone scuro, da lontano, sembrava un altro tronco cresciuto dalla quercia per capriccio della natura' (31) [From afar his body, clad in dark brown velvet, looked like another trunk, which by

---

64   The intersectionality between gender, class and ethnicity is a rich theme in *L'arte della gioia*, which would deserve specific attention. For the purpose of this book, I limit my analysis to gender constructs. For a discussion of *L'arte della gioia* as a 'postcolonial' novel, see Goffredo Polizzi, 'The Art of Change. Race and the Body in Goliarda Sapienza's *L'arte della gioia*', in Bazzoni, Bond and Wehling-Giorgi, *Goliarda Sapienza in Context*, 163–77.

some quirk of nature had sprung up from the oak. 42]; Carmine speaks a popular language, a mix of Italian and dialect, rooted in the ancient traditions of Sicily. It is Carlo, the positivist doctor originally from Lombardy, who breaks the connection between men and nature, so that rather than between men and women the distinction appears to be between Sicily and Northern Italy. Sicilian traditions are presented as closer to natural rhythm and passionality and are set against rational Northern positivism: 'il contrasto fra la mia lingua cupa di passione e la sua – chiara elegante – che tanto amavo, ma che non riuscivo ad amalgamare con la mia fantasia' (228) [the contrast between my dark language of passion and his – lucid and elegant – which I loved so much, but which I could not reconcile with my imagination. 305]. The contrast between passion and rationality, body and mind, is displaced from the stereotypical distribution of traits between men and women and interacts with the geographical and ethnic axis. *L'arte della gioia* makes space for different positions, attitudes and identities to exist; it represents female characters who are more 'masculine', like Gaia, more traditionally 'feminine', like Beatrice and Stella, or a varied combination of both, like Modesta, Joyce and Nina; the same is true of male characters, who range from Prando's stereotypical masculinity to different degrees of reconfiguration of masculinity itself, for example in the cases of Mattia, Carlo, Jacopo and Carluzzu – even though, overall, more variation is afforded to women. Interestingly, a figure who is entirely missing in *L'arte della gioia* is that of the effeminate and/or the homosexual man, which conversely is well present in the narrative from other Italian women writers of the time, as for example Morante and Ginzburg.[65]

A great openness of possibilities beyond constrictive categories is afforded in the novel to – female – sexual orientation, for Sapienza does not only question patriarchal power, but heteronormativity as well. Even

---

65   We can think, for example, of Wilhelm Gerace (Arturo's father) in Morante's *L'isola di Arturo* (1957), and Manuele, the protagonist of *Aracoeli* (1982); As far as Ginzburg is concerned, see Valentino and Kit from the short story *Valentino* (1951) and Gigi from *Le voci della sera* (1961); for a comprehensive list and discussion, see James Michael Fortney, 'Con quel tipo lì: Homosexual Characters in Natalia Ginzburg's Narrative Families', *Italica*, 86 (December 2009).

though, as Ross cogently argues, the representation of homosexual desire in Sapienza's narrative overall presents many self-contradictory aspects, and Modesta expresses even 'rather homophobic views, dismissing her relationship with Beatrice as mere "carezze di femmine" once she has slept with Carmine and experienced "real" sexual intimacy with a man', the representation of homosexual desire is immune from any charge of deviance.⁶⁶ Through the multiple homosexual and heterosexual relationships represented in the novel, Sapienza questions the alleged naturalness of the link between sex, gender and sexual orientation, as well as the exclusivity and stability of a person's sexual orientation. This is certainly the aspect of the novel that most closely anticipates the critique of heteronormativity and theory of fluid desires and identities later developed by queer thinkers.⁶⁷

In the first part of the novel, female homosexuality, in the relationship between Modesta and Beatrice, is described as a preparatory stage for heterosexuality, as Carmine tells Modesta: 'Che credi che sei la prima a passare all'inizio per mani di femmine? Niente c'è di male, figghia. [...] Quello che imparavo da Carmine cercavo di comunicarlo a Beatrice. [...] E poi, come Carmine diceva, la preparavo a quando avrebbe incontrato l'uomo giusto' (AG 111) [What do you think, that you're the first to be initiated by a woman's hand? There's nothing wrong with it, *figghia*. [...] What I learnt from Carmine I tried to relay to Beatrice. [...] Besides, as Carmine said, I was preparing for when she would meet the right man. AJ 156]. Modesta's relationship with Beatrice has much in common with the representation of homosexual desire in *Lettera aperta* and *Io, Jean Gabin*. Goliarda's relationships with Nica in *Lettera aperta* and with Jean in *Io, Jean Gabin* are characterized as bonds that allow the protagonist to experience reciprocity and communication beyond the distorting effects of

66 Ross, 'Eccentric Interruptions', 16. The argument recalls the discussion developed in Chapter 1.
67 See Teresa de Lauretis, 'Queer Theory: Lesbian and Gay Sexualities', *Differences*, 3, 2 (1991), iii-xviii; Eve Kosofsky Sedgwick, *Epistemology of the Closet* (Berkeley: University of California Press, 1990); Butler, *Gender Trouble*; Rich, 'Compulsory Heterosexuality and Lesbian Existence'.

power imbalance. These equal and 'resonant' relationships, in the sense of a communication founded on mutual recognition of unique subjectivities proposed by Cavarero, enable the protagonist to access and strengthen a more authentic sense of the self. Homosexuality is thus preparatory in the sense that it is represented as a productive step in the formation of the self and in establishing bonds with others. The relationship between Modesta and Beatrice is recounted in very similar terms, which stress reciprocity, self-recognition and confidence:

> Così, per la prima volta in vita mia, fui amata amando, come dice la romanza. [...] Abbandonandomi a lei, uscivo da quell'inferno di dubbi e bende e muri di lava. [...] Una tenerezza mai conosciuta mi faceva essere tranquilla fra quegli alberi che giravano intorno al sole, sicura di non sprofondare. Se mi spogliavo sapevo da lei che colore aveva la mia pelle, quanti nei la mia schiena. (AG 79–80)

> [And so, for the first time in my life, *fui amata amando*, I loved and was loved in return, as the aria goes. [...] Surrendering to her, I left behind that inferno of qualms and bands and lava walls. [...] A tenderness I had never known before made me feel serene among the trees that revolved around the sun, confident that I would not fall. When she undressed me, I learned from her what colour my skin was, how many moles I had on my back.] (AJ 113–14)

Contradicting the dialogue between Carmine and Modesta cited above, and commented by Ross, the development of the characters' sexuality does not follow the idea, there formulated, that mature sexuality corresponds to heterosexuality. Homosexual relationships are a maturational stage for the construction of identity, but they do not dictate that future orientation shall be heterosexual, nor that it shall be univocal and stable. Indeed, in Modesta's relationship with Joyce this 'preparatory' aspect of homosexuality, which would confine it in an underdeveloped stage of sexuality, disappears. In long – slightly didactic and melodramatic – dialogues between the two women, Joyce voices a Freudian interpretation that pathologizes non-hetero sexualities – 'Ogni rapporto omosessuale è senza futuro. [...] sei malata' (AG 352) [No homosexual relationship has a future. [...] you're sick. AJ 464–5]. On the contrary, Modesta claims the right for herself and for others to enjoy a fluid sexuality beyond any definition of hetero/homosexuality: 'sono donna, Joyce, e per me la normalità è amare l'uomo e la donna' (409) [I'm a woman, Joyce, and for me being normal means loving men and women. 537].

Fluid sexuality is not Modesta's exclusive prerogative, but rather a widespread phenomenon in the novel: 'E Beatrice? Per anni ci siamo amate e poi lei ha amato Carlo. E chissà quante altre donne e uomini' (AG 352) [And what about Beatrice? For years we loved each other and later she loved Carlo. And the same can be said for countless other men and women. AJ 464]. Likewise, Mela and Bambù have a homosexual relationship, after which Bambù falls in love with Mattia, while Mela appears to settle into a lesbian relationship, which is not problematized either: 'Chi ci capisce con la natura! Credo che lei amerà sempre solo le donne' (436) [Who can understand nature! I think that she will always love only women. 572]. Nina moves from lover to lover, from both genders, often having more than one relationship at the same time. Even more freely than with gender identities, *L'arte della gioia* makes space for a multiplicity of possibilities for female sexuality, strenuously refusing to fix and close reality into a single, stable category. What is particularly surprising in the text is that sexual fluidity is presented as perfectly natural and unproblematic not only for Modesta but also for her surrounding environment. Except for Joyce, who struggles with her own identity, no other character questions or stigmatizes the sexual conduct of anyone else. The heteronormativity that Sapienza is questioning pertains to the author's socio-historical context rather than the fictional world, where sexual fluidity is represented as largely accepted. Modesta mentions social discrimination against homosexuality,[68] but, apart from the case of Joyce, this curiously does not play any significant role in the novel.

The Primacy of Rebellious Desire

Modesta's yearn for freedom has in patriarchal power and women's submission its primary obstacle, as it takes place largely in the terrain of gender identity and fluid sexuality. Although material conditions of oppression

---

68   See AG 352.

(i.e. patriarchal structures, as well as class conditions) are clearly identified and acknowledged in the text, Sapienza's main focus is on cultural oppression deriving from the social construction of the role of women. This consideration may explain why, within the overall structure of the novel, the representation of patriarchal power takes so little space compared to the narration and the discussion of forms and strategies of rebellion. With the exception of the initial rape, male characters are never really an obstacle for Modesta. They do not succeed in actively dominating or controlling her (even though they do so with other women, such as Carmine and Prando with their respective wives). Quite the opposite, after initial attempts to impose themselves, they invariably surrender to her will and are all willing to learn from her. Similarly, once Modesta escapes from the convent walls, her sexual fluidity – whether in the form of homosexual desire or multiplicity of lovers – is not really questioned by anyone.

Fortini points out this absence of a foregrounded clash between Modesta and patriarchal power, and discusses specifically the quick disappearance and ultimately the irrelevance of the figure of the father after the rape.[69] She interprets this absence as related to the extreme originality of the novel compared to patriarchal tradition, as it appears to have no roots or models.[70] On the basis of such an absence of the father figure and this unclassifiable originality, Fortini suggests a comparison between Sapienza's, Morante's, and Anna Maria Ortese's works. Fortini's argument recalls Irigaray's understanding of the relationship between women and patriarchal power put forward in *Speculum of the Other Woman* and *This Sex Which is Not One*. According to Irigaray, the female sex is not opposed to the male sex, but outside the binary logic of masculine thought. The opposition between 'One' and 'Other' is all internal to the masculine signifying economy, while the female sex is neither 'One' nor 'Other', it is many, or an absence. In *L'arte della gioia*, according to Fortini, this would be reflected in the absence of frontal opposition between women and men, or between victims and perpetrators, because the privileged point of

69   Laura Fortini, '*L'arte della gioia* e il genio dell'omicidio mancato', in Farnetti, *Appassionata Sapienza*, 101–26.
70   Ibid. 110.

view is external to the logic of opposition itself. As far as Modesta's story is concerned, however, the extraneousness to the binary logic of masculine thought suggested by Fortini must be understood within the precise limits pointed out here, consisting in the initial, primary necessity for subaltern subjects to access a locus of agency.

The focus on the agency of the oppressed rather than the structures of oppression could potentially be interpreted as a sort of nonchalance towards material conditions on the part of Sapienza. The parable of Modesta is in no way a realistic representation of women's actual opportunities, and *L'arte della gioia* at times displays a superomistic liberation, as though freedom could depend only on the individual's determination to be free. Destiny is dismissed as 'tutte chiacchiere inutili di donnette' (AG 60) [The idle prattle of silly women! AJ 86], or, in Carmine's words, 'parola per acquietare i miserabili è! Il destino te lo puoi maneggiare come vuoi, se valente sei' (216) [A word to reassure those who are miserable! You can control destiny as you please, if you're determined. 290]. In fact, Modesta accomplishes a complete liberation from any internal and external cultural conditioning within the space of a lifespan, without paying the price of insanity, social marginalization and loss of identity usually befalling on those who transgress well-established traditions and social roles.[71] After all, as a reviewer observed, 'Modesta wins the benefits of marriage – money, a title, and a cover for her indecencies – and avoids any of the burden. Just eighteen, she has engineered for herself a handful of rare freedoms: liberty without loneliness, money without work, and sex with whomever she wants.'[72]

Nonetheless, once the superomistic and symbolic feature of the character of Modesta has been acknowledged, defining *L'arte della gioia* as indifferent towards material conditions would not be accurate and would not do justice to Sapienza's political and philosophical substance. First, Sapienza appears to be fully aware of the role of economic privilege and how women's emancipation is largely dependent on it. In *L'arte della gioia*, the accumulation of wealth is not held as a value, but a certain degree of

71 As discussed in Chapter 1, this was conversely the fate of Maria Giudice and, partially, of Sapienza herself.
72 Cooke, 'Disobedience is a Virtue'.

economic independence is recognized as necessary. Obviously, the stress on economic independence is of particular importance with regards to women's struggle for freedom and equality, considering their historical seclusion from access to money and the administration of their own patrimony. Modesta's rapid rise to power is the most evident manifestation of the primary importance of material independence for freedom and joy to be pursued, and throughout the text Modesta never forgets to acknowledge how her freedom rests upon her economic privilege: '– Mi piaci, Mody, mi piace come riconosci il tuo privilegio. – È il primo dovere, mi sembra, per quelli che la pensano come noi' (AG 435) ['I like you, Mody, I like the way you acknowledge your privilege.' 'It's the primary duty, it seems to me, for those who think like we do.' AJ 571]. Second, Modesta's symbolic liberation is counterbalanced by the overall structure of the novel, and specifically by the secondary characters, who are much more closely affected by historical and socioeconomic conditions. If Modesta can achieve complete liberation from oppression and traditions in the arc of a single lifetime, for the other characters it is not possible to ignore historical conditions that are not changeable by individual will and from which individual will is itself conditioned. Finally, and perhaps more importantly, *L'arte della gioia* is concerned with a transformation that needs to take place first and foremost in the cultural and psychological structures of the subaltern subjects. This is why the present analysis started from the very foundation of the individual subject, the desiring matter of the body, and this is why *L'arte della gioia* begins and finishes with an orgasm, for it expresses the centrality of desire in constituting a subject who can recognize and oppose structures of oppression.

In *L'arte della gioia*, the primary subjects who need to retrieve this desiring dimension are women, but the liberation entailed in the deconstruction of patriarchy concerns both women and men. Women, in order to become subjects, need to retrieve that primordial desire that constitutes the foundation of agency and nourishes strength, independence and 'positive' pride. Surely, without material liberation, little change is possible. But if there is not an initial desire to want to modify those material conditions, the struggle cannot even begin. As Martha Nussbaum explains with great clarity,

When society has put some things out of reach for some people, they typically
learn not to want those things; [...] sometimes adaptation happens after the person
wanted the thing initially [...]. Sometimes, however, people learn not to want goods
in the first place, because these goods are put off-limits for people of their gender,
or race, or class.[73]

Psychological liberation, in the form of nourishing desire, and the related
process of 'becoming a subject', is not a sufficient condition, but is a necessary one. Here lies the sense of Modesta challenging a destiny of oppression and encouraging others to do the same: 'In un lampo capii che cosa
era quello che chiamano destino: una volontà inconsapevole di continuare
quella che per anni ci hanno insinuato, imposto, ripetuto essere la sola
strada giusta da seguire' (AG 122–3) [Suddenly I knew what that thing
called destiny was: the unconscious desire to continue what for years has
been insinuated, imposed and repeated to us as being the only right path
to follow. AJ 171]; '"Lei dice, principessa, ca un destino si può cangiare?"
"Tutto si può cangiare, Stella"' (235) ['Do you mean that a person's destiny can be changed, Princess?' 'Everything can be changed, Stella.' 315].
In *L'arte della gioia*, Sapienza realizes what Manuela Vigorita cogently
defined 'a book that teaches to yearn',[74] seeking to inspire other women to
rebel, instilling in them the primordial desire to fight oppression, to stop
thinking of themselves inescapably as victims.

The focus on the agency of the oppressed helps us understand why
Sapienza addresses particularly women and often puts responsibility primarily on them for their own oppression, to the point, at times, of verging
on blaming the victims themselves. In *L'arte della gioia*, Modesta voices
a bitter condemnation not only of women who join men in positions of
power, like Joyce, but also those who, in fully accepting a submissive role
for themselves, force other women to do so:

73   Martha Nussbaum, *Creating Capabilites. The Human Development Approach* (London:
     The Belknap Press of Harvard University Press, 2011), 54.
74   Manuela Vigorita, 'Omaggio a Goliarda Sapienza: se l'arte della gioia diventa libertà',
     Buddismo e società, 93 (July/August 2002).

Come in convento, leggi, prigioni, storia edificata dagli uomini. Ma è la donna che ha accettato di tenere le chiavi, guardiana inflessibile del verbo dell'uomo. In convento Modesta odiò le sue carceriere con odio di schiava, odio umiliante ma necessario. Oggi è con distacco e sicurezza che difende Bambolina dai maschi e dalle femmine, in lei difende se stessa, il suo passato, una figlia che col tempo potrebbe nascerle ... Ti ricordi, Carlo, quando ti dissi che solo la donna può aiutare la donna, e tu nel tuo orgoglio di uomo non capivi? (AG 265)

[Like in the convent: laws, prison, history erected by men. But it's women who have agreed to be the keeper of the keys, uncompromising guardians of men's word. In the convent, Modesta hated her jailers with a slave's hatred, a humiliating but necessary hate. Today, she defends Bambolina from men and women, impartially and confidently; by defending her she is defending herself, her past, a daughter she might some day give birth to ... Remember, Carlo? Remember when I told you that only women can help women, and you, with your masculine pride, didn't understand?] (AJ 354)

If patriarchal structures are dominated by men, Modesta says, women too play a role in guaranteeing their continuity, by accepting their own submission and perpetrating the oppression of other women. Through Modesta's voice, Sapienza declares her hostility towards women who are implicated in the perpetration of oppression and clearly argues that a struggle against patriarchal structures can only be started by women themselves. Sapienza's hostile attitude towards other women has been defined by Monica Farnetti as 'amorous misogyny',[75] in Ross's words 'a sentiment experienced by women who, while holding their sex in great esteem, feel a disdain for other women who, in their view, taint the *image* of woman in some way'.[76] Similarly, according to Providenti the homicides committed by Modesta are directed against the symbols of femininity that those women (the mother, Tina, Leonora and Gaia) represent.[77] Likewise, Ross comments: 'Here it is evident how Sapienza's writing and politics can cause discomfort, since she seems to judge and blame other women, rather than

75   Monica Farnetti, "'L'arte della gioia" e il genio dell'omicidio', in Farnetti, *Appassionata Sapienza*, 89–100, 92.

76   Ross, 'Eccentric Interruptions', 15. My emphasis.

77   Providenti, *La porta è aperta*, 43.

considering the conditions that might have resulted in their having a different view or situation to her ideal of womanhood.'[78] The contradiction that Farnetti, Ross and Providenti point out between solidarity and hostility towards women needs to be integrated by an important consideration concerning the specific object of Sapienza's criticism. In fact, within the narrative economy of the story, Leonora and Gaia are not killed for the model of femininity they embody, but for their perpetration of oppression of other women, including Modesta herself.[79] In other words, they are not only *symbols* of femininity or *images* of woman, but also and mainly Modesta's 'jailers'. Whereas Modesta fiercely – and violently – opposes the oppression exerted by women on other women, like any other form of oppression, it is significant to stress that *L'arte della gioia* actually makes space for different ways to be a woman. For example, Beatrice, Stella and Bambù have very little in common with Modesta's rebellious and proud attitude, but certainly she does not kill or condemn them. Instead, because they do not constitute a direct threat to her independence, she actively tries to educate them to freedom. In this way, Sapienza's 'misoginia amorosa' becomes more legible when the rebellious, anarchist spirit of the book is taken into account. As Bakunin writes,

> No man can emancipate himself without also emancipating all the men around him. [...] I am incessantly the product of what the last among men are: if they are ignorant, miserable, slaves, my existence is determined by their slavery. [...] I, who want to be free, cannot be, because all the men around me do not yet want to be free, and by not wanting it, they become instruments of oppression against me.[80]

78 Ross, 'Eccentric Interruptions', 15.
79 The discourse is different for the homicide of Modesta's mother, which was discussed in the first part of this chapter. Nevertheless, none of the existing interpretations, including mine, can convincingly account for the killing of Tina, Modesta's sister who has Down's syndrome. Such an act remains brutally inexplicable within the signifying economy of the text, and psychoanalytic hypotheses on what Tina might symbolize to Sapienza herself appear to be the only practicable direction for an interpretation, although I am not endeavouring to do so.
80 Michail Bakunin, cited in Errico Malatesta, *L'anarchia. Il nostro programma* (Rome: Datanews, 2001), 28–9.

The main focus in *L'arte della gioia* is the oppression exerted by patriarchal structures on women and men and the protagonist's rejection of imposed identities and social roles. Change, for Sapienza, needs to sediment within the consciousness of the oppressed and start from them, possibly from someone who, like Modesta, is in the position of helping others. Hence, it can be argued that Sapienza's novel does not function primarily as a judgement of the victims, but rather as a defence of one's independence against oppression, including that which is perpetrated by other women, and a call to boycott normative roles and aspire to individual and social transformation.

Against Ideology: An Engagé Anarchist Novel

The inequality between men and women is doubtless the most prominent context in which power takes place and is contested in *L'arte della gioia*, but the rebellious spirit of the novel is much broader, embracing any form of internal and external oppression. Through Modesta's behaviour, as well as through explicit remarks, Sapienza attacks a series of centres or structures, at the same time originating multiple and creative responses to them. For example, she subverts the structure of the family, 'quella fortezza di prima linea che, fascismo o no, è sempre la famiglia' (AG 481) [that first line of defence which – Fascism or not – is still the family. AJ 632];[81] she contests marriage, 'un contratto assurdo che umilia l'uomo e la donna insieme' (399) [an absurd contract that debases both the man and the woman. 523], and the idea that love is singular and lasts for the whole life. In line with Epicurean ethics, according to which 'you're never too young or too old to know happiness',[82] Sapienza questions the exclusion of the elderly from

---

81   On Sapienza's subversion of the family structure, see Aureliana Di Rollo, 'Reforging the Maternal Bond', in Bazzoni, Bond and Wehling-Giorgi, *Goliarda Sapienza in Context*, 33–45; Susanna Scarparo and Aureliana Di Rollo, 'Mothers, Daughters and Family in Goliarda Sapienza's *L'arte della gioia*', *The Italianist*, 35, I (2015), 91–106.

82   Epicuro, *Lettera sulla felicità*, 5.

active life and the representation of old age as negative: 'Anche la parola vecchiaia mente, Modesta, è stata rimpinzata di fantasmi paurosi come la parola morte per farti stare calma, ossequiosa di tutte le leggi costituite (481) [Even the term 'old age' is a lie, Modesta. It's been crammed with scary ghosts, like the word 'death', to make you be quiet, deferential to the established rules. 632].

Similarly, Modesta refuses any activity or ideal that demands absolute dedication and subordinates the enjoyment of life, including the goal to improve one's wealth and power beyond the need. In this rejection of the capitalistic spiral of economic growth, Sapienza distances herself from the Sicilian literary tradition of Giovanni Verga, Federico De Roberto, Luigi Pirandello and Giuseppe Tomasi di Lampedusa, which conversely presents the thirst for richness and power as the principal human drive. Modesta achieves the status of princess, only to sell most of her properties, ultimately sustaining herself by working in a bookshop. Modesta's trajectory reverses the path of Mazzarò in *La roba* (1893), of Mastro-don Gesualdo in the homonymous novel (1888), of Consalvo Uzeda in *I Vicerè* (1894), of Flaminio Salvo in *I vecchi e i giovani* (1913), of Tancredi and don Calogero Sedàra in *Il Gattopardo* (1957). By exalting the enjoyment of life and rejecting the ideal of power, prestige and wealth as fundamental drives and ultimate goods, Sapienza consciously and explicitly presents her novel as subversive with respect to the Sicilian literary tradition, with which nonetheless she clearly dialogues.[83] Modesta challenges the core principle of capitalism, defined as 'l'atroce notte insonne dell'efficienza a tutti i costi' (AG 471) [atrocious sleepless nights: efficiency at all costs. 618], and, in a dialogue with Carmine, she overtly deserts her class – dismissing with it the patriarchal Sicilian tradition of the Traos, the Uzedas, the Laurentanos and the Leopards:

---

83   For a more detailed discussion of Sapienza's relationship with the Sicilian literary tradition, see Bazzoni, 'Gli anni e le stagioni: prospettive su femminismo, politica e storia ne *L'arte della gioia*', in Providenti, *Quel sogno d'essere*, 33–52, and Polizzi, 'The Art of Change'.

'Non sono come te, Carmine! I tempi stanno cambiando, e spero che i tuoi figli, i
tuoi nipoti e tutti gli altri giovani vi facciano saltare teste e poderi!'
    'Sentitela! E chi ti ha messo queste idee in testa, tuo cognato? O l'hai letto nei
libri? E che interesse ci avresti tu, eh? Principessa Brandiforti?'
    'L'interesse di farmi una bella risata.' (AG 207)[84]

['I'm not like you, Carmine! Times are changing, and I hope that your sons, your
grandchildren and all the other young people will overthrow you landowners and
do away with your estates.'
    'Listen to her! And who put these ideas into your head? Your brother-in-law? Or
did you read about them in books? And what would you gain from it, eh, Princess
Brandiforti?'
    'I would have a good laugh over it.'] (AJ 280)

From marriage to capitalism, from love to literary tradition, Sapienza questions any centre or structure of power that can limit individual freedom.
Scarpa highlights the rebellious anarchism that characterizes *L'arte della
gioia*: 'The ideology that really counts in this novel, and that goes beyond
its pedagogical intention, is an ideology of anarchist behaviour. [...] The
ideology of the novel is, more properly, an ethics; it is an energy, deployed
in defence of one's physical and mental freedom, which propels the book
forward at full tilt.'[85] Scarpa is right in pointing out the anarchist ethics and
energy that constitute the fundamental drive of *L'arte della gioia*. However,
by limiting the novel's anarchist perspective to Modesta's individual behaviour, he is again fairly dismissive of the political and historical dimension
of Sapienza's work. Sapienza, who comes from a politically committed
family and fought as a partisan, dialogues with her own political tradition
with full awareness of its social context. In fact, anarchism is also present in
the text as a specific political subject with a specific historical consistency,
and the complex relationship between anarchist ethics and the political
arena is an important aspect of *L'arte della gioia*. Sapienza mentions the

84   Carmine's reply, 'mai niente di buono fuori dall'isola è venuto' (AG 207) [noth-
      ing good ever came to island from outside. AJ 280] directly recalls don Fabrizio
      Salina's position in the famous dialogue with Chevalley in Tomasi di Lampedusa's
      Il Gattopardo.
85   Scarpa, 'Senza alterare niente', 521–2.

founding thinkers of anarchism, such as Bakunin and, in the Italian context, Malatesta;[86] the movement's cultural tradition, like the lyrics of the song 'Son nostre figlie le prostitute, son ...' (425) [the prostitutes are our daughters. 557];[87] and its historical memory and militants, described as 'persone dolci, morali e sventate' (154) [Individuals who are gentle, moral and impetuous. 211].

Through Nina, the principal referent for the representation of anarchy in the novel, Sapienza voices the conflict between anarchism and socialism (and later communism) that so deeply marks her narrative. Such a conflict is represented in its historical dimension, for example in the anarchists' refusal to support Italy's participation in World War I, unlike some socialist 'traditori' (AG 424) [traitors. AJ 556],[88] and the infamous episode of the massacre of anarchists by the communist militias during the Spanish civil war, in 1937. Yet, this is also a conflict that concerns Sapienza's relationship with her own historical and political context. Sapienza is critical of the PCI, the dominant intellectual referent for the left until the late 1970s and specifically in her circle of friends. On several occasions, Sapienza manifests discomfort towards the rigidity, pervasiveness and strength of the communist agenda among the Roman left-wing intellectuals in the years when she was writing *L'arte della gioia*, and in turn she was not taken seriously by the same circle due to her anti-conventional, heretic views. The polemic against the PCI, already raised in *Lettera aperta* and *Il filo di mezzogiorno*, is explicitly declared in *L'arte della gioia*. The Communist Party is represented as reluctant, when not overtly hostile, towards gender equality, and it is at the same time subservient to the Catholic electorate. In a bitter argument with Joyce, who has become a party executive, Modesta accuses the PCI of having betrayed Marxism and of being a compromised, ultimately conservative force: 'siete una massa di traditori, Joyce. [...] era sempre quel potere a tutto tondo nella sua divisa elegante di altero guerriero' (472–3)

---

86   See AG 180.
87   Lines from the song *Inno dei pezzenti. Marsigliese del lavoro* (1895).
88   Maria Giudice herself was arrested, together with Terracini, for her anti-interventionist position. See Santino, 'Maria Giudice'.

[you're a gang of traitors, Joyce. […] still the same power in every respect, wearing the elegant uniform of an arrogant warrior. 619–21].

The conflict between Sapienza's anarchism and the PCI is political as well as more broadly philosophical. Sapienza articulates the relationship between anarchism and the PCI as a conflict between individual freedom, connected with the fluidity of a materialist approach to reality, and an abstract, dogmatic and intransigent attitude. Communist commitment and ideology are charged with relying on a restrictive notion of the individual, reason and history, which prevents real freedom and replicates the mistakes of the enemies it fights. Modesta explains clearly her position to Carlo: 'Io non nego nessuna lotta! Critico l'atteggiamento del pensiero che è troppo poco differente da quello del vecchio mondo che voi volete combattere' (AG 168) [I'm not denying any struggle! I'm critical of a mindset and way of thinking that is not very different from the old world that you seek to oppose. AJ 230]. In the socialist and then in the communist militants Modesta does not find 'la libertà del materialismo' [the freedom of materialism], but only 'la ferocia del dogma per nascondere la paura della ricerca, della sperimentazione, della scoperta, della fluidità della vita' (168) [a ferocity of dogma hiding a fear of investigation, of experimentation, of discovery, of life's fluidity. 230]. Likewise, as Nina tells Modesta, 'In Russia hanno accantonato tutto quello che contava per la nostra libertà individuale' (436) [In Russia, they've discarded everything that mattered to our individual freedom. 572]. While Sapienza does not disavow class emancipatory struggle, she nonetheless associates communism – in the way it is represented by its political referent, the PCI – with a logocentric and patriarchal perspective that reduces the fluidity of reality to abstract categories and thereby oppresses individual freedom. Anarchy would be, in Sapienza's view and in line with Bakunin's and Malatesta's political tradition, the truest realization of socialism, which socialist and communist parties keep betraying.[89]

---

89 'Anarchy, like socialism, has in the *equality of conditions* its foundation, its starting point and its necessary environment; *solidarity* is its core value and *freedom* its method', Malatesta, *L'anarchia. Il nostro programma*, 57.

In *L'arte della gioia*, political, ethical and philosophical perspectives are closely interconnected, having in the notion of freedom and in Epicurean ethics their common ground. There is a continuity between the awareness of the corporeal dimension of existence, the liberation of desire and the realization of political freedom. Such a perspective brings *L'arte della gioia* close to the epistemological and political project of Braidotti's feminist nomadism, with its 'rejection of hierarchical differences and negation of the hegemonic power of reason.'[90] Since there is an 'unavoidable connection between metaphysics and domination,'[91] opposing power is linked to questioning abstract and universal notions of reason, making space for other dimensions of existence that are neglected, oppressed or expelled by metaphysics – body, desire, imagination and ethics. The material ground of existence must be kept present, frequented and acknowledged, in order not to get lost 'nelle ali menzognere della ragione per la ragione, nelle teorie, le utopie a tutto tondo, perfette delle più crudeli delle perfezioni: quelle che la mente disegna astrattamente, senza tenere conto del pane, la cacca, il desiderio carnale' [in the deceitful wings of reason for its own sake, in theories, in all-round utopias, which are perfect in the cruellest form of perfection: the ones that the mind draws in complete abstraction, without taking into account bread, excrement, or sexual desire].[92] Whereas 'il leninista non legge per autocensura' (AG 480) [a Leninist doesn't read out of self-censorship. 630], Sapienza's anarchist thought maintains that 'per prepararsi alla rivoluzione si deve bere tanta e tanta fantasia' (438) [to prepare for the revolution one must soak up lots and lots of fantasy. 575]. In addition to claiming the freedom of imagination from ideology within the artistic field, as Vittorini did in his well-known quarrel with Palmiro Togliatti on *Il Politecnico*, Sapienza also aspires to contaminate politics itself with imagination, voicing a perspective that is close to the students'

---

90   Braidotti, *Nuovi soggetti nomadi*, 151.
91   Giuseppe Stellardi, '*Pensiero debole*, Nihilism and Ethics, or How Strong is Weakness?', in Pierpaolo Antonello and Florian Mussgnug, eds, *Postmodern* Impegno (Oxford: Peter Lang, 2009), 83–98, 87.
92   Sapienza, unpublished diaries, cited in Providenti, *La porta è aperta*, 76.

slogan 'l'immaginazione al potere' [all power to the imagination] in the late 1960s and 1970s.[93]

In *L'arte della gioia* anarchism goes together with the criticism of logocentrism and the oppression it perpetrates by expelling body and imagination from abstract rationality, and by reducing the multiplicity of reality to one, absolute and dominant structure. What must be overcome, in Sapienza's view, is the reification of a single perspective and the systematization of a fluid reality into absolute categories. On this ground, Modesta confronts the definitory and categorizing applications of Freudian psychoanalysis, which she compares to religion, like socialism is compared to the Church.[94] If, in Vattimo's words, 'anti-foundationalism itself is at risk of hardening into metaphysics',[95] Modesta states, 'mentono le parole, appena hai detto la parola questa ti ricade addosso come il coperchio di una bara. [...] una negazione assoluta non è esattamente uguale a un'affermazione assoluta?' (AG 397) [Words are deceiving: as soon as you utter a word, it falls on you like the lid of a coffin. [...] isn't an absolute denial exactly the same as an absolute affirmation? AJ 521]. Anarchism is at the same time a political perspective and a philosophical approach, connecting Sapienza to the fundamental inspiration of weak thought, post-structuralism and feminist nomadism.[96] As Braidotti argues,

> The nomadism I am talking about has to do with a critical conscience that does not subscribe to socially codified forms of thought and behaviour. [...] The nomadic condition does not identify with the physical act of travelling but is rather defined by an awareness and desire to overturn established norms. It is a political passion for radical change and transformation.[97]

93   Elio Vittorini, 'Politica e cultura. Lettera a Togliatti', *Il Politecnico*, January–March 1947.
94   See AG 350.
95   Gianni Vattimo, *Nihilism and Emancipation. Ethics, Politics and Law* (New York: Columbia University Press, 2004), xxviii, cited in Stellardi, '*Pensiero debole*, Nihilism and Ethics', 87.
96   For a joint consideration of anarchism, post-structuralism and nomadism, see Jamie Heckert and Richard Cleminson, 'Ethics, Relationships and Power', in Heckert and Cleminson, eds, *Anarchism and Sexuality: Ethics, Relationships and Power* (Oxon: Routledge, 2011), 1–22.
97   Braidotti, *Nuovi soggetti nomadi*, 14.

Significantly, this political passion for radical transformation is described by Braidotti as a '*joyful* nomadic force.'[98] Sapienza voices a pluralistic and anti-metaphysical perspective and applies it from the figuration of identity to the ethics of materialism and Epicureanism to the anarchist political perspective, composing a libertarian picture that remains unique in the Italian literary context for its breadth and radicalism.

In order for freedom, multiplicity and fluidity to take place, Modesta needs first to build a sense of self and to reject oppression, adopting a strongly oppositional attitude that has little to do with the anarchist and post-structuralist view just described. In order to access a right to weakness, a subject needs firstly to develop a positive confidence, originating in the desire to reject oppression. As Giuseppe Stellardi points out, freedom is the necessary condition for an epistemological and political paradigm based on weakness to work: 'freedom must at some point become something more than a consensually agreed and negotiated "good", since it is at the same time a necessary condition for the negotiation of identities, positions and interests to take place.'[99] Likewise, in Vattimo's words, 'there are no ultimate *foundations* before which our freedom should stop, which is instead what authorities of every kind [...] have always sought to make us believe.'[100] However, we must pursue the 'ideal of *founding* every law and social behaviour on the respect of everyone's freedom.'[101]

In fact, the parable of Modesta in *L'arte della gioia* shows the margins of post-structuralist thought itself, which rests upon a condition of freedom that is not granted within the social system itself, but must be achieved through a struggle. Overall, the novel features two perspectives, which can be read as in contradiction with one another, or as two different 'moments', 'strategies' or 'positions.' On the one hand, Modesta resorts to direct opposition to power, in order to establish the conditions for exerting her freedom; whenever this attitude prevails, life is represented as a struggle,

98   Braidotti, *Nuovi soggetti nomadi*, 21. My emphasis.
99   Stellardi, '*Pensiero debole*, Nihilism and Ethics', 91–2.
100   Vattimo, 'Nihilism as Emancipation', *Cosmos and History*, 5, I (2009), 20–3, 21. My emphasis.
101   Ibid. 22. My emphasis.

a clash between opposite and irreducible positions. It is the strategy of the oppressed, the moment of rebellion and violence. On the other hand, *L'arte della gioia* endeavours to resist the replication of a system of oppression, a binary logic, the opposition of an ideology with another ideology, and makes space for plurality and change. The revolutionary is replaced by the nomad, the 'preghiera dell'odio' gives way to the 'arte del dubbio'. Ross remarks that Sapienza's texts, 'like many autobiographical writings by women, seek not to install a sovereign subject, but to push to the margins of the rational subject.'[102] In Sapienza's words, 'rivoluzione significa legittima difesa contro chi ti aggredisce con l'arma della fame e dell'ignoranza' (AG 379) [Revolution means legitimate self-defence against those who abuse you with the weapons of hunger and ignorance. 499], but 'anche la parola rivoluzione mente o invecchia. Bisognerebbe trovarne un'altra' (482) [Even the word 'revolution' lies or grows old. We need to find another one. 633].

In its questioning of power structures, *L'arte della gioia* is explicitly conceived as an engagé novel. From the title, it presents itself as a pedagogical narrative, with Modesta as a model of female emancipation, an exemplary embodiment of anarchist and Epicurean ethics. While within the fictional world of the novel Modesta achieves agency and freedom through violence, Sapienza entrusts to literary communication a liberating message, creating a narrative that seeks to inspire a desire and passion for freedom in the readers. The pedagogical relationship between the narrative discourse and the readers is exemplified in the text by Modesta's attitude towards other characters – like Beatrice, Carlo, Stella, Joyce, and all the children living in Villa Suvarita – whom she tries to educate to freedom. For her anarchist inspiration, thus, *L'arte della gioia* is suitably ascribable to the category of 'Italian postmodern *impegno*' and 'progressive art' discussed by Mussgnug and Antonello:

> Progressive art, in this context, is not defined as a struggle for a new hegemonic affirmation – the transformation of plurality into a *habitus* – but a challenge of any form of hegemony. The alternative to rigid ideological definitions, in other words, is an

102 Ross, 'Eccentric Interruptions', 2.

'emancipatory' or 'reformistic' impegno, a shift from macropolitics to micropolitics, or perhaps – in Simon Critchley's terms – an 'ethical anarchy'.[103]

The postmodern aspect of *L'arte della gioia*, its 'systematic distrust of historically grounded power, combined with a de-naturalizing critique of ideology',[104] combines and collides with Modesta's own trajectory of violence and frontal opposition to power, rooted in her strong and subversive bodily desire. Where a 'sovereign subject' is with no doubt what Sapienza questions and deconstructs in this novel, nomadism cannot take place without the subject's achievement of a preliminary condition of agency. *L'arte della gioia* thus exposes the margins, if not the potential limits, of post-structuralist and postmodernist discourses with respect to the position of oppressed subjects, and places body and desire as an important site of resistance.

In conclusion, from the construction of the self to the ethical and political level, Sapienza applies a deconstructive gaze on reality that invests any social, political and cultural structure, aimed at rethinking the very foundations of society. Anarchy is the aspiration to achieve individual and social freedom, founded on the restless movement of the material and bodily domain of existence, which defies any systematic ideology and institutional power. Modesta is a subject who claims the right to self-determination, rejecting oppression in any form, but does not use this determination to establish a new rigid identity or to dominate others, turning emancipation into a new system. Conversely, her identity and position as well as her intellectual categories keep developing, as she never fully embraces any final interpretation of reality and strenuously refuses to settle. Her trajectory can be thought of as a commitment in two movements, that of strength and that of weakness, with the freedom of the body at the beginning and at the end of this troubled, but also joyful, emancipatory journey.

103   Antonello and Mussgnug, 'Introduction', in Antonello and Mussgnug, *Postmodern Impegno*, 1–22, 11.
104   Ibid. 8.

Living and Narrating, Living as Narrating

Mimesis of the Present in Action: A Non-teleological Narrative

In *Lettera aperta* and *Il filo di mezzogiorno*, the autobiographical narrator, by telling her own story, performs a process of self formation. This operation, which simulates the production in the present of a past story that is, in fact, concluded, retains an element of fiction, although a fiction with very real and material effects. In the passage to *L'arte della gioia*, Sapienza gives up the illusion of autobiography to embrace fiction overtly, fiction in which the narrator can actually be the creator, rather than the actor, of a story. If in *Lettera aperta* Sapienza proclaimed the impossibility of autobiographical truth – 'credo proprio che questo mio sforzo per non morire soffocata nel disordine, sarà una bella sfilza di bugie' [I'm afraid that my struggle to not die suffocated by this mess will be a series of lies] (LA 16) – at the beginning of *L'arte della gioia* Modesta asserts: 'Lasciamo questo mio primo ricordo così com'è: non mi va di fare supposizioni o d'inventare. Voglio dirvi quello che *è stato* senza alterare niente' (AG 5) [Let's leave this early memory of mine just as it is: I don't want to correct or invent things. I want to tell you how it was without changing anything. AJ 5]. Once the element of fiction is assumed as the explicit frame of the text, within the fictional world the narrator can, indeed, tell the truth, for she is the actual author and source of it.

In this respect, Sapienza can be seen to follow a path that is diametrically opposed to that of Ginzburg, who, after extensive production of fictional works, gradually approached autobiography as a liberating opportunity to write about her own reality. In the 'Avvertenza' [Introductory Note] that precedes *Lessico famigliare* (1963), Ginzburg asserts her complete adherence to reality: 'Luoghi, fatti, persone sono, in questo libro, reali. Non ho inventato niente' [Places, facts and people in this book are real. I didn't invent anything].[105] At the same time, however, she warns the readers

---

105   Ginzburg, 'Avvertenza', in Ginzburg, *Lessico famigliare*.

about the faltering and selective nature of memory, and suggests that the work should be read like a novel. From different perspectives, then – as Sapienza overtly embraces fiction and Ginzburg moves from fiction to autobiography – both writers express the limits of autobiography to tell the truth. As Farnetti writes, 'It is no longer possible to narrate life as one experienced it. We are no longer talking in terms of an overlap between experience and writing, but rather in terms of a transposition from experience to creation. We now acknowledge the element of invention that any act of writing comprises.'[106]

Within the transition from autobiography to overt fiction in *L'arte della gioia*, there is nonetheless a substantial continuity with *Lettera aperta* and *Il filo di mezzogiorno* in the configuration of the narrating voice and her position in the story narrated. *L'arte della gioia* is a fictional autobiography that adopts an internal focalization, as the narrating voice belongs to the protagonist herself. The point of view is strictly limited to her experience, and she has no access to the other characters' thoughts nor to events beyond her personal knowledge. The story is told mainly in the past tense, suggesting a traditional narrative structure in which a character recollects his/her life and composes it into a meaningful story. The narrator is supposed to speak from a position located at the end of the story, from which she would look back at past events. However, the location of the narrating voice is not stable, as there is a constant fluctuation between present and past tense. As in *Lettera aperta* and *Il filo di mezzogiorno*, this alternation in the tenses influences the structure of the plot and the relationship between story narrated and narrative discourse. From the very beginning, the present tense alternates with the past, something which characterizes the work as a whole: '*Ed eccovi me* a quattro, cinque anni in uno spazio fangoso che *trascino* un pezzo di legno immenso. [...] Voglio dirvi quello che *è stato*' (AG 5. My emphasis) [*I'm* four or five years old, in a muddy place, dragging a huge piece of wood [...] I want to tell you how it *was*. AJ 5].

106 Farnetti, *Il centro della cattedrale. I ricordi d'infanzia nella scrittura femminile* (Mantova: Tre Lune Edizioni, 2002), 9. For a comprehensive perspective on recent criticism and theory on autobiography, see Linda Anderson, *Autobiography* (London: Routledge, 2001).

In addition to the pervasive use of the present in place of the past tense, in the first part of the novel the metaphorical references are limited to the world known by Modesta as a child and adolescent. The mountains are 'nere come i capelli della mamma' [black as Mama's hair] and 'azzurre come il vestito della domenica' (AG 6) [blue, like the Sunday dress. AJ 7]. Not only the metaphors but the whole system of perceptions is that of the child, who narrates from her limited and naïve perspective. The almost total absence of prolepses further reduces the distance between the narrator and the character, as the former does not tell more than the latter can know. Modesta's adult narrating voice presents herself as strongly sympathetic with the character who is living and not recollecting her experiences, situating herself in the middle of, rather than after, the events.

In the last part of the novel, there is an overt reference to the act of writing memories, accompanied by a reference to notes that Modesta would have written down in the past, which suggests the form of re-elaboration of diaries. The statement is followed by a sudden return to the present tense, which marks a time where the character, not the narrator, is located:

> E come *in quel lontano* 1945 il silenzio calò sui brevi appunti della mia vita, ammutolisco di nuovo *ora che scrivo*, e tremo cercando il nome di Jacopo fra le carte. Temo d'aver perduto la data del suo ritorno. L'attesa rende sordi, distratti ... Ecco, 6 agosto 1945. Hiroshima. Jacopo tornò proprio in quei giorni, si vede che fu per questo che non appuntai la data, l'Atomica ebbe la capacità di distrarre anche me. [...] Chiudo gli occhi e ascolto soltanto il ricordo di quell'attesa che dilata i secondi, i minuti in un solo suono buio. *E non mi accorgo* di 'Ntoni che mi viene incontro sulla spiaggia di villa Suvarita. (AG 453. My emphasis).

> [And just as silence fell over the brief reminders of my life *in that distant* 1945, I fall silent again *now as I write*, trembling as I search for Jacopo's name among the papers. I'm afraid I've lost the date of his return. Waiting makes us impervious, distracted ... Here it is: 6 August 1945, Hiroshima. Jacopo returned at just that time. Clearly that was why I didn't note the date. The A-bomb was able to distract even me. [...] I close my eyes and hear only the memory of that waiting, which draws out the seconds and minutes in a single bleak sound. *And I don't notice* 'Ntoni coming toward me on the beach at Villa Suvarita.] (AJ 595)

In the passage above, the narrating voice shifts from Modesta as the narrator of her past to Modesta as the actor of her present, for the two subjects come

to coincide in the subject of the expression 'non mi accorgo'. The mimesis of
the present in action is overtly stated by the narrator in one of her frequent
appeals to the readers: 'Sicuramente voi che leggete state pensando che la
mia conquista comportava di necessità qualcosa di molto sgradevole [...].
Il fatto è che voi la leggete questa storia, e mi anticipate, mentre io la vivo,
la vivo ancora' (AG 99) [Those of you who are reading are surely already
thinking that my triumph would necessarily require something very dis-
tasteful. [...] The fact is that you're reading this story, and you're ahead of
me, whereas I'm living it. I am still living it. AJ 140]. Furthermore, the very
moment of the end is not pronounced, as the novel finishes on a scene in
which Modesta's lover, Marco, asks her to carry on telling her story as she
continues to live, in a scene that recalls Scheherazade's affabulatory effect:
"'Dormi, Modesta?" "No." "Pensi?" "Sì." "Racconta, Modesta, racconta"'
(511) ['Are you sleeping, Modesta?' 'No.' 'Are you thinking?' 'Yes.' 'Tell me,
Modesta, tell me.' 670]. The narrator thus creates a present in fieri. To use
Sapienza's own words, her narrative reproduces life in the moment of its
happening, 'la nitidezza del momento stesso in cui la vita-azione sboccia,
fiorisce, cresce, cresce ancora, muore' [the clarity of the exact moment in
which life-action blossoms, blooms, grows, grows more, dies] (JG 9).

By voicing the present in action, the narrator of L'arte della gioia seeks
to express the primary, constantly renovated encounter between the body
and the world. Turning again to Coquet's reflections, Sapienza gives voice
to the body's primary 'production of meaning': 'The body [...] reveals its
existence by feeling, talking, acting, tracing drafts of knowledge, etc. Its
privilege, as well as its function, is to be the first to enunciate its contact
with the world.'[107] Hence, the constant oscillation between activity and
passivity, instincts and rational control, perception and imagination that
characterize Modesta, as the narrator reproduces the unstable moment of
the present, before the organization of experience through memory and
reflection.

While telling a story that has already happened belongs to the
domain of memory, to narrate a story as it happens belongs to the field of

107   Coquet, Le istanze enuncianti, 24–5.

production, in a continuous oscillation between 'return to' and 'return of' the past, diegesis and mimesis.[108] In *L'arte della gioia*, the twofold origin of the discourse deeply affects the structure of the novel, since positioning the narrating voice at the end or in the middle of the story entails a different organizing principle of the plot. On the one hand, the narrating voice looks back at the past from a mature point of view, to which the significance and consequences of the events are already known. Memory re-presents the past by selecting and organizing events into teleologically constructed meaning. According to Brooks, this is the traditional structure of the plot, in which events are held together by their overall meaning in a concluded system:

> The beginning presupposes the end, since the concept of an ending is necessary to that of a beginning. The idea of 'adventure' has to do with what is to come, the ad-venire, so that an adventure is a piece of action in which beginnings are chosen by and for ends. The very possibility of meaning plotted through sequence and through time depends on the anticipated structuring force of the ending. [...] We read the incidents of narration as 'promises and annunciations' of final coherence.[109]

On the other hand, the production of experience as it happens is not subject to teleology but only provisional interpretation of ongoing events. Unlike the sense of time developed through memory, the present does not contain in itself the idea of the end and is therefore the bearer of an open structure. The character who is still living is not able to select and organize her present on the basis of its following consequences. Hence, many details are provided which do not have any actual influence on the plot, and others are conversely omitted and then instrumentally retrieved following the character's realization of their initially underestimated importance. The positioning of the narrator in the middle of the story thus accounts for the non-cohesive, wandering narrative structure of *L'arte della gioia*.

In his analysis of the mechanism of plot, Brooks describes narrative as a repetition of the past aimed at retrospectively organizing events whose

---

108 Brooks, *Reading for the Plot*, 98.
109 Ibid. 93. On the function of the end in the structuring of narratives, see also Frank Kermode, *The Sense of an Ending: Studies in the Theory of Fiction: With a New Epilogue*, new edn (Oxford: Oxford University Press, 2000).

original production was beyond a subject's control. In this way, narrative would establish mastery over the past by composing it through memory:

> If repetition is mastery, movement from the passive to the active, and if mastery is an assertion of control over what men must in fact submit to – choice, we might say, of an imposed end – we have already a suggestive comment on the grammar of plot, where repetition, taking us back again over the same ground, could have to do with the choice of ends.[110]

In *L'arte della gioia*, Sapienza challenges this model by mimicking the present in action. Whereas narrative in the past has to do with the acceptance of a destiny and the assumption of a story that has already happened, Sapienza engages with the freedom of the present moment, full of potential and constantly renovated. Instead of achieving mastery and control through repetition of the past, that is, through memory, in *L'arte della gioia* Sapienza looks for the agency contained in the moment of production. Modesta's movement towards agency is thus constructed as a movement towards the freedom to experience the present and the presence of the body in action.

The Involvement of the Readers: Empathetic Narrative Tension and the Political Dimension of the Voice

If the narrator does not organize the narrative material from a space located *after* the events narrated, how does the plot proceed? How is the narrative tension produced? The focus on the present does not allow the readers to activate a system of expectations. With no guarantee of closure, the elements put in place are unreliable to the readers and thus cannot be read in a chain of memory and anticipation, which, following Wolfgang Iser and Brooks, normally constitutes the fundamental mechanism of plot.[111] And yet, the novel succeeds in engaging the readers in Modesta's story, throughout the over 500 pages of the narration. It does so by establishing

110   Brooks, *Reading for the Plot*, 98.
111   Wolfgang Iser, *The Act of Reading: A Theory of Aesthetic Response* (London: Routledge & Kegan Paul, 1978).

a close connection between readers and character, as the adoption of the character's point of view creates an emotive and empathetic rather than properly narrative tension. The readers are captured by the hectic sequence of Modesta's feelings, perceptions, reflections and metaphorical descriptions. As Hernández observes, 'the protagonist changes before the reader's eyes; she forges herself through a constant metamorphosis that produces a sense of vertigo, defined as feverish, frantic or hectic narration.'[112] Instead of developing a deterministic system of expectations, the readers follow Modesta's free movements, participating in her vitality and self-regeneration, the expansion of her experience and her achievement of the freedom to constantly evolve and change.

Similarly to *Lettera aperta*, character, narrator and readers are represented as sharing the same theatrical space. Modesta is repeatedly described as a 'cantastorie' (AG 8; 243) [troubadour. AJ 9; 324] and the narration is configured as Modesta's voice reciting her life. The presence of these theatrical modes reinforces the impression that Modesta is telling her story as she lives it rather than recollecting events from the past, and involves the readers in a dialogical and empathetic structure. Appeals to the readers mark the entire work, beginning from the opening scene in which the narrator presents the character (Modesta as a child) as if before an audience: 'Ed eccovi me' (5).[113] On numerous occasions, the narrator involves the readers in the story narrated by introducing to them the voices of other characters: 'Questa voce dolce, non sentite quanto è dolce? È la voce di madre Leonora' (16) [This sweet, gentle voice – can't you hear how sweet it is? – is the voice of Mother Leonora. 20]; 'Avete sentito la voce di Beatrice?' (134) [Did you hear how Beatrice talks? 186]; 'Ascoltate, anche se non ne avete più voglia' (43) [Here's more, even if you no longer care to listen. 60]. Here Modesta directly addresses the readers as a collective audience present in the same space as hers.

In addition to the appeals to the readers, Sapienza also blends the space of narration and that of the story narrated by virtue of another, possibly

---

112 Hernández, 'La fortuna literaria de Goliarda Sapienza', 148.
113 Unfortunately, in the English translation – 'I'm four or five years old' – the theatrical exposition of the character to the readers is lost.

unique, narrative technique. This can be seen, for example, in these dialogues between Modesta and Tuzzu and between Modesta and Carmine, in which the characters are represented as able to hear the narrator's thoughts: 'Non dovevo lasciarlo andare via, dovevo chiedergli perché – quando lo guardavo prima, e ora che tenevo il suo braccio – mi nasceva dentro quel desiderio di accarezzarmi là dove … "Ma guarda se sono domande da fare!"' (AG 9) [I couldn't let him go away, I had to ask him why – when I was watching him before, and now that I was holding his arm – why I felt that urge to touch myself in the spot where … 'What kind of question is that to ask!' AJ 10]; 'Quando è l'alba Carmine se ne va … Nel sonno lo vedo allontanarsi come un'ombra. Come faceva ad apparire e sparire ed essere sempre presente? "È che mi hai nel cuore, Modesta"' (204–5) [When dawn comes, Carmine goes away … In my sleep I see him slip away like a shadow. How did he manage to appear and disappear, yet still be ever present? 'It's because you have me in your heart, Modesta.' 277]. What at first sight appears to be a silent thought belonging to the narrating voice often turns out to be words actually spoken aloud by Modesta, with intensely disorientating effects. These episodes, frequent throughout the novel, break down the boundaries between different temporal and spatial domains. This narrative technique also expresses the attraction to oral speech that characterizes Sapienza's works. Here, language is irresistibly attracted to the oral dimension of the pronounced word, to the point that the characters are able to 'hear' the narrator's thoughts.

The text is, indeed, populated by voices. Drama deeply influences the narrative structure, especially if we consider that more than half of the novel is made of pure dialogues. These take up more and more space as the narration proceeds, and in the third and fourth parts they come to occupy almost the totality of narration. The other characters are mainly present on the scene through their voices, the defining qualities of which Sapienza carefully notes. Particularly conspicuous in this respect is Modesta's habit of dialoguing with characters who are absent or dead but whose voices are represented as physical and vibrant, as if they were actually present.

In the realization of a present *in fieri*, the performative, oral dimension of narration plays a crucial role. The voice constitutes the embodied and relational dimension of language, for it is always someone's voice; it links together speaker and listener and roots language in a material exchange. The voice is also, in Cavarero's philosophy, the marker of a person's uniqueness, which resists the universalizing feature of disembodied rationality: 'In the uniqueness that is audible in the voice, an embodied being, or, in other words, a "being" in its radical finitude – here and now – expresses itself. The sphere of the voice refers to an ontological dimension and links it to the existence of singular beings who call one another, contextually.'[114] In *L'arte della gioia*, Sapienza states the contemporaneity of action and narration, in the presence of an audience. Through the qualification of narration as oral speech, she seeks to create with the readers an inter-corporeal and empathetic community, rooted in the vocal dimension of communication. Cavarero uses the notion of 'risonanza' [resonance] to qualify this type of communication, and Coquet provides a definition that itself resonates with Cavarero's: 'Intersubjective communication [...] entails corporeality, that is, a musical foundation, so to speak. It means tuning with the note of the person before us and who participates in the same fundamental key.'[115] Differently from the dimension of the voice, abstract and universal rationality ties together individuals by virtue of its laws and erases the bodily and unique existence of each individual. As Cavarero argues, 'Free and equal individuals, who have nothing in common, finally find their community in the communicative relationality of a language that binds them together, because it binds them to its procedural norms. Language ties together those who have no other ties.'[116]

Clearly, a completely different way to look at the voice is possible, for example and most notably in Derrida's theory. According to Derrida, the voice, with its illusion of presence, does not represent a resistance against metaphysics but rather its ally, against the *différant* feature of writing and the 'trace'.[117] However, in Cavarero's theory the voice is not the expression

114   Cavarero, *A più voci*, 189.
115   Coquet, *Le istanze enuncianti*, 68.
116   Cavarero, *A più voci*, 205.
117   See Jacques Derrida, *Speech and Phenomena*, trans. David B. Allison (Evanston, IL: Northwestern University Press, 1973); *Of Grammatology*, corrected edn, trans. Gayatri Chakravorty Spivak (Baltimore, MD: Johns Hopkins University Press, 1997).

of an abstract *logos* that prescinds from the material, iterated acts of the constitution of knowledge, as in Derrida, but is considered in its relationship with the body, as the rooting of language in the ephemeral, embodied, situated and relational position of the speakers. As such, it is not opposed primarily to writing, but to the a-temporal and video-centric feature of metaphysics, which realizes a disembodied and universalizing *presence*:

> The transition from the centrality of the ear to that of the eye gives rise to a form of thought that crystallizes sounds into abstract and universal images. These are endowed with objectivity, stability, and can be organized in a coherent system.
> Sounds are not perceived simultaneously but in succession. It is this characteristic that prevents hearing from becoming the foundation of an unlikely acoustic metaphysics.[118]

Against abstract thought and its illusion of eternalized time, the voice represents a way to rethink the category of *presence*, defined by the co-presence of the interlocutors in a shared, contingent and unstable present:

> The presence of those who look at each other 'face to face', far from being functional to the eternity of *being*, guarantees the empirical contingency of the context. [...] Such a presence 'face to face' evokes a discontinuous becoming, characterized by the constantly renovated present of the 'nows' that cross their gazes, instead of indicating the atemporal dimension of an unchanging permanence.[119]

Cavarero's and Derrida's perspectives do not seem to be in a relationship of symmetrical opposition, but rather express incommensurable positions, for they attach very different roles to the voice within their overall systems, which are nonetheless equally opposed to metaphysics and logocentrism. The relationship between the two different approaches to the voice would deserve specific investigation, but for purposes of the present discourse what matters is that in Sapienza's works, as in Cavarero's philosophy, the voice plays an anti-metaphysical and anti-logocentric role, reinstating the body and its contingent and relational presence.

118   Cavarero, *A più voci*, 49, 94.
119   Ibid. 193.

The centrality of the voice has, thus, a political dimension, for it grounds communication in the embodied dimension of language and the mutual recognition of singular and unique subjects. Coquet writes that the linguistic community of human beings 'presupposes an agreement involving the *physis*, the physical sphere, and therefore is founded on the experience of a corporeal relationship with the other, that is, on empathy.'[120] Coquet's perspective could not express any more cogently the anti-metaphysical and anti-ideological stance put forward by Sapienza in *L'arte della gioia*, and the empathetic relationship she seeks to establish with the readers. *L'arte della gioia* is a novel with a strong performative and transformative power. Its pedagogical stance – anti-ideological, rebellious and liberating – involves the readers not only, and possibly not mainly, through its explicit content, but also through its language and narrative structure, engaged in the communication of a living body.

120 Coquet, *Le istanze enuncianti*, 70.

Io, Jean Gabin: Staged Identities and Anarchist Love

Introduction

After *Lettera aperta* and *Il filo di mezzogiorno*, Sapienza wrote a third text
on the recollection of her childhood in Catania, *Io, Jean Gabin*, which
was interrupted before being finished and was published posthumously by
Einaudi in 2010. There is some uncertainty about the period when the text
was written. One hypothesis, maintained by Pellegrino, suggests that it was
written in from 1979 to 1980, after Sapienza finished *L'arte della gioia* and
before her incarceration in the prison of Rebibbia.[1] In her investigation
of the evolution of Sapienza's autobiographical narrative, Andrigo accepts
Pellegrino's proposed period.[2] Relying on the analysis of textual structures,
she places *Io, Jean Gabin* in a transitional phase immediately preceding the
prison works, midway between Sapienza's effort of self-reconstruction in
the previous texts and the focus on outer reality in *L'università di Rebibbia*
and *Le certezze del dubbio*. Andrigo suggests that the abrupt interruption
might be due to the author's own incarceration. Conversely, Providenti
suggests that *Io, Jean Gabin* was written before *L'arte della gioia*, from
1968 to 1969, and then interrupted due to the urge to work on this major
project.[3] Yet, Providenti does not rule out the suggestion that Sapienza
might have worked on *Io, Jean Gabin* at two different times, before and
after *L'arte della gioia*. As the critic herself remarks, only more detailed

---

1   See Pellegrino, 'Postfazione', in JG 113–24, 117.
2   See Andrigo, 'L'evoluzione autobiografica di Goliarda Sapienza'.
3   See Providenti, 'Introduzione', in Providenti, *Quel sogno d'essere*, 13–30, 23–4.
     Providenti does not bring evidence in support of her argument, which rests upon
     the mentioning of unspecified 'some sources'.

research into Sapienza's archive may provide a definitive answer. Waiting for the archive to be made available to the public, Pellegrino's hypothesis seems to be confirmed by the reference, in the text's opening lines, to Margaret Thatcher, who was elected prime minister in the UK precisely in 1979. Pellegrino recounts that a previous version of the text featured Nilde Iotti in place of Thatcher, and indeed 1979 is also the year in which Iotti became president of the Italian Chamber of Deputies. Although *Io, Jean Gabin* was published posthumously and with no editorial note, thus leaving the hypothesis of interpolation open, the reference to Thatcher is present in one partial version of the original typescript.[4]

   Io, Jean Gabin is a short novel written in the first person. Here Sapienza combines fiction and autobiography, focusing again on the recollection of her childhood in Catania in the 1920s and early 1930s. As in *Lettera aperta*, there is a young female protagonist, Goliarda, in search of her positioning in the world. The character's formative experience is represented through her physical wandering around the neighbourhood of San Berillo ('Civita' in the author's words) and her meetings with various characters. At the beginning of the story, Goliarda pushes and hurts her friend Concetta, who, during the screening of the film *Pépé le Moko (Il bandito della Casbah)*, made trivial comments about the female character.[5] Identifying herself with Jean Gabin (the protagonist hero of the film), Goliarda acts to protect the insulted female character from her detractor, Concetta. Learning about the episode, Goliarda's mother reprimands the child and suggests she atone for her misbehaviour by giving some money to Concetta to pay for the medical care she needs following the incident. Goliarda finds out that her sister Musetta has stolen her savings and wanders through the neighbourhood looking for small jobs to earn some money. Such a task is perceived by the child as a heroic adventure, as she looks at the events through her identification with Jean Gabin. She visits a number of people – uncle Giovanni, 'il gelsominaro' [jasmine seller], the Brunos and 'il puparo

---

4   The partial typescript was given by Sapienza to the journalist Adele Cambria, who kindly allowed me to see it (Rome, September 2013). It comprises only the first part of the novel (to page 17), and presents several divergences from the Einaudi edition.
5   *Pépé le Moko (Il bandito della Casbah)*, dir. Julien Duvivier (France, 1937).

Insanguine' [Insanguine the puppet master]. After a series of encounters and vicissitudes, partially through her work in Insanguine's shop and thanks to a donation by her uncle Nunzio, she can pay Concetta back and buy the ticket for the new film starring Jean Gabin, *Il porto delle nebbie*, to which she was ardently looking forward.[6] Overall, the story covers a timespan of approximately three days, which offer the narrator the time to include portrayals of the protagonist's family and everyday life. It is significant to point out that at the time of the release of *Pépé le Moko (Il bandito della Casbah)* in Italy in 1938, Sapienza was in fact thirteen or fourteen years old, while in the text she is still a small child. Moreover, Laura Ferro indicates that *Il porto delle nebbie* was only released in Italy in 1943.[7] On other occasions too Sapienza's autobiographical accuracy proves faltering. This approximate attitude towards temporal and geographical references suggests that the author's imagination intervenes to deeply alter the strictly faithful recollection of her past, making space for fictional creativity.

Io, Jean Gabin touches upon many of the core issues explored in *Lettera aperta* and *Il filo di mezzogiorno*, such as the coexistence of different models of gender identity and social roles, the possibility of an experimental attitude towards sexual orientation and the search for personal agency, all combined with lively family portraits and extra-diegetic remarks about political events and cultural reflections. In addition, Sapienza devotes specific attention to the tension between artistic work, which is perceived by the protagonist as problematically individualistic, and moral duty, aimed at social equality at the expense of personal freedom and authenticity. Unlike *Lettera aperta* and *Il filo di mezzogiorno*, in *Io, Jean Gabin* the representation of the narrator's own present situation is virtually absent, while a central plot can be identified, revolving around the child's endeavour to find some money. Although the centrifugal tension is still predominant, some minimal cohesion and coherence make their appearance.

6   *Quai des brumes (Il porto delle nebbie)*, dir. Marcel Carné (France, 1938).
7   Ferro, 'Changing Recollections. Goliarda Sapienza and Fabrizia Ramondino Writing and Rewriting Childhood', in Bazzoni, Bond and Wehling-Giorgi, *Goliarda Sapienza in Context*, 181–98, 190.

The different structure of this novel, with a recognizable organization of foreground and background narrative materials, is the manifestation of a significantly changed relationship between the text and the protagonist's identity formation. Indeed, *Io, Jean Gabin* marks a development towards a detachment from the past, which is favoured by the narrator's acquisition of an identity of her own. This consists in the creative activity and the marginal social position of a rebellious artist. The changed formative tension in the protagonist's identity affects tone and style of narration. *Lettera aperta* and *Il filo di mezzogiorno* centre on a protagonist who struggles to make sense of her position in the world as a girl who is taught to be different from the dominant gender model but is not provided with a successful alternative; she is educated and wealthy but called to egalitarian commitment, forced to please her family to obtain love but also fights to foster and protect her personal independence. While in those works the narrator is in the middle of the process of becoming a subject through the very act of remembering and narrating, in *Io, Jean Gabin* she knows the outcome of the little girl's formative experience and is able to structure her story accordingly. Such a strengthened position of the narrator allows her to recollect memories from her childhood without re-experiencing the feelings and openness of life 'as you are living it', resulting in a much more ironic, light and linear narrative.

Although the adult narrator is almost absent in *Io, Jean Gabin*, here too the narrating voice represents a multiple gaze, comprising the child protagonist's perspective and her identification with the male characters played by the French actor Jean Gabin. Gabin is connected with a multiplicity of referents, for he represents not only a man, as different from a woman, but also the power of dream and imagination, as opposed to the limits of reality, and the outcast hero, as opposed to conformist society. This multiplicity of semantic functions of Jean Gabin further enriches (and adds complexity to) the protagonist's self-identification with him. In other words, to the little girl Jean Gabin means much more than the model of a male identity. Hence, when analysing the protagonist's identification with her hero it is important to distinguish between his different aspects and their respective influence on her identity formation and search for freedom.

Io, Jean Gabin continues the autofictional journey of previous texts, but also presents noticeable differences; this chapter investigates similarities as well as developments. The first section analyses the protagonist's identity formation from the perspective of gender and sexual orientation, which play a crucial role in the character's search for agency and authenticity, and the role of the body in the figuration of identity. The second part considers the semantic functions of the identification with Jean Gabin that relate to imagination and marginality, focusing on alternative figurations of identity and modalities of communication and their political implications. Finally, the narrator's detachment from the past and her acquisition of a more definite identity, that of the anarchist artist, and its consequences on the level of the text's narrative structure and narrating voice, are discussed in the concluding part.

A Staged Freedom

The Absent Mother: Alternative Models of Gender Identity

In the opening to *Io, Jean Gabin*, the narrator, seeing a picture of Margaret Thatcher on a newspaper, deplores a state of affairs in which women adopt allegedly male features and roles: 'lady di ferro, donne poliziotte, soldate e culturiste' [iron ladies, police women, female soldiers, female bodybuilders] (JG 3). In the afterword to *Io, Jean Gabin*, Pellegrino notes that Sapienza was worried by an evolution of the relationship between the sexes that, in her view, was erasing the difference between men and women by simply assimilating the female to the male. According to Pellegrino, she felt sorry for women when she saw them being possessed by a desire to conform to a male identity.[8] *Io, Jean Gabin* seems to start as an endeavour to understand why 'qualcosa non è andato per il verso giusto in questi ultimi trent'anni

---

8   Pellegrino, 'Postfazione', in JG 122.

di democrazia' [something has gone wrong in these last thirty years of democracy] (3) and to re-establish a more traditional articulation of the difference between men and women. Nonetheless, from the very beginning something disturbs the linearity of this operation, as the narrator places herself alongside men by identifying with Jean Gabin. While the narrator criticizes women who replicate male attitudes, the child protagonist identifies with a man and looks at women from a male viewpoint. As in *Lettera aperta* and *Il filo di mezzogiorno*, Sapienza returns to her childhood memories, but, differently from previous autobiographical novels, she does not look for the model of woman she wants to become, but for the kind of woman she *as a man* would love. This double gaze, of a young girl and a man, complicates and destabilizes the representation of gender identities and thereby the protagonist's search for freedom.

Through the characters' opinions and examples and through the narrator's own extra-diegetic comments, Sapienza presents different models of how women are and how they should be. A striking novelty in this respect is the very marginal space afforded to the parental figures and the protagonist's detached attitude towards them: 'Di Maria non mi soffermo a parlare perché anche lei, esattamente come mio padre, è conosciutissima qui nella Civita e io non ho tempo da perdere' [I will not waste my time talking about Maria because everybody knows her here in the Civita, exactly like my father] (JG 11). Both the painful sense of a task related to the mother and the fear of sexual violence associated with the father, which were central to previous works, are replaced with the protagonist's bold and perky adoption of a male role and a male perspective on women. The first and most important model of gender identity in *Lettera aperta* and *Il filo di mezzogiorno* was Goliarda's mother Maria. *Io, Jean Gabin* confirms the portrait of a nonconformist, clever and morally intransigent woman, who is devoted to her studies and committed to the socialist cause. Yet, the painful conflict between the model of woman embodied by Maria and the social condition of women, which lacerated Goliarda in the previous works, no longer bothers the protagonist of *Io, Jean Gabin*, as her mother is here important mainly for her absence and emotional distance. Maria retains the role of undisputed authority on moral issues, but is too busy with her own work and too focused on intellectual and political concerns to take care of the little girl's practical and emotional needs: 'mia madre Maria voleva conferire con me. [...] deve essere importante se così di buon'ora ha deciso di sacrificare il suo tempo con me. Studia sempre' [My mother, Maria, wanted to talk to me. [...] It must be important if she decided to sacrifice her time with me this early in the morning. She studies all the time] (11). When Goliarda interrogates Maria about the issue of love, the girl finds her response utterly inadequate. Maria's approach is confined to an intellectual and abstract perspective, the only sphere that seems to provide a channel of communication between mother and daughter:

> L'unica che ammetteva che l'amore era qualcosa degno di essere preso in considerazione era mia madre, ma la faceva così complicata: doveva essere un amore libero da convenzioni, da ricatti psicologici o finanziari eccetera. Insomma la faceva così ufficiale che era meglio stornare il discorso sulla Grecia antica, la politica o la filosofia che, anche se difficili, applicandosi almeno si potevano capire ... (JG 52–3)

> [The only person who would concede that love was something worthy of consideration was my mother, but she made it so complicated: love had to be free from social conventions, psychological or financial blackmail, and so on. She would make the whole thing so official that it was better to just talk about ancient Greece, politics or philosophy instead. These subjects were hard, but at least I could understand them by applying myself.]

Neglected by her mother, the little child is raised by men, mostly by her brother Ivanoe. He guaranteed her survival as a newborn by feeding her artificial milk when she rejected breast milk: 'io sono stata allattata da un uomo – il mio primo ricordo sono due braccia forti e pelose che mi sollevano' [I was breastfed by a man. My first memory is two strong and hairy arms that pick me up] (JG 60).[9] From the early stages of her life, the little child feels a closer connection with men, which the narrator attributes to the mother's absence. As Goliarda grows up, this connection with men turns into identification and is seconded by other members of her family. For example, her brother Carlo teaches her boxing,[10] she wears a boy's jacket, and for a party her sister Licia gives her a flower to put in the

9   The episode is also narrated in FM 67–8.
10 The girl's training to be 'like a boy' also features in LA 110 and FM 108 (see Chapter 1).

button-hole as a typically male ornament. While in *Lettera aperta* and *Il filo di mezzogiorno* the conflicted relationship with a female identity never led the protagonist to identify with the male gender, in *Io, Jean Gabin* this identification is well established and sustained throughout the whole text. The identification with the model of woman represented by the mother is no longer at the centre of Goliarda's personal research, while rage and pain are turned into irony.

In addition to the protagonist's detachment from Maria and her identification with the male gender, the disappearance of the character of Nica is also remarkable, compared to the prominent role she played in *Lettera aperta* and *Il filo di mezzogiorno*. In those texts, Nica represented a source of creative imagination and allowed the protagonist to access her true emotions; she was both the positive model of a girl to imitate and the object of Goliarda's love. However, Nica's marriage and premature death in childbirth narrated in *Lettera aperta* sanctioned the impracticality of a free and joyful way of being a girl. Thus, in *Io, Jean Gabin* Nica makes just a fleeting appearance, when Goliarda meets her in a street and, albeit tempted, declines her invitation to play together and runs away. In this sense, *Io, Jean Gabin* is not just a different exploration of Sapienza's childhood, but a subsequent stage in its interpretation, as the narrator now knows that Nica is not a viable model of woman and that a true communication with her will be impeded – hence she lets her protagonist run away. The distance from Maria and the absence of Nica mark a clear departure from the formation of gender identity in the earlier works. In *Io, Jean Gabin*, reconciliation with female identity is given up from the beginning, thus opening the space for the protagonist to identify with a male viewpoint.

A further element in this transition is the removal of male violence, which goes together with the displacement of mental illness from Maria to other female characters and its conjugation with female violence. Male-exerted domestic and sexual violence, which obsessed the narrator of *Lettera aperta*, no longer plays a significant role. The only form of violence used by men is political – uncle Alessandro who beats up a group of fascists or the fascists who beat up Goliarda's brothers. While the narrator makes no reference to Maria's own insanity, she recounts three stories of mad women, two of which are also associated with murder. There is for example the maid Tina, 'con gli occhioni nero seppia sempre terrorizzati – la sua pazzia era causata, sembra, dall'avere ucciso la sorella e il suo fidanzato che se la faceva con la sorella' [with her ink black eyes that were always full of terror – apparently her madness started after she killed her sister and her boyfriend, who was fooling around with her sister] (JG 10); and there is Zoe, the other maid who occasionally replaces Tina at work in the Sapienzas' house. Zoe killed her mother and hurt her lover with a knife, for which she spent eight years in prison. 'Per difendere il suo onore di fanciulla pura' [In order to protect her honour as a pure girl] she always carries a knife, called 'misericordia' [mercy], hidden close to her breast, terrorizing Goliarda and her siblings (99). For this reason, Goliarda's sister, Musetta, considers Zoe a heroic feminist:

> Musetta asseriva che Zoe era la punta estrema del movimento per la causa della donna. [...]
>   'Io ti porterò ad agire per la nostra causa.'
>   'La nostra causa signorina? E in cosa consiste?'
>   'Spazzare via l'uomo e il mondo cattivo che ha costruito!'
>   'E con chi ci sposiamo, chi ci mantiene?' (JG 102)

> [Musetta used to say that Zoe was the extreme champion of the struggle for women's rights. [...]
>   'I will make you participate in our struggle'
>   'Our struggle, Miss? And what is it about?'
>   'Sweeping away men and the evil world they have created!'
>   'But then, who will we marry, who will support us?']

Here, there is obviously an ironic and light tone on the narrator's part. Nonetheless, a suggestion is made, which relates an extreme form of feminism to female violence, with an explicit polemic against that feminist approach. Compared to *Lettera aperta* and *Il filo di mezzogiorno*, the problem of female mental insanity and male violence undergoes a spectacular distortion and is reformulated as a problem of mad women committing violent crimes of passion. The adoption of a patriarchal viewpoint seems here to belong to the narrator herself, as she shifts the blame from the violent power of men (central to *Lettera aperta* and *Il filo di mezzogiorno*) to the violence of women, associated with subversive feminism. Sapienza even resorts again to the image of the blade, used in all previous works in relation to male aggressiveness and abusive power, and re-deploys it to describe Musetta's and Zoe's 'unghiacce e strilli acuti come lamine' [long nails and shrieks as acute as blades] (JG 104).

The narrator makes a single reference to male sexual violence, and specifically to the actions of men who show their genitals and stare menacingly at women, also narrated in *Lettera aperta*. In this way, *Io, Jean Gabin* reconnects to the discourse on the constant threat of men against women there addressed, but, after a moment of fear, the child simply disregards the problem to focus on something else:

> Il culo mi fa ridere, non è come quei grossi cosi che hanno davanti, flaccidi topi violacei sembrano, che continuamente ti mostrano a scuola, nei parchi o nel buio fondo dei numerosi cantoni del nostro quartiere tutto giri e giravolte nere di lava. Loro hanno l'aria di fare un gesto necessario e consueto: quello di fare la pipì, ma si vede che lo fanno apposta, altrimenti perché ti fisserebbero con quello sguardo ironico e duro che pare un colpo di stocco o di pugnale? Ma lasciamo le manie che tutti i cittadini di una città hanno. (JG 78)

> [Their asses make me laugh. It's not like those big things they have on the front, which look like floppy purple mice. They show them off all the time, at school, in the park, or in the dark depths of the many alleys and corners in our neighbourhood, with its twists and turns of black lava. They do it as if they are just doing something necessary and common, as if peeing, but you can tell that they do it on purpose. Otherwise, why would they stare at you with that ironic, hard gaze that feels like being hit by a pointy stick or a dagger? But let's leave aside the obsessions that all city dwellers have.]

Sapienza returns to this core issue, but displays a deeply changed attitude, as she does not engage with these memories, circumventing the pain attached to them. In other words, she looks at this disturbing issue from a distant, safe position. The act of recollecting is no longer 'active' on the narrator's present. Nonetheless, the passage above, although circumscribed, when it is read together with *Lettera aperta* and *Il filo di mezzogiorno*, shows Sapienza's suggestion of a different way to look at the relationship between the sexes and her deliberate will to ignore the issue at the same time.

In *Io, Jean Gabin* Goliarda is neglected by her mother, raised by her brothers and considered one of them, and is looked after by maids who are mad murderers. On top of that, she is surrounded by a sexist and even misogynistic culture. The little girl assimilates gender difference from the way it operates in her social context, and develops quite a strongly sexist perspective on women. The novel features an extensive list of patriarchal stereotypes, from the definition of women as sentimental, malicious and deceitful, to the specular exaltation of the figure of the angelic woman. For example, the teacher Jsaya manifests overtly misogynistic views that depict women from an extremely negative perspective: 'ecco tutto il veleno di tutte le femminacce castigo di Dio. Vomitavano invidie, e quello che era peggio piccoli pettegolezzi, per spargere zizzania nella nostra comunità' [here is all the poison of all the nasty wenches who are a punishment from God. They vomited jealousy and, what's even worse, bits of petty gossip to sow discord in our community] (JG 16). Few references are made to the connection between such a perspective on women and patriarchy. For example, Ivanoe explains that a woman has a '"basso intuito femminile" [...] non connaturato ma sviluppato nei secoli per imbrogliare il padrone maschio che l'ha sempre tenuta in prigionia ...' ['low female intuition' [...]] that is not innate in her, but which she developed over the centuries to cheat the male master who kept her as a prisoner] (15); and Musetta asserts that love is 'l'arma che usavano gli uomini non solo per ridurre in schiavitù le donne ma per annientarle completamente' [the weapon used by men not only to reduce women to slavery but also to completely annihilate them] (53). Nonetheless, even these etiological accounts simply reinforce the idea that being a woman is ultimately an undesirable condition, in the protagonist's eyes.

In all the environments surrounding Goliarda's family the rules are the same. The girl is confronted with middle-class women, 'madri spaurite, schiave' [frightened mothers, slaves] who never leave their home, where 'o friggevano o pregavano' [they would either fry or pray] (JG 18; 19), and with Southern women who, in Licia's words, have 'una vocazione al lutto' [a vocation for mourning] (64). Goliarda's uncle Giovanni refuses to teach her the artisan craft of manufacturing shoes because 'le donne sanno solo indossarle, queste scarpine' [women can only wear these little shoes] (27), and in the eyes of fascism 'le donne non contano, non sono degne d'essere arrestate' [women don't count, they're not worth arresting] (32). Not surprisingly, Goliarda herself looks at gender roles through a deeply patriarchal conceptual frame. Ross notes that 'she distances herself from the category of women, through disrespectful, frankly misogynistic remarks.'[11] The narrator makes use of a variety of sexist expressions such as 'femminucce' [silly females] (11), 'ragazzette pigre e melense' [lazy, vapid girls] (10), 'sentimentalismi da donnette' [silly women's sentimentalism] (15), 'una donna fragile indifesa' [fragile and defenceless woman] (74) and 'lacrime femminili' [feminine tears] (76). In the opening to the novel, Sapienza's criticism of women who efface their femininity and imitate men is followed by the representation of 'la donna' [woman] as a territory for men's action, 'spazio immenso in cui misurare il nostro coraggio di individualisti incalliti' [immense space where we can test our courage as hardened individualists] (3). The narrator identifies herself as an active male subject who exerts his agency on women, who are deemed to be a passive complement to his action. Such an articulation of sexual difference as a binary of agency and passivity closely reflects what Cavarero calls the 'androcentric arrogance that gives Man the role of subject', typical of a patriarchal symbolic system in which 'woman is in the position of the object – she is thought, represented and defined from Man's perspective.'[12]

There are only a few exceptions to the negativity of women's condition, for instance in the figures of Angelica, the epic woman-warrior, and Marie Curie, who elicit a different attitude towards the female gender from the protagonist.[13] The main example is the scene set in Insanguine's workshop, where Goliarda is looking for a way to earn some money. She is given a small job to do, consisting of repairing the puppet's clothes, a type of work that was usually carried out by women. On this single occasion, Goliarda is unproblematically integrated into the female gender: 'noi donne eravamo intente all'ago e al filo' [we, the women, were busy with needle and thread] (JG 46. My emphasis). Similarly to the manufacturing of chairs recounted in Lettera aperta, here the carrying out of an artisan job provides the girl with a space of serenity and self-reconciliation. In this context, the scene suggests that,

11   Ross, 'Eccentric Interruptions', 9.
12   Cavarero, Tu che mi guardi, 69.
13   See JG 41, 43.

where she is allowed to play an active role, she could reconcile herself with her female identity, otherwise the transgression of the limitations of her gender becomes a preferred strategy to access freedom and agency.

Loving Other Women

The exceptions to the negativity of the condition of women do not suffice to provide an alternative model of gender and rather reconfirm the importance of the role played by female submission in the formation of the child's gender identity. If the protagonist does not look at women, and especially at her mother, as gender models, how does she relate to them? Through the identification with Jean Gabin, women are perceived as objects of love and a territory for male action, as is made explicit in the text's opening statement cited above. For example, Maria is emphatically described by the little girl as the object of her adoration; similarly, her older sister Licia, who could have provided a valuable female example by virtue of her positive traits as an intelligent and independent woman, is regarded as an object of love and conquest, as the child even engages in a competition for Licia's attention with the unsuccessful admirer Cesare.

In her relationship with Maria and Licia, Goliarda gives voice to a twofold need for love and care. On the one hand, she expresses the need for love of a neglected child, to whom women represent potential carers. On the other, through her adoption of a male viewpoint, she confines women to the passive role of the recipients of male desire and the territory of male action. The two gazes on women, that of the needy child and that of the self-referential man, converge on the figure of the idealized angelic woman, which is suggested to Goliarda in an imaginary dialogue with Jean Gabin:

> Finché vi saranno delle Tine grassottelle e generose siamo in salvo, Goliarda, da tutte le guerre possibili, da tutti gli astii e le intolleranze ... Mi ricordo, alla fine della guerra, sperduto e affamato, fu proprio una donna come questa che mi salvò la vita con un pezzo di pane e il sogno – cosa importante come il pane – e con un sorriso. Sapessi com'era bella! Portava una treccia bionda intorno alla testa a mo' di corona e ogni volta che sorrideva era come se un faro le si accendesse davanti e la illuminasse tutta. Guardarla dava l'illusione che una grande pace fosse scesa sulla terra. (JG 105)

[As long as there are some chubby and generous women like Tina, we're safe from all possible wars, hostility and intolerance, Goliarda. I remember, at the end of the war, I was hungry and lost; a woman like this one saved my life with a piece of bread, with a dream – which is no less important than bread – and with a smile. If only you knew how beautiful she was! She had a blonde braid wrapped around her head like a crown, and every time she smiled it was as if a beam of light illuminated her from the front. Looking at her you had the illusion that an immense peace had descended on the Earth.]

It is interesting to note that this passage closely follows the scene of Musetta and Zoe conspiring against men, so that the image of the angelic woman works as an anti-feminist model as proposed by a male perspective, which considers the female subject 'as belonging *to*, and a function *of*, Man.'[14] Through the adoption of a patriarchal standpoint, the narrator aspires to reinstate a traditional role of care for women, while at the same time she does not include herself in the category. Considering that the text is constructed on the absence of the figure of the mother, the protagonist's stated nostalgia for women's role of care can be interpreted as the expression of a child's longing for affection and solicitude rather than the definition of a model of gender for herself.

From Jean Gabin – or rather from a combination of the French actor and the models of masculinity she assimilates from her social context – the little girl learns 'come ci si comporta con le donne, come le si fa innamorare e come le si protegge' [how to deal with women, how to make them fall in love and how to protect them] (JG 109). In this way, the protagonist's self-representation as a man borders on homosexuality.[15] If her mother is forbidden to her as an object of love, as declared at the beginning of the novel, the same is not true for the other women. The novel makes a few references to the protagonist's homosexual desire for other girls;[16] moreover,

14   Cavarero, *Tu che mi guardi*, 67.

15   In *Appuntamento a Positano*, too, Sapienza's narrating 'I' looks at a woman, Erica, through the identification with a male gaze, that of the young man Nicola, and uses such a gaze as a vehicle to express her own desire. See *Appuntamento a Positano*, 17–18, 100.

16   See, for example: 'Perché diavolo seguo così intensamente questa bella ragazzina dai capelli biondi mai vista prima in giro?' [Why on earth am I following so intensely this beautiful blonde girl I've never seen before?] (JG 43). See also JG 50–1.

in the same chapter in which Goliarda describes her upbringing amidst men, while talking about her dream to be a storyteller she declares that she wants to become like Sappho, which is at least an ambiguous statement considering that Sappho is not only a woman poet, but also the author of poems voicing female homoerotic desire. The most explicit and at the same time ambiguous reference to homosexual desire, however, belongs to a separate section of the novel, set in a different time and place. This is the story of Goliarda's friendship with an American girl, Jean, under the Nazi occupation of Rome, when she is around twenty years old. The terms used to describe Goliarda's relationship with Jean have little in common with the tangle of sexism and the child's need for love related to her identification with Jean Gabin in the rest of the novel. Conversely, an idea of communication, reciprocity and respect for the other's independent will makes its appearance, marking a different way of conceiving human relationships. The representation of reciprocity and accordance in the relationship with Jean closely recalls the scene of Goliarda's play with Nica in *Lettera aperta* and Modesta's discovery of love with Beatrice in *L'arte della gioia*, which were analysed through Cavarero's notion of 'resonance'. In *Io, Jean Gabin*, too, Sapienza carves out a little space for a modality of communication that is not founded on power imbalances – and its correlatives: need, dependence, distribution of active and passive roles – but on the dialogue between two girls who become subjects precisely thanks to their mutual recognition. It is noteworthy that Sapienza links such a reciprocity to the context of the two girls telling each other the story of their lives. In fact, through this very narration the protagonist becomes aware of having a past, that is, of being the subject of a personal story:

> Jean sa tutto di me, forse per questo l'amo tanto? È la prima persona alla quale ho raccontato il mio passato, o meglio la prima con la quale ho scoperto di avere un passato. [...] Avevo la giornata per poi la sera, quando tutti dormivano, raccontarla a lei fissandola negli occhi. Avevano la capacità di spalancarsi immensi e raccogliere le mie esperienze, le mie fatiche, i miei sogni, la mia vita stessa e ridarmela attraverso un sorriso quieto più ricca e viva. Pensare le stesse cose. Non mi era mai accaduto con una carusa e per questo l'amavo. (JG 98)

> [Jean knows everything about me. Maybe that's why I love her so much? She's the first person I told about my past, or, to put it better, the first with whom I discovered

I had a past. [...] I had the day so I could tell her about it looking her in the eyes, in the evening, when everyone was sleeping. Her eyes were able to open wide and receive my experiences, my struggles, my dream and my life itself, which they returned richer and livelier, with a calm smile. Having the same thoughts – it had never happened to me with a girl before, and that's why I loved her.]

The brief passage about Goliarda's relationship with Jean links two macro concepts elaborated by Cavarero, the notion of 'resonance' and that of 'narration' (the latter is explored by the philosopher in *Tu che mi guardi, tu che mi racconti*). Resonance is the accordance of voices that produces communication before and beyond the exchange of semantic content. It allows the interlocutors to communicate their 'chi' [who] (unique identity, embodied in the uniqueness of each individual's voice) and not their 'che cosa' [what] (their attributes, their belonging to categories). Remaining in a similar conceptual frame, but with a shift in focus, narrative is what turns life into a story through, and only through, the intervention of an external gaze on a person's life. In her rich exploration of the narrative discourse, Cavarero draws particular attention – and it is an innovative point, which has its roots in Arendt's thought – to the intrinsically relational constitution of a personal story, not much or not only because personal identity is embedded in social relationships, but because personal identity depends on someone else's recognition: 'The person who is walking on the ground cannot see the figure traced by her steps, but needs someone else's perspective'; 'The category of personal identity always postulates the other as necessary.'[17]

In the scene with Jean, Sapienza captures the core of Cavarero's argument and combines it with a 'resonant' communication. Identity cannot be known through the categories to which it belongs, but can be narrated as the unique story of a unique human being: 'the identity of a unique being has its only tangible unity – the *unity* that it needs as a *unique* being – in the narration of its story.'[18] In Sapienza's representation, the locus of such a founding narration is precisely a scene of resonant communication, in

17   Cavarero, *Tu che mi guardi*, 10, 31.
18   Ibid. 56.

which each person is at the same time unique and able to dialogue with the other. This exchange of personal stories between the two girls allows Goliarda to gain a sense of herself, independently of any identification with external models (either her mother or Jean Gabin) and irrespective of any *dover essere*. It is significant that in both *Lettera aperta* and *Io, Jean Gabin* Sapienza carves out the space for minor scenes in which she gives voice to a conception of identity and human relationships that represents an alternative to the dominant one in the rest of the text. Even more interestingly, these 'islands of communication' take place with other female characters, for which the protagonist develops feelings that border on homosexual desire. Differently from the rest of the novel, Goliarda's love for Jean does not rest on her identification with Jean Gabin but conversely facilitates the protagonist's access to her own story and sense of the self.

The novel thus features two different representations of homosexuality. One derives from the protagonist's adoption of a male perspective on women, which indirectly replicates a heterosexual dynamic; the other one appears to have its roots in the character's unmediated desires, free from what Ross defines 'her self-conscious construction of gender identity based on imitating the performances of others.'[19] While the first modality is exalted by the protagonist in her bold identification with Jean Gabin, the second possibility is denied to her, by Maria's slaps in *Lettera aperta*, and by the character's anticipation of Jean's likely rejection in *Io, Jean Gabin*: 'Potrei prenderla fra le braccia ma sarebbe un atto troppo carnale, lei non si aspetta questo, Gabin non l'avrebbe fatto. Da qualsiasi amore sei posseduto devi scrutare l'altro, sapere quello che la sua natura vuole, rispettarlo' [I could hold her in my arms, but it would be too carnal a gesture, that's not what she expects, Gabin wouldn't do it. Whatever love possesses you, you must observe the other to learn what her nature wants, and you must respect her] (JG 68). In this passage, Goliarda's reasoning, which is expressed in the second person, suggests the idea of an internalized ban rather than the actual protagonist's will, so that her physical desire for Jean is at the same time uttered and blocked. The character of Jean is also present in *Il filo di*

---

19   Ross, 'Eccentric Interruptions', 12.

mezzogiorno, under a slightly different name, Jane. Whereas in *Io, Jean Gabin* the name 'Jean' overlaps with Gabin's first name, in *Il filo di mezzogiorno* Sapienza plays on the correlation between 'Jane' and 'Giovanna', the nurse who was assisting her during her recovery, and associates the two figures as they both take care of her: 'Giovanna Jane ... E quegli occhi che mi guardavano, come Jane mi aveva guardata erano occhi di madre, di sorella, di amica' [Giovanna-Jane ... And those eyes that were looking at me, like Jane had looked at me, were the eyes of a mother, a sister, a friend] (FM 183). In *Il filo di mezzogiorno* there is also a scene in which the relationship with Jane appears to include a sexual connotation:

> ... gli alleati bombardavano Anzio ... nella notte lei passava nel mio letto, chiudevamo i lenzuoli neri di polvere e ragnatele che separavano letto per letto ... [...] studiavamo ...
> 'What is this?'
> 'This is a flower'
> 'Do you know the name of this flower?'
> 'Yes, its name is geranium'
> 'Come si sente forte il rumore delle bombe questa notte ... presto saranno qui ... And, do you like this flower?'
> 'Yes, I like it very much, but I prefer ...' (FM 132–3)

> [... the Allies were bombing Anzio ... at night, she would come into my bed, we closed the sheets, black with dust and spiderwebs, that separated each bed ... [...] we studied ...
> *'What is this?'*
> *'This is a flower'*
> *'Do you know the name of this flower?'*
> *'Yes, its name is geranium'*
> 'The noise of the bombing is so loud tonight ... soon they'll be here ... *And, do you like this flower?'*
> *'Yes, I like it very much, but I prefer ...']*

The therapist does read the relationship in this direction, defining Jane 'morbosa' [sick] (FM 138), but the narrator denies that there was ever a sexual element and adds (in contrast to *Io, Jean Gabin*), that she enjoyed Jane's physical detachment. The relationship with Jane/Jean, then, confirms the narrative of an 'interruption' of homosexual desire pointed out by Ross. While the text boldly exhibits a form of 'external' homosexuality, which is related to the protagonist's instrumental adoption of a male identity, Sapienza includes a little episode that appears to be more problematic for a binary and heteronormative system, but again this possibility is only suggested and not further explored.

In Male Shoes: Freedom and Constraints

Goliarda's identification with the male gender originates as a response to the limits imposed on women and widespread misogyny in her social context. With her uncle Giovanni she puts aside conversations about family anecdotes, deemed to be feminine, and just entertains 'rapporti da uomo a uomo, che è come dire d'affari' [man to man relations, that is to say, business relations] (JG 26), thus stating the relevance of money to a male domain and her access to it. She happily accepts the definition of 'maschiaccio' [tomboy] and enjoys the sense of freedom that comes with the performance of a male role:

> 'È vero, Nino, che non s'addice a una signorina quel galoppo continuo con tutte le gambe di fuori?' [...]
>   'Ti pare una signorina? Un maschiaccio!'
>   E io, sbrigativa per tagliare quel ritornello che a loro sembra intensamente offensivo ma che a me fa ridere, semplicemente ridere:
>   'Signorine siete voi due! Dove andate a mostrare le vostre grazie verginali?' (JG 19–20)

> ['Isn't it true, Nino, that galloping all the time like that, with legs all exposed, is inappropriate for a young lady?' [...]
>   'Does she look like a young lady to you? She's a tomboy!'
>   So I replied quickly to cut them short with that refrain that they thought was offensive, but that made me laugh, only laugh:
>   'You two are the young ladies! Where do you go to show off your virginal graces?']

The little girl's self-representation as a man even shapes the perception of her own body, of which she 'emphasizes the "masculinity"',[20]

20　Ross, 'Eccentric Interruptions', 9.

characterizing it as strong, with big shoulders, long and firm arms, fit muscles and rapid pace.[21]

Although it is presented as a liberating and joyful strategy, in fact the adoption of a male identity is more troubled than the protagonist wants to believe. For example, the rejection of female identity is represented through Goliarda's physically cold and scared response to the prospect of becoming an adult woman and having to fulfil a procreative role, for which she feels that her body is inadequate:

> Davanti a un mare bianco d'inverno che torceva il suo corpo fra gli artigli di lava seppi la storia più incredibile della mia biologia di bambina … un sangue a volte doloroso ma necessario per la perpetuazione della specie striava le nuvole al limite estremo del mare, dove il mio corpo del futuro – chi poteva immaginarlo? – possente e delicato, così diceva Ivanoe, sarebbe divenuto, come quello di nostra madre, la fonte, culla, matrice di tante vite belle e forti se avessi voluto. 'Sì, sì' – ripetevo presa dal freddo del vento che s'era alzato potente e gelido intorno a noi alla notizia di questo nuovo compito che attendeva il mio corpo. – 'Sì, certo, ma a parte che non so come sia possibile, sono così magra!' (JG 34)

> [Facing a white winter sea, which twisted its body among lava claws, I learnt the most incredible story of my childhood biology … blood, painful at times, but also necessary to the continuation of our species, striped the clouds at the extreme limit of the sea, where, according to Ivanoe, my powerful and delicate future body, like that of my mother, – who could imagine it? – would become the source, the cradle, the matrix of many beautiful and strong lives, if I so desired. 'Yes, yes,' I repeated, feeling cold as a strong, freezing wind rose around us at the news of this new task that awaited my body. 'Yes, sure, but apart from the fact that I don't see how this is possible, I'm so thin!']

The setting of this dialogue with Ivanoe by the sea, which throughout the novel is overtly assumed as an image symbolizing women, offers the narrator the possibility of expressing the protagonist's uneasiness through highly dense metaphors. It is important to note that, unlike *Lettera aperta* and *Il filo di mezzogiorno*, which make wide use of metaphors, this is one of the few occasions in *Io, Jean Gabin* in which the narrator distorts the linearity

---

21   See JG 17, 63.

of sentence referentiality, thus reconnecting this passage to the knots of anxiety dominating previous works.

We have seen how male violence is only superficially exorcized and a small but significant reference to its constant threat surfaces anyway. Similarly, the menstrual cycle appears here to be at the core of the little girl's troubled relationship with her own body, as it is in *Lettera aperta*. Menstruation marks the transition from childhood, a stage of life in which Goliarda is left free to interpret her gender as she likes, to being a woman, who is strictly constrained in her social role. The passage cited above suggests that the protagonist's rejection of the female identity is not as plain as she describes it. In fact, it turns into her refusal to grow up, in the impossible hope of controlling her biological development to escape an imposed destiny of submission: 'Ma io ormai ho deciso [...]: farò in modo di non diventare mai grande, così non avrò bisogno dei loro consigli e non mi sposerò mai!' [Now I've decided [...]: I'll make sure I never grow up, so I won't need their advice and will never get married] (JG 24). Although the child claims a joyful adoption of a male role, the narrator provides several clues hinting at a much more intricate connection between biological sex, gender identity and gender role.

In her discussion of gender and sexuality in *Io, Jean Gabin*, Ross interprets Goliarda's adoption of a male identity as a liberating move:

> Here masculinity is seen as a powerful and liberating identity that she can assume independently of her sex, and redefine, thereby reshaping her body in her desired image. Ultimately, Sapienza's is a masculinity without maleness that denaturalizes and reveals masculinity as a construction, challenging the assumption that biological sex inevitably leads to a predestined gender identity (Halberstam 1998). Gendered behaviour and biology are linked, but queerly.[22]

While I overall agree with Ross's considerations on Sapienza's deconstruction of gender essentialism, the liberating feature attached to the protagonist's masculinity is quite nuanced and complex and is therefore worth further qualification. First, the little girl's freedom to adopt male behaviour does disconnect biological sex and gender identity, showing such a

22   Ross, 'Eccentric Interruptions', 10.

connection as a social construct. Yet, albeit dismantled on a theoretical level, this construct exists in practice, as a result of social imposition, and *Io, Jean Gabin*, in continuity with Sapienza's earlier works, provides an articulated representation of the relationship between social norms and personal freedom. Indeed, the protagonist's transgression of her gender identity is allowed in childhood but not outside its boundaries, so that Goliarda must reject adulthood in order to refuse to play the gender role superimposed on her biological sex by social norms. The sense of freedom deriving from the adoption of a male identity can only be enjoyed by isolating it from its future development. The second point concerns the protagonist's freedom to choose her gender identity 'independently of her sex'. This is a highly problematic issue, since not only is the adoption of a male identity limited to childhood, it is also, and perhaps more importantly, embedded in a hierarchical organization of the sexes. The little girl assumes a male identity precisely because this allows her to escape the constraints of being a woman. Even in the rejection of female identity, the choice is not 'independent' from the biological sex, but originates as a strategic response to it. In other words, the protagonist longs for the benefits associated with the male identity, as is made evident in the representation of the patriarchal and misogynistic confinement of women into a passive role. Finally, the definition of 'maleness without male', which points to the 'queer' link between sex and gender, is theoretically relevant, but, in my view, it fails to capture an important aspect of the protagonist's performance of gender. In fact, Goliarda's interpretation of a male role is not the expression of her personal identity, but rather a straightforward replication of male gender stereotypes. She is not creatively interpreting a personal identity that disrupts binary categories with its transgressive hybridism and fluidity; instead, she is playing a pre-existing role, the very traditional role of a man in a patriarchal society. By incorporating the male construct, the protagonist, rather than constructing the freedom to be herself, ultimately achieves a staged freedom.

In the polarizing distribution of features between the genders in *Io, Jean Gabin*, the male role comprises the notions of freedom, strength and independence, which are set against constrictions, weakness and dependence typical of the female role. Thanks to the imitation of a male stereotype, Goliarda accesses a position from which she can be active and express herself freely, but at the same time such a freedom to be herself is built upon the strategic negation of what she is, i.e. female, with far reaching consequences for the articulation of her own identity. An example of this active vitality that comes with the male identity can be seen when the protagonist runs downstairs in her building, which earns her the label of 'tomboy' by the Brunos; likewise, in the first part of the novel, terms referring to action and energy recur: 'Sola, bilanciandomi su passi brevi ed energici sprizzanti coraggio altezzoso, adattavo i miei piccoli piedi alla camminata piena d'autosufficienza virile di Jean Gabin' [On my own, balancing myself on quick and energetic steps full of haughty courage, I adapted my small feet to Jean Gabin's manly and self-sufficient walk] (JG 3); 'Con mossa energica m'infilai un maglione [...] mi precipitai fuori dal mio covo per agire' [With an energetic movement I put on my sweater [...] and ran out from my hideout to take action] (10). However, the expression of vitality is built upon the character's explicit intention to mark a distance from weakness, which is seen as pertaining to female behaviour. The insertion of sentences about female weakness and emotionality as the counterpart of male strength causes the expression of vitality to undergo a subtle but crucial shift in meaning. Vital action becomes the result of the protagonist's effort to discard her own emotions, needs and weaknesses, and to play the role of the 'tough guy', rather than giving vent to uncontrollable vital energy: 'Per poco non mi prendo a schiaffi, nello specchio, nel vedere lagrime che a mia insaputa se ne vanno in giro per le mie gote rivelando a tutti la mia impotenza [...] reazione questa da signorinella scema' [I almost slap myself when I see in the mirror unwanted tears running down my cheeks, revealing my helplessness to everyone [...] this is a silly girl's reaction] (17). Here, what is uncontrollable is not a form of vitality that would require the freedom of a male role, but the tears 'da signorinella scema'. In this respect, the protagonist of *Io, Jean Gabin* is amazingly ambiguous, as she constantly oscillates between the bold and joyful attitude of the 'tough guy', overall active and energetic, able to overcome her own momentary weaknesses, and a fragile little girl who struggles to hide her own vulnerability behind a virile mask, because 'boys don't cry'.²³ In one scene in particular the self-imposition of a strong attitude emerges as belonging to a male construct, in sharp contrast with the character's own emotions:

> Maledetto sia il momento che crescendo (dolore dell'uomo crescere) fui scaraventata giù nel pavimento a guadagnarmi il pane col sudore della mia fronte ... Non avevo ancora realizzato quanto grande era la sventura di reggersi sulle proprie gambe che una marea di voci dure, dinieghi, occhiatacce e chi più ne ha più ne metta m'impalarono col culo al pavimento, decisa nel mio piccolo intimo (non credete che anche i piccoli hanno un intimo?) a non muovermi più per l'eternità. [...]
> Il pavimento come una voragine precipita sotto i miei piedi [...]. Io fatico come un mulo e loro ridono ... maschiacci, si sa. Ma questa è acqua passata, non è da 'ommini' sguazzare nelle sofferenze e ormai sono in grado, appena aperti gli occhi, di balzare dal letto e sussurrando a me stessa: 'Piccole insulse traversie di picciriddi', accantonare i pensieri fastidiosi, con gambe salde andare su e giù per la mia soffitta e fronteggiare il presente. (JG 61–2)

> [Cursed be the time when, growing up (growing up is the suffering of mankind) I was cast down onto the ground to earn my daily bread by the sweat of my brow ... I hadn't yet realized how great was the misfortune of standing on my own legs, when a flood of hard voices, denials, nasty looks and so on stuck my ass on the floor. In my little child's soul (don't you think children also have a soul?) I was determined not to move ever again. [...]
> The floor collapses under my feet like an abyss [...]. I struggle like a mule and they laugh ... boys, you know. But this is water under the bridge, indulging in suffering isn't manly, and now I'm able to jump out of bed as soon as I open my eyes. I tell myself, 'these are just stupid childish problems', so I put aside annoying thoughts, walk up and down my attic with firm legs, and face the present.]

I quote the passage almost in its entirety because it comprises the core elements involved in the relationship between the character's emotions and normative gender constructs. In contrast to other parts of the text, this primary scene of the experience of walking is marked by the protagonist's lack of vital drive, as she is forced and directed in her movements by her brothers, rather than supported in her wishes. From the outset, action is not the expression of the character's impulse but the result of an external

---

23   The reference is to the title of the film *Boys Don't Cry*, dir. Kimberly Peirce (US, 1999).

demand, which gives rise to what Winnicott defines as 'False Self', set against the 'True Self' that is rooted in the desiring matter of the body: 'The True Self comes from the aliveness of the body tissues and the working of body functions, including the heart's action and breathing [...] and is, at the beginning, essentially not reactive to external stimuli, but primary.'[24]

The external imposition of action takes place in the context of the brothers' pressing attitude, which the child perceives as hostile and normative. In interpreting the conditioning imposed by Goliarda's brothers and her reaction to it, a relevant insight is provided by Miller's illustration of the child's adaptation to adult norms. Adaptation derives from the child's need for love and care, and results in the repression of his/her own emotions and desires. Exposed to the power of adults, the child attempts to disregard his/her own weakness and endeavours to comply with the self-control required of him/her: 'Contempt is the weapon of the weak and a defense against one's own despised and unwanted feelings. And the fountainhead of all contempt, all discrimination, is the more or less conscious, uncontrolled and secret exercise of power over the child by the adult.'[25] According to Miller, the repression and contempt for emotions and weakness affects girls more severely than boys, a view that is also endorsed by Elena Gianini Belotti.[26] In her analysis of the social construction of gender identities in the upbringing of children, carried out in Italy from the late 1960s to the early 1970s, Gianini Belotti describes the formative process of young girls as the inculcation of a sense of inferiority with respect to the male population, coupled with a re-channelling of vitality from self-expression to the performance of a duty of self-sacrifice and care. When a girl displays stronger resistance, such a formative process culminates in the repression of vitality. The adaptation of boys to their gender role would be less problematic, as they are expected and therefore encouraged to express themselves freely: 'Pushing an individual toward his own development is easier than repressing the impulse to self-realization that is present in all

---

24   Winnicott, *The Maturational Processes and the Facilitating Environment*, 148.
25   Miller, *The Drama of Being a Child*, 90.
26   See Elena Gianini Belotti, *Dalla parte delle bambine* (Milan: Feltrinelli, 1973).

individuals, regardless of their sex.'[27] However, this applies only partially
to the relationship between gender and vitality in the scene of the little
girl who learns to walk. In this episode, Goliarda manifests contempt for
weakness and emotions, which are deemed to be feminine, but she reacts
to it by forcing herself into a strong and active position, the one belonging
to the *ommini* and *maschiacci*, which remains nonetheless the result of self-
discipline as opposed to self-expression. Hence, this scene questions the
naturalness of *any* behavioural model that conditions action and represses
emotions and weakness, including the male construct. As Gianini Belotti
herself concedes, boys' upbringing is also conditioned and constrained by
the binary gender system: 'Nobody can tell how much energy and how many
talents are destroyed in the process of forcing children of both sexes into
male and female patterns as they are conceived in our culture.'[28] Reflecting
on the formation of the male gender role, Ciccone argues that the upbringing of boys entails a type of repression that is equally damaging, inasmuch
as it is based on detachment from emotions and weakness. The canon of
virility, in other words, is constructed on the negation of parts of the self.
Therefore, it results in a male subject who is split between his body and
his rationality, between instincts and control. Borrowing Ciccone's words,
the 'canon of virility' prescribes 'a male identity that is founded *against the
corporeal sphere* and on the ability to dominate the body, its instincts and
emotions.'[29]

In *Io, Jean Gabin*, Goliarda, by attempting to overcome her own weakness, resorts to a virile attitude that is ultimately equally constructed on
repression. However, while stressing the elements of constraint and power,
at the same time it is not productive to force an interpretation of the text
that rigidly separates a true from a false self, as both coexist in the child
protagonist, in an alternation and blend of weakness and strength that
is a dominant trait of Sapienza's narrative. In fact, at the end of the passage cited above, Goliarda has learnt to walk and enjoys the freedom of
action achieved thanks to it. Overall the character's weak side and the

27   Gianini Belotti, *Dalla parte delle bambine*, 24.
28   Ibid. 9.
29   Ciccone, *Essere maschi*, 61, 99.

instrumentality of the male role seem to prevail, even though they are possibly not the most evident elements. The text devotes great attention to the child's emotional sphere, which from all directions reveals the adoption of strength and energetic action as constraining rather than expressing the little girl's desires. On a single occasion the expression of vital action is associated with free enjoyment and not with effort: 'Io volo per le strade felice, certo non sono le cinque lire che avevo, ma è qualcosa. La strada! La strada apre tutte le occasioni e le avventure!' [I run happily in the street. Sure, it's not the five liras I had before, but it's something. The street! The street opens the way to every opportunity and adventure] (JG 21). Significantly, this energetic happiness does not pass through the mediation of the virile role.

In conclusion, the little protagonist's adoption of a male role, with its emphasized masculinity, confirms rather than challenges the attribution of independence and agency to the male gender. Hence, Goliarda's transgression does not affect the patriarchal structure of gender dualism, but works as an indication of its constraints. Not only is Goliarda's transgression dictated by the need to access agency in a patriarchal system and temporally limited to childhood, it also remains confined within the binary and heteronormative structure of the patriarchal symbolic system. In other words, the little girl who identifies as a boy does undoubtedly break the alleged naturalness of the connection between biological sex and gender identity, but, by simply incorporating a normative male identity, she does not threaten the overall system.[30] From this perspective, the contradiction between the condemnation of women's adoption of male features pointed out in the opening to the novel, and Goliarda's own behaviour, appears to be wholly internal to the patriarchal viewpoint. Arguably both options – to stick to women's traditional roles or to impersonate a male role – fall within a traditional binary system of gender; in both cases, women are not allowed a space of autonomous expression. If they adopt a male role, they efface themselves as women; if they do not replicate male constructs, they

---

30   On the concept of different types of transgression – of role and of symbolic structure – in female homosexuality, see Nerina Milletti, 'Donne "fuori della norma"', in Nerina Milletti and Luisa Passerini, eds, *Fuori della norma. Storie lesbiche nell'Italia della prima metà del Novecento* (Turin: Rosenberg&Seller, 2011), 21–41.

are confined in a passive and submissive role. The dilemma that tormented the protagonist of *Lettera aperta* and *Il filo di mezzogiorno* is not solved in *Io, Jean Gabin*, as no real alternative of independence is envisaged for women, but is set aside to enjoy the provisional and precarious freedom deriving from the performance of a male role. The problem of women's autonomy does not find a solution in *Io, Jean Gabin*, but is uttered in its contradictions and impasses, although with parody and irony. The only truly transgressive experience on a structural level is Goliarda's relationship with Jean, and it is extremely significant that this is attached to the protagonist's discovery of her own personal identity, but it is blocked by Goliarda before it develops.

Food, Sleep and Love

The notions of staged freedom, performed identity and imitation of a heteronomous model implicitly point to their opposites, namely the possibility of agency and authenticity. What is at work in *Io, Jean Gabin* is the exposition of the conflict between different layers or instances of the character's identity, some of which are represented as belonging to a sphere that is closer to her inner instincts. More specifically, bodily impulses, emotions and the need for love occupy the centre of the character's self, which is prevented from becoming static by its own mutability and instability on a first level, and, on a second level, by its constitutive interaction with others, in a representation of identity which recalls the 'materialistic, dynamic, vitalistic and post-humanistic notion of the subject' theorized by Braidotti.[31] In *Io, Jean Gabin*, the body performs a twofold function: first, it undermines the achievement of a crystallized identity deriving from the adherence to heteronomous constructs (to which playing the role of the 'tough guy' belongs). While rational will seeks to establish a fixed and stable identity, the corporeal dimension, with its drives and desires, constantly unsettles established identity patterns. However, the body is

31   Alessia Ronchetti, 'Postmodernismo e pensiero italiano della differenza sessuale', in Antonello and Mussgnug, *Postmodern* Impegno, 99–119, 112.

also, phenomenologically, a living body, an irreducible material entity, which works as a limit to the deconstruction of identity and a source of vital impulses. The ontology of the body prevents identity from utterly dissolving, by anchoring it to its driving centre and situated locus of primary interaction with the world. In her autobiographical works, Sapienza uses narrative as a means to establish renewed contact with such a bodily foundation, traversing and deconstructing oppressive layers of identity. Differently from a phenomenological reduction or *epoché*, however, this operation is never fully achievable, and the desire to reconnect with a bodily and instinctual dimension runs in parallel with the story of its obfuscation and modification through time.

In this novel, gender constructs constitute one fundamental way of determining identity. The protagonist's incorporation of a heteronomous model within the context of power imbalance between men and women cannot be considered fully autonomous. To say this does not invalidate the outcome of a liberating effect for the protagonist, but defines its limits as traced in the text itself. In other words, this is not a theoretical argument against the possibilities of liberation incidental to the access to a male role, but rather an examination of the limits of this operation as they are specifically represented in Sapienza's work. Indeed, a close textual analysis has demonstrated the permanence, in the character's adoption of a male role, of normative stereotypes that do not only shape but also constrain her own identity. The child's assimilation of a stereotypical male behaviour and viewpoint – chosen as a response to the restrictions of the female model, carried out without a creative reinterpretation and limited to childhood – constitutes a 'staged freedom', at times overtly disconnected from the protagonist's own desires.

While in order to be free to be herself the protagonist needs to be something she is not, she is constantly drawn to do otherwise, by indulging in a passive attitude toward her own emotions and in the free enjoyment of the present. Similarly to what *L'arte della gioia* realizes on a wider scale, *Io, Jean Gabin* displays a conflicting succession of vitalistic impulses and voluntaristic actions, uncontrolled emotions and detached rationality. The bodily foundation of identity is alternately uttered and repressed, searched for and silenced. In parallel, the protagonist's relationship with the other characters is deeply conflicted, crossed by a struggle for autonomy, on the one hand, and emotional dependence, on the other. Analogous conflicts are at work in *Lettera aperta* and *Il filo di mezzogiorno*, in which the protagonist's role of 'child entertainer' inhibits her liberty to develop her own identity and hinders the possibility of an authentic relationship with the others. It is in the problematic dialogue between personal instincts and the others, characterized by power imbalances and normative identity constructs, that the protagonist's split and alienation originate. Similarly, in *Io, Jean Gabin* the exposure of the impositions endured by the protagonist goes together with the opening of spaces where she can access her own instinctual domain. The text gives voice to a desire for rooting the self in a corporeal dimension that constitutes the fundamental horizon of freedom in Sapienza's narrative.

Through the articulation of the character's perceptive and emotional world, the narrator approaches the expression of that bodily foundation of the self which is to be reconstructed beyond staged identities. The main staged identity in the novel is that of the tough boy, who is characterized by strength and vital action. However, these characteristics of strength and vital action alternate in Goliarda with uncontrolled emotions and weaknesses, so that strength and action are the result of an effort rather than the expression of the protagonist's vital self, to the point that action is described as functioning to dominate deeper fragilities: 'L'azione calma l'ansia e la paura' [action calms down anxiety and fear] (JG 32). Moreover, the narrator associates the need for action with family pressure, thus marking its heteronomous feature. Even playing and daydreaming, which the child should be able to enjoy irrespective of any concern for purposes, are linked to a duty: 'A casa mia avevano sempre tutti tanto da fare. Così tanto che *eri costretta* anche tu a inventarti cento cose da trafficare, sbrigare, leggere, giocare, perché anche giocare e fantasticare a casa mia era considerato un "fare"' [In my family they were always all very busy, to the point that *you also had to* come up with hundreds of things to do and take care of, reading, playing – because my family considered playing and daydreaming also to be forms of 'doing something'] (13. My emphasis).

Such a duty of action can be set against a series of images of passivity, in which the narrator, remembering her early childhood, conceptualizes her body as an object that is lifted and carried by other people who take care of her. This memory is pleasant and is associated with a sense of strength and protection: 'mi ricordo del mio corpo come di un pacco trasportato da grandi braccia nell'aria e posato in posti precisi dove restava passivo in attesa che altre braccia venissero a rimuoverlo' [I remember my body like a package that was carried in the air by big arms and then put down in specific places where it remained passive, waiting for other arms to come and move it from there] (JG 36);[32] 'Le sue braccia erano così sicure nel trasportarmi da una stanza all'altra che mi ci sentivo come in una culla e così dall'alto tutto mi sembrava possibile e non avevo più paura di nulla, nemmeno del mare, anche se era un po' mosso' [His arms were so safe, carrying me from room to room, that I felt as if I were in a cradle. From that position high up, everything seemed possible and I wasn't scared of anything anymore, not even of the sea, even if it was rough] (60). These passages point to a dimension of the self that resists the accomplishment of a task and the exercise of self-imposed control. Likewise, syntactical constructions where emotions and physical instincts are in the position of agents affecting the character abound throughout the text: 'Il silenzio complice si fa così intenso che mi spuntano le lacrime dalla gioia' [the complicit silence is so intense that I burst into tears of joy] (31); 'Un'eco di allegrezza mi scorre nelle giunture' [an echo of happiness runs into my joints] (30); 'Il desiderio di burro e marmellata conditi dalle ciance del mio fratellone mi vince completamente' [the yearning for jam and butter, accompanied by my big brother's chatter, totally wins me over] (37).

In these scenes involving a pleasurable experience of bodily instincts, the biological functions of eating and sleeping, with their correlate references to hunger and tiredness, stand in a prominent position. Food and sleep partition the narration and weave a complex relationship with the character's self-imposed discipline. Significantly, food and sleep are often present in scenes in which the little girl is in a state of harmony with members of her family, especially her siblings. As regards sleep, for example, Goliarda suddenly falls asleep after her brothers Carlo and Arminio return from the police station where they had been brought and beaten up by fascists. She also relaxes and

---

32   The metaphor of the package also features in the opening scene of UR, when the protagonist is being taken to prison (see Chapter 4).

almost falls asleep when her sister Licia chooses her company and cuddles her at a house party: 'Una vampa d'orgoglio mi stravolge talmente che tutta la fatica del giorno mi cade addosso e quasi ho voglia di dormire lì abbracciata a lei' [a burst of pride shocks me so deeply that I suddenly feel all the tiredness from the day and almost want to fall asleep there in her arms] (JG 55). Food too is linked to harmony and love with her siblings in a number of scenes. For instance, Sapienza describes a moment of perfect happiness when cooking fried polenta in the kitchen with Ivanoe, and an equally joyful breakfast with Carlo after boxing training.[33] On this occasion, however, Sapienza also voices a conflict between will and desires, between duty of action and enjoyment of pleasures: 'Ma non ce la faccio a dire di no a Carlo quando ride sotto i baffetti neri e mi solleva da terra facendomi volare. Non ce la faccio a "volere proprio". Dev'essere questa la mia contraddizione intima' [I can't say no to Carlo when he laughs behind his thin black moustache and lifts me from the floor making me fly. I just can't 'really want'. This must be my inner contradiction] (37). In the context of Goliarda's highly split self, the impulses of hunger and sleep are represented as pertaining to a sphere of the protagonist's self that is characterized by naturalness, enjoyment and truthfulness. Conversely, the insertion of the expression 'volere proprio' between inverted commas suggests that it is an acquired ethical norm.

Sapienza's narrative only knows a few moments of rest and adherence to an unproblematic present, as enjoyment is constantly marred by the character's will to accomplish a task, which in this case is the endeavour to find money. *Io, Jean Gabin* displays a real war between will and the temptation of abandoning oneself to pleasures, alternating the enjoyment of the present and the projection towards the accomplishment of a *dover*

---

33   A similar description of happiness involves Tina: 'Ragazzi, fu magnifico! Da Tina si dormiva su materassi di crine fresco in un silenzio così completo che solo la sazietà era capace di svegliarci. In quel piccolo dado bianco di calce sperduto nel verde degli aranci si mangiava all'ombra della pergola fichi freschi, ulive e miele' [Guys, it was wonderful! At Tina's place we slept on fresh horsehair mattresses, in such a complete silence that only fullness was able to wake us up. In that small white dice, in the middle of the green orange trees, we used to eat fresh figs, olives and honey in the arbour's shade] (JG 105).

essere. 'Io non sono carusa che quando s'è messa uno scopo in testa ceda alla fame o al sonno prima di averlo raggiunto, questo scopo, per dio Ulisse! Io sono così, decisa e senza mollezze, ma nondimeno spero proprio che ci sia qualcosa da mettere sotto i denti' [I'm not the kind of girl who, having an objective in mind, gives in to hunger or sleep without first achieving her goal, for god Ulysses' sake! I'm like this, determined and without weaknesses; however, I really hope there's something to eat!] (JG 29). Inner instincts are characterized as physical drives, which are in a conflicting relationship with will and self-discipline. In this respect, *Io, Jean Gabin* provides an effective representation of a lively debate between will and desires, a struggle which is at the same time *for* and *against* instincts. While the character attempts to control her instincts to accomplish a *dover essere*, through writing the narrator reconstructs a space for the expression of those instincts behind the layers of falsifying identities consolidated over time. The contrast could not be any clearer, and much of the dynamism, contradictions and instability of Sapienza's narrative is rooted in it: 'Era questa forse la mia contraddizione? Sapere perfettamente quello che mi abbisognava, avere deciso una linea d'azione e nello stesso tempo lasciare che tutto andasse in malora per qualche morso della fame o per una visita dei fascisti? [Maybe this was my contradiction – knowing exactly what I needed to do, deciding on a plan of action, and at the same time letting everything fall apart because of hunger or a visit from the fascists?] (35); 'Ecco un altro difetto imperdonabile per un condottiero, un uomo di scienza, un ricercatore: perdere tempo a ciondolarsi senza meta' [Here is another unforgivable flaw for an adventurer, a man of science, a researcher: wasting time lazing about without a purpose] (43).

Emotional Dependence and Misunderstandings

After discussing the protagonist's adoption of a male role and the components of the self that appear to be rooted in her primary instinctual domain, it is now possible to put these elements together to answer the question of where the duty to accomplish a task, the need for a self-imposed discipline and the contrast between instincts and will originate. Similarly to *Lettera aperta* and *Il filo di mezzogiorno*, *Io, Jean Gabin* also features a protagonist who is painfully seeking love and attention from her family, especially from her mother. In *Lettera aperta*, the initiation of a *dover essere* is related to Maria and takes the shape of Goliarda's endeavour to become an independent woman like her mother. At the beginning of *Io, Jean Gabin*, a dialogue between the little girl and Maria sets up the protagonist's task to find some money and repair the damage her aggression against Concetta has caused. Within the analogy in the structure, an important development takes place from the first autobiographical works to *Io, Jean Gabin*. In *Lettera aperta*, the tasks to which the protagonist felt called were in mutual conflict and overall too demanding compared to her resources as a little girl. This resulted in her utter inadequacy to cope even with the simplest aspects of life and was expressed through a narrative deeply affected by pain and suffering. Conversely, in *Io, Jean Gabin* the duty to find some money is much more specific and achievable for the little girl. Rather than paralysing her with its overwhelming difficulty, the task to find some money triggers her vital and cheerful wandering through the *casbah* (even though this vitality must be interpreted within the limits outlined above).

In the context of an improved balance of resources available to the protagonist to master her own identity, she is however still in a position of severe emotional dependence on her family. Starting from her relationship with Maria, who is distant and cold, the little girl fights against her own need for affection, which is felt as a major threat to her will and action:

> Una furia infernale contro il mio lato amorevole 'troppo dipendente', come diceva Arminio, aggiungendo – che vergogna! – 'morbosamente dipendente!', mi prese a tal punto da costringermi a dare calci e pugni nell'aria contro non so chi. [...]
> 'Non sarò mai un guerriero, zio!'
> 'e com'è 'sto fatto?'
> 'troppo dipendente affettivamente.' (JG 41–2)

> [I feel furious at the part of me that is too loving, 'too dependent,' as Arminio used to say, and then he would add, 'insanely dependent!' – I feel so ashamed! Anger makes me kick and punch the air, against I don't know whom. [...]
> 'Uncle, I'll never be a warrior!'
> 'And why is it so?'
> 'I'm too emotionally dependent.']

There is a real tension between Goliarda's own self-expression and her relationship with the others, whenever this is not available in the form of shared happiness (as in the scenes involving food and sleep analysed above) and is marked instead by need and asymmetry. Behind the little girl's emphasis on her will to be independent, she suffers from feeling neglected by her family and from the constrictions brought about by such a state of emotional dependence.

Miller and Winnicott describe the formation of a False Self as the result of a process of adjustment to parental expectations, as discussed regarding the protagonist's accomplishment of a task in *Lettera aperta* and *Il filo di mezzogiorno*. In *Io, Jean Gabin* the task is established and achievable, yet the fundamental dynamic shaping the relationship between the protagonist and her family members is the same as in previous works. Miller's illustration of different strategies of coping with the need for love and its potential distorting effects on the self also provides useful insights to analyse the entanglement of emotional dependence and quest for freedom in *Io, Jean Gabin*. Goliarda's attitude finds some direct correspondences in Miller's description of the 'reversal' strategy: 'I am breaking down under the constant responsibility because the others need me ceaselessly.'[34] Through the reversal strategy, the suffering that derives from dependence on the love of others is turned into impatience towards their request for attention. This mechanism is present in the novel through different nuances. For example, the protagonist consciously experiences her own need for love as limiting her independence, as in the passage cited above. However, in the same dialogue with uncle Nunzio, she also pictures a reversed situation, in which she must escape from her family's need for her. Significantly, the effort to be independent is described in terms that recall the strong male construct, while the heroic projection is so grandiose that it creates an ironic rather than painful contrast:

> Lui [Ulisse] aveva la volontà di non curarsi della moglie, dei figli e solo al suo scopo pensava, ai suoi viaggi, la sua conoscenza ... Io basta che Carlo o Arminio o Licia mi facciano un cenno, corro appresso a loro come una mentecatta qualsiasi. [...] Tutti contro di me. Tutti a chiamarmi, a volermi ... Ma anche Ulisse era voluto da tutti eppure ce la faceva sempre a ripartire. (JG 42–3)

34 Miller, *The Drama of Being a Child*, 27.

[He [Ulysses] had the determination not to care about his wife and children. He only thought about his aim, his travels, his knowledge ... All it takes with me is for Carlo or Arminio or Licia to nod at me and I run after them like an imbecile. [...] They were all against me, calling me, wanting me ... But Ulysses was also wanted by everyone, and yet he still always managed to leave again.]

In another scene, Goliarda, after learning that Tina is about to leave, goes through a rapid succession of feelings and degrees of self-consciousness, alternating need and impatience, ultimately uncovering the fictional feature of the pressuring need of the others, constructed through the reversal strategy. Indeed, she wriggles away from Tina's hug, who is subsequently revealed as actually ('in verità') not holding her back and absorbed in thought:

'Eh, Tina, sono proprio disperata!'
'Perché me ne vado, picciridda?!'
Lo dice con tanta ansia d'una conferma che non mi sento di deluderla. Jean non lo farebbe mai, di deludere una donna fragile indifesa. [...]
'Eh sì, mi spiace che parti.'
Avevo intenzione di dire una *bugia* ma, complessità della natura umana!, nel dirla capisco che *è vero*, mi dispiace e in un batter d'occhio, proprio come al cinema, mi trovo abbracciata alle sue spallone immense – sembrano cuscini, oh! – a singhiozzare e, cosa veramente vergognosa, a implorarla di non partire. [...]
Meglio prenderla a ridere, eh Jean!, allontanando le braccia di tutte queste donne – una folla, Jean – che ti braccano, ti vogliono, ti allacciano con mille carezze e graffi.
Allontanando le braccia paffute di Tina che *in verità* in quel momento se ne stava quieta a fissare la finestra [...]. (JG 74–5. My emphasis)

['Eh, Tina, I'm really sad!'
'Is it because I'm leaving, you little one?'
In saying it, she is looking forward to my confirmation so much that I don't feel like disappointing her. Jean would never do that, disappointing a fragile, defenceless woman. [...]
'Oh yes, I'm sorry that you're leaving.'
I meant to *lie* but – complexity of human nature! – in saying it I realize *it's true*, I'm sorry that she's leaving, and suddenly, just like in a movie, I find myself hugging her huge shoulders, which feel like pillows. I'm crying, and what's even more embarrassing, I'm begging her not to leave. [...]

> I better have a laugh, right Jean?, and push all these women's arms away – such
> a crowd, Jean! – who chase you, want you, tie you up with a thousand caresses and
> scratches.
>   I push away those plump arms of Tina's, who in that moment was *actually* staring
> quietly at the window [...].]

Emotional dependence causes the protagonist to experience her relationship with her family as deeply conflicting with her inner instincts. Self-
repression and inauthentic communication are the price for obtaining
love, a relational trouble that marks many of Sapienza's pages. Compared
to the earlier texts, the protagonist of *Io, Jean Gabin* is much more aware
of her own feelings and emotions, which are nonetheless put aside or misunderstood by her family.

In the dialogue between Goliarda and Maria which opens the novel,
we have an explicit account of this combination of need for love and impossible communication. While Maria is reproaching Goliarda, the little girl
wants to show to her mother the love she feels for her but also perceives
that this contact is forbidden to her, and avoids expressing it 'serrando le
braccia al torace per non fare gesti incauti' [by pressing my arms against
my chest in order to avoid thoughtless acts] (JG 12). Maria, who notices
Goliarda's gesture, misinterprets its meaning: 'Perché taci, cara? [...] Non
rispondi? O forse stai male con lo stomaco che ti stringi così le mani al pan-
cino?' [Why don't you speak my darling? [...] Don't you want to answer?
Or perhaps you have a stomach ache and that's why you're pressing your
hands on your tummy?] (12). This is the first of many occasions where
Goliarda is not understood by her family members. For example, when
she weeps out of joy for the 'silenzio complice' [complicit silence] (31) in
the kitchen with Ivanoe, he takes it for a worried cry. More dramatically,
when she bursts into tears during the house party because she is thinking
about the inequality between wealthy and poor people, everybody con-
gratulates her for being such an impressive actress: '"una vera attrice, un
tempo incredibile ... [...]" "Ma io soffrivo veramente!" osai sciocamente
replicare' ['what an actress, what perfect timing! [...]' 'But I was suffering
for real!', I stupidly dared to reply] (59). This scene closely recalls the episode of the bulletin of Goliarda's cries in *Lettera aperta*, where her repeated
weeping, faked in order to attract attention and recorded by her family,

was set against her real crying out of fear of losing her family's attention, which conversely went unnoticed. On the whole, even though in *Io, Jean Gabin* the narrative tone is much more joyful and light than in *Lettera aperta* and *Il filo di mezzogiorno*, references to self-repression and interrupted communication are overt.[35] The problem of being misunderstood also affects the adult narrator, in one of her very few explicit appearances in the text: 'La consapevolezza di non essere capiti è un tranello mortale per sé e per gli altri. Anch'io forse caddi in quel tranello ... Fermati Goliarda, non ascoltare il tuo futuro che s'apre come una fossa di fangose bugie tue e degli altri' [The awareness of being misunderstood is a fatal trap for yourself and for the others. I, too, may have fallen into this trap ... Stop, Goliarda, don't listen to your future, which opens up like a muddy grave full of your and others' lies] (81).

Goliarda's Positioning in Society

The Culpable Love: Shortcomings of Left-Wing Political Commitment

Goliarda's relationship with her family is affected by the child's unsatisfied need for love. With Maria, the protagonist perceives love as an egoistic and culpable drive, 'l'amore colpevole che poteva offenderla' [the culpable love that could offend her] (JG 14), in contrast to self-sacrifice for the cause of socialist struggle. Love is inextricably linked to guilt: 'È questo il guaio, io amo quella donna che con dolcezza certo, ma con una fermezza terrorizzante, mi sta dicendo che sono colpevole [...] verso tutta l'umanità povera, ignorante e umiliata' [This is the problem. I love this woman who, kindly but with frightening firmness, is telling me that I'm guilty [...] towards all the poor, ignorant and humiliated people] (11). In fact, the episode that

---

35   See also, for example, JG 38, 53.

triggers the plot of *Io, Jean Gabin* is precisely Goliarda's aggression against Concetta, who belongs to an underprivileged class.

While Maria is described as capable of altruism and generosity, Goliarda rather positions herself as closer to the Sapienzas' lineage, which is portrayed as radically individualistic and dominated by animal instinct: 'sprofondavo muta nell'ignominioso cinismo e spocchia, passionalità bestiale e indifferenza al grande dolore del mondo, dei Sapienza. Questo era il male di noi Sapienza, levantini libidinosi, protesi solo alla ricerca del nostro io, incalliti individualisti' [I was silently sinking into the shameful cynicism, haughtiness, bestial lust and indifference to the world's great suffering that were typical of the Sapienzas. This was the Sapienzas' fault, we were libidinous Levantines, hardened individualists pursuing our own self-realization exclusively] (JG 12–13). This opposition belongs to the same conceptual frame shaping the virile construct, which separates rationality from the body and will from instincts, where rationality and will allegedly overcome the exclusively egoistic nature of bodily instincts and emotions. Yet, in *Io, Jean Gabin* Sapienza overturns this paradigm and overtly charges it with failing to account for personal needs, feelings and emotions. Maria is represented as detached from reality, unable to take care of her daughter and to communicate on an emotional level. Maria's language is that of a moral duty that relies on abstract rationality, ultimately inapt in achieving real care for the others. By contrast, there is Carlo, Goliarda's brother, who, despite being considered not particularly smart by his family, is nonetheless able to take care of the little girl:

> Di Carlo in casa si diceva che non era intelligente, ma io non condividevo quella loro convinzione. Forse non parlava un italiano perfetto, non sapeva polemizzare, non leggeva abbastanza, ma nei fatti della vita era imbattibile, sapeva tutto. Che anche questa non era intelligenza? A volte li odiavo, come adesso che lui mi aveva preso in braccio. (JG 82–3)

> [At home, they used to say that Carlo wasn't intelligent, but I disagreed with their view. Maybe he didn't speak perfect Italian, he couldn't argue, he didn't read enough, but as far as the facts of life were concerned, he was the best, he knew everything. Isn't this also a form of intelligence? Sometimes I hated them, like now when he picked me up in his arms.]

The disparity of behaviours existing between the clever but cold Maria and
Carlo's loving attitude leads Goliarda to feel increasing resentment towards
her parents' socialist commitment, as she feels neglected 'perché "loro" avevano cose ben più importanti e vitali: "Il bene del popolo", "Il progresso",
"Il dolore del mondo"' [because 'they' had much more important and vital
commitments: 'The Common Good', 'Progress', 'The World's Suffering']
(JG 108). The polemic is personal and intense, directly addressing the price
she and her siblings are paying for their parents' political activity. Following
the story of her siblings' suffering as children while their parents were in
prison, the narrator's expression of anger and resentment reaches its apex in
a provocative criticism of the emotional consequences of political activity:
'Marx aveva cominciato a sacrificare i figli, non so se tre o quattro gliene
erano morti di fame per scrivere *Il capitale* e dare pane all'operaio ... l'operaio
dalla grande bocca spalancata stava lì a ricevere in pasto figli di marxisti e
mai si saziava ...' [Marx had started sacrificing his children. Three or four
of them, I'm not sure, had starved to death while he was writing *Capital*
so he could feed the workers ... the workers who were there with their big
mouths open wide to ingest the children of Marxist militants and were
never sated] (98).[36] This statement links directly to the dialogue between
Goliarda and her uncle Giovanni in the first part of the text, from which it
marks a significant change of perspective: '"È tuo padre che affama i suoi
figli con quelle balle del socialismo." "Noi non siamo affamati! E se qualche
volta ci mancano i soldi è perché non sfruttiamo nessuno, caro zio. E poi
anche Marx soffriva la fame per scrivere *Il capitale*"' ['It's your father who
starves his children with that socialist bullshit.' 'We're not starving! And if
sometimes we don't have money, that's because we don't exploit anyone, dear
Uncle! Besides, Marx too was starving when he was writing *Capital*'] (27).
     The criticism expressed in the first passage clearly belongs to the narrow
perspective of the neglected child. However, Sapienza's conflicting relationship with left-wing commitment in *Io, Jean Gabin* is not limited to the
child's personal resentment, but also assumes a properly political dimension.

36   Here, Sapienza also alludes, ironically, to the popular belief that the communists
     eat children, first spread by fascism and then, after World War II, encouraged by
     opponents of the PCI.

Sapienza speaks from a peculiar position, as she shares her family's opposition to all forms of oppressive power, from fascism to the Catholic Church and capitalist exploitation, but is also very critical of the attitude of left-wing intellectuals, including that of her family. She uses other characters, such as uncle Giovanni, Jsaya and Carlo, to voice a criticism of her parents. Jsaya, for example, offers a radically pessimistic view, close to the Sicilian literary tradition of Verga, De Roberto, Pirandello and Tomasi di Lampedusa. He does not believe in any emancipatory struggle and shakes the little girl with a criticism of her parents which points out the discrepancy between their class condition and their egalitarian belief:

> 'La miseria è una dannazione senza riscatto!' urla la voce del professor Jsaya all'orecchio della mente: 'Non credere alle balle liberali di tuo padre e di tua madre! Balle! Utopie di intellettuali viziati! Dalla miseria alla gloria ... Nessuno esce dalla miseria, sinonimo di ignoranza, e diventa un genio. Se non ci credi, va' a guardare da dove vengono tutti i loro scrittori, pittori, musicisti ... Da famiglie agiate, se non ricche, agiate! Hai capito?!' (JG 56)

> ['Poverty is a damnation without redemption!', Professor Jsaya's voice shouts into my mind's ear; 'Don't buy into your father's and your mother's liberal lies! Bollocks! Spoiled intellectuals' utopias! From poverty to glory ... No one escapes poverty, which is a synonym of ignorance, and becomes a genius. If you don't believe me, go and check where all their writers, painters and musicians come from ... From well-off families, if not rich, well-off. Do you understand?!']

Similarly, Carlo detects a dangerously naïve attitude in left-wing intellectuals, and especially in Maria. By attempting to improve society, such a naïve attitude turns into ideology and oppression: 'Maria in fatto di vita è un'ingenua, Iuzzetta mia, un'ingenua. Ne ho conosciuti a bizzeffe di questi ricchi che per svagarsi si fanno il passatempo di cambiare la società, servire il popolo, e giù a tagliare teste e opprimere. [...] io intelligente fino a fissarmi in un'idea tanto da diventare ingiusto non ci voglio arrivare' [With regard to life, my little Iuzza, Maria is just naïve. I've met plenty of these rich people who take up the hobby of changing society and serving the people, just to do something different, and then down to chopping off heads and oppressing. [...] I wouldn't want to be so intelligent that I fixate on an idea to the point of becoming unjust] (JG 83).

While on several occasions the protagonist professes her solidarity with her parents and their ideal of a more equal and just organization of society, she also marks a distance from them, especially from Maria, based on a deep difference in their respective understanding of human needs and the role of individual emancipation. By interpreting Sapienza's criticism of left-wing struggle as aimed mainly against its ideological intransigence rather than against its egalitarian objectives, there is here of course the risk of domesticating her individualistic and controversial charge. However, Sapienza never really questions the rightness of aspiring to a more equal and just society. Rather, she closely scrutinizes the strategies that are believed to lead to those objectives, noting limits and mistakes, at times to the point of embracing a very argumentative and provocative attitude against left-wing political struggle. In *Io, Jean Gabin*, Sapienza's main polemical objective is the notion, represented by Maria, that collective good is a moral duty necessarily founded on the detachment from personal emotional needs. To borrow Miller's words,

> The usually accepted judgemental contrast between self-love and object-love, and their portrayal as opposites, springs from naïve and uncritical usage in our everyday language. Yet, a little reflection soon shows how inconceivable it is really to love others (not merely to need them) if one cannot love oneself as one really is. And how could a person do that if, from the very beginning, he has had no chance to experience his true feelings and to learn how to know himself?[37]

A similar perspective is expressed by Husserl, who employs a system of thought that offers important insights to understanding Sapienza's connection between selfhood and political emancipation in *Io, Jean Gabin*. According to Rocco Donnicci, who carried out a vast analysis of the relationship between body, ethics and politics in Husserl's philosophy, 'An ethical value would not be of any value if I did not love it, and if, in appreciating it, I did not feel any satisfaction also for myself as I am realizing it. Love for one's own set of values, which ultimately is "self-love", is an indispensable condition for an ethical life.'[38] In Sapienza's view, it is in this split between self-love and object-love that the shortcomings of the rational language

37   Miller, *The Drama of Being a Child*, 14.
38   Donnicci, *Intenzioni d'amore, di scienza e d'anarchia*, 261.

spoken by Maria reside, as it is a language that fails to grasp a fundamental dimension of existence that resists the detached and abstract nature of ideology. This point of view is clarified in a dialogue between Goliarda and her anarchist uncle Nunzio:

'Oh, tu non sei nemico dell'amore?'
'E perché dovrei essere nemico dell'amore?'
'Non lo so, tutti sono nemici di questa parola. Dicono ca il Novecento è un secolo scientifico e l'amore, dicono, non c'entra niente con la scienza. Ivanoe sostiene che l'amore è l'esatto contrario e perciò ha una sola prerogativa: far perdere tempo.' (JG 90)

['Oh, aren't you an enemy of love?'
'Why would I be an enemy of love?'
'I don't know, everyone is an enemy of this word. They say that the Twentieth Century is a century of science, and they say that love has nothing to with science. Ivanoe maintains that love is exactly the opposite and therefore its only prerogative is to waste your time.']

Sapienza expresses a very similar criticism in *Il filo di mezzogiorno*, 'in questo secolo di religiosità scientifico-tecnica, l'emozione, l'amore, la scelta morale, la fedeltà e finanche la memoria cadono in sospetto di malattia' [in this century of technological and scientific religiosity, emotions, love, moral choice, loyalty and even memory are under suspicion of illness] (FM 60). In the separation realized by ideology between individual and collective good, emotions and rationality, Sapienza identifies a dead end of the left-wing struggle as she sees it conceived by her parents.

To her family's socialism, Goliarda prefers her uncle Nunzio's anarchist perspective, reflecting Stalin's radical distinction between socialism as founded on class and anarchism as founded on the individual:

The cornerstone of anarchism is the *individual*, whose emancipation, according to its tenets, is the principal condition for the emancipation of the masses. [...] The cornerstone of Marxism, however, is the masses, whose emancipation, according to its tenets, is the principal condition for the emancipation of the individual. [...] Clearly, we have here two principles, one negating the other.[39]

39   Joseph Stalin, 'Anarchism or Socialism?', in *Works, Vol. 1, December 1906–January 1907* (Moscow: Foreign Languages Publishing House, 1954), Marxist Internet Archive

However, anarchy, in Sapienza's narrative, is represented as having the potential to overcome the dichotomous opposition between individual and collective interest that is proper to Stalinist ideological thought. From the protagonist's perspective, anarchy does not need to split the individual between egoistic instincts and altruistic moral duty. Individual instincts, and specifically the feeling of love, offer a potential common ground on the basis of which social hierarchies and ultimately power can be challenged. In fact, love is the 'umanissimo bisogno che tutti ci accomuna, poveri, ricchi, fascisti e antifascisti e forse anche i reali' [very human need that brings us all together, poor, rich, fascists, antifascists and perhaps even royals] (JG 80). Whereas rationality is intrinsically separative – in categories, classes, parts of the self – bodily instincts, emotions and feelings offer resources to construct different, more authentic and therefore subversive relationships. The anarchist uncle Nunzio, who is not 'nemico dell'amore', suggests a materialist and anti-ideological political ideal, which does not repudiate the embodied singularity of individual existence and its fundamental needs.

Sapienza's exploration of the bonding potential of parts of the self and modalities of communication that are excluded by abstract rationality forms the constructive nucleus of her narrative. This perspective places Sapienza at the intersection of different strands of thought which share an interest in overcoming ideology, metaphysics and abstract rationality by rooting identity and communication in a bodily ontology. Sapienza's resistance against ideology can be productively read through Arendt's argument for the irreducible plurality of political subjects, whose individual uniqueness cannot be subsumed by universalizing ideologies.[40] A suggestion towards a joint reading of Sapienza and Arendt through the mediation of Cavarero has been firstly advanced by Anna Carta, who focuses on the relationship between life and narrative.[41] However, the points of contact between these authors from a political perspective still stand unaddressed. Sapienza's

---

(2008) <http://www.marxists.org/reference/archive/stalin/works/1906/12/x01. htm> [Accessed 22 August 2015].

40 See Arendt, *The Human Condition*.

41 Anna Carta, 'Finestre, porte, luoghi reali e spazi immaginari nell'opera di Goliarda Sapienza', in Providenti, *Quel sogno d'essere*, 261–76.

anarchist subject derives its rebellious strength and its communicative openness not from abstract rationality but rather from the re-integration of emotional components of the self into the subject. Beside the reading of Sapienza's representation of identity through Miller's and Winnicott's psychoanalytic perspective, parallels can also be drawn with the research carried out by Damasio from a neurological point of view and by Lakoff, Johnson and Turner in the field of cognitive studies. While Damasio questions the Cartesian split between rationality and emotions, phenomenological cognitivism looks at the rooting of thought and language in the material and dynamic dimension of the body. What these studies have in common is an attempt to recompose identity by reintegrating those elements of existence that are neglected or negated by abstract rationality.

A theoretical elaboration that is transversal to these studies and particularly congruent with Sapienza's narrative is Husserl's formulation of anarchy, insofar as it endeavours to place a theory of the subject at the foundation of his political perspective. Donnicci illustrates the fundamental connection sought for by the German philosopher between individual cognitive structures and collective political structures. Three points in particular place Sapienza within a conceptual frame that is close to the one employed by Husserl. The first is the attempt to enlarge the notion of rationality to include bodily impulses and desire within individual cognitive and ethical structures. While Husserl's initial project was aimed at grounding ethical values in the same scientific laws that were supposed to govern rationality, he ends up reshaping his notion of rationality according to the functioning of ethical values, which call vital impulses, emotions and positions into question. Instead of making ethics rational, he makes rationality ethical. Second, equipped with such an enlarged understanding of rationality, Husserl redefines intersubjective communication by founding it on empathy, which bonds together subjects who are at the same time irreducibly unique. What allows communication is not a shared and universal rational structure but a shared and universal condition of irreducible and corporeal individuality, known through the mechanism of analogy: 'The apperception of the other *as a living body* (Leib) that is *analogous to mine* takes place by attributing my sense of my own body to the other body, *by analogy*.' 'The recognition of the other as radically different from natural objects and analogous to my properties ultimately coincides with the awareness of the other as an end in itself.'⁴² The possibility of authentic human relationships is thus rooted in empathy, which recognizes the centrality of each subject. Finally, Husserl endorses an ideal of anarchist communism, but this must emerge as the result of an autonomous ethical transformation of all subjects. Communism, in Husserl's and Sapienza's view, cannot be imposed by institutional power and must be achieved through the progressive decline of any state authority, because it reflects the structure of empathetic relationships that are established by the transformed subject: 'The progress of ethical development must go together with a gradual decline in the power of the state.'⁴³ If political and social transformation is not founded on a transformed notion of the subject and human relationships, it necessarily replicates the system it is attempting to change. Specifically, power will change place and actors, but not structure. This happened, in Husserl's view, with Marxism and the Russian revolution, to which he addresses a criticism that is very much in tune with Sapienza's own approach to her parents' and her friends' ideological attitude.

The Outcast Hero

Sapienza, in a way that is ascribable to Husserl's phenomenological perspective, connects an enlarged notion of identity and communication with an anarchist political aspiration, which is the constructive nucleus of her narrative. Nevertheless, while in *Io, Jean Gabin* the criticism and deconstructive attitude endorsed by the protagonist against socialism is properly political, the same is not true of the constructive pole of anarchy. While for Husserl the ultimate horizon of individual emancipation is intrinsically collective, in *Io, Jean Gabin* Sapienza only marginally exploits the potentials of the empathetic subject to move beyond individualism and construct different types of human bonds. In other words, in *Io, Jean Gabin* there is no

42   Donnicci, *Intenzioni d'amore, di scienza e d'anarchia*, 292, 302. My emphasis.
43   Husserl, Hua XXVII, 58, cited in Donnicci, *Intenzioni d'amore, di scienza e d'anarchia*, 335.

positive investigation of the nexus between what the narrator calls 'love' and social transformation. Here, Sapienza's anarchy is rather connoted by individual resistance and does not seek to re-found social structures on a different basis, which is conversely crucial for Husserl's political perspective. The articulation of a constructive link between individual and collective emancipation remains unexplored potential, while the stress on individual difference occupies the foreground.

The second aspect of the protagonist's identification with Jean Gabin, the solitary hero, comes into play here. Indeed, on top of signifying a male identity, the French actor represents an individualistic and anarchist perspective, set against egalitarian commitment, as well as romantic imagination, opposed to mass conformism. The protagonist of *Io, Jean Gabin* does not only voice a polemical view against socialist ideology, but also against the 'bruttezza e crudeltà meschina della massa' [ugliness and vile cruelty of the masses] (JG 4). The despised mass includes the underprivileged class and the conformist middle class, which are both the target of sour expressionistic deformation, reminiscent of Emilio Gadda's satirical and contentious vein.[44] As regards the representation of sub-proletarian and working class, for example, Goliarda's friend Concetta is 'piccola deforme beghina' [small deformed bigot] and 'occhialuta' [bespectacled]; Concetta's mother, 'detta la Cagna' [called the Bitch], is 'scema' [dummy], and mother and daughter are both 'scimunite' [fool] (4–5). Peppino's study room is crowded with 'clienti cenciosi ma parati dignitosamente come per apparire a un funerale' [clients dressed in rags but embellished and dignified as if going to a funeral] (6), and the indigent people sitting in the cinema stalls are 'veri e propri animali che sputano in terra e in aria' [proper animals who spit on the floor and in the air] (76). The same grotesque tone characterizes the portraits of 'quei dolcissimi delinquenti falliti che mio padre ha sistemato' [those sweet failed delinquents who were helped by my father], such as Zoe, Tina 'la pazza' [crazy] and 'il commesso' [the errand boy], who eats raw onions and makes the house smell (77).

44   Here, I am thinking in particular of *L'Adalgisa. Disegni milanesi* (1944) and *La cognizione del dolore* (1963).

Even though the protagonist shares her parents' conviction that these classes should be offered opportunities of improvement, she is less certain that this can actually happen: 'è possibile che cambieranno? Non mi sembra possibile ma ognuno ha il suo sogno e io rispetto il sogno di mio padre' [Is it possible for them to change? It doesn't seem possible to me, but everyone has a dream and I respect my father's dream] (JG 76). Moreover, when discussing Maria's trust in the educational and emancipatory potential of cinema (something which we can assume to be a sensitive topic for Sapienza, considering her own involvement in Neo-realist film making),[45] the protagonist insinuates a criticism of the idea of progress as conformism that closely recalls Pasolini's critique of progress:[46]

> 'Il cinema col tempo diventerà un mezzo formidabile per diffondere cultura e pro-
> gresso, Goliarda ...' – queste, oramai l'avete capito, sono frasi di mia madre – 'cultura
> e progresso non ai soliti, pochi privilegiati, ma a masse intere di popolo.' In America
> sembra ci siano già sale da diecimila persone, incredibile! [...] diecimila persone che
> godono e si nutrono di cultura per uscire dallo stato di semibestie come queste qui
> sotto e mutarsi in cittadini modello con giacca stirata, camicia pulita e cravatta di
> seta! (JG 77)

> ['Someday, cinema will become a formidable means to spread culture and progress,
> Goliarda ...' – these are my mother's sentences, by now you recognize them, – 'cul-
> ture and progress not for the usual privileged few, but for whole masses of people.'
> Apparently in America there are already cinema theatres for ten thousand people,
> it's incredible! [...] ten thousand people who enjoy and feed themselves with cul-
> ture in order to leave behind their semi-animal state, like the ones below here, and
> metamorphose into model citizens with ironed jackets, clean shirts and silk ties!]

The reference to the US in relation to consumerism and conformism is not unique in the text. In the short chapter dedicated to her friend Jean,

---

45   For an account of Sapienza's work in cinema, see Emma Gobbato, 'Un primo piano di
      profilo', in Providenti, *Quel sogno d'essere*, 277–84; 'Goliarda Sapienza: The Unknown
      Scriptwriter', in Bazzoni, Bond and Wehling-Giorgi, *Goliarda Sapienza in Context*,
      75–86; Palieri, 'La Sapienza e lo scrivere'.
46   I am referring here in particular to Pier Paolo Pasolini's journalistic articles and short
      essays collected in *Lettere luterane. Il progresso come falso progresso* (1976) and *Scritti
      corsari* (1975).

in a dialogue between the two women set after World War II, the narrator
discusses the failure of 'il grande sogno americano' [the great American
dream], which has turned into brutal consumerism: 'Al posto di rari gruppi
d'ufficiali tedeschi compassati nelle loro divise, folle osannanti una libertà
magnereccia ora sguazzavano nell'oro calante del tramonto romano' [In
place of sporadic groups of German officials, all composed in their uni-
forms, there were crowds singing the praises of a succulent freedom and
wallowing in the declining gold of Rome's sunset] (JG 69).[47]

Sapienza's polemical attitude is also directed against the middle class,
and raises the problem of what kind of progress should be pursued. Yet,
well before the economic boom and the advent of mass consumerism, the
little protagonist rejects any complicity with the middle class, described as
conformist, bigoted and fascist, in this case perfectly in line with her family's
anti-institutional example. As in *Lettera aperta*, the privileged polemical
objective is the state school, where false fascist rhetoric fosters middle-class
conformist mentality and serves to maintain institutional power:

> 'Lascia i pallidi rampolli della borghesia come i Bruno e compagni baloccarsi e venire
> a patti con false idee, false parole, storia e avvenimenti storici travisati a comodo dal
> potere ... solo le date sono giuste ... e forse neanche quelle ... lascia ai Bruno quella
> brodaglia di cultura.' [...] Andate, andate a scuola, voi! Che altro potete fare se non
> trovarvi un piccolo o grande impiego statale dove ingrassare oscenamente in mezzo
> a tutti i parassiti, ladri legalizzati, dello stato fascista! (JG 18–19)

> ['Let the pale sons of the bourgeoisie, like the Brunos and their friends, play and
> agree with false ideas, words, history and historical events, distorted to serve the
> interests of power ... only the dates are right ... and perhaps not even those ... leave
> this slop of culture to the Brunos.' [...] Go, go to school! What else can you do, apart
> from finding a small or big state job, where you can grow obscenely fat among all the
> parasites, the legalized thieves of the fascist state!]

To middle-class rhetoric and conformist power, the protagonist opposes
Jean Gabin's romantic heroism, resorting to the identification with the

---

47   The economic boom that followed World War II inspires a similar expressionist pas-
      sage in FM 18–19. Sapienza will further develop this theme in the representation of
      Rome in CD (see Chapter 4).

French actor to perform the role of a proud solitary rebel. The isolation resulting from her conflicting relationship with society is endured thanks to the exaltation of a radically individualistic position: 'tutti d'accordo su una precisa breve frase: "sempre fuori da tutti i poteri costituiti", soli, ma con l'orgoglio di sapere la rettitudine che soltanto nell'outsider alligna' [we all agree on a short, precise sentence: 'always outside all established powers', alone, but proud to know the uprightness that you find only in an outsider] (JG 3).

Interestingly, in the incipit of the text the narrator uses the first person plural, 'noi ribelli' [we rebels] (JG 3), thus suggesting that, while positioning herself as an individualistic outsider, she is at the same time attempting to insert herself into a community of people who understand and share her values, namely the readers. A similarly sympathetic attitude towards the readers is also present in the episode in which the protagonist learns to walk, precisely the occasion that introduces her to power inequality, the falsification of the self and the duty to be strong. It is important to note here the continuity between the child's adoption of a virile, active and self-sufficient attitude, her troubles in establishing a communication with her context and the narrator's displacement of this communication towards the readers. The protagonist's disdainful and contemptuous individualism actually coexists with the research of other, different bonds, entrusted to the readers' solidarity. While the protagonist has an antagonistic relationship with society, a cooperative attitude is reserved for the readers, with whom the narrator constructs a dialogue that her protagonist finds impeded.

Art, Work, Money and Gifts

The relationship with the readers relates to the final point of Goliarda's identification with Jean Gabin, that is, the element of creativity and dream in relation to the protagonist's self-positioning as an artist. On top of being male and rebellious, Jean Gabin is also an actor, who represents the power of imagination against the constraints of reality. These constraints are on the one hand the moral duty of a political engagement ideologically conceived as conflicting with individual needs, and, on the other, mass conformism.

The element of imagination allows Sapienza to add one last perspective on the character's construction of identity and search for freedom, a perspective that is centred on the role of the artist. This aspect also constitutes an important innovation compared to previous texts, which did not achieve any positive definition of identity but rather aimed at liberating vital energies that were hidden beyond layers of inauthentic identity constructs.

The role of the artist is explored in *Io, Jean Gabin* as one that allows the protagonist to resist the duty of carrying out a useful job and reflect on the mediation with social conformism represented by money. Goliarda is urged on by her mother's teachings on the moral duty of social usefulness and economic self-sufficiency: 'Un individuo deve guadagnarsi da sé i soldi che gli abbisognano, altrimenti si diventa parassiti della società, che è come dire più vigliacchi dei vigliacchi' [An individual must provide for himself, otherwise you become a parasite of society, that is to say, more cowardly than the cowards] (JG 90). Indeed, the plot of *Io, Jean Gabin* is constructed around the protagonist's endeavour to earn some money, and such a task follows from her wrongdoing against members of the working class, as Maria stresses. In her wandering through the neighbourhood of the Civita and in her meetings with various characters, the child reflects on the means that are appropriate for earning money and the relationship between her 'profession', its social legitimacy and its acknowledgement in the form of money. It is not difficult to read here the expression of Sapienza's own concerns, for she had descended into poverty during the long time she spent writing *L'arte della gioia*, and her eccentric novel was then rejected by all publishers. In *Io, Jean Gabin* Sapienza voices the question of the tense relationship between artistic work and its economic dimension, which particularly preoccupied her in that period – and which ultimately resulted in her act of theft and her incarceration in Rebibbia.

While the child protagonist clearly has no problem with earning money through her artisan work in Insanguine's workshop, she is uncertain whether it is acceptable to receive financial compensation from the Brunos in exchange for her acting performances. After an initial agreement, in order to avoid compromising her artistic independence she returns the money given to her by the Brunos. The artist that the protagonist chooses to be is therefore in an antagonistic position towards the average and the common, represented by the Brunos, because 'solo l'eccezione entusiasma' [only the exception is exciting] (JG 80), and she lays claim to independence from the fulfilment of a duty. In other words, the protagonist interprets her creative activity as the expression of personal authenticity, to be preserved from any mystification and distortion that may be induced by compliance with social expectations. The protagonist's choice in favour of an antagonistic position is resolute and radical, expressed in a programmatic declaration of poetics:

> Quel sogno d''essere' era così coraggioso e libero che l'idea di andare a raccontare anche solo qualche pezzetto di quelle meraviglie a quei borghesucci del primo piano mi disgustò in tal modo da farmi fare quella che forse mi appariva come la prima vera presa di posizione verso la volgarità, la norma: non guadagnare riducendo il sogno a raccontino commerciabile, non accettare compromessi. (JG 93–4)

> [That dream of 'being' was so brave and free that the idea of telling even small bits of those marvels to those petty bourgeois on the first floor deeply disgusted me. So I made what seemed to me my first real choice against vulgarity and the norm: I would not earn money by reducing the dream to a marketable silly story. I would not accept compromises.]

There are two different artistic professions pursued by the protagonist, acting and writing. Through the figure of the 'child entertainer', acting is represented as the site of an impossible negotiation between personal expression and communication with the others. Differently from acting, the activity of writing gives free rein to the protagonist's imagination and suspends the sense of time and the moral duty of work and social usefulness. When she is busy writing in her notebook, 'il tempo si sfalda' [time flakes off] (JG 72). The same happens in Insanguine's workshop, reinforcing the similarity already suggested in *Lettera aperta* between writing and artisan work, both rooted in the *poiesis* which momentarily reunifies all the discordant tensions concerning identity and position: 'non si sentiva più né la fame né la sete, tutti i pensieri venivano afferrati in un'unica direzione, i sentimenti stralunati dai cento ritmi e voci e lamenti dei pupi immobili. Tutto si dimenticava ... anche Jean, e non dico poco' [you no longer felt hungry or thirsty; all thoughts were concentrated in a single direction, and feelings were stupefied by the hundred rhythms and voices and groans of the still puppets. You forgot everything ... even Jean, and this is no little thing'] (48).

The narrator explicitly poses the problem of a conflicting relationship between art and economic compensation, creative independence and material need for subsistence: 'Lascia perdere le parole, Goliarda, anche le più preziose non si possono mettere sotto i denti' [Forget words, Goliarda. Even the most precious ones, you can't eat them] (JG 30).[48] Yet, imagination is decidedly preferred, for it is the carrier of that strength, autonomy and authenticity that lies at the core of the protagonist's construction of identity and search for freedom. Albeit risky, 'non bisogna lasciare che la vita distrugga il sogno' [don't let life crush your dream] (30); 'tenersi stretti al sogno sempre, e sfidare anche la morte per non perderlo mai' [always hold on to your dream, and challenge even death so as not to lose it, ever] (75). Reversing conventional meaning, creative writing and imagination are described as having the role of producing a discourse that is truer than those supposedly founded on truth, namely ideology and social norms. While the middle class is permeated with rhetoric and lies, creative writing is characterized as the production of 'bugie' [lies] which turn into 'verità' [truth] as they give voice to other aspects of reality that are neglected or compressed in everyday life, which is governed by pragmatism, and in ideology, which is the expression of universal and abstract rationality. A dialogue between Goliarda and Jsaya clarifies the relationship between truth and lies, where imagination really is what Elio Franzini defines 'altra ragione' [other reason]:

> 'Non sei che una bugiarda, così bugiarda che forse sarai poeta.' [...]
> 'Ma io, professore, non dicevo bugie. Lei mi ha chiesto di raccontare e io ho cercato ...'
> 'Nel raccontare bisogna attenersi alla realtà! Che minchia mi frega a me del colore che aveva il sole al tramonto o il vento che spirava ... cose oscene e inutili che insoz- zano il mondo ... paesaggismo da quattro soldi! Va', almeno scrivile queste porcherie, che divengano bugie vere sulla carta ...' (JG 64)

48   See also: 'devo aver perso tutta la spinta su quel quaderno [...] di botto ti accorgi che sono passate ore e non hai fatto niente per la tua sussistenza' [I must have consumed all my energy on this notebook [...] suddenly you realize that hours have passed and you didn't do anything for your subsistence] (JG 72).

['You're just a liar, so much a liar that maybe you'll be a poet [...]'
'But professor, I didn't lie. You ask me to tell a story and I tried ...'
    'In telling a story you must stick to reality! What the fuck do I care about the
colour of the sun at sunset or the blowing wind ... disgusting and useless things that
besmirch the world ... cheap landscapes! Go and write this filth at least, so it can
become true lies on paper ...']

Sapienza's overturning of the relationship between truth and lies is very
important to all her narrative.[49] While the autobiographical texts claim the
right to lie, the overtly fictional novel *L'arte della gioia* is inaugurated by
the narrator's declaration of strict adherence to reality. In *Io, Jean Gabin*,
the opposition between lies and truth is related to the representational
relationship between discourse and reality. Imagination is not false, but
has a different relationship with reality, of which it allows perception of
hidden and deeper aspects. The idea of a special relationship between creative imagination and reality is suggested in the text through Maria's words.
In patent contradiction with the position held by Maria in the rest of the
text, on a single occasion she criticizes the limits of socialist revolution
and attributes a special status to the role of the artist. Even more interestingly, Maria establishes a connection between art and women, and charges
the Russian revolution with having failed to make space for such *different
discourses*: 'negano la causa della donna e dell'arte e in questa negazione
strangolano la rivoluzione' [they deny women's struggle and the importance
of the arts, and with this denial they strangle the revolution] (JG 39). The
judgement expressed by Maria recalls Husserl's critique of Bolshevik communism, in that the Russian revolution is said to rest on the same conceptual
structures that it questions. Conversely, art and women would constitute
two elements of deep discontinuity with the social and discursive order to
be dismantled. If social change is not grounded in a transformation of the
relationship between the sexes and a transformation of human relationships, based on a different understanding of the components of the self, it
is doomed to fail – and create oppression on its way to failure.

49   Bond analyses extensively the twist of values between truth and lies in *Il filo di mez-
     zogiorno* from a psychoanalytic perspective. See Bond, 'Zeno's Unstable Legacy'.

A final consideration concerns the role of dependence on others in relation to the need for money. The protagonist's search for money ends with her acceptance of a donation from her anarchist uncle Nunzio, which she had conversely rejected from the 'capitalist' uncle Giovanni and from the 'bourgeois' Brunos. Similarly, in the analectic chapter dedicated to her friendship with Jean, the adult Goliarda allows Jean to pay for her drink in a café. In this episode, the narrator comments on the legitimacy of depending on others: 'Jean paga per me la consumazione da Doney. Come allora non ho il becco di un quattrino e lei ha sempre un pezzo di pane o una manciata di zucchero da mettermi in bocca ... l'amore è anche questo, saper accettare di essere nutriti senza sentirsi umiliati' [Jean pays for my order at Doney's. As in the past, I'm flat broke, and she always has a piece of bread or a handful of sugar to feed me ... love is also this, accepting to be fed without feeling humiliated] (JG 70) While with her family she had to conform to their expectations in order to obtain care – 'fui scaraventata giù nel pavimento a guadagnarmi il pane col sudore della mia fronte ...' [I was cast down onto the floor to earn my daily bread by the sweat of my brow] (61) – her relationship with Jean comprises an element of 'free' love and care, of which the donation of money is an expression. Once again, Sapienza destabilizes images and meanings, so that money is here not the unacceptable medium of social conformism, but rather the manifestation of love, according to the logic of the gift that replaces the one of economic exchange. Unlike her dependence on her family, her dependence on Jean is not perceived as falsifying and oppressive. What has changed in the meantime is Goliarda's fierce rejection of any sort of compromise, so that she is open to accept what comes from the others without falling into subservience to their expectations, an approach that recalls Modesta's entrustment to Nina's caring attitude in *L'arte della gioia*.

In conclusion, the protagonist's choice to be a writer appears to be her strongest answer to the problem of constructing personal identity and positioning herself in society. Freedom is characterized as the possibility of being loved independently of the accomplishment of a task and of the adjustment of personal identity to obtain love or money, as in Goliarda's friendship with Jean. The *dover essere* established by Maria is turned by Goliarda into the active 'dream of being', which she pursues through artistic creation. Whereas in the imitation of a male role she came across a falsifying stereotype, in the role

of the artist she finds a form of freedom, although it is an ambivalent one:
'è stato faticoso ma ora è bello saper usare le proprie gambe e andare dove si
vuole' [It's been hard, but now I enjoy being able to use my legs and go wher-
ever I want] (JG 62). The possibility of communication with society, which
the protagonist finds impeded, is searched for by the narrator through the
literary text. For the protagonist of *Io, Jean Gabin*, artistic creation implies
the rejection of a dialogue played out on a level that is perceived to be distorting, and opens up the possibility of experiencing personal authenticity
and momentary reconciliation of inner conflicts, even though for the real
author such an identity remains unavoidably suspended between reality and
fiction, rooted in a *mise en abyme* of the artistic creation.

Wandering Away from the Past

Central Plot and Wandering Thoughts

After the fictional journey of *L'arte della gioia*, in *Io, Jean Gabin* Sapienza
goes back to the autobiographical genre, although in a form that is strongly
contaminated with fiction. This work, set in the same years as *Lettera aperta*,
presents a distinct departure from Sapienza's previous writings, in terms of
narrative structure and relationship between past and present. Compared
to the fragmented and centrifugal structure of *Lettera aperta* and *Il filo
di mezzogiorno*, a central plot with a chronological development emerges
in *Io, Jean Gabin*. The child's task to find some money, concentrated in a
compact and intelligible unity of space and time, provides the *fil rouge* of
the narration. The central story covers a period of a few days, marked by a
succession of meals and sleep. However, in quantitative terms the central
and chronological story covers only a limited portion of the text. Several
episodes from other periods of time (some preceding the events of the story,
others following it, others situated in a non-specified temporal location),
interfere with the linearity and cohesiveness of the central plot. Moreover, the
narrator repeatedly interrupts the story with extra-diegetic remarks, usually

motivated by elements of the plot but neither functional to its development nor strictly constrained by criteria of relevance. Sapienza often uses the text as a space in which to freely develop and link her wandering thoughts, not a stream of consciousness per se but, rather, the expression of juxtaposed ideas and episodes. Between stream of consciousness and this other discursive structure, which I term 'wandering thinking', there is no qualitative difference – both in fact follow a free association of ideas and images – but rather a difference in intensity, as Sapienza's wandering thinking lacks aim and organization, but not intelligibility. It is a technique that allows the narrator to address topics she cares about (politics, the arts, society etc.), without the constraint of relevance for the plot or the organization of such topics into narrative form. An analogous mechanism governs many of the dialogues in *L'arte della gioia*, and *Lettera aperta* also features a similar use of wandering thoughts, in particular in the essayistic reflections that were partially excluded from the edited work, even though the majority of the text is subject to a much more radical and intense fragmentation. Even though in quantitative terms the central plot takes less narrative space than that dedicated to digressions, the very presence of a distinction between foreground and background distinguishes *Io, Jean Gabin* from the radically disrupted narrative of *Lettera aperta* and *Il filo di mezzogiorno*.

Overall, *Io, Jean Gabin* presents similar structural features to previous texts, but manipulation of the narrative discourse is realized to a lesser extent, so that the disorientating effects produced by *Lettera aperta*, *Il filo di mezzogiorno* and *L'arte della gioia* are here mitigated. What remains unaltered throughout all the works, and characterizes the later prison diptych as well, is the attention paid by Sapienza to the sensorial dimension of the voice, the expression of an embodied and relational approach to language. We hear, for example, Licia's 'voce delicata' [delicate voice] (JG 7), Ivanoe's 'voce cullante' [soothing voice] (8), but also his 'dura voce lombarda' [hard Lombard voice] (43); the 'curva armoniosa' [harmonious curve] of Maria's voice (12); Peppino's 'bella voce fonda' [beautiful deep voice] (58); Carlo's 'canti ora lenti ora cullanti, ora alti e argentini come il rincorrersi dei ciottoli smossi dalla risacca' [singing voice, slow and soothing at times, or high and silvery like clashing pebbles in the undertow] (36); and, when Nica speaks, we hear 'la dolcezza di quelle sillabe scivolanti nel sangue' [the sweetness of those syllables, flowing through our veins] (44). As in *Lettera aperta* and *L'arte della gioia*, the characters are mainly present on the scene through their voices, and the memory of their opinions and teachings is never detached from their actual words. For Sapienza, remembering figures from the past always coincides with listening to their voices: 'Sento ancora la mia vocina di un tempo belante come una pecora' [I can still hear my past little voice, bleating like a sheep] (56) and Jsaya's voice shouts 'all'orecchio della mente' [into my mind's ear] (56).

The theatrical setting, connected to the prevalence of voices and oral speech, is further reinforced in the characterization of the readers as a collective audience, to which the narrator addresses her speech. The narrator refers directly to them and to her own act of narrating: 'Avete sentito che voce decisa?' [Did you hear this strong voice?] (JG 45); 'Già, non ve l'avevo detto' [That's true, I didn't tell you] (89); "'Allora, carusa, oramai p'aviri l'unuri d'avirti tocca aspettare c'hai la febbre?" [...] È Nunzio, ormai lo conoscete, questo è il bello di parlare a vecchi amici, non c'è bisogno di spiegare troppo, di raccontare tutto da capo' ['So, *carusa, oramai p'aviri l'unuri d'avirti tocca aspettare c'hai la febbre?*'[50] [...] This is Nunzio speaking, at this point you must know him – this is what I like about speaking to old friends: I don't need to explain too much, or to tell everything again from the beginning] (89). The configuration of narrative as oral speech is analogous to the one highlighted in previous writings, with the readers present in the same space of the narrator's. The tendency of Sapienza's works towards theatrical and vocal discourse finds here further confirmation. However, in contrast to previous texts, in *Io, Jean Gabin* the readers are not invited to play any active role in the narrative discourse. Here, narrator and readers do not actually interact beyond the appeals mentioned above, which then appear more like residual markers of a performance, ultimately inessential to the development of the narration. Nonetheless, the readers have become, in *Io, Jean Gabin*, the narrator's elective company, a sympathetic circle of friends, distinguished from the rest of conformist society which the rebellious protagonist fiercely opposes and despises.

50   'So, girl, shall we wait for you to be ill to have the privilege of seeing you these days?'.

Goodbye, Childhood

The greatest difference between *Io, Jean Gabin* and Sapienza's previous works, however, concerns the narrator's relationship with her past. Indeed, here the points of view of adult and child remain clearly distinct, as do the different spatio-temporal domains where narrator and protagonist reside. Unlike in *Lettera aperta* and *Il filo di mezzogiorno*, the protagonist's formative process is represented as lying in the past and it no longer involves the narrator. We have seen that *Lettera aperta* and *Il filo di mezzogiorno* are structured as a twofold discourse, with one focus on the recollected past and the other on the narrator's present. They are active, performative texts, which stage a dialogue and a relationship of mutual influence between the two narrative spaces. The adult narrator intensely identifies with the young protagonist, and even blends her point of view with the child's. The same structure features in *L'arte della gioia*, where the narrator places herself in the middle of the developing present. Conversely, in *Io, Jean Gabin* the narrator's present plays a marginal role, and the narrative discourse remains almost constantly focused on the recollection of the past. In terms of linguistic markers of time, past and present tenses alternate, but the alternation happens with much less frequency and, overall, the past is by far the more prevalent tense. The narrator does not dialogue with her past, for the act of recollecting and narrating does not affect her present any longer.

The evolution of Sapienza's works recalls Virginia Woolf's considerations on the role that writing *To the Lighthouse* (1927) had in her relationship with her own past – and with her mother in particular:

> When it was written, I ceased to be obsessed by my mother. I no longer hear her voice; I do not see her. I suppose that I did for myself what psycho-analysts do for their patients. I expressed some very long felt and deeply felt emotion. And in expressing it I explained it and then it laid to rest.[51]

---

51   Virginia Woolf, *Moments of Being*, ed. Jeanne Schulkind (London: Chatto & Windus for Sussex University Press, 1986), 81. Hernández suggests a parallel between Sapienza and Woolf in 'Orlando and Modesta: Two Voices for the Freedom of Women', in Bazzoni, Bond and Wehling-Giorgi, *Goliarda Sapienza in Context*, 115–27.

The only occasion in *Io, Jean Gabin* where the voices of the narrator and the characters are actually blended, thus recalling the performative structure and present *in fieri* of previous works, concerns, quite paradoxically, a passage that states the utter separation of the present from a concluded, already determined and exhausted past:

> Rassicurandomi con la mano della presenza delle due lire dimenticate nel fondo della tasca, filo via in cerca della mia vita. Ma io l'ho vissuta già la mia vita, penso, almeno tre quattro volte! E per quanto faccia, per quanta volontà, intelligenza, fantasia sprigioni intorno a me per incanalarla e sottometterla al mio volere, mi si delinea davanti quell'unico teorema possibile che è il risultato di mia madre, mio padre, mio zio, i miei fratelli eccetera. Risultato matematico o destino, essa è lì e io ci giro intorno come un asino bendato intorno alla macina. Asino o non asino, con scatto agile salto sul tram che mi porterà lontano. (JG 104)

> [Making sure with my hand that those two liras are in the bottom of my pocket, I run away in search of my life. But, I think, I've already lived my life, at least three or four times! And whatever I do, whatever strength, intelligence, imagination I display in order to channel life and subdue it to my will, I have in front of me the only possible theorem that is the result of my mother, my father, my uncle, my brothers etcetera. Mathematical result or destiny, it is there, and I keep circling around it like a blindfolded donkey going around the millstone. Donkey or not, with a rapid movement I jump on the tram that will take me far away.]

The passage above is strikingly ambiguous. Not only do child's and adult's perspectives conflate and merge in the subject of the expression, 'l'ho già vissuta la mia vita', but its definitive stance is also immediately contradicted by the plurality expressed by the clause 'almeno tre quattro volte'. Moreover, whilst the narrator would be doomed to keep re-enacting the same destiny, 'come un asino bendato intorno alla macina', the child protagonist contradicts the circular repetition by affirming her vital action, marked by a linear movement: 'con scatto agile salto sul tram che mi porterà lontano'.

Despite the intricate relationship between present and past featured in this passage, in the rest of the work such a relationship is actually quite straightforward. Even though the present is acknowledged as the product of the past, the narrator looks at her past as a closed and stable set of memories. Past and present are finally separated. Narration does not have the creative, assertive and performative power with which it was bestowed in *Lettera aperta* and *Il filo di mezzogiorno*, but functions as a means of recollection of a past that is over. In other words, *Io, Jean Gabin* departs from the formative and performative tension of previous works, for the narrator is no longer asking the act of remembering and narrating to act upon her present life.

Strengthened by her conquered identity of an anarchist artist, the narrator stands at a safe distance from her past. Originating in the crossing of textual and experiential layers of reality, such an identity is precisely what Sapienza created through her previous 'performances', namely the identity of the artist, the storyteller, at the margins of society (in Sapienza's self-representation) and determined to use such a position as a space enabling personal freedom. It is from this space that the narrator of *Io, Jean Gabin* tells the story of her own evolution towards it. Therefore, the character's formative experience does not proceed in parallel with the narrator's own path of personal reconstruction, as it did in *Lettera aperta* and *Il filo di mezziogiorno*, but rather is recollected from a concluded, resolved point of observation. Pellegrino convincingly argues:

> *Io, Jean Gabin* integrates *Lettera aperta*. [...] But it concludes Goliarda Sapienza's autobiographical cycle. The girl who walks hand in hand with the bandit of the *Casbah*, through the streets and the people of her beloved and terrible neighbourhood, is no longer the same as the one in *Lettera aperta*. Now she is the *tosta carusa*, the tough girl of *L'arte della gioia*.[52]

The difference between *Io, Jean Gabin* and Sapienza's previous works is connected to the position she has achieved in society as an artist, a writer, a storyteller – an identity she had been looking for in and through writing. With all the problems annexed to the coincidence of the outcome of the protagonist's formative process with her assumption of the identity of storyteller, such a 'conclusion' is achieved and can provide the starting point of *Io, Jean Gabin*, this time in concordance with Brook's reflections on the necessity of the end for narration to begin. Since she already knows the outcome of her search for identity, narration can depart from

52   Pellegrino, 'Postfazione', in JG 123.

the concern with the formative process itself. Indeed, after *Io, Jean Gabin* Sapienza moves away from the recollection of her childhood to delve into the exploration of her present, and from an endeavour of self-reflection and self-reconstruction to a gaze predominantly focused on external reality.

Liberated from the effort to master the present by re-traversing the past, the narrator of *Io, Jean Gabin* constructs a text that constitutes a direct and ironic response to her own search for identity in *Lettera aperta* and *Il filo di mezzogiorno*. Parents are mostly ignored, sexuality and male violence largely removed, the oppressive features of the construction of the female role in a patriarchal society are neutralized through the assumption of a male identity, and the duty of social usefulness is discarded in favour of a proudly oppositional anarchism. Nonetheless, beyond the joyful and ironic tone, the fascination and depth of the text – and of Sapienza's literary production more broadly – lies in its ambiguity between the evolution attained and the ongoing presence of knots of anxiety, between having put the past 'to rest' and having put it 'between brackets'. At the same time, the narrator appears to be able to detach herself from her past, without re-experiencing its painful and upsetting features. The decision to ignore the troubles involved in the construction of identity (and its future descent into depression and loss of self) is exhibited as a deliberate act. She cannot change the conditions that constituted her upbringing and led to mental illness, for these belong to a concluded past. She then moves away from that reality and delves into autofiction, at the same time pointing to the limits of fiction itself by occasionally allowing the reality of material oppression and childhood troubles to surface. Although closely interconnected with the other works, *Io, Jean Gabin* also constitutes an *unicum*, as the text is no longer a space of interaction with the past but a space of playful experimentation, as Sapienza creates here the child she never was. And yet, the apparent fiction of *Io, Jean Gabin* has behind it, and beneath it, the journey into the past carried out in *Lettera aperta* and *Il filo di mezzogiorno* and the desire for self-creation voiced in *L'arte della gioia*. Treading this fragile line, *Io, Jean Gabin* constructs its narrative play of staged identities and bodily desires, recounted by a narrator whose achieved identity coincides with that of an anarchist artist, marked by precariousness and marginality.

Both regressive and evolutionary tendencies are present in Sapienza's works, and this is one of the many aspects of her narrative that require the critic to select what to emphasize. This analysis has focused extensively on elements of discontinuity, showing how Sapienza's works bear the trace of the healing process performed through writing, especially with respect to narrative structures. Clearly, another approach, which stresses the persistence of knots of anxiety, repressed rather than resolved issues, and the recurrence of the same obsessions, is certainly legitimate. For example, Emma Bond's analysis of *Il filo di mezzogiorno* pursues this direction. Discussing the fictional nature of the relationship between narrator and therapist staged in this work, and drawing parallels with *La coscienza di Zeno* (1923) by Svevo and *Il male oscuro* (1964) by Giuseppe Berto, Bond describes these authors' use of 'curative narrative' as an improper substitute for analytic therapy. Since the relationship with the therapist is, ultimately, fictional, narration, instead of curing, would actually provide the writer with the possibility of re-enacting defence mechanisms. Where Bond's analysis is very productive and insightful into the complex relationship between narrative, fiction and cure in *Il filo di mezzogiorno*, overall Sapienza's writings maintain a performative power that exceeds fiction and escapes the re-enactment of similar dynamics. It takes *L'arte della gioia*, with its overt fictionality, to take the decisive step towards narrative evolution. Thereafter, the emergence in *Io, Jean Gabin* of a – limited and fragile – central narrative, the detachment of the present from the past, the replacement of a generic and overwhelming task (to understand who she is) with a specific and achievable task (to find some money), and the side-lining of the parental figures are all elements that can be interpreted as markers of fruition. Her subsequent production, focused on the narrator's present and mainly concerned with other characters, rather than with processes of identity formation, confirms such a shift in her narrative.

A final, essential consideration must be made, concerning the qualification of the type of identity and maturation at play in Sapienza's works. To say that through her writing Sapienza constructs her own identity and can therefore depart from the investigation of her past does not imply that her formative process as an adult comes to an end. As we have exhaustively explored regarding *L'arte della gioia*, identity, in the context of Sapienza's work, should not be equated with a fixed and stable set of characteristics and a fixed and stable way to inhabit the world. Quite the opposite; the type of identity Sapienza looks for throughout her narrative is configured as an open self, sustained by its constantly renovated contact with the vitality of a living body and therefore subject to continuous evolution and change. Cavarero's words can once again provide useful insights into the type of identity represented by Sapienza's works:

> A relational and exposed identity, immersed in the flow of life and by definition unmasterable, cannot give origin to the life story of a self whose identity is character-ized as *simple* and the coherent development of an immutable substance. Instead, the unity of the self lies in the becoming through time of a unique existence, which, by continuing to manifest itself, becomes a story; in other words, it is the configuring of a unique self through time.[53]

Sapienza's narrative of self-construction, rich in counter-movements and contradictory undercurrents, follows a path that takes it from a painful exploration of the past in order to make life possible in the present, to a liberation of desires and imagination in fictional stories. The identity of the anarchist artist, whose orientating values lie in the auscultation of bodily instincts and the rejection of any form of imposition, allows her to make space for continuous self-renovation, which closely recalls Bono and Fortini's definition of the 'romanzo del divenire'. The titles of Sapienza's last published works, with their allusion to a formative experience (*L'università di Rebibbia*) and to the impossibility of a perspective that is rigid and definitive (*Le certezze del dubbio*), express well the openness of identity proposed by Sapienza. Ultimately, the subject emerging from Sapienza's literary production reflects the relationship that, to quote Maraini's fit-ting description, she always entertained with the world, a relationship 'da zingara e girovaga' – a joyful 'wandering nomad'.[54]

---

53   Cavarero, *Tu che mi guardi*, 96.
54   Maraini, 'Ricordo di Goliarda Sapienza', in LA 9–11, 11.

Speaking from the Margins: *L'università di Rebibbia* and *Le certezze del dubbio*

Introduction

On 4 October 1980, Sapienza was arrested for theft and incarcerated in Rebibbia prison, in Rome, where she spent five days.[1] In *L'università di Rebibbia*, published by Rizzoli in 1983, Sapienza provides a fictionalized account of her experience in prison, giving voice to other inmates and their stories. *Le certezze del dubbio*, published by Pellicanolibri in 1987, is the sequel to *L'università di Rebibbia*. It recounts Sapienza's friendship with some ex-convicts she met in Rebibbia, and in particular her love and attraction for Roberta, a young terrorist, heroin addict and social activist who had spent most of her adult life in and out of prison. These novels, the last ones published by Sapienza during her life, are closely interconnected and can be fruitfully described as a 'prison diptych', as both focus on prison, marginality, and the stories of the women Sapienza met there. However, while *L'università di Rebibbia* centres on the protagonist's experience of being detained and on the representation of the prison environment and its inhabitants, in *Le certezze del dubbio* the focus shifts towards the intimate, erotic and densely ambiguous relationship between Sapienza and Roberta, with the recollection of prison and the reality of urban marginalization as the story's background. Critical readings thus far have privileged a focus on the theme of prison and marginalization, which certainly provides a productive key for looking at

---

1   Providenti, *La porta è aperta*, 160. Sapienza narrates her experience as if it lasted a few months, which misled several reviewers and critics about the actual length of her detention.

these novels together; however, this focus needs to be complemented by reserving a specific space for the main theme of *Le certezze del dubbio* – the relationship of attraction and care between Sapienza and Roberta.

L'università di Rebibbia and *Le certezze del dubbio* stand in a relationship of continuity with Sapienza's previous works, but they also present significant developments. Featuring a combination of autobiography and fiction, they reconnect to the autobiographical project carried out in *Lettera aperta*, *Il filo di mezzogiorno* and *Io, Jean Gabin*, of which they constitute the final episode. They also share a number of common themes with these works, as well as with *L'arte della gioia*, such as the investigation of the relationship between individual freedom, community and society; marginality, especially in relation to women; sexuality in its various forms, including a variety of sexual orientations, identities and incest dynamics; the prominence of the corporeal dimension of experience and relationality; and a formative tension, connected to a socially and politically committed view of literary communication. On the other hand, these novels represent a turning point compared to Sapienza's previous production, as the main focus changes from the recollection of the past to the narration of the present, and from the narrator's own search for identity to the representation of the reality surrounding her.

Even though about thirty years have passed since the first publication of *L'università di Rebibbia* and *Le certezze del dubbio*, criticism on these novels is still very limited. While *L'università di Rebibbia* generated some interest at the time of its publication, especially in connection with the 'scandal' of a relatively well-known intellectual being convicted of theft, and as a documentary testimony of a female prison, *Le certezze del dubbio* went almost unnoticed and has remained so up to today. Recent critical interventions on Sapienza's prison diptych include Giulia Bicchietti's and Andrigo's essays, which focus mainly on the works' formal and stylistic features and consider these novels as the most mature results in the evolution of Sapienza's writing towards clarity and objectivity.[2] Clotilde Barbarulli reflects on the role of the body in

2   Giulia Bicchietti, 'Esperienze dal carcere', in Providenti, *Quel sogno d'essere*, 181–90; Andrigo, 'L'evoluzione autobiografica di Goliarda Sapienza', and 'Goliarda Sapienza's Permanent Autobiography', in Bazzoni, Bond and Wehling-Giorgi, *Goliarda Sapienza in Context*, 17–31.

establishing empathetic relationships and relates *L'università di Rebibbia* to feminist discourses on the body, human interactions and community.[3] Ross is the only critic to focus specifically on *Le certezze del dubbio*, which she reads from the perspective of queer theory, evidencing the contradictions inherent in Sapienza's depiction of sexual desire, both in this novel and in her previous autobiographical works.[4] Finally, two recent interventions open up a comparative perspective on these novels. Bond develops a parallel reading of *L'università di Rebibbia* and Joan Henry's *Who Lie in Gaol*, focusing on the role of shame and affect in the narrators' relation to the prison community,[5] while Maria Morelli investigates conformist and subversive expressions of gender and sexuality in *L'università di Rebibbia* (and, marginally, in *Le certezze del dubbio*) and Maraini's *Memorie di una ladra*.[6] Another important source when analysing these novels is represented by Sapienza's own accounts of her experience as provided in letters, diaries and interviews, and her interview with Enzo Biagi, which distils her vision of prison as a space of both regression and vitality.[7]

A first way of approaching these novels is to focus on the representation of prison as an institution. In this respect, it is particularly productive to read them together with an analysis of the female inmates' testimonies developed in *Recluse*, where *L'università di Rebibbia* itself is cited as an 'extraordinary book' that convincingly describes 'this universe of people oppressed by *moral* crimes.'[8] Reading them in parallel in this way reveals the punctual correspondence of

3   Clotilde Barbarulli, 'Essere o avere il corpo. "L'università di Rebibbia"', in Farnetti, *Appassionata Sapienza*, 132–47.
4   Ross, 'Eccentric Interruptions' and 'Identità di genere e sessualità'.
5   Bond, '"A World without Men": Interaffectivity and the Function of Shame in the Prison Writings of Goliarda Sapienza and Joan Henry', in Bazzoni, Bond and Wehling-Giorgi, *Goliarda Sapienza in Context*, 101–14.
6   Maria Morelli, '"L'acqua in gabbia": The Heterotopic Space of the (Female) Prison in Goliarda Sapienza's and Dacia Maraini's Narratives', in Bazzoni, Bond and Wehling-Giorgi, *Goliarda Sapienza in Context*, 199–214.
7   Enzo Biagi, *Film Story: la giustizia*, 1983. Part of the episode is available on YouTube <https://www.youtube.com/watch?v=ojXxjHr6MU0> [Accessed 11 August 2016].
8   Franco Corleone, 'Postfazione. Quali garanzie e diritti nel carcere femminile', in Susanna Ronconi and Grazia Zuffa, eds, *Recluse. Lo sguardo della differenza femminile sul carcere* (Rome: Ediesse, 2014), 263–72, 267.

scenes, stories, dynamics and themes. Most importantly, it shows two key points
of contact. First, there is a convergence in method, based on giving voice to
women themselves by way of interviews in the case of *Recluse* and long reported
dialogues in *L'università di Rebibbia* and *Le certezze del dubbio*. Second, it also
reveals a convergence in their political approach, which aims at restoring the
inmates' agency by highlighting both the negative, degrading, infantilizing and
depersonalizing features of prison, and the practices of resistance and resilience
adopted by the inmates to transform their experience of detention into a positive opportunity. In a mosaic of scenes, dialogues, stories and reflections, the
narrator conveys the rich complexity of the condition of being imprisoned,
its themes, ambivalence, protagonists and relation with the outside world.
A second approach focuses on the representation of the problems affecting
society outside the carceral institution. Narrating her experience in prison is
an opportunity for Sapienza to reflect on society at large. She criticizes social
conformism, individualism, and the marginalization of the most vulnerable
sections of society; this criticism goes hand-in-hand with her scrutiny of the
failure of left-wing discourses and ideologies. She responds to this failure with
a political engagement that is much more defined and proactive compared
to that of previous works, as its foundation lies in elements of civic and social
activism, feminism and anarchist thought. Finally, a third way of reading these
novels is to focus on the protagonist's own experience, investigating the role
and meaning attributed to prison within her existential path and, interlaced
with that, the role and meaning of narrating prison within her artistic path.
Sapienza's experience is indeed in no way typical of that of most inmates –
she is imprisoned only for a few days, she comes from an economically and
intellectually privileged background, and, above all, she approaches detention
as an adventure full of regenerative potential. The theme of Sapienza's own
experience provides the thread that links *L'università di Rebibbia* to *Le certezze
del dubbio* and the relationship with Roberta narrated there.

A common element to the various aspects analysed in this chapter –
prison, criticism of modern society, Sapienza's vital journey and love relationship with Roberta – is represented by the body: the perceptive and
phenomenological body of the protagonist, the bodies of the other inmates,
and their relationship of mutual and mimetic affection. The centrality of
the body pertains to the modalities of narration, with the prevalence of

voices and gazes and the emphasis on the sensorial domain, heightened by the enclosed space of the prison and the narrator's emotive involvement. But the body is also itself a theme of the novels, as a sexed, relational and imprisoned body, which Sapienza puts back in the centre of individual and collective existence. We shall see that Sapienza's discourse on prison and social conformism has some important points of connection with Foucault's most renowned work on the subject, *Discipline and Punish*.[9] Yet, Sapienza goes beyond Foucault in representing the body as a situated, active and relational force, and not as a 'docile',[10] disciplined and anonymous object of power. This perspective distances her narrative from post-structuralist thought and brings it close to the political thought of Arendt and Cavarero, as well as to the work of scholars, jurists and activists currently engaged in promoting ideals and practices of correctional justice, thus contributing to the advancement of our understanding of these issues.

The Ambivalence of Prison between Regression and Resistance

Regression and Degradation

L'università di Rebibbia and *Le certezze del dubbio* combine the story of Sapienza's own experience, a portrait of the prison institution and a wider reflection on modern society, its dynamics and its margins. While the author's own experience is a positive and vital response to the challenges posed by her incarceration, the meaning of prison within her own existential path never overwhelms her ability to record and give voice to the reality of prison itself, with its positive potential but also its degrading, tragic aspects. The representation of prison interweaves with the narrator's reflections on her own condition and with a number of episodes that see

9   Foucault, *Discipline and Punish: The Birth of the Prison*, trans. Alan Sheridan, 2nd edn (New York: Vintage Books, 1995).
10   Ibid. 135.

her as the protagonist, but also with her observations on the functioning
of the institution and its inhabitants' stories and tales, which overall take
up most of the narration. The result is the travel or ethnographic narrative of a 'sconosciutissimo pianeta' [totally unknown planet] (UR 690),
of which the narrator progressively becomes an inhabitant. In line with
Sapienza's approach to identity and power highlighted in previous works,
these novels expose the constraints and oppression exerted by power on
the subject, here observable in its most explicit form. However, instead of
resulting in a tale of victimhood and 'panoptic' control (to cite Foucault's
well-known definition of the total institution),[11] Sapienza's works explore
the subjects' active and rebellious responses to their condition. While still
stressing the dehumanizing mechanisms of prison, she gives space to the
prisoners' voices and practices of resistance and resilience.

In *L'università di Rebibbia* and *Le certezze del dubbio*, prison is an ambivalent space: on the one hand, it is characterized by regression and degradation, to the point of assuming infernal traits; on the other, it is a protected
environment, which enables empathetic communication and individual
recognition, which contrast with the mass conformism, individualism and
depersonalization of modern society. As such, prison is not only an experience
of suffering and penance, but also an opportunity for regeneration. As Maria
Luisa Boccia points out about female inmates, 'women themselves have an
ambivalent view of their condition. On the one hand, they are aware of the
infantilized state in which they live, and they are clear about it; on the other
hand, detention is a turning point that can represent an *opportunity*'.[12] Let
us start by looking at the unequivocally negative aspects of prison as portrayed in *L'università di Rebibbia* and *Le certezze del dubbio*. First, prison is
described as an infantilizing space: 'il carcere regredisce all'infanzia' [prison
makes you regress to childhood] (UR 35). Sapienza observes such a regression in the inmates' behaviour, especially in the repeated manifestations of
hysterical laughing: 'Come può una battuta così sciocca provocare in loro

---

11   Foucault, *Discipline and Punish*, 195.
12   Maria Luisa Boccia, in 'Il filo della differenza, fra il "dentro" e il "fuori". Conversazione
      fra Maria Luisa Boccia, Susanna Ronconi, Grazia Zuffa', in Ronconi and Zuffa,
      Recluse, 239–61, 256.

contorsioni e boccacce bambinesche? Anche quelle vecchie donne in quel quadrato cintato di reti ricadono nell'infanzia più ebete' [How can such a silly joke spark contortions and childlike grimaces on their faces? Inside that fenced square, even those old women fall into the most idiotic childhood] (38). In *Le certezze del dubbio*, Roberta, who spent many years in prison, also bursts into similarly uncontrolled laughter: 'sghignazza proprio come là a Rebibbia quando il *fou rire* tipico della regressione coatta all'infanzia ci afferrava' [she sneers just like there, in Rebibbia, when the *fou rire* typical of the forced regression to childhood seized us] (CD 127). Regression is expressed also through recurring comparisons to school, which involve the space of the prison, 'uno stanzone [...] che ha l'aria famigliare di un'aula di scuola comunale' [a large room [...] that has the familiar look of a classroom in a local school] (UR 40); the female guards, 'bidelle di scuola elementare' [primary school janitors] (UR 8); the warden Santomauro, 'come a scuola, nessuno osa parlare davanti alla maestra' [just like in school, nobody dares to speak in front of the teacher] (108); the prisoners' attitude, 'Come a scuola quel bailamme non finirà più a meno che non intervenga una bidella' [like in school, that din will not stop unless a janitor intervenes] (39); and the narrator's own perception that 'come allora, nel primo giorno di scuola, sto cadendo in preda alla sensazione panica di dover entrare in un luogo misterioso e potente del quale non so niente, e dove niente ormai dipenderà più dalla mia volontà' [like then, on my first day of school, I'm falling prey to the irrational feeling of having to enter a mysterious and powerful place, about which I know nothing, and where nothing will depend on my will anymore] (9).

Prison induces a regression to childhood by taking away the prisoners' autonomy and forcing them into a state of complete dependence on others, which achieves the opposite effect to that of a responsible participation in society. It is 'a sort of reiterated infantilization, a dependence on others' actions and will, which brings with it the paradoxical outcome of a constant tendency to induced passivity'.[13] The language of the institution plays an important role in this process, as the infantilization of prisoners translates

13   Ronconi and Zuffa, *Recluse*, 45.

into a childlike language, 'well exemplified by the procedure of the famous "teeny question".[14] Sapienza notes the role of language, with its widespread use of childish diminutives, in enforcing regression: 'Domandina, educatore, guardiana, spesina … La riforma carceraria ha dato un tono di grazia infantile al suo linguaggio' [teeny question, educator, guard, just a bit of shopping … The prison reform gave its language a tone of child-like graciousness] (UR 118). Another way in which prison infantilizes the inmates is by excluding them from handling money: 'la detenuta non ha il diritto di toccare più la moneta che, come sappiamo, è simbolo d'autonomia, identità, misura del tuo valore e del tuo posto nella società. Un'altra spinta per farti regredire nell'infanzia coatta' [the detainee is no longer allowed to handle money, which, as we know, is a symbol of autonomy, identity, the measure of your worth and of your place in society. It's another push to make you regress to enforced childhood] (77). The issue of money is an opportunity for Sapienza to reflect on the specificity of the female experience of prison and its continuity with the patriarchal system. If prison is intrinsically paternalistic, it is even more so in relation to women, who at least since Aristotle have been portrayed by patriarchal discourses as passive and weak subjects, in need of guidance and protection. Sapienza notes how the infantilization that is forced on women by the carceral institution through the ban on money is just the continuation of their usual condition:

> donna di casa o bambina, come volete, alla quale è sempre stato evitato di avere – attraverso i soldi guadagnati e poi spesi – contatto diretto con la realtà del mondo. Se per l'uomo è punizione, per la donna non è nemmeno questo, solo un mantenerla ancora nella condizione di ignavia e di ignoranza di tutti i problemi che essere un cittadino comporta. (UR 77)[15]

> [housewife or girl, as you please, who has never been allowed to have direct contact with the world by earning and spending money. If for men it's a punishment, for women it's not even that, it's just maintaining condition of passivity and her ignorance of all the problems that being a citizen entails.]

14   Ronconi and Zuffa, *Recluse*, 219.
15   See also Roberta's discourse on the continuity between prison and women's role in patriarchal societies, UR 176–7.

There is thus an insidious continuity between prison and patriarchy, which makes women's regression more acute and subtler at the same time:

> Female infantilization [...] tends to be read as an intrinsic feature of women, connected to their 'fragility'. [...] With the result that women are more at risk of 'losing themselves': on the one hand, the institutional mechanisms of reduction of women to a minority/infantilized/passive status are less readable. On the other, paternalism can more easily be exercised on women.[16]

In this respect, it is relevant to note that the idea of correctional prison – as opposed to punitive imprisonment – was first conceived in relation to women and minors, and only subsequently applied to adult men, reinforcing the idea of prison as a paternalistic institution that serves to educate a minor subject.[17]

Insofar as it imposes a minority status on women, prison is represented as the expression of male domination. While female guards are described by Sapienza as humane and sympathetic, the carceral institution is seen as being governed by, and the emanation of, a distinctively male power. The *carabinieri* who take Sapienza to prison in the opening scene of the novel cause her to feel deep 'paura della loro forza fisica' [fear of their physical strength] and 'terrore d'essere fra uomini ostili' [the terror of being among hostile men] (UR 8); later in the novel, she observes: 'lì dentro si perde l'abitudine quotidiana al maschio, la sua assenza fisica ingigantisce la sua immagine, mitizza la sua forza' [in prison you're no longer used to male presence, his absence magnifies his image, mythologizes his strength] (180). As Bond notes, 'the physicality of male bodies seems only to communicate a potential menace'.[18] Indeed, when a revolt explodes, the female guards retreat and in their place male guards intervene to suppress the revolt with the use of violence. As noted in *Recluse*, 'When the relational approach

---

16   Ronconi and Zuffa, *Recluse*, 220.
17   See Esther Heffernan, 'Gendered Perceptions of Dangerous and Dependent Women: "Gun Molls" and "Fallen Women"', in Barbara H. Zaitzow and Jim Thomas, eds, *Women in Prison. Gender and Social Control* (Boulder, CO and London: Lynne Rienner Publishers, 2003), 39–64.
18   Bond, 'A World without Men', 105.

does not work as a governing strategy, at some point they call the male guards, who "put things right"; that is how it works in the sections, if conflict explodes, the men come."[19] While the female 'governing strategy' is described as relational, the carceral institution is seen as the ultimate expression of male power, exerted through the use of force and violence and in continuity with the patriarchal imposition of a minority status on women.

In addition to regression, Sapienza also represents a process of human degradation that takes place in prison, which she expresses for example through the widespread use of animal metaphors. These occur in reference to smell, 'acre lezzo stagnante di gabbia dei leoni' [acrid stench of a lion cage] (UR 153); voices, 'muggiti' [moos] (54); 'un ennesimo grido inarticolato' [another inarticulate cry] (76); the physical location of the cells, 'giaciglio di un animale' [animal's bedding] (54); and the prisoners themselves, 'un branco di scimmie in piena foresta' [a troop of monkeys deep in the forest] (160), 'qualche viandante o cane randagio che vaga ancora senza pace' [a traveller or stray dog who still wanders restlessly] (111). Human degradation reaches its peak in the portrayal of prison as an inferno, pervaded by the looming lure of death. The path that takes Sapienza inside the prison is depicted as an infernal *catabasis*, where the detainee's former identity is progressively lost:

> Questi camminamenti d'immersione alla pena sono di una perfezione gelida. [...] si scende ancora, si scende sempre. A ogni passo senti che vai verso il basso e che non potrai più tornare a essere come prima. Quei camminamenti sotterranei parlano di morte e conducono a tombe. Infatti, per la legge dell'uomo un tuo modo di essere è stato cassato, [...]: quella che eri prima è morta civilmente per sempre. (UR 9–10)

> [These paths that lead into the depths of punishment are of an icy perfection. [...] You are descending further, you are always descending. With each step, you feel that you're going down and that you will never be able to go back to what you were. Those underground passages speak of death and lead to tombs. In fact, by law of man your way of being has been crossed out, [...]: the person you were before is dead to society forever.]

19   Ronconi, in 'Il filo della differenza', 252.

Sapienza provides an impassioned and detailed description of the degrading practices, what Foucault terms the 'micro-physics of power',[20] that introduce the convict to the world of prison upon her arrival. She describes the ritual of assuming a squatting position while totally naked, carried out to check for 'la droga, potrei averne nascosta nella vagina' [drugs – I could have some hidden inside my vagina] (UR 8). She goes on to depict the prison environment, the squalor of her first cell in solitary confinement, a smelly blanket, a window that is too high up and narrow to see outside, but with a handle that suggests suicidal thoughts: 'la prima cosa che vedi appesa a quel manico è la tua testa penzoloni' [the first thing you see hanging from that handle is your head, dangling] (14). Similarly she describes a voice shouting in the dark, 'M'ammazzo, voglio uscire!' [I'm going to kill myself, I want to get out!] (13). This is a path of 'autodegradazione' [self-degradation] (10), which for some women, particularly those least equipped with personal and social resources, leads to depression and self-annihilation, as Sapienza can observe in many women around her: 'donne e donne buttate sui letti, immobili' [women, many of them, lying on their beds, still] (73). The brief and sporadic encounters with the outside world that take place in the meeting room only reinforce the feeling of shame that infiltrates the prisoner, and the sense of having fallen into a condition like death: 'una porzione di morte viene qui distribuita, a chi poche gocce come a me, a chi per la vita, per venti anni, per dieci. [...] Molti visitatori infatti hanno l'espressione indescrivibile di chi conversa con un malato condannato da una malattia senza speranza' [a portion of death is distributed here: some only get a few drops, like me, others get a whole life, twenty years, ten. [...] In fact, many visitors have the indescribable expression of those who are speaking to a sick person, doomed by a hopeless disease] (67).

In this respect, Sapienza's work recalls Primo Levi's ethnological approach in *Se questo è un uomo* (1947). Recounting his experience in the Nazi concentration camp of Auschwitz, Levi focuses on the dehumanizing mechanisms of the Lager and the prisoners' different reactions to that condition of extreme human degradation, which range from cruelty and

20   Foucault, *Discipline and Punish*, 26.

annihilation to solidarity and ingenuousness. However, although the commonality of approach and theme with *Se questo è un uomo* is evident, most notably in the description of a process of de-humanization and in the recurring use of animal metaphors, Sapienza never explicitly refers to Levi's work. In this way, she reconnects to Levi's ethnographic and witnessing project, at the same time avoiding to reduce the distance that separates the radical horror of the concentration camp and her experience in a modern prison.

School or University? Ambivalence of the Carceral Institution

Amidst the challenges posed by the carceral condition, Sapienza also gives space to positive elements, which are rooted not so much in the institution itself as in the women's responses to it. Human relationships are truly at the centre of Sapienza's prison world, and they represent the main source of vitality in this otherwise infernal space. They are relationships of care and solidarity, often shaped according to a maternal or familial pattern, as for example that between Marrò and Annunciazione, who 'si fa chiamare mamma e le fa la spremuta' [is called mom by Marrò, and makes orange juice for her] (UR 87). As the authors of *Recluse* note, 'among the strategies of "resistance", the maternal element stands out, which [...] also gives shape to the relationships between women inside prison. [...] To create "a family home", offering warmth, protection and safety, is a way to fight against the degradation and depersonalization of prison.'[21] Moreover, inmates also develop relationships founded on intellectual exchange, as in the group of women who gather in Susie Wong's cell. It is here that Sapienza discovers a new world, where people of different ages and backgrounds interact in a way she had never experienced before (and that she will discover again in the meeting of a group of activists narrated in *Le certezze del dubbio*). It is 'un ambiente vivificante di scambi mentali e meditazioni' [an enlivening environment of intellectual exchange and meditation] (104), where conversations about politics, sex and love flourish freely, recalling, as Barbarulli

21   Ronconi and Zuffa, *Recluse*, 32.

points out, the feminist practice of 'autocoscienza' [self-awareness].[22] Sapienza's description of relationality has a parallel in what is observed in *Recluse*, pointing out not only the aspect of resistance, which is a static strategy, but also a component of resilience, which entails a proactive and transformative attitude:

> Relationships among women represent an exceptionally important factor of affective and psychological endurance, and often evolution, development and learning. [...] These friendships also represent unusual encounters, across different generations, cultures and social backgrounds. [...] They soothe loneliness and allow narratives which liberate experiences and feelings and lead to self-reflection.[23]

As Bond illustrates, drawing on a fitting combination of phenomenological and queer theories of 'affect', human relationships are characterized by the 'interpersonal traffic of emotions and their bodily expressions',[24] which in prison, due to the circumscribed space and interconnectedness of prisoners' lives, are particularly heightened. This leads to a warm sense of safety and solidarity, with inmates feeling and depending on each other's emotions in a way that allows them to act as one, harmonic organism. The narration in both novels takes note of gazes, voices, expressions, gestures, and even minimal bodily movements, in an orchestration of corporeal actions and reactions: 'appena ho cominciato a riascoltarle, le loro presenze fisiche ed emotive si rifanno vive con movimenti e sguardi' [as soon as I started listening to them again, their physical and emotive presence came back to life through movements and gazes] (CD 88). Sapienza explains this interconnectedness of an affective community as a form of mystical punctuality:

---

22 See Barbarulli, 'Essere o avere il corpo', 141.
23 Ronconi and Zuffa, *Recluse*, 100–1.
24 Bond, 'A World without Men', 101. Bond refers to Sarah Ahmed, *The Cultural Politics of Emotions* (New York: Routledge, 2004); Melissa Gregg and Gregory J. Seigworth, eds, *The Affect Theory Reader* (Durham, NC and London: Duke University Press, 2010); and Eve Kosofsky Sedgwick, *Touching Feeling: Affect, Pedagogy, Performativity* (Durham, NC: Duke University Press, 2003).

In quel posto [in carcere] c'è un'altra puntualità non temporale ma interna, rispondente alle esigenze emotive e spirituali delle compagne: quando spegnere la propria luce se l'altra ha troppo sonno, non fare raffreddare il caffè che l'altra gentilmente t'ha preparato, eccetera. Puntualità mistica che probabilmente muoveva i gesti dei frati. (CD 54)

[In prison, there is a different punctuality, not temporal but internal, which responds to the emotive and spiritual needs of your mates: when to turn off the light if she is too tired, not to let the coffee get cold when she kindly prepared it for you, and so on. Mystical punctuality that probably used to coordinate friars' movements.]

This inter-corporeal empathetic communication is defined by Sapienza as the *linguaggio primo* [*primary language*] (UR 130), which binds together all members of a community through the shared materiality of the body, beyond social differences: 'linguaggio profondo e semplice delle emozioni, così che lingue, dialetti, diversità di classe e di educazione sono spazzati via come inutili mascherature dei veri moventi (ed esigenze) del profondo' [profound and simple language of emotions, so that languages, dialects, class and education differences are swept away like useless masks covering our true inner reasons (and needs)] (129–30). The *linguaggio primo* of emotions is the most important and enriching 'lesson' that can be learnt in prison, turning detention into a transformative 'university'.

The constant empathetic communication and mutual influence has, however, also more worrying aspects, as individual will is constantly at risk of dissolving into an uncontrollable collective energy, which Sapienza describes as a 'centrifuga alimentata dalle radiazioni energetiche di cento corpi esasperati' [centrifuge fuelled by the energy radiated by a hundred bodies] (UR 75). When in the last section of *L'università di Rebibbia* a revolt explodes, for example, despite her best intentions not to get involved Sapienza falls prey to the 'insana logica della centrifuga' [insane logic of the centrifuge] and finds herself caught 'fra spinte e grida a urlare' [between pushes and cries, shouting] (186). The prison world is 'a collective well, with behaviours, gestures, smells, sadness, jealousy, neurosis: because bodies, especially when locked in prison, are heavy.'[25] It is constantly on the edge

---

25   Barbarulli, 'Essere o avere il corpo', 142.

of excessive emotions, which can suddenly shift from joy and laughter to aggressiveness or desperation. As the authors of *Recluse* describe it, emotions in prison are governed by 'a micro-physics of words, signals, movements and actions that [...] create and radiate tension and anxiety, or on the contrary create a calm and friendly environment'.[26] It is a world of excess, where all prisoners' emotions are interwoven and intensified by the compressed space of the prison.

The role of the community is similarly ambivalent. On the one hand, in Sapienza's view the existence in prison of a close-knit community is what makes it a vital and enriching environment, in contrast to the desolate atomization and conformism of modern society. Within the prison community, the individual, who in the outside world is isolated and marginalized, finds a form of recognition, a role. As Roberta explains to Sapienza, 'Si torna a vivere in una piccola collettività dove le tue azioni sono seguite, approvate se sei nel giusto, insomma riconosciute. Tutte capiscono perfettamente chi sei – e tu lo senti – in poche parole non sei sola come fuori ...' [you go back to living in a small community where people observe your actions, approving of them when you're in the right, recognizing them, in other words. Everyone understands perfectly who you are – and you feel it – in a word, you're not lonely like outside] (UR 194–5). However, such a recognized role, exercised in a sort of pre-modern community, can also be limiting, as it does not comprise evolution nor make space for individual initiative – it is, indeed, a fixed role. As Fred Albort explains, the prison community is 'something closer to a primitive society';[27] a definition that resonates with Sapienza's own description of prison as 'un villaggio primitivo' [a primitive village][28] and a 'regno degli archetipi eterni' [reign of eternal archetypes] (168), where 'ogni iniziativa personale viene punita come il delitto più efferato' [any personal initiative is punished like the most heinous crime] (167). Instead

26   Ronconi and Zuffa, *Recluse*, 77.

27   C. Fred Alford, 'What Would It Matter If Everything Foucault Said About Prison Were Wrong? *Discipline and Punish* After Twenty Years', *Theory and Society*, 29 (2000), 125–46, 132.

28   Sapienza, interview with Grazia Centola, 'Orrore e fascinazione di Rebibbia', *Il Manifesto*, 15 February 1983, cited in Barbarulli, 'Essere o avere il corpo', 139.

of leaving all social masks behind, as the *linguaggio primo* promises, each member of the community is also constantly pushed into a more restrictive and fixed role: 'non c'è scampo neppure in galera dalla atroce condanna di dover sempre a ogni cantone prendere un partito (degli altri), una posizione, una maschera, eccetera, eccetera: infernale! [there's no escape, not even in jail, from the atrocious sentence of always having to take (someone else's) side, a position, a mask, etcetera, at every step: infernal!] (71). The protective, womb-like condition of the affective community, is reversed into an infernal, tomb-like one, where the prisoner is trapped in a timeless, archetypical and unidimensional role.[29] As a nameless prisoner puts it, 'Non c'è redenzione in questo luogo' [there's no redemption in this place] (187).

Only in Susie Wong's elitist circle does Sapienza seem to find a micro-community that does not crush individuality but rather fosters enriching relationships, and it is indeed here that the idea of Rebibbia as a university comes into play. The notion of the university, which features in the title, draws attention to the aspect of existential education that can take place in prison, where the atomized individual of modern society can apprehend the *linguaggio primo* of empathetic and caring relationships. Viviana Rosaria Cinquemani points out that Sapienza's positive view of her interpersonal experience in Rebibbia prison is clear in the title, although the text also contains a strong criticism of the Italian penitentiary system.[30] In this sense, the notion of a university can be read in contrast to that of the school, which conversely represents the regressive and infantilizing feature of the carceral institution. The university of the inmates, with its empathetic language, battles against the infantilizing school of the institution. Moreover, this places the university against those exclusively negative views of prison that would reinforce the depiction of women as passive victims, as Roberta claims: 'Non c'è libro di donna, o conferenza o altro che non sia una mera enumerazione di

29   On the womb-like feature of prison and the threat it poses to individuality, see also Morelli, 'L'acqua in gabbia', 203.
30   See Viviana Rosaria Cinquemani, 'Da *Lettera aperta* a *Le certezze del dubbio*: la voce autobiografica di Goliarda Sapienza', *Revista Internacional de Culturas & Literaturas*, 2015 <http://www.escritorasyescrituras.com/da-lettera-aperta-a-le-certezze-del-dubbio-la-voce-autobiografica-di-goliarda-sapienza/> [Accessed 11 August 2016].

rimostranze, torti subiti ... Ma questo nel nostro caso è scartato già nell'idea di parlare di Rebibbia come di una università, invece che di un luogo di sole sofferenze' [there's no book by a woman, nor a conference or anything else that is more than a mere list of grievances, injustices suffered ... But in our case, this is rejected in the very idea of talking about Rebibbia as a university instead of as a place only of suffering] (UR 139). However, the possibility of experiencing prison as a 'higher education' clearly depends on the women's own resources – class, education, and interpersonal skills, which women in Susie Wong's circle possess in abundance. Without these resources, the *linguaggio primo* of emotions is always at risk of morphing into inarticulate cries, the university regresses to a school, and the affective community becomes an immobile, infernal village.

Institutional Syndrome: destini coatti

The ambivalent characterization of the prison environment is at the centre of Sapienza's reflection on institutional syndrome. In *L'università di Rebibbia* and *Le certezze del dubbio*, Sapienza is particularly interested in the problematics of institutionalization, linked to her interest in the mechanisms of repetition compulsion. Throughout her whole corpus, Sapienza shows a fascination with the idea of repetition compulsion, how it can be challenged, and how conversely it can become an ineluctable destiny. *Destino coatto* [Compulsory Destiny] is the title of her collection of short stories, which portray several characters who are trapped in their obsessions, representing forms of inescapable 'compulsory destinies'. Sapienza is enormously attracted to the ambivalent space of prison – a womb, a tomb – as a space that is at once limiting and protective, vital and infantilizing. In the destiny of the other prisoners, this psychoanalytic interest in repetition compulsion also comes to coincide with a sociological and political interest in institutional syndrome, which is a result of the ineffectuality of prison – 'the failure of the prison', in Foucault's terms.[31]

---

31   Foucault, *Discipline and Punish*, 265.

The very structure of the prison, both in its infantilizing and protective features, is at high risk of producing recidivism rather than effective rehabilitation, an aspect that Sapienza emphasizes both in relation to the other characters and herself. In fact, detention is founded on a contradiction that both her writing and the prisoners identify clearly, the paradox of attempting to educate people into freedom and responsibility through captivity and infantilization. It is 'the paradox of detention to produce reintegration'.[32] In the expressive words offered by two inmates who are interviewed in *Recluse*, 'how can you rehabilitate me, if you keep me locked in my cell all day staring at the ceiling?';[33] 'They say that "prison rehabilitates", but what? when I get out of here – excuse my language – I'm fucked'.[34] Prison isolates convicts from society, making their position even more marginalized and precarious, and creates a subject who is thus dependent rather than empowered. At the same time, prison is a protected environment that shields the prisoner from the challenges of society. Furthermore, once the convict has gone through her first 'prison education', prison is no longer an unknown threat, but a world where she has learnt to live. Prison becomes a reassuring and even exciting opportunity, set against the lack of support and individualism that dominate outside society, where the ex-inmates would occupy a marginal and anonymous place. Most of the prisoners Sapienza meets keep going in and out of detention, having lost – or having never had – the ability to lead a satisfactory life outside, and conversely having adjusted successfully to their life inside.

The tension between desire for freedom and addiction to prison is neatly captured in the words of Marrò, 'delinquente abituale' [habitual delinquent] (UR 91): 'Da quando avevo sedici anni è che me bevono e me sputano. [...] Ho la vita che me s'è cambiata in altalena ... ma non me dispiace proprio ... Quando ero apprendista parrucchiera la noia me se magnava tutta ... [...] Voglio usci'!... Voglio usci'!... Voglio usci'!...' [Ever since I was sixteen they keep drinking me down and spitting me back out. [...] My life has turned into a swing ... but it's not like I'm sorry ... when I was training

32   Ronconi and Zuffa, *Recluse*, 13.
33   Ibid. 83.
34   Ibid. 83.

as a hairdresser I was consumed with boredom ... [...] I want to get out!...
I want to get out!... I want to get out!...] (113). Similarly, Marrò recounts
how Annunciazione keeps going in and out of prison in a repetitive cycle of
desire to get out and desire to return (121). And it is of course Roberta, the
co-protagonist of *Le certezze del dubbio*, who represents the most dramatic
example of 'affezione carceraria' [institutional syndrome] (194). Her case
differs significantly from those of Marrò and Annunciazione in that she
is educated, politicized, and can rely on the support of a social network
outside; however, she has been in and out of prison since she was a teenager
and has come to consider prison her home. She rationalizes her existential
condition, defined by an addiction to prison as well as to heroin, capturing
the ambivalence of the carceral institution as a protective community that
is set against the loneliness of her life outside:

> Vedi, qui la giornata è così piena di avvenimenti che alla fine diviene come una
> droga ... [...] Anch'io adesso fremo tanto d'uscire perché è un anno che sono dentro,
> ma dopo due o tre mesi di libertà nell'anonimato – libertà che ha il solo vantaggio
> d'esser lasciati a morire soli – so che mi riprenderà il desiderio di qui. Non c'è vita
> senza collettività ... (UR 194–5)

> [You see, here the day is so full of events that in the end it becomes like an addition ...
> [...] Now I'm yearning to get out because I've been inside for a year, but after two or
> three months of freedom in anonymity – a freedom whose only advantage is letting
> you die alone – I know that the desire to come back here will seize me again. There's
> no life outside of community ...]

Prison, like heroin, paradoxically becomes a liberating escape from a reality in which Roberta cannot live: 'Nessuno può dare quella sensazione di
liberazione che si prova al momento che ti "chiudono" fuori dalla società e
da te stesso' [nobody can explain that sense of liberation that you feel when
they 'lock' you out of society and out of yourself] (CD 136–7). Sapienza
thus foregrounds addiction to prison to stress both the failure of the carceral
institution in rehabilitating inmates and, at the same time, the problems of
modern society – individualism and conformism, to which prison paradoxically constitutes an alternative. Ultimately, Sapienza acknowledges
women's strength and their creative response to the prison environment,
and she highlights the positive aspects of relationality and solidarity that

248 CHAPTER 4

take place there. All the same, the overall portrait of the institution is one of tragic failure – and this is a failure that calls into question the broader problem of the relationship between prison and society.

Prison and Society: Subversion, Mirroring and Margins

Subversion and Urban Inferno

What is the relationship between society and prison in Sapienza's novels? A first way in which Sapienza articulates this relationship is by portraying prison as a space of resistance against the ills of modern society. She sets the prison's affective community against the isolation, solipsism and divisions that reign outside:

> Sono da così poco sfuggita dall'immensa colonia penale che vige fuori, ergastolo sociale distribuito nelle rigide sezioni delle professioni, del ceto, dell'età, che questo improvviso poter essere insieme – cittadine di tutti gli stati sociali, cultura, nazionalità – non può non apparirmi una libertà pazzesca, impensata. (UR 103)

> [Because I have escaped so recently from the immense penal colony that is in force outside, a social life sentence distributed into strict categories of profession, class, and age, this sudden possibility of being together – citizens of all social classes, cultures, nationalities – can't help but look to me like an incredible, unexpected freedom.]

With her usual taste for paradox and provocation, Sapienza affirms that prison is dominated by 'la regola della fantasia, della sperimentazione e dell'azzardo' [the rule of imagination, experimentation and chance] and the 'libertà di inventarsi la vita' [freedom to invent your life] (UR 163). Women in Susie Wong's circle exchange conversations with a passion and freedom that are 'impensabili per chi è abituato alla distrazione e al sordo mutismo senza speranza degli intellettuali, fuori nel mondo cosiddetto libero' [unthinkable for someone who is used to the intellectuals' hopeless distraction and deaf muteness, outside in the so-called free world] (125). For Sapienza, this freedom to experiment with human exchanges across social differences and generations is 'l'unico potenziale rivoluzionario che ancora soprav-vive all'appiattimento e alla banalizzazione quasi totale che trionfa fuori' [the only revolutionary potential still standing amidst the almost complete homologation and banality that dominate outside] (103–4). Prison would not only be a space of resistance and resilience but also subversion of the reality outside. As Bond puts it, reporting Davies' reflections on prison and linking them to Bakhtin's carnivalesque subversion, 'it is precisely the fact that prison is removed from everyday culture that can allow it to become a space of creative potential'.[35]

In this respect, Sapienza's view of prison as a space of unexpected encounters and experiences differs significantly from Foucault's under-standing of a pervasive 'panoptic' power and of a subject that is utterly constituted by it. As several critics have pointed out, Foucault's view of the panoptic prison – that is, an institution that disciplines every single aspect of the inmates' life, soul and body, and that uses intimate knowledge of the 'delinquent' to exert complete control on him/her (what Foucault terms 'power-knowledge') – leaves no space for individuality, agency or rebellion, as all subjects are equally and uniformly constituted by a faceless and time-less power. As C. Fred Alford observes, for example, Foucault 'mistakes the utopian discourse of prison reform for its practice',[36] thus missing out on any possibility of subjectivity that can arise in the folds of power, thanks to the novelty and uniqueness that each individual brings into the world, to use Arendt's concept. Whereas Arendt 'retain[s] a conception of individu-ality capable of being endangered',[37] Foucault's notion of panoptic power leads to 'a distinctly ambiguous position on the possibility and means of

---

35   Bond, 'A World without Men', 112. See Ioan Davies, *Writers in Prison* (Oxford: Basil Blackwell, 1990).

36   Alford, 'What Would It Matter If Everything Foucault Said About Prison Were Wrong?', 134.

37   Ibid. 135. Alford refers in particular to Hannah Arendt, *The Origins of Totalitarianism*, 3rd edn (London: Allen & Unwin, 1967), and *The Human Condition*.

emancipation'.[38] In contrast to Foucault's view, and much closer to Arendt's, Sapienza narrates her subjective experience of prison, and gives space to prisoners' own experiences; this is in itself a way of resisting the totalizing and silencing aspects of discourses that consider individual subjectivity as irrelevant or actually non-existing beyond its social constitution. On different occasions, this practice of 'giving voice' allows subjects to talk back and challenge dominant discourses that see them only in the position of silent objects. For example, when Sapienza, looking for empathetic communication, inadvertently imitates Giovannella's Roman dialect, which is here a marker of underprivileged class belonging, the girl stops her, reclaiming the reality of class difference that Sapienza's approach sought to mystify (UR 43). Similarly, Marrò proudly reclaims her story against the version spread by newspapers that depicted her as a rape victim, while she actually managed to fight and escape (122).

Sapienza's approach is thus founded on reporting subjects' own words, and her broader aim is that of challenging a unilateral view of prison, which itself reinforces the actual oppression of the carceral institution by silencing the prisoners' subjective responses to it. This approach is integral to the project of *Recluse*, where the investigation of the reality of a women's prison is based on giving voice to the prisoners' personal experiences. As we read in *Recluse*, the authors choose 'to let women talk about their experiences [...] to fully regain possession of their subjectivity'.[39] Likewise, Sapienza's narration restores the prisoners' agency – precisely what prison takes away from them – and challenges the common view that sees them exclusively as passive victims. As Susanna Ronconi notes, 'whenever women are given the possibility of talking [...] new perspectives emerge, which differ from a certain representation of women in prison as victims'.[40] To give women the possibility of talking about their experiences is a way to highlight the 'difference between the way in which they talk about themselves and how

38   F. Driver, 'Power, Space and the Body: A Critical Assessment of Foucault's *Discipline and Punish*', *Environment and Planning D: Society and Space*, 3 (1985), 425–46, 438.
39   Ronconi and Zuffa, *Recluse*, 18.
40   Ronconi, in 'Il filo della differenza', 241.

they are represented'.[41] We see then how Sapienza's choice to construct a nuanced narrative which also features positive elements is not only the result of her personal – and rather unusual – experience of prison as a vital journey, but also the attempt to render the manifold and ambivalent aspects of the carceral institution, including the unexpected resources and forms of resistance and subversion that inmates are able to create.

While Sapienza sees in the space of prison a possibility of resistance and even subversion, her criticism of modern society as itself constituting a prison is very much in tune with Foucault's. She describes society as a carceral environment, an 'immensa colonia penale' [immense penal colony][42] and 'ergastolo sociale' [social life sentence] (UR 103), which closely recall Foucault's notion of a 'carceral archipelago'[43] – no longer the explicit dictatorship of fascist, Nazi or communist regimes, but the insidious totalitarianism of pseudo-democratic capitalism. In *Le certezze del dubbio*, Sapienza provides a hallucinatory and expressionistic depiction of the urban inferno of the city of Rome, which mirrors the infernal condition of the prisoners in Rebibbia. City dwellers are 'ergastolan[i] della metropoli' [metropolis lifers] (103) and are compared to animals who wander around the city like lost, dying creatures: 'un bestiario esotico ora sonnolento, ora agitato da sbandamenti inesplicabili come quelli che s'impossessano di un branco sperduto in una foresta' [a herd of exotic, sleepy animals, suddenly agitated by inexplicable staggering movements, like those that seize a flock lost in the forest] (CD 114–15); 'Teorie di animali antidiluviani in fila si trascinano fingendosi giovanissimi ma sostenendosi a vicenda come veri e propri morituri' [Trajectories of antediluvian animals, dragging themselves in a line, pretending to be young, but hanging on each other like the dying] (118).

Roberta takes Sapienza to new peripheral neighbourhoods and old ghettos, in a crescendo of alienation and degradation, often under the

---

41   Boccia, in 'Il filo della differenza', 240.
42   The expression 'colonia penale' recalls the title of a short story by Franz Kafka, 'Nella colonia penale', in Kafka, *Racconti* (Milan: Mondadori, 1970). The same expression is also in CD 102.
43   Foucault, *Discipline and Punish*, 298.

CHAPTER 4

sinister and spectral light of the moon. The city itself is transfigured into an infernal animal creature, explicitly linked to a prison: 'Il grande carcere intorno a me mugghia furioso come un bisonte insofferente dei tracciati coatti delle strade' [the big prison around me roars like a buffalo impatient at the forced layout of the streets] (CD 176). The hallucinatory depiction of Rome reflects the narrator's feverish state – she is falling in love, and is often drunk – but also expresses a distorted reality, which is the effect of the human and environmental degradation brought about by modernity. The infernal urban prison is exemplified by the image of the pines trapped in concrete, under a sinister moonlight: 'Una luna immensa, indolente mi fissa sardonica dalle grandi finestre che danno su un mare di pini sempre agitati [...] nella loro prigione di cemento ... presto anche quei pini saranno spazzati via dall'esercito di cemento che li assedia da tutte le parti' [A giant, indolent moon stares at me sardonically through the large windows that look onto a sea of pines, restless [...] in their concrete prison ... soon, these pines too will be swept away by the army of concrete that besieges them from all sides] (15). So-called free society is nothing but another prison, inhabited by 'poveri esseri assediati' [poor besieged beings] whose life is just 'una guerra atroce già perduta in partenza' [an atrocious war, already lost as soon as it has begun] (107). Sapienza's negative view of modern society recalls Pier Paolo Pasolini's criticism of the anthropological destruction carried out by the 'false progress' of capitalism,[44] and the inferno of modern life through a hallucinatory and distorted picture of the city and its inhabitants can also be associated closely with Pier Vittorio Tondelli's work. It resonates in particular with his narration of marginality – including homosexuality, drug addiction and urban degradation – in *Altri libertini* (1980). Even though Sapienza evidently belongs to an entirely different generation and cultural background, her novels are nonetheless fully immersed in the problems of the present and provide a rich portrait of life at the margins in Italian society of the 1980s, capturing the same sense of anxiety and degradation through a feverish and expressionistic narration that is also in Tondelli's work.

44 See Pasolini, *Lettere luterane* and *Scritti corsari*. Sapienza returns to the theme of an anthropological and environmental destruction in *Appuntamento a Positano*, 142–3.

The Margins of Society

Whereas in many respects prison works as a space of resistance against mass conformism, it is at the same time a magnified mirror of society, in which it occupies the margins. Rebibbia is 'la sintesi chiara e inappellabile del mondo di fuori col suo, ora per ora, eterno riprodursi del vinto e del vincitore, del servo e del padrone ...' [the clear and incontestable synthesis of the world outside, with its continuous and eternal reproduction of winners and losers, servants and masters] (UR 72–3). Despite the possibility of enriching and unexpected friendships, in prison class difference is more evident than ever: 'La differenza di classe vige qui come fuori, insormontabile: il carcere è lo spettro o l'ombra della società che lo produce' [class difference is in force here like it is outside, insurmountable; prison is the spectre or shadow of the society that produces it] (156). Prison stands at the margins of society, and as Alford points out, 'We see at the margins more clearly the brutality, tyranny and charisma of everyday life.'[45] The majority of inmates are women who have been 'spinte verso la galera dal bisogno' [pushed toward prison by necessity] (40); they are poor and uneducated, drug addicts, and often women with experiences of violence and marginalization in their past. This is the case of Giovannella, who at the age of seventeen already has a four-year-old son and is expecting another one, but due to indigence cannot keep her baby and is in prison because it is easier to get an abortion there. Her mother, Giovannella tells Sapienza, had twenty abortions herself. Marrò is addicted to heroin, and was almost raped by a friend, while Annunciazione was raped as a child by her mother's partner, and when she is not in prison she works as a prostitute. Roberta is from a relatively privileged background, but her father is a criminal too, and her life, after many years spent in prison, is characterized by poverty, violence and marginality: her friend/lover/father figure Albert almost strangles her to death while they are arguing; she works as a prostitute in a hotel, sells and uses drugs, and eventually is arrested again for plotting a terrorist attack. Beside being a space of resistance and subversion, then, prison

45   Alford, 'What Would It Matter If Everything Foucault Said About Prison Were Wrong?', 140.

is the 'febbre che rivela la malattia del corpo sociale' [fever that reveals the disease of the social body] (158), a disease consisting in conformism and individualism, but also in the stark reality of class difference and social marginalization, which prison emphasizes and reproduces.

Crime, in this context, and in line with a long tradition of anarchist and socialist thought, is understood by Sapienza as a legitimate – although ultimately unproductive – form of rebellion against social injustice. In this view, the law is not the democratic expression of justice but only the concealed instrument of class oppression and the social control of deviance. Foucault cites, for example, socialist and anarchist magazines from the first half of the nineteenth century, in which the existence of crime is seen as 'a fortunate irrepressibility of human nature' and an 'outburst of protest in the name of human individuality'.[46] In the second half of the nineteenth century, Foucault continues, 'the anarchists posed the political problem of delinquency; [...] they thought to recognize in it the most militant rejection of the law; [...] they tried not so much to heroicize the revolt of the delinquents as to disentangle delinquency from the bourgeois legality and illegality that had colonized it'.[47] The distinction between political dissent and common delinquency becomes blurred, as they are both expressions of a rebellion against a social order that is perceived as unjust.[48]

Sapienza describes the prison population in Rebibbia as 'centinaia di individui eccezionali – politici e no – che solo perché dissentono nei modi che da sempre sono stati quelli primari di dissentire, vengono segregati' [hundreds of exceptional individuals – politically involved or not – who are segregated only because they express their dissent differently from what have always been the primary ways of dissenting] (UR 158). Furthermore, prisoners are a 'masnada di bucanieri che in un modo o nell'altro non s'è piegata ad accettare le leggi ingiuste del privilegio' [gang of pirates who, in one way or another, didn't yield to the unjust laws of privilege] (72). It is interesting to recall here that, according to Pieter Spierenburg, the origins

46   *La Phalange*, 10 January 1837, cited in Foucault, *Discipline and Punish*, 289.
47   Foucault, *Discipline and Punish*, 292.
48   See Sapienza's discourse on common offenders and political consciousness in CD 164.

of the carceral institution are not rooted in the judicial punishment of violent crimes, but rather in the non-judicial control and reformation (that is, normalization) of deviance, broadly understood: 'The prison originated as a non-judicial institution. [...] During the early years of the institution's existence, beggars and vagrants constituted the majority of inmates in most places. [...] Next to beggars and vagrants, the early prisons often housed disobedient children or recalcitrant spouses.'[49] The aim of prison was that of normalizing the marginal individual and bringing society back to 'normal' by expelling that marginal individual from it. It thus enforced whatever the dominant view of normality was and pushed 'recalcitrant' subjects to the margins. If society, Sapienza's texts say, is going further and further in the direction of conformism, capitalism and neo-liberalism, it is at its margins, where deviance is confined, that she looks to find the resources to resist. Prison, then, 'non è che un territorio chiuso o riserva di minoranze destinato a ingrandirsi in questa nostra era di omologazione totale' [is just an enclosed territory or reservation of minorities, which in our times of complete homologation is destined to expand] (CD 67). The ambivalence between the view of prison as a magnifying glass that reveals the ills of society and the view of prison as a space of alterity that resists social ills reflects the ambivalence of the carceral institution itself, for prison realizes social oppression and division to its extreme, but due to this extreme condition it also opens unexpected and creative spaces of resistance.

In the last section of *Discipline and Punish*, titled 'The carceral', Foucault discusses recidivism in relation to the role of prison as an instrument of class oppression and the normalization of deviance. In his view, prison itself fabricates the figure of the delinquent as a way to control those sections of society that pose a threat to the social order. Differently from politically organized parties, in democratic systems the figure of the delinquent is easily controllable and not particularly dangerous to the system itself. Crime, for as much as it is a form of vital dissent, is nonetheless fatally trapped in the game of power, for it makes it easy for the system to isolate

---

49   Pieter Spierenburg, 'The Origins of the Prison', in Clive Emsley, ed., *The Persistent Prison: Problems, Images and Alternatives* (London: Francis Boutle Publishers, 2005), 27–47, 29–30.

and neutralize the dissident. Sapienza's representation of the figure of the
woman terrorist in the character of Roberta works along the same lines. In
a dialogue with Barbara, Roberta describes her choice to engage in violent
opposition as a reaction to political power and its perpetration of social
injustice: 'Senti, non scoprire l'acqua calda dell'ingiustizia sociale! Se non
fosse così che forse *noi* ci saremmo sognati di passare alla disobbedienza per
puro capriccio o noia? Cazzo, ci hanno spinto "loro" a prendere il partito
della guerriglia, con la loro terroristica spocchia di potere ...' [Listen, don't
reinvent the wheel of social injustice! If it weren't so, would *we* have just
turned to disobedience as a whim, or out of boredom? Fuck, it's 'them',
and their terroristic haughtiness of the powerful, that have pushed us to go
the way of armed struggle] (CD 104). Howevr, in the expression 'ci hanno
spinto "loro"' lies the necessary defeat of the choice itself. Young political
dissidents such as Roberta, Sapienza says, have been swindled by political
power, manoeuvred to join terrorism and therefore pushed outside of the
law, where they can be imprisoned and neutralized. In Roberta, Sapienza
gives the portrait of a defeated generation who has been played by power:

> il suo visetto di creatura tradita da trame occulte, disegnate in altra sede (e tanto in
> alto da far venire le vertigini solo a pensarci). [...] Nessuno di loro *sa* dove agisce la
> direzione vera di quella macchinazione. Ancora una volta questi giovani sono stati
> strumentalizzati dall'alto esattamente come molti di noi, della generazione resisten-
> ziale, illusi a combattere per un mondo migliore. [...] Non c'è male come piano per
> far maturare preventivamente il bubbone del dissenso: farlo esplodere alla luce così
> che spurghi ben bene. Che sono tremila, quattromila individui 'infetti' da sacrificare
> alla nobile utopia della pacificazione mondiale, ora tutti in carcere per centinaia di
> anni? (UR 144–5)

> [her small face of a creature who was betrayed by hidden plots, designed somewhere
> else (and so high up that just the thought of it is dizzying) [...]. None of them *knows*
> where the true direction of that scheming is heading. Once again, these young people
> were exploited from above, exactly like so many of us, from the generation of the
> Resistance, who were deluded into fighting for a better world. [...] Not bad as a plan to
> make the swelling of dissent grow quickly – causing it to burst in the light so it clears
> out everything. What are three, four thousand 'infected' individuals to be sacrificed
> to the noble utopia of world pacification, now in prison for hundreds of years?]

Sapienza is plainly uninterested in expressing a moral view of terrorism, although through repeated comparisons to her own experience in the Resistance she appears to legitimize it. On the one hand, she depicts Roberta as a sort of gentle thief, who steals a car but makes sure it will be returned to the owner, and who only exercises violence as a masquerade. But on the other hand, Roberta is in effect a terrorist, which surely was a particularly sensitive and controversial topic in the Italy of the 1980s, just then painfully emerging from the Years of Lead. In this respect, *Le certezze del dubbio*, and in particular the figure of Roberta, can be productively compared to another work from the same period, centred on the figure of a female terrorist and set in England in the early 1980s, *The Good Terrorist* by Doris Lessing (1985). Both works engage in the representation of a new subject, that of middle-class women who join terrorism, focusing not so much on the legitimacy of terrorism as a form of political action, but rather on its social context, slogans, paths of radicalization and new protagonists.

In the passage cited above, Sapienza is arguing with Roberta, trying to show her that terrorism, whether or not it is a legitimate act of resistance against mass conformism and oppression, essentially serves the interests of the status quo. Here, Sapienza appears to shift from an understanding of crime as vital resistance to one of crime as an instrument of power itself. In this way, she draws close to Foucault's view that the prison is a function of political control, a space where dissent is channelled and neutralized. Sapienza's last image of Roberta and her partner Riccardo is indeed that of two 'amanti braccati' [hunted lovers] (CD 182), two poor young people crushed by society – an image of defeat, equally distant from the glorification of crime and its moral condemnation.

Within this rather bleak picture of modern society, in *Le certezze del dubbio* Sapienza opens up a space of positive political action that differs significantly from the exaltation of crime as a form of resistance, an element of her work that criticism so far has not identified. Such a space is represented by feminism and social activism. If *L'università di Rebibbia* opens with a scene that foregrounds male power, with Sapienza sitting in a car between two terrifying *carabinieri*, at the beginning of *Le certezze del dubbio* we have conversely a scene centred on women's fight against

patriarchal power, as Sapienza is going to Court to report on a trial in
which 'l'avvocatessa Tina Lagostena Bassi difende l'ennesima ragazza stu-
prata' [the lawyer Tina Lagostena Bassi is defending yet another girl who
was raped] (CD 8).[50] While in previous works Sapienza's relationship to
feminist activism was partially overshadowed by her troubled and conflicted
feelings towards her mother's feminism, we have here an unequivocal and
convinced endorsement of its principles and practices. Sapienza says she
collaborates with the *Quotidiano donna* [Woman's Newspaper],[51] a left-
wing feminist magazine, frequents the feminist group of *Pompeo Magno*,
and defines herself straightforwardly as a feminist: "'Tu sei una comune,
ma almeno femminista lo sei?'. "Certo", la rassicuro, "come no!"' ['You're
not political, but at least you're a feminist, aren't you?' 'Yes', I reassure
her, 'of course!'] (154). In *Le certezze del dubbio*, Sapienza seems to finally
meet a form of political activism that, unlike the one she associated with
her mother and the communist intellectuals of the 1950s, is not founded
on ideological inflexibility and self-sacrifice: 'Eh, caro Fellini, l'epoca delle
tue femministe trucide è finita' [Well, dear Fellini, the time of your cruel
feminists is gone] (8). The new type of feminist woman is represented
by her friend Ginevra, who is described as sweet and beautiful, is openly
lesbian, and 'sa combattere per le sue idee ma tenendo sempre conto del
valore della libertà e perché no, della gioia di vivere' [is able to fight for
her ideals but always keeping in mind the value of freedom and, why not,
of the *joie de vivre*] (10). Here, the complex and suffering anti-ideological
stance she put forward in *Lettera aperta* and *L'arte della gioia* becomes a
clear and direct message, as she has found a context where her ideas are
understood and shared.

50   Tina Lagostena Bassi was a lawyer renowned for defending women in rape cases, at a
     time when rape was still largely accepted in the Italian society. In 1978 she defended
     a victim of rape in a famous trial, which was filmed and turned into a documentary
     broadcast on national television. The documentary was seen by 9 million people
     and caused great shock in the Italian population. See *Processo per stupro* [A Trial
     for Rape], dir. Loredana Rotondo, RAI (Italy, 1979) <https://www.youtube.com/
     watch?v=Kj2qyo8xQ8w≥ [Accessed 31 July 2016].
51   *Quotidiano donna* was a weekly magazine, issued from 1978 to 1981.

The second space of political engagement opened up in *Le certezze del dubbio* is that of social activism, represented by a group, to which Roberta introduces Sapienza, that is dedicated to fighting for prisoners' rights. The description of the group is devoid of the irony and sarcasm that usually accompany Sapienza's representation of political initiatives and ideologies. On the contrary, she sets the meeting of the activists' group in opposition to official, high-brow Roman intelligentsia, as well as to the compartments in which modern society is divided, thus reconnecting this group to Susie Wong's circle in Rebibbia: 'Non era dunque un'eccezione quel consesso interclassista cosmopolita che allignava in carcere, né un risultato anomalo della coazione come temevo. Quel nuovo esperimento continua anche fuori!' [That cosmopolitan, interclass gathering that flourished in prison wasn't an exception, nor the anomalous effect of detention, as I feared. That new experiment continues outside, too!] (CD 160). This passage from a revolutionary potential inside the space of prison to outside society is significant, as it breaks the continuum of the 'carceral archipelago'. As Driver points out, one of the problems with Foucault's view of rights exclusively as a means of domination is that it leaves no space for emancipation nor change *through* the law.[52] Conversely, in feminist and social activism Sapienza envisages another possible form of resistance against the pervasive destruction operated by modern society, one that is also an alternative to crime and terrorism. Looking beyond the strictly political perspective, these groups of activists also represent a fundamental point of pacification for Sapienza herself, as for the first time in her long autobiographical journey, she appears to have found an elective community of people 'che proprio vanno addosso come un bel paltò caldo quando comincia la cattiva stagione ...' [who fit just like a nice, warm coat, when the cold season is starting] (UR 173).

52   Driver, 'Power, Space and the Body', 438.

Sapienza's Experience: Prison as a Vital Journey

Before Prison: Looking for a Social Suicide

One way of looking at Sapienza's prison diptych, as we have seen, is to concentrate on the representation of the carceral institution, its population and relationship with modern society. But these works are also autofictional novels that continue the narrative of Sapienza's 'autobiography in progress'. We can thus also focus on Sapienza's own experience of prison and its significance within her existential and artistic path. What does prison mean to the author? Or, in other words, how does she interpret the reasons behind her theft and subsequent incarceration? Prison, for Sapienza, is part of a life-long interest in margins, laws and outlaws. And female detention can be said to suffer from a double marginality – with respect to society, but also with respect to male detention, since criminality and prison were and remain largely a male issue.[53] Throughout all her works, Sapienza always presents herself as a subject 'outside the norm', starting from her unique name, Goliarda, and her 'bastard' identity within her family in *Lettera aperta*. In that text she also recounts that her father, a lawyer, used to defend common criminals, and that both her parents and several siblings were repeatedly incarcerated. She grows up in a context, Catania in the 1920s and 1930s, where the law is seen as the expression of fascist power, which incarcerates its opponents. Modesta's abnormal behaviour in *L'arte della gioia*, and the young protagonist's adoption of the romantic delinquent Jean Gabin as a role model in *Io, Jean Gabin*, reflect such a view of the law. Sapienza is irresistibly fascinated by social margins, by the figure of the outcast, the outlaw, by madness and mental institutions; likewise, she is interested

---

53   See Ronconi and Zuffa, *Recluse*, 19. In 2016, in Italy, women represent only 4.2 per cent of the overall prison population. See the website of the Italian Ministry for Justice, <https://www.giustizia.it/giustizia/it/mg_1_14_1.wp?previsiousPage=mg_1_14&contentId=SST126108> [Accessed 1 August 2016].

in queer figures that blur the boundaries between male and female and in forms of sexuality that contest normative limits between licit and illicit – bisexuality, homosexuality, sexual fluidity and incest. Her works are a relentless investigation of the margins of society, those expelled and repressed and yet constituting the frame that shapes society itself.

The reasons Sapienza provides for her act of theft are multiple, but all have at the centre the notion of prison as a place at the margins of society, to which she feels she belongs. She defines herself as a 'criminale per protesta civile' [criminal by civil disobedience],[54] and records in her diary the enthusiasm she felt when she arrived in Rebibbia, as she experienced 'una pace e soddisfazione etica indicibile, come qualcuno che finalmente abbia rimesso piede nel suo paese d'origine da cui un evento nemico l'aveva sradicato. Questo paese era quello dei poveri, umiliati e offesi' [an unspeakable peace and ethical satisfaction, like someone who finally comes back to her country of origin, from which adverse circumstances had uprooted her. This was the country of poor, humiliated and hurt people].[55] From the various explanations she provides in letters, interviews, diaries and the novels themselves, two main sets of reasons emerge. The first one is personal, and has to do with her suffering, her discouragement after the repeated rejections of *L'arte della gioia*, her material poverty, and her frustration with a social environment she perceived as hypocritical, conformist and snobbish. Going to prison is a response to this personal impasse, a 'social suicide' that brings with it the possibility of a new adventure, with its reinvigorating and regenerative potential. As she explains in a letter to Sergio Pautasso (and with a significant reference to Pirandello, whose Mattia Pascal and Henry IV also commit forms of 'social suicide'), 'il Pirandello che c'è in me ha capito – a posteriori – che cercavo un funerale, cosa che ho avuto in pieno' [The Pirandello who is in me understood – a posteriori – that I

---

54   Interview with Roberta Tatafiore, in *Noi donne*, April 1982, cited in Providenti, *La porta è aperta*, 160.

55   Taccuini 1989, cited in Providenti, *La porta è aperta*, 160.

was looking for a funeral, which I have had, fully].[56] On a second, different level, Sapienza is also moved by a 'thirst for first-hand knowledge',[57] that is, the desire to experience and document the reality of prison as a privileged point to observe society. As she explains in an interview to a rather perplexed and scornful Enzo Biagi, 'la mia è stata un'esperienza [...] mossa da un desiderio di testimonianza. [...] a casa mia si diceva che il proprio paese si conosce conoscendo il carcere, l'ospedale e il manicomio [...]. In casa mia erano anarchici' [my experience [...] was motivated by a desire to be a witness. [...] in my family they used to say that in order to know your country you need to look at prisons, hospitals and mental institutions. [...] They were anarchists, my family].[58]

The two reasons – personal and political – are inextricable, and Sapienza cannot come to a clear-cut explanation of her act: 'fra le tante motivazioni che mi hanno spinto in quel posto, alcune sono state comprese [...], le altre ci vorrebbe un Pirandello per andarle a scovare una per una' [Among the many reasons that led me to that place, some were understood [...], the others would need a Pirandello to uncover them one by one].[59] What is more important, however, is that the vital encounter with the prison environment makes the genealogy of reasons irrelevant, as she expresses in a very ironic dialogue with Giovannella in *L'università di Rebibbia*, one of the most lively of the novel:

> 'Sai che cosa ho fatto per finire qui?... [...] Da dodici anni non riuscivo più a pubblicare una riga, ho lavorato per dieci anni a un lungo romanzo e nel frattempo tutto cambiava, tutto: amici, situazioni, rapporti ... L'inferno della società italiana di questi ultimi anni ... Poi lo sfratto, la miseria, o comunque l'indigenza davanti a me sicura! Ma devo dire: m'ha fatto bene, m'ha aperto gli occhi ... Ero scivolata da ultimo in un ambiente pseudo-libero, pseudo-elegante, pseudo-tutto ... [...] e così ho rubato a una di queste pseudo-signore per punirla. O per punirmi? Insomma un bell'acting-out da manuale ...'
> 'Ma che stai a di'? 'Na pazza me pari! E chi t'ha chiesto cotica?' (UR 31–2)

---

56   Letter to Sergio Pautasso, Rome, 27 October 1981. Sapienza's unpublished letters are kept in the Sapienza-Pellegrino Archive in Rome. I thank Angelo Pellegrino for providing me with a copy of part of the epistolary.
57   Morelli, 'L'acqua in gabbia', 200.
58   Sapienza, in Biagi, *Film Story*.
59   Letter to Sergio Pautasso, Rome, 27 October 1981.

['Do you know how I ended up here?... [...] I hadn't managed to publish anything
in 12 years, I worked on a long novel for 10 years and everything changed in the
meantime, friends, situations, relationships ... The inferno of Italian society in the last
years ... then the eviction, misery, or anyway the indigence that was surely awaiting
me! But I have to say: it was good for me, it opened my eyes ... Lately I had slipped
into a pseudo-free, pseudo-elegant, pseudo-everything environment ... [...] and so I
stole from one of these pseudo-ladies to punish her. Or to punish myself? In short,
a textbook case of *acting-out* ...'
'What are you talking about? You sound crazy! Who asked you anyway?']

In this long, hectic confession, Sapienza traces a picture of her existential
situation before going to prison, mixing social criticism and psychoanalytic
insights. But Giovannella's reply, with its expressive Roman dialect, comi-
cally highlights the incongruence between Sapienza's preoccupations and
her present reality in prison, where this self-absorbed analytical attitude,
and the sophisticated language that belongs to it, are no longer relevant.
Instead, they are replaced by the uncovering of the prison world.

Inside Prison: Negotiating a Carceral Identity

In crossing the prison walls, Sapienza leaves behind her reasons and preoccupations from outside and fully delves into the discovery of this new world.
Prison represents a suspension of her search for identity, or rather a temporary and contextual re-adjustment of the coordinates of such an identity
search within the confined space and time of the prison. The dimension of
memory – 'non è tempo di ricordi' [it's no time for memories] (UR 11) –
and that of the future – 'non pensare mai al futuro in questo posto' [never
think about the future in this place] (36) – are both excluded, replaced by
the absolute dominance of the present. And it is a present that soon loses
the precise measure of objective time and expands into 'un ritmo senza
tempo' [a rhythm out of time] (35).

Inside the enclosed space of the prison, all the questions that oriented
her identity construction up until *Io, Jean Gabin* lose their pertinence, as
'qui sai subito chi sarai nella vita, non ti è concesso crogiolarti nel falso
problema di sapere chi sei, di cercare "la tua identità"' [Here, you know

immediately who you're going to be in life, you're not allowed to indulge
in the false problem of knowing who you are, of looking for 'your identity']
(UR 72–3). This relenting of the tiresome search for identity is evident in
the ironic tone she uses when talking about her unusual name, Goliarda.
While in *Lettera aperta* the uniqueness of her name carried a painful sense
of isolation and difference, in *L'università di Rebibbia* it is at the centre of a
comical series of mistakes and misunderstandings that do not emotionally
affect the narrator. Prison is thus a break from the demands of everyday
life and from a social environment perceived as hostile and alienating. As
Sapienza declared in an interview, 'stavo così male fuori che, entrata dentro,
in questa nave in mezzo al mare da cui non puoi fuggire, che è la galera,
sono stata meglio. Meglio rispetto alle angosce quotidiane' [I was feeling so
bad outside that, when I got in, into the sailing ship from which you can't
escape that is prison, I felt better. That is, better compared to my everyday
anguish].[60] Within the established boundaries of the prison, it is possible
for Sapienza to liberate new energies, no longer involved in the task of
finding out 'who she is', but rather all projected toward the discovery of
this new world. Barbarulli points out that prison 'calms her psychological
suffering'[61] and, by reassuring her, 'paradoxically allows a form of vitality
to remerge'.[62] Comparing her experience to that of Stendhal's characters,
Sapienza reads her own incarceration as a reinvigorating and strengthening adventure:

> Ecco che cosa avviene in quello stato che si chiama detenzione: la realtà, ricerca di
> soldi, doveri, etiche, viene tagliata fuori ripotenziando al massimo la forza e la sicurezza
> interna di tutti i nostri spiriti vitali, riportandoli alla esuberanza autonoma dell'ado-
> lescenza ... Questo intendeva Stendhal ogni qual volta riduceva il suo protagonista
> in una cella per metterlo in grado di ritrovare la sua integrità perduta. (CD 136)

> [That's what happens in that state called detention! Reality, the search for money,
> duties, ethics, everything is cut out, reinforcing the internal strength and determi-
> nation of all our vital drives, bringing them back to the autonomous exuberance of

60   Interview with Roberta Tatafiore, in Providenti, *La porta è aperta*, 160.
61   Barbarulli, 'Essere o avere il corpo', 136.
62   Ibid. 144.

adolescence .... This is what Stendhal meant anytime he put his protagonist in a cell, to enable him to rediscover his lost integrity.]

The opposition between the negativity of modern society outside and the vitality of her experience of detention is reflected in the epic transfiguration that colours episodes and characters. Inmates are often described through various heroic, cinematographic or sacred associations: a nameless prisoner has 'una massa di capelli color rame a foggia d'elmo barbarico' [a mass of copper coloured hair shaped like a barbarian helmet] (UR 139); Marrò's movements have 'l'eleganza orgogliosa del guerriero' [the proud elegance of a warrior] (84); Annunciazione is a 'sacro eunuco' [sacred eunuch] (84), and Marcella is a 'cavaliere errante' [knight errant] (165). As far as cinema is concerned, she meets for example 'una piccola James Dean' [a small, female James Dean] (56) as well as a 'Marilyn invecchiata' [old Marilyn] (27), and Barbara calls herself and her partner 'Bonnie e Clyde' [Bonnie and Clyde] (135).

Similarly to *Io, Jean Gabin*, everyday reality is intensified and trans-figured through heroic projection, which creates an ironic contrast with the simplicity of the context represented, and liberates a child-like joyful vitality. This is most evident in Sapienza's relationship with Annunciazione and Marrò: 'In un balzo sono fuori. Ho una missione segreta per un'amica: gli adulti non permettono alle ragazzine di bere il vino e io li devo frodare. Questa è la vita!' [I quickly jump out. I'm on a secret mission for a friend: adults don't allow girls to drink wine, and I have to trick them. This is life!] (UR 94). And again, after Annunciazione and Marrò succeed against another inmate who wanted to move Sapienza to another cell, they spend the afternoon in glorious tales of the comical episode: 'è un pomeriggio di racconti sulla grande battaglia sostenuta, la quasi sconfitta subito seguita dalla vittoria improvvisa, chi è stato più valente, eccetera' [the afternoon is spent remembering the great battle, the near defeat followed straight away by sudden victory, who was more valiant, etc.] (110). The ironic epic projec-tion, together with the inmates' lively accents and dialects, contributes to significantly lightening the tone of narration in *L'università di Rebibbia*, conveying the feeling of an adventurous journey. On the contrary, in *Le certezze del dubbio* narration does not undergo heroic projection but rather hallucinatory and feverish distortion, which considerably reduces the ironic and joyful tone of Rebibbia and emphasizes the distance between the protective space of the prison and the stark reality of everyday life.

Beside illustrating the ambivalence of prison, Sapienza narrates her own journey and traces the trajectory of a successful – and perhaps too successful – adaptation. When she is taken into the prison 'come pacco di poco conto' [like a package of little significance] (UR 8), she feels like a child, and is first tempted to lose herself into regression and degradation: 'L'autodegradazione che genera quella lunga discesa [...] è così potente da apparirmi come una sorta di piacere al quale abbandonarsi' [The self-degradation induced by that long downhill path [...] is so powerful that it feels like a sort of pleasure to embrace] (10). The temptation soon takes the shape of voluptuous self-annihilation, but her response is immediately one of vital action: 'Il desiderio di richiudere gli occhi, non fare più un gesto, è immenso. [...] Invece salto in piedi' [The desire to close my eyes and not move is powerful. [...] Instead I jump up] (15). The allure of regression is one of the 'sirene carcerarie' [prison Sirens] (14) that Sapienza is determined to fight from the outset. Another Siren is the temptation to fully accept the identity of the delinquent and endorse the 'soddisfazione autolesiva nel sentirsi perduta completamente' [self-harming satisfaction of feeling completely lost] (18). But again Sapienza appears to be equipped with sufficient determination to resist the Siren – in this case, a rude guard – and reaffirm her dignity: 'anche se sono lì per pagare la mia trasgressione, loro – "personalmente", dico – non hanno alcun diritto di umiliarmi' [even if I'm there to pay for my transgression, they – I mean 'personally' – have no right to humiliate me] (18).

In prison, Sapienza finds a circle of friends; however, Bond points out that, before achieving recognition and acceptance, her first interactions with the other inmates actually feature an acute sense of difference, fear and shame. In Bond's view, the sense of shame that Sapienza feels in these initial interactions manifests a 'partially failed desire for integration and belonging,'[63] which she is able to overcome only when she 'ultimately

63   Bond, 'A World Without Men', 108.

discovers a true "paradiso" of affective communication with Suzie Wong's select tea-party group'.[64] Although it is true that it is only when she meets Susie Wong's circle that she forms that special 'paradisiac' empathetic communication, even in her previous encounters she is actually ready in identifying the unspoken rules of conduct and in adapting to the new demands of prison, creating bonds that cut across differences of age, class and education. With the women in the prison yard, with Giovannella, with the guards and with Marrò and Annunciazione she always succeeds in establishing friendly and sympathetic relationships, exemplified by the 'intesa da ragazzacce di strada' [gangster girls' mutual understanding] she accomplishes with Marrò (UR 94), although the difference that separates them cannot be effaced.

While she can adjust her behaviour, and she does so successfully, what she cannot change is her class belonging, and this is the main factor at the root of her sense of shame. Sapienza notes that, unlike most inmates, she can afford a lawyer (although her friends pay for it), and resorts to the vocabulary of shame in noticing the complicity of the wealthy inmates working at the commissary: 'Mi vergogno della mia dovizia soprattutto perché la capa ingioiellata m'ha rivolto uno sguardo complice da ricca a ricca' [I feel ashamed of my wealth, especially because the boss, covered in jewellery, gave me a complicit gaze, from one rich lady to another] (UR 98). In her dialogue with Giovannella, as Bond notes, Sapienza imitates the girl's accent, seeking an identification that the girl rejects. Giovannella forces Sapienza to accept their class difference, which is also a difference from the identity of the prisoner, as Sapienza is only there for a very short period of time: 'Non devo fingere un'identità carceraria o proletaria che sia. [...] Non si sfugge alla propria classe, penso con amarezza, e la bocca mi si chiude umiliata' [I mustn't fake a carceral or proletarian identity. [...] You can't escape your class, I think with bitterness, and my mouth shuts, humiliated] (43).

Sapienza thinks of herself as an outlaw, and her entire relational investment is concentrated within the prison community, which she has

64   Bond, 'A World Without Men', 109.

elected as her 'country of origin'. At the same time, she is also aware of not being a common inmate, and she feels shame whenever this becomes an impediment to her identification with the other prisoners. Bond notes how Sapienza's narrative differs from Joan Henry's *Who Lie in Gaol* in that Henry feels shame vis-à-vis society, while Sapienza's shame is concentrated within the prison community. Both narrators, however, would be able to 'experience shame as a productive process which will ultimately allow them to reconnect with the wider community outside'.[65] Although through shame Sapienza realizes her difference from the average prison population, I would argue that she does not achieve, and does not even seek, any reconnection with the community outside, having chosen prison as her elective community. Sapienza's sense of shame, and the process of overcoming shame in finding her place, is all confined within the prison walls. As Marcella tells her, people outside will no longer consider her 'una di loro' [one of them] (UR 187). Instead, Sapienza says she feels proud and happy like a child when Roberta accepts her into her group and calls her 'una di noi' [one of us] (188), thereby acknowledging her carceral identity. Sapienza does adapt successfully to prison, to the point of showing the early signs of institutional syndrome, as Roberta points out to her, and *Le certezze del dubbio* voices Sapienza's longing to return to prison, seeking to recreate with Roberta and Barbara 'quei muri escludenti il malessere sinistro e indifferente della metropoli' [those walls that keep out the sinister and indifferent unease of the metropolis] (CD 113).

    While it is true that Sapienza presents her experience in prison as vital and reinvigorating, it is important nonetheless to stress that the 'freedom' she encounters there is such only because the experience is temporary, and because it is, to some degree, chosen. In other words, the idea of prison as having a freeing potential essentially rests upon and presupposes a wider freedom, that of not being there in a near future. If that freedom is taken away forever, the protective, womb-like space turns into an infernal one, where the prisoner is stuck in a timeless condition of regression. Sapienza expresses this view very clearly in *Le certezze del dubbio*, when with Roberta

65   Bond, 'A World Without Men', 111.

and Barbara she discusses the idea that prison would be wonderful, if you could get in and out as you please. But then, as the three friends acknowledge, it would be a holiday or a journey, and not the tragic reality that it actually is for the majority of prisoners (CD 104–5). Sapienza's experience is therefore not representative of the prison condition itself, but is rather to be inscribed within her personal – existential and political – search for freedom, of which prison constitutes an enriching but temporary step. However, the view of prison as a temporary step can also be appropriated by common prisoners, using the prospect of a future outside to foster a constructive approach to the time spent inside. In this sense, Sapienza's view of the positive potential of a fostering and sympathetic community resonates with many of the inmates' stories recounted in *Recluse*, centred on aspects of learning and empowerment achieved through the relationship with other women.[66] In other words, Sapienza not only recounts her vital journey, but she also counters a unidimensional narrative of prisoners as passive victims with those elements and responses that strengthen their subjectivity.

After Prison: Whiskey and Queer Love in Rome

Towards the end of *Io, Jean Gabin*, Sapienza proudly asserts that she has finally decided where she stands and what role she wants to play in society. She takes up the identity of an anarchist artist, at the margins of society, approaching life as a succession of adventures and experiences, a cycle of death and regeneration. In *Le certezze del dubbio*, the child protagonist of *Io, Jean Gabin* is now an adult, whose identity is precisely that of an outlaw, anarchist woman who wanders around Rome on the metro, by taxi or in stolen cars, smokes countless cigarettes, drinks coffee and whiskey, and is irresistibly caught up in a new, dangerous adventure. This is her ambiguous

---

66   See, for example: 'I didn't know who I was. No, because I was always conditioned; in prison, I discovered the desire to get up in the morning and the will to live despite all difficulties', Ronconi and Zuffa, *Recluse*, 152; and 'It's sad to say, but in prison I grew up', ibid. 153.

and extremely intense relationship with Roberta, the co-protagonist of
the novel. Alternating first and third person narration, like Modesta in
L'arte della gioia, Sapienza recounts the development of her relationship
with Roberta, which is characterized by exceptional intensity, dramatic
emotional changes and fluctuating roles. The bond between Roberta and
Sapienza can be aptly described as 'queer', as it constantly crosses and blurs
boundaries between multiple categories commonly used to read human
relationships – friendship, identification, eroticism and maternal care.

Roberta is a physically small, aggressive and intelligent young woman,
who is affected by incurable addictions to both prison and heroin. Biographical
details differ slightly in the two novels – in *L'università di Rebibbia* she is
twenty-six, while in *Le certezze del dubbio* she is twenty-four[67] – but we know
that she was incarcerated for the first time at the age of fourteen, and after
that she spent overall about six years in prison, fully absorbing its regressive
life and different temporality: '*lei* c'è cresciuta nella reclusione, in quella scac-
chiera interminabile di ore sezionate fino allo spasimo in minuti e secondi'
[*she* grew up in detention, in that endless chessboard of hours, spasmodi-
cally dissected into minutes and seconds] (CD 67). Roberta is a childish
and rebellious young woman, who is now incapable of living a stable life
outside of prison. She rejects the very idea of legal work, and expresses anger
and scorn at Barbara's desire for a normal, middle-class life. She is also gifted
with talents, sensitivity and intelligence, which allow her to establish a rich
emotional and intellectual exchange with Sapienza. But the narrator increasingly pictures her as a defeated figure, trapped in her addictions, played by
political power, and ultimately arrested once again.

The first element that composes this multifaceted relationship is the
linking between Sapienza's attraction to Roberta and her regressive fascination with prison. From the beginning of the novel, which opens with the
ironic sentence 'm'avevano sbattuta fuori' [they had kicked me out] (CD
7), the narrator expresses a strong desire to identify with the prison population and feels drawn towards repeating the experience of being detained.
Initially, and any time Roberta disappoints her, she associates Roberta with

one of the prison Sirens that must be resisted, and tries to convince herself that she must not be drawn in by 'effimere nostalgie carcerarie' [ephemeral prison nostalgia] (10) and should leave behind that 'appendice perniciosa di Rebibbia' [pernicious continuation of Rebibbia] (33) represented by Roberta. But when the relationship works, by virtue of its association with Roberta prison also becomes a mythical space of bliss, an 'era dell'oro' [golden age] (18), which it would be pointless to resist.

As the relationship between the two women develops, Sapienza increasingly comes to trust Roberta, feels accepted as part of a shared carceral identity, and finally gives in to her feelings of attraction and their promises of a deep and enriching encounter, as well as likely suffering. Indeed, Roberta, as the object of Sapienza's desire, represents all the enlivening and destructive potential of erotic passion, with its extreme polarity of life and death. Roberta is a figure of *thanatos* – she helps Barbara cut her wrists, and promises to give Sapienza a lethal injection, should she ever ask her to.[68] But she also embodies a vital principle, as Sapienza decides to call her 'Vita' [Life] (CD 59), possibly alluding to another intense and ambiguous relationship of love and friendship between two women of different ages and backgrounds – the one between Virginia Woolf and Vita Sackville-West.[69] When Roberta unexpectedly kisses Sapienza on the lips, throwing her into a feverish state of emotional turmoil, she reflects on the likely consequences of that passion:

> continuare a seguirla così come sto facendo, presto significherà per me riaffrontare ancora una volta la completa distruzione di quello che sono oggi 10 aprile 1980 e la conseguente *risurrezione* che purtroppo segue sempre (quanto è più facile morire una volta per tutte!) le *piccole morti per amore* che perseguitano noi miseri mortali. (CD 100)[70]

68   In 'Identità di genere e sessualità', Ross points out the link between Roberta and death and puts it in relation to lesbian desire: 'Lesbian desire is associated with madness and death: *eros* and *thanatos* are joined together', 70. I read it instead as a polarity between death and erotic desire in general, that is, not specific to lesbian desire.

69   See Vita Sackville-West and Virginia Woolf, *The Letters of Vita Sackville-West to Virginia Woolf*, ed. Louise A. DeSalvo and Mitchell Alexander Leaska (London: Virago, 1992).

70   The date, 10 April 1980, is presumably a mistake, as it precedes Sapienza's imprisonment.

[to keep following her like I'm doing will soon mean that I'll once again have to face the complete destruction of what I am today, 10 April 1980, and the subsequent resurrection that unfortunately (it's so much easier to die once and for all!) always follows the *small deaths by love* that persecute us poor mortals.]

Roberta represents the possibility of a joyful, new encounter, but also the endless re-enactment of fixed patterns, that 'destino coatto' against which Sapienza is fighting. In the end, however, Sapienza succeeds in separating her relationship with Roberta from a regressive attraction to prison, as she achieves a form of carceral identity that does not coincide with institutional syndrome and is expressed instead in taking the prisoners' side through activism and writing. While Roberta is trapped in her compulsory destiny, Sapienza, despite her nostalgia and regressive tendency, escapes the prison Sirens and continues her life as an anarchist, whiskey-drinker and wandering writer.

On a different level, however, Sapienza also protects herself by suppressing her sexual attraction for Roberta and shaping their relationship according to amical and maternal feelings. While in the first part of the novel their relationship is characterized by mutual resistance, mistrust and marked difference – 'Sapienza e Roberta che si conoscono così poco, si somigliano così poco e probabilmente avrebbero tutte e due cose più importanti a cui badare' [Sapienza and Roberta, who know so little of each other, are so different, and probably would both have more important things to do] (CD 29–30), difference progressively gives way to similarity and then to imitation and identification. The merging of their identities is anticipated in the final scene of *L'università di Rebibbia*, when Sapienza imitates Roberta's posture, and their cell is described through the womb-like image of a protective submarine (UR 195). This merging likewise features in several scenes in *Le certezze del dubbio*. There, the mutual identification is both stated explicitly in their dialogues, such as in Roberta's assertion that 'Con te Goliarda è come parlare con se stessi' [with you, Goliarda, it's like talking to myself] (CD 36), and in the flux of actions and reactions in which their separate identities become undiscernible. Their progressive identification goes together with intense feelings of erotic attraction and love. Their encounters, in bars, in Barbara's shop, or just wandering around Rome, all have the feverish quality of passionate love, with dramatic oscillations between opposite emotional states, an 'altalena d'esultanza e terrore' [alternation of jubilation and terror] (129), in which 'una gioia densa come onda calda d'estate' [a dense joy like a warm summer wave] (12) can suddenly turn into 'un panico assoluto' [absolute panic] (24). The relationship between Sapienza and Roberta presents all the symptoms of romantic love and erotic desire. Although some critics have focused only on the elements of motherhood and friendship,[71] others have acknowledged the homoerotic nature of the relationship, calling things by their name: Ross rightly talks about 'lesbian desire'[72] and sexually charged friendship;[73] similarly, Barbarulli claims that Roberta unsettles Sapienza's sexuality.[74] Sapienza's attraction to Roberta is indeed unequivocally sexual; and it is recounted through the intense physical reactions of her body, which throughout the novel keeps escaping her control.

Despite the strength of their emotional and physical involvement, Roberta and Sapienza do not act upon their erotic desire, and instead divert it towards other forms of love, such as friendship and maternal care. Ross, and later Morelli, interpret Sapienza's repression of her own sexual desire in *Le certezze del dubbio* as related to a problematic internalization of heteronormative discourses, and in particular her mother's repressive slaps that are recounted in *Lettera aperta*, which Sapienza replicates here by slapping Roberta. It is certainly true that, differently from Modesta's multifarious experiences, in her autobiographical texts Sapienza is never the protagonist of fully lived homosexual relationships. However, I would disagree with the contention that her works display a heteronormative view and 'encourage us to hide secrets rather than contesting normative models that prevent us from saying and expressing certain desires.[75] On the contrary, homosexual desire is dealt with very explicitly and outside any pathologizing frame, both in terms of Sapienza's desire and as a recurring

---

71 See, for example, Cinquemani, 'Da *Lettera aperta* a *Le certezze del dubbio*', and Bicchietti, 'Esperienze dal carcere', 188.

72 Ross, 'Identità di genere e sessualità', 240.

73 Ross, 'Eccentric Interruptions', 5.

74 Barbarulli, 'Essere o avere il corpo', 145.

75 Ross, 'Identità di genere e sessualità', 241.

topic in the characters' conversations.[76] When Roberta kisses her, Sapienza
is surprised by the strength and novelty of homosexual desire, which unsettles her perception of herself and, most of all, threatens her personal stability. She wonders why, having reached a mature age and built a satisfactory
relationship with a man, she is now being discombobulated by such a
powerful erotic desire for Roberta. If she hesitates, though, it is because
of the threat of destruction posed by such a late formed passion and the
unreliability of Roberta's behaviour, rather than the refusal or mystification of homosexuality. As she states clearly, Roberta is awakening her 'lato
omosessuale' [homosexual side], which she had closeted 'nel cantuccio
sereno della sublimazione' [in the serene nook of sublimation] (CD 100).
Furthermore, despite her hesitation, she comes to recognize her desire as
unequivocally erotic: 'Esagero, forse? [...] No, non è esagerazione. L'eco
piena di brividi travolgenti che quelle labbra tumide m'hanno stampato
addosso facendomi perdere la nozione di me stessa e la fame ne sono un
segno inequivocabile' [Am I exaggerating? [...] No, it's not an exaggera-
tion. The echo brimming with overwhelming shudders that her full lips
have impressed on me, making me lose my sense of self and my hunger, are
an unequivocal sign of it] (100). Sapienza could not be any more explicit
about the nature of her desire, which she communicates straightforwardly
to her readers.

Why, then, do Roberta and Sapienza repress their mutual attraction?
On the level of the plot, it is Roberta who asks Sapienza for a different type
of relationship, based on intimacy, care and friendship, instead of passion.
When Sapienza asks her what she wants, her reply is 'pace' [peace] (CD
124). It is only after this clarification of their relationship, when Roberta
again tempts Sapienza into an erotic embrace, and then laughs at her, that
Sapienza slaps her. Ross rightly reads these slaps as a re-enactment of Maria's
slaps, aimed at repressing a homosexual desire towards which Sapienza
feels at the same time attracted and inhibited.[77] However, within the text
the reason why Sapienza has to repress her homosexual desire does not lie
in her internalization of heteronormativity, but in the relationship with

76   See, for example, UR 148–9; CD 61, 84, 168.
77   See Ross, 'Eccentric Interruptions', 16–17.

Roberta, who asks her for something different: 'Roberta non vuole passione, erotismo, avventure più o meno amorose da me' [Roberta doesn't want passion, eroticism, more or less romantic adventures from me] (185). And it is significant that Sapienza, in the same novel, recounts another episode involving slapping, when she hits Santomauro, the warden of the prison who is presented in terms that closely recall Maria Giudice: 'quella donna tutta ferro, intellettuale intendo' [that iron woman, intellectual I mean] (43). Sapienza slaps Santomauro in the attempt to prolong her detention and thus remain with Roberta. In this case, the slaps represent rebellion against the interdiction of homosexuality, and they replicate the ones she gave to her therapist in *Il filo di mezzogiorno*, in response to his attempt to pathologize homosexual desire. While Sapienza in *Le certezze del dubbio* represses her homosexual desire, she is nonetheless very explicit about it, and her representation of such a desire does not appear to display any pathologizing element.

In exchange for her demanding request for 'peace', which is closely followed by the revelation that she has fallen in love with a man, Roberta gives Sapienza a sort of compensatory gift, entrusting her story to her. Sapienza accepts this new role, which she interprets as an act of 'giving birth' to Roberta by writing about her.[78] As Barbarulli notes, 'after descending into the abyss of desire and pain, she seems to exalt/accept the ambiguity of her relationship with Roberta, friend/lover/daughter.'[79] Motherhood is indeed the ultimate form taken by the relationship between Sapienza and Roberta, but it manifests a very unusual understanding of the maternal bond, given that sexual attraction – although not acted upon – is not excluded but rather considered central to it. Most relationships in the novel, and not just the one between Roberta and Sapienza, comprise an element of parental care, for example between Roberta and Albert, who the narrator defines 'suo papà' [her dad] (CD 42) and between Roberta and her Chilean lover, for whom she feels at the same time powerful sexual attraction and maternal feelings.[80] In this respect, *Le certezze del dubbio*

78   See CD 186.
79   Barbarulli, 'Essere o avere il corpo', 146.
80   See CD 87.

reconnects to the centrality of parental love, and its proximity to incestuous dynamics, that recurs in all of Sapienza's works and that here is stated
explicitly by Roberta, who compares her love for Sapienza to the kind of
absolute and incestuous love she feels for her mother.[81]
    Moreover, and again in continuity with Sapienza's earlier works, the
maternal bond is shaped by the reversibility of roles. On a first, more evident level, Sapienza plays the role of Roberta's mother. Roberta, despite her
aggressive and independent attitude, acts like a child in need of guidance
and help, while Sapienza is an adult woman, who in the end manages to
swallow her erotic passion, and even her jealousy, to give Roberta what she
needs – peace, protection, care. On the other hand, Roberta is also a maternal figure for Sapienza, a figure who is connected to the sense of protection
and warmth Sapienza felt in prison. When Roberta defines her 'una di noi',
her joy is that of a child, while when she leaves prison, Sapienza feels 'come
se qualcuno mi strappasse dal ventre di mia madre' [as if someone tore me
from my mother's womb] (CD 42). In one of the many oneiric passages in
the novel, Roberta is even associated with Maria Giudice herself: 'Roberta
mi appare come fotografata in bianco e nero dietro grosse sbarre [...] la foto-
grafia di mia madre in carcere' [I see Roberta as in a black and white photo,
behind big bars [...] the picture of my mother in prison] (44). Again, the
maternal bond is filled with eroticism, as when Roberta tells her that she
has '"mani esili, morbide [...] da bambina". Quella parola accende un fuoco
pieno di brividi nel nodo compatto delle nostra dita intrecciate' ['small,
soft hands [...] like a child'. This word lights a fire full of shudders in the
tight knot of our interlaced fingers] (121). The reversibility of roles of care
creates a profound and innovative equality within the hierarchic nature
of parental roles, neutralizing what constitutes the dangerous 'exercise of
power in the relationship of care'[82] that Sapienza investigates extensively in
previous works. In her novels, Sapienza represents, and to a certain extent
invents, relationships of care of a mother-like type, which however do not
contain a threatening imbalance of power. Attitudes of protection and care
on the one side, and regression, vulnerability and infantilism on the other,

---

81   See CD 123.
82   Ronconi, in 'Il filo della differenza', 248.

change depending on time and context, resulting in a bond in which two people effectively take care of each other. In conclusion, although the relationship between Sapienza and Roberta is diverted towards maternal care, the boundary between eroticism, identification, incest and motherhood is constantly blurred, giving rise to a 'queer' relationship that escapes any usual definition. *Le certezze del dubbio* is a novel about homosexual love, but even more it is about the freedom to experiment with queer, multifarious relationships, beyond their codification in usual categories.

The Encounter with the Present

Linearity of Narration and the Expanded Present

L'università di Rebibbia and *Le certezze del dubbio* continue Sapienza's autobiographical journey, but they depart from the investigation of the past and delve into the narrator's present. Both novels are first-person intradiegetic narrations; but, compared to previous novels, the focus has shifted from the work of memory and the narrator's investigation of the self to the encounter with an unknown, extraordinary reality, taking place in the present. Andrigo points out that 'this new relationship with reality is the crucial difference between these last two, stylistically similar works and those of her previous production.'[83] Furthermore, she specifies: 'After recreating her own *self*, in the first phase of her writing, now Goliarda Sapienza finally inserts her person in her present context.'[84] Similarly, Bicchietti remarks: 'With *L'università di Rebibbia* Goliarda Sapienza seems to leave behind the obsessive investigation of the self and its complex contradictions, adopting instead a new, open attitude to the world.'[85] The existential question that dominated previous works, who am I?, is reformulated in contextual

83   Andrigo, 'Goliarda Sapienza's Permanent Autobiography', 26.
84   Andrigo, 'L'evoluzione autobiografica di Goliarda Sapienza', 127.
85   Bicchietti, 'Esperienze dal carcere', 182.

and provisional terms, who am I in prison? Who am I after prison? Who am I in this unfolding love relationship? And the question itself retreats to the background, giving centre stage to the new context in which she is immersed. According to both Andrigo and Bicchietti, such a change in focus brings about a difference in language and narrative structures, which become more linear: 'language is unadorned, without the long digressions and oneiric divagations that characterize previous works. There is a new narrative approach, that of the almost documentary description of social reality.'[86] Andrigo and Bicchietti are right in locating the main discontinuity with Sapienza's previous work in the changed narrative focus, which is now on the present and the other characters; however, the present analysis also suggests that their views of a narrative that is linear and entirely projected on the outside world requires partial reassessment as regards *Le certezze del dubbio*.

The narrator of *L'università di Rebibbia* is mainly present as an observer, as most space – especially in the second part, when Sapienza is moved from solitary confinement to the general population section – is dedicated to the prisoners' monologues and dialogues, the detailed description of the prison, and the lively, cinematographic narration of a number of episodes. *Le certezze del dubbio* also engages in the representation of Sapienza's contemporary reality – the city of Rome and the lives of her new friends. Significant space is given to the description of Roberta and to her own words, as she discusses her past and political opinions at length. When the narrator is not emotionally involved, she comfortably retreats into the position of an external, unobserved observer: 'Parlando le due amiche hanno gradualmente abbassato la voce e si sono avvicinate l'una all'altra (di me non parlo perché mi hanno dimenticata completamente)' [As they were talking, the two friends gradually lowered their voices and came closer to one another (I say nothing of myself because they completely forgot my presence)] (CD 77–8). However, compared to *L'università di Rebibbia*, *Le certezze del dubbio* features a much more prominent presence of the narrator, whose feverish emotional state colours most episodes, and

86   Bicchietti, 'Esperienze dal carcere', 182.

whose reflections and physical reactions alternate with the recording of events and external reality. The narrator is here closely implicated in the story narrated, as she is exposed to a relationship that threatens to destroy her sense of the self, and is engaged in the effort to understand and direct her own emotions and reactions. The narrating voice is therefore more precarious, and Sapienza resorts again to narrative techniques she used in previous works to explore the uncertainty and complexity of identity and desire, such as the alternation of first and third person narration, the representation of bodily reactions that escape rational control, and the overlapping of the narrator's distorted or dreamlike perception with the reality that is represented.

In both novels, the present tense prevails, and it is a present that marks the 'actual temporal proximity' between narration and the events narrated – as opposed to childhood memories.[87] In *L'università di Rebibbia*, the exclusive focus on the present is explicitly linked to the prison condition, which suspends both the dimension of memory and that of the imagined future. The only flashforward is the prophecy that an inmate, Mamma Roma, tells Sapienza, anticipating the theme of *Le certezze del dubbio*: 'Deve resistere a tutte le sofferenze perché un essere vivente ha bisogno di lei, e per altro che non riesco a "vedere"... ma lo sapremo questo "altro"... col tempo lo sapremo ...' [you must fight back against your suffering because a human being needs you, I can't 'see' anything else ... but we'll know it, this 'something else'... with the passage of time we'll know it ...] (UR 61–2). But the very fact that the future is told in the form of a prophecy actually reinforces the restriction of time to the present. In *Le certezze del dubbio*, the present opens up in the direction of the past, but it is a very recent past, consisting of the memories of Rebibbia that Sapienza shares with Roberta and Barbara. It also opens toward the immediate future, in the form of Sapienza's preoccupation for her work, for the possible outcomes of her relationship with Roberta, and for Roberta's life itself. The future and the past however maintain a strict relationship with the present, and ultimately

---

87   Andrigo, 'Goliarda Sapienza's Permanent Autobiography', 26.

the novel features the same enclosed temporal quality that characterizes *L'università di Rebibbia*. Differently from the disrupted narratives of *Lettera aperta* and *Il filo di mezzogiorno* and the wandering thoughts of *Io, Jean Gabin*, the prison novels are structured as linear narratives, with a clearly recognizable succession of events. However, within the overall linearity of structures and stability of narrating voice, which set the prison novels apart from Sapienza's previous production, a certain degree of manipulation of time and narrating voice remain. The linearity of narration is subjected to the distortion of time as it is lived, subjectively, in the present, with its movements of dilatation and contraction. In *L'università di Rebibbia*, the passage of time is marked by a series of episodes, nights, meals and encounters, in which the narrator, and the readers with her, loses the sense of quantifiable, objective time, in favour of a form of suspended or iterative present, a 'ritmo senza tempo' [rhythm out of time] (UR 35), a form of carceral temporality described by Alford as 'sacred time, all the time in the world, time out of mind'.[88] The manipulation of time is conspicuous in *Le certezze del dubbio*, where narration reproduces the distorted and heightened perceptions of an unsettled self. The novel is structured as a series of encounters between Sapienza, Roberta and other characters (Albert, Barbara, the group of activists, Riccardo), set apart by long periods (weeks and months) which are summarized by the narrator in a few lines. Time is here affected by her altered emotional state, which intensifies and expands the perception of the present, to the point that less than one day, when she and Roberta visit Barbara, is narrated over more than sixty pages. Befuddled by the emotions aroused in her by Roberta, and exhausted after long conversations with her friends, Sapienza asks Barbara what time it is, pointing out the difference between subjective and objective time: 'Barbara tira fuori dalla sua borsa un orologino minuto e mi risponde "Le cinque e un quarto". Perché, penso io, per tutta la sera ha tenuto nascosta quella possibilità di tempo reale che aveva a portata di mano?' [Barbara takes a small watch out of her handbag and replies 'It's 5.15'. Why, I wonder, had she kept hidden for the whole

---

88		Alford, 'What Would It Matter If Everything Foucault Said About Prison Were Wrong?', 132.

night that possibility of real time she had at hand?] (CD 106–7). Each encounter recreates the suspended time of *L'università di Rebibbia*, where objective time is replaced by an intensified and unquantifiable duration that alters the linear and objective features of narration.

The linguaggio primo *of Gazes and Voices*

L'università di Rebibbia and *Le certezze del dubbio* are the final episodes within Sapienza's long autofictional journey. After the painful reconstruction of her identity and agency, she now speaks from the position of an anarchist artist, proudly inhabiting and recounting the margins of society. This identity is not fixed and closed-off; on the contrary, it embraces openness to change through the constantly renovated encounter with the world. A performative element is retained, comprising the centrality of the present and the oral dimension, but in a rather changed setting. Indeed, narration is no longer the space of the narrator's performance of the self, but a set or stage she shares with the other characters, where action unfolds under her and the readers' eyes. Emma Gobbato points out that these novels 'tend towards figurative representation in a way that is closely related to her cinematic gaze'.[89] Such a cinematic approach is reinforced by the recurring references to cinema and theatre, such as the comparisons to actors, which are part of a heroic projection conveying the sense of an adventurous journey into a new world. As one inmate, Marcella, comments, 'O siamo in uno zoo o in un teatro underground' [Either we're in a zoo or an underground theatre] (UR 95). Likewise, the table where inmates can buy necessities is portrayed as a prop, turning the prison into a big stage: 'chi poteva immaginare che quel tavolo nudo simboleggiasse

---

89   Gobbato, 'The Unknown Scriptwriter', 80. On the cinematic aspects and intertextuality of Sapienza's works, see also Ortu, 'Visi dischiusi ad ascoltare: Goliarda Sapienza narratrice di visioni', in Lucia Cardone and Sara Filippelli, eds, *Cinema e scritture femminili. Letterate italiane fra la pagina e lo schermo* (Rome: Iacobelli, 2011), 93–105; and Maria Rizzarelli, 'Schermo, schermo delle mie brame... La formazione dello sguardo di Goliarda Sapienza', *Arabeschi*, 9 (2017), 32–47.

tutto un mercato?' [Who could imagine that that bare table symbolized a whole market?] (97). *Le certezze del dubbio*, too, includes repeated references to acting, cinema and theatre, as for example in the description of a dialogue between Roberta and Barbara, in which the 'cinematic gaze' is doubled – we watch Roberta watching Barbara 'come se fosse a teatro, il visetto appeso ai gesti [...] della primadonna' [as if she were watching a play, her gaze following the *primadonna*'s movements] (CD 103).

The modality of representation still relies on the centrality of the present and presence of the body, principally in the form of voices and gazes. Sapienza's representation orchestrates a play of gazes through which narrator and characters see and affect one another. The narrator applies her cinematic gaze to her surrounding and the other characters, 'Mi attardo a notare ogni particolare' [I pause to observe every single detail] (UR 111) and in turn she is observed and penetrated by their gazes, thus creating the image of a mirroring and reciprocally affective community. For example, Sapienza writes about the deep mutual understanding between her and Marrò, which takes shape as an exchange of gazes: 'lei, prendendomi il viso fra le mani, mi costringe a fissarla. I suoi occhi pieni di ombre mi scrutano così a fondo da mutare i secondi in un tempo senza memoria' [Holding my face between her hands, she forces me to look at her. Her shadowy eyes gaze at me so deeply that they turn seconds into a time without memory] (123–4). Similarly, Santomauro scrutinizes her eyes 'come un cavatappi che si insinua nel sughero' [like a corkscrew creeping into the cork] (109), and Sapienza in turn looks into Santomauro's eyes, where 'appare come un lieve spiraglio di divertita commozione' [a glimmer of amusement surfaces] (109). In *Le certezze del dubbio*, Sapienza's relationship of love and identification with Roberta is represented through a series of mutually affective bodily signs, and especially gazes: 'Vorrei fissarla nel suo sguardo che s'allarga avvolgendomi tutta e risucchiandomi dentro di lei' [I would like to keep looking into her gaze, which expands wrapping me around and sucking me into her] (CD 135).

Together with these gazes, the narration also avails itself of a detailed recording of voices and spoken language. The narrator describes for example Marrò's 'nitida, calda voce romanesca dall'erre un po' moscia' [limpid, warm Roman voice with its soft 'r's] (UR 85); Annunciazione's 'voce adenoidea' [adenoidal voice] (82); Roberta's 'voce cavernosa e dolce' [cavernous and sweet voice] (CD 76) and her 'canto a onda lunga nel quale modulava il racconto' [chant in long waves, through which she modulated her story] (72). In the prison novels, Sapienza realizes the representation of a polyphonic, multilingual community of voices to a degree never achieved before, with an accurate recording of the auditory quality of the characters' voices, and the skilful reproduction of oral language and dialects, especially the Roman dialect.[90] Here, too, writing irresistibly tends toward orality, and thinking toward spoken communication: 'tutto questo devo averlo detto ad alta voce' [I must have said all this out loud] (UR 63); 'La bella voce virile che ha risposto ai miei pensieri non mi meraviglia. Come al solito ho continuato a comunicare senza saperlo' [The beautiful virile voice that replies to my thoughts does not surprise me. As usual, I kept on communicating without realizing it] (CD 156). The political dimension of the voice is here brought to the fore explicitly, as it represents the corporeal and empathetic relationships, the *linguaggio primo*, that Sapienza values against modern society's conformism and individualism. The voice, as Cavarero explains, is the marker of the uniqueness of each individual and the means of anchoring abstract thought to the intersubjective communication of emotions and meaning at the same time. Once again, Sapienza puts the body back in the centre of individual and collective existence, as a foundation for the possibility of agency and resistance.

In *L'università di Rebibbia*, the narration is not called on to perform a formative and empowering process for the narrator, as the present tense, although closer to the story narrated, does not coincide with the narrator's own 'present in action' – as it was in *Lettera aperta* and *L'arte della gioia*. However, the narrative is still sustained by an active force that fosters not the narrator's own agency but that of the other women, which it does by allowing them to speak. Likewise, it aims at fostering the agency of the readers by drawing them into the immediacy of the unfolding action and putting them in contact with a marginalized reality and an affective community. In *Le certezze del dubbio*, some aspects of identity formation return

---

90 For the analysis of plurilingualism in the prison novels, see Andrigo, 'Goliarda Sapienza's Permanent Autobiography', 26–8.

in the context of the challenges posed by the narrator's relationship with Roberta and in her elaboration of a 'carceral identity'. But on the whole, the performative tension of narration does not consist in the narrator's identity formation, but in her expression of desire. The text is filled with erotic and caring desire, which culminates in the metaphoric gesture of giving birth to Roberta through writing, after their relationship is abruptly interrupted. As Barbarulli points out, Sapienza also writes as a way to 'remain attached to Roberta and the attraction she feels for her, at the same time attenuating the intense confusion aroused by her body'.[91] Overall, these novels are far from the process of constructing identity through writing that characterized previous works. Nonetheless, in continuity with the project of an autobiography in progress and with Modesta's 'art of joy', the prison novels are infused with a transformative and liberating desire – the desire for testimony of an exceptional reality, in *L'università di Rebibbia*, and the desire to continue an interrupted relationship of love and care through writing, in *Le certezze del dubbio*. The notion of a performative narrative through which identity is constituted is here replaced by writing as a form of desire and care, which is aimed at giving voice to a neglected and silenced reality.[92] Writing is conceived as an active force, inhabited by the body and projected towards the achievement of a liberating impact on the world – that of the narrator and that of the readers. Whether it comes from the deconstruction of an oppressive past, Modesta's rebellious journey, the affective community of prison or a queer relationship of love and care, Sapienza's writings foster and communicate a liberating desire.

Sapienza's prison novels comprise elements of both political memoir and the documentary collection of testimonies, but overall they belong unequivocally to the genre of fiction. She develops a properly political understanding of her crime and crime in general, along the lines of an anti-capitalist criticism of modern society. However, she also distances

---

91 Barbarulli, 'Essere o avere il corpo', 146.
92 Most notably, *L'università di Rebibbia* inspired the creation of a literary prize for prisoners' writings, 'Premio Letterario Goliarda Sapienza. Racconti dal Carcere' [Goliarda Sapienza Literary Prize. Stories from Prison] <http://www.raccontidal carcere.it/> [Accessed 6 September 2016].

herself from an elevated notion of politics and political crime, identifying a 'revolutionary potential' not in direct political action, including terrorism, but in the regenerative potential of relationships of solidarity that take place at the margins of society, and other forms of political engagement, such as feminism and social activism. In *L'università di Rebibbia*, Sapienza discusses the difference between political prison writings and the reality of prison for common delinquents: 'Solo il politico si attarda a raccontare del carcere, ma la ragione per la quale c'è stato è troppo "onorevole" per poter dare la misura del vero carcere: quello dei ladri, degli assassini, dei maledetti per intenderci. Il politico ne esce rafforzato nell'orgoglio e il suo racconto è viziato dall'epicità' [Only the political prisoner pauses to speak about prison, but the reason why he's been there is too 'honourable' to give the idea of real prison – that of the thieves, the murderers, the cursed. The political prisoner emerges strengthened in his pride, and his tale is flawed by its epic nature] (UR 69–70). However, Sapienza, albeit not a political prisoner, is not a common delinquent either – if not because of her petty crime, theft, certainly because of her background and approach to prison. As Bond points out, Sapienza is neither a '"normal" prisoner in terms of class, education and privilege' nor a '"normal" prison *writer*, as a large proportion of prison writing as a genre is produced by those who perceive themselves to have been unjustly detained, political dissidents, for example.'[93]

Because of their testimonial component, Sapienza's prison novels also reconnect to the projects of documenting and giving voice to the realities of various marginalities, especially in relation to women's life, carried out for example by Maraini in *Memorie di una ladra* (1993) (as suggested by Morelli) and Giuliana Morandini in *Allora mi hanno rinchiusa* (1977), which collects women's testimonies in mental institutions. At the same time, it is important to acknowledge that *L'università di Rebibbia* and *Le certezze del dubbio* are not documentaries or collections of testimonies, but properly

93   Bond, 'A World without Men', 103. Based on these coordinates, another significant parallel is that with Piper Kerman's *Orange is the New Black. My Time in a Women's Prison* (2010) and the web television series based on it, which brought the marginal theme of the female prison to a wider audience. The series started in 2013 and is streamed on Netflix.

works of fiction, in which the reality of prison and the carceral identity are appropriated and transfigured into creative forms. Sapienza's experience in Rebibbia is the autobiographical nucleus around which she constructs her autofictional narrative, turning her five days of detention into 'pochi mesi' [a few months] (CD 15). Rather than a political prison *memoir*, in which the Italian tradition – from Silvio Pellico to Antonio Gramsci – is rich, or the documentary recording of women's stories, *L'università di Rebibbia* and *Le certezze del dubbio* constitute a vital journey into the margins of society, from the perspective of an anarchist artist who found in the margins her elective, affective community, and for this community she writes.

Conclusion

This study has traced the evolution of Sapienza's writing over twenty years, from her endeavour of self-reconstruction in *Lettera aperta* and *Il filo di mezzogiorno* in the 1960s to the narration of female imprisonment and marginality in the prison diptych of the 1980s. What has emerged is the portrait of an artist who was ahead of her times in many respects, both with regard to themes and literary forms. Her articulation of subjectivities that are rooted in the experience of a living body full of desires, engaged in a struggle for freedom, and radically anti-essentialist, brings her work close to the main principles of nomadic ethics. Furthermore, the tight link she establishes already in her early texts between individuals and their socio-political context prefigures the feminist notion that 'the personal is political', while her deconstruction of normative categories of gender and sexual orientation anticipates the core inspiration of queer theory. Finally, her performative and dialogic use of the text is the manifestation of her profound trust in the power of literature as a transformative force, thus providing an original way of overcoming the scepticism and intellectual play of postmodernism.

In this investigation, several thematic and structural connections have emerged that link her works together. The overarching inspiration of Sapienza's narratives lies in the notion of freedom, which guides her representation of identity construction as an ongoing negotiation between body and power. Maintaining the close relationship between the analysis of the self and its social, political and historical context, attention has been drawn to the major factors influencing Sapienza's narrative of a struggle for freedom, namely gender, sexuality and political ideology. On these grounds, patriarchal and heteronormative structures of society occupy a central position in her works, together with a left-wing political commitment perceived as reductively ideological, and the power involved in interpersonal relationships. Overall, in light of the prominence of the bodily dimension and the radical opposition to normative structures, I have defined Sapienza's works as Epicurean and anarchist, accounting for their peculiar position at the intersection of a number of discourses shaping contemporary critical debate, such as psychoanalysis, post-structuralism and Marxist-feminism.

It is my hope that this book will provide a solid basis for advancing the interest in, and appreciation of, this author's literary production, also broadening the field of Sapienza studies by opening up new perspectives and directions for future research. The numerous parallels with other Italian and international authors as well as philosophical perspectives suggested here represent further promising areas for future investigation. In addition, this book will hopefully generate interest in Sapienza's works that engage with literary forms other than the novel, such as the plays and film subjects collected in *Tre pièces e soggetti cinematografici*, the short stories of *Destino coatto*, and the poems of *Ancestrale*, as well as her varied contribution to cinema.

I want to conclude here by reflecting on the position that Sapienza's works occupy in the context of modern Italian literature. Their troubled publishing history suggests a double location for her texts, which should be contextualized both in the period of their composition or first publication (mainly from the 1960s to the 1980s) and in that of their critical and popular reception (projected into the twenty-first century). The trajectory followed by Sapienza's works links them to the tension between centre and margins pointed out by Alberto Asor Rosa in *Letteratura italiana del Novecento*.[1] The critic describes the evolution of an important part of Italian literature in the twentieth century according to a dynamic of initial marginality and later reconsideration. He mentions for example Svevo, Gadda, Campana, Slataper and Michelstaedter as authors who diverged from the canon – or canons – of their time and rather spoke to a future reader. Marginal authors, Asor Rosa argues, are worthy of particular attention, because they contribute to defining the contours and limits (in other words, the 'margins') of an established dominant canon, inasmuch as they

1   Asor Rosa, 'I fondamenti epistemologici della letteratura italiana del Novecento', in
     Asor Rosa, *Letteratura italiana del Novecento: bilancio di un secolo*, 5–33.

are 'the carriers of the most intense dynamism between form and conscious-ness'.[2] Marginal authors, defined by Asor Rosa as 'dis-assati' [misaligned],[3] are of central importance: 'Central of course does not mean that they can be reinserted into the historical and critical debate of their time, where on the contrary they were so often neglected; it means instead that they repre-sent what, within twentieth-century Italian literature, survives beyond the chronological end of the century and builds a bridge toward the future.'[4]

Similarly to the authors mentioned by Asor Rosa, Sapienza's life and works, which 'from the very outset [...] have appeared as excessive, eccentric and bizarre' (to borrow Fortini's words),[5] were fated to be understood only after much time. The eccentric features characterizing her works overlap with her position as a woman writer, for women authors have historically occupied, and continue to occupy, a marginal position in the Italian liter-ary canon.[6] 'The relationship between female writers and critics', Fortini writes, is still 'an unresolved matter', as 'in Italy, the debate regarding the admission of female writers into the canon of Italian literature is always open.'[7] Literary texts written by women often do not conform to the

2   Asor Rosa, 'I fondamenti epistemologici', 24.
3   Ibid. 24.
4   Ibid. 25.
5   Fortini, 'Beyond the Canon', 131.
6   On women's writing and the Italian literary canon, see also Alba Amoia, ed., *20th Century Italian Women Writers. The Feminine Experience* (Carbondale: Southern Illinois University Press, 1996); Ornella Marotti and Gabriella Brooke, eds, *Gendering Italian Fiction* (Rutherford, NJ: Fairleigh Dickinson University Press; London: Associated University Presses, 1999); Letizia Panizza and Sharon Wood, eds, *A History of Women's Writing in Italy* (Cambridge: Cambridge University Press, 2000); Rita Wilson, *Speculative Identities: Contemporary Italian Women's Narrative* (Leeds: Northern Universities Press, 2000); Sharon Wood, *Italian Women's Writing 1860–1994* (London: Athlone Press, 1995); Marina Zancan, *Il doppio itinerario della scrittura: la donna nella tradizione letteraria italiana* (Turin: Einaudi, 1998); Anna Maria Crispino, ed., *Oltrecanone. Generi, genealogie, tradizioni* (Rome: Iacobelli, 2014); Alessia Ronchetti and Maria Serena Sapegno, eds, *Dentro/fuori, sopra/sotto: critica femminista e canone letterario negli studi di italianistica* (Ravenna: Longo, 2007).
7   Fortini, 'Beyond the Canon', 133.

canon, and are rather characterized by the subversion of its hierarchical values. As Asor Rosa puts it, 'Women, then, are not inside that "canon". Perhaps, they could be in this other one, which is determined by the specificity of each writer's epistemological discovery, that is, the discovery of a worldview that is different from the past and that does not conform to any dominant view of reality.'[8] If, as Asor Rosa argues, it is not possible to go back and reinsert an author in the critical debate of his or her time, we can nonetheless address their marginalization and turn their exclusion based on their 'nonconformity' into the acknowledgement of their original contribution, giving them the place they deserve inside the literary canon.

Sapienza's narrative can be situated in a position of continuity with the investigation of identity that is typical of modernism, such as, in the Italian context, in the works of Pirandello and Svevo, their focus on a split self and the ultimately unresolved relationship between truth and lies, reality and consciousness. Similarly, she shares with postmodernist authors such as Italo Calvino and Umberto Eco the renunciation of a comprehensive and organic representation of reality and the heightened attention to the reader.[9] However, her works do not pursue the direction of intellectual play, lucid dissection of rationality and dissolution of reality into 'an autonomous world of signs',[10] which largely characterize Italian literary modernism and postmodernism. Compared to Svevo's and

8   Asor Rosa, 'I fondamenti epistemologici', 26.
9   I refer to the interpretation of main strands of twentieth-century Italian literature suggested by Renato Barilli in *La linea Svevo-Pirandello* (Milan: Mondadori, 2003); see also Guido Guglielmi, *'Tradizione del romanzo e romanzo sperimentale'*, in Franco Brioschi and Costanzo Di Girolamo, eds, *Manuale di Letteratura italiana. Storia per generi e problemi*, 4 vols (Turin: Bollati Boringhieri, 1999), IV, 556–615; and Vittorio Spinazzola, *La modernità letteraria* (Milan: Il Saggiatore, 2001). For critical accounts of Italian postmodernism, I refer to JoAnn Cannon, *Postmodern Italian Fiction* (Rutherford, NJ: Fairleigh Dickinson University Press, 1989); Dino S. Cervigni, ed., 'Italy 1991: the Modern and the Postmodern', special issue of *Annali d'italianistica*, 9 (1991); Remo Ceserani, *Raccontare il postmoderno* (Turin: Bollati Boringhieri, 1997); Romano Luperini, *Lezioni sul postmoderno: architettura, pittura, letteratura*, ed. Franco Marchese (Palermo: G. B. Palumbo, 1997).
10   Asor Rosa, *Stile Calvino* (Turin: Einaudi, 2001), 138.

Pirandello's representations of a split self and their linguistic 'transparency and functional neutrality',[11] and compared to Eco's intellectual play and Calvino's limpid use of imagination in his 'structural narrative',[12] Sapienza's writing, characterized by contradictions and syncretism, voices the passionate and painful struggle for freedom of a subject in a subaltern position. Sapienza's effort to reinstate a bodily dimension establishes a different relationship with rationality, which is exalted in the very moment it is denied an abstract and universal role and is pushed back into the context of a fleshy body, desiring and situated. And it is perhaps significant to note that even a philosopher such as Derrida and a writer such as Calvino, after following the investigation of reality as a textual relationship between signs, re-direct their attention towards the physical dimension of a perceptive body – Calvino with his project of *I cinque sensi* and subsequently *Palomar* (1983),[13] and Derrida with his reflections on touch.[14] Through her writing, Sapienza gives voice to a primary, foundational desire to become a subject and access a locus of agency, whilst modern and postmodern discourses on the falling apart of identity remain wholly internal to the history of a dominating, universalized male subject. In Sapienza's narrative, freedom is thus exposed as the unrecognized margin or condition of possibility of postmodernism, for which subjects in a subaltern position have to fight. The tight relationship she establishes between narrative, agency and bodily presence, in the context of an emancipatory struggle for freedom, brings about a strong form of desire that is extraneous to the novels of modern crisis and postmodern intellectualism.

The analysis of Sapienza's autofictional narrative and the focus on the emergence of a new subjectivity and an anti-ideological stance in her works can serve as a productive key to link together the works of other writers, from Aleramo to Maraini, Ramondino, Ortese, Morante, and, more recently, Ferrante, who employ literary communication in a similar

11   Barilli, *La linea Svevo-Pirandello*, 6.
12   Asor Rosa, *Stile Calvino*, 138.
13   Ibid. 140.
14   See Derrida, *On Touching – Jean-Luc Nancy*, trans. Christine Irizarry (Stanford, CA: Stanford University Press, 2005).

way.[15] For example, Maraini's *La lunga vita di Marianna Ucrìa, Bagheria* and *Memorie di una ladra*, and her theatrical production in the 1970s, with their focus on women's struggle and negotiation of identity, are particularly congruent with this approach. The same is true of Ramondino's texts *Althénopis* and *Guerra d'infanzia e di Spagna*, which provide autofictional recollections of the author's childhood and her socio-historical context. Ramondino's works have been analysed from a similar perspective by Burns in her *Fragments of* Impegno,[16] and have recently been associated with Sapienza's writings by Ferro.[17] Ortese's oneiric and syncretic semi-autobiographical narrative of *Il porto di Toledo*, and her acute perception of gendered power dynamics in *L'iguana*, are another significant component in this web of affinities. But it is certainly Morante who represents the most significant example of a creative and original use of literature that has much in common with Sapienza's, as I suggested elsewhere in a comparative reading of *L'arte della gioia* and *La storia*.[18] Despite undeniable differences existing between these two authors – most notably, Sapienza's perspective is integrally materialist, while Morante's work incorporates a transcendent dimension – both authors explore at length the complex dynamics of power and desire, within family relationships and in the broader context of history. Morante, like Sapienza, puts forward a radically anti-ideological stance, while also displaying a strenuous faith in the expressive and communicative possibilities of literature. This book therefore offers a framework to bring together Sapienza's distinctive voice with those of other writers such as Maraini, Ramondino, Ortese and Morante, whose works show how the modernist and postmodernist 'narrative of crisis' is *one* version of the story, to which other narratives can be opposed, thus modifying and

---

15   On Italian women writers' use of autobiographical and historical genres, see, for example, Carol Lazzaro-Weis, 'Stranger than Life? Autobiography and Historical Fiction', in Marotti and Brooke, *Gendering Italian Fiction*, 31–48, and Graziella Parati, *Public History, Private Stories: Italian Women's Autobiography* (Minneapolis: University of Minnesota Press, 1996).

16   Burns, 'Fabrizia Ramondino: The Politics of Identity', in *Fragments of* Impegno, 81–98.

17   See Ferro, 'Changing Recollections'.

18   Bazzoni, 'Agency and History'.

enriching our modern literary canon. This is one of the important critical tasks which I hope this book will contribute to advance.

Sapienza brings to twentieth-century Italian literature a remarkably mature and original voice. In their deconstructive and constructive effort, her works are characterized by multifarious, complex and at times contradictory tensions, proper to a form of writing that is itself in search of something, not in possession of an answer or a definitive perspective. Her writing is indeed defined by the same dissonances it represents, alternating passionate and rationalistic attitudes, uncertainty and strong determination. It is discontinuous and syncretic, shaped by the effort to represent and elaborate a new subjectivity, ahead of its time in many respects and thus moving, tentatively, in a plurality of directions. As Scarpa notes, through her representation of a radical yearning for freedom Sapienza 'evokes future values', meeting Braidotti's call for new ways of thinking about identity and politics: 'The search for new forms of political practice is indissolubly linked to creativity. We must learn to think about our subjectivity in ways that are radically different from the ones we are used to. We need a supplement of creative energy in order to realize such a breakthrough.'[19] Projected towards the future and yet rooted in the desiring matter of the body, Sapienza's narrative responds to the political and artistic challenge posed by post-structuralism by creating new ways of thinking the relationship between the self and the world that, without replicating the essentialist and logocentric understanding of the subject, are still able to produce agency and emancipation.

19   Braidotti, *Nuovi soggetti nomadi*, 20.

Bibliography

Goliarda Sapienza's Works

Sapienza, Goliarda, *Lettera aperta* (Milan: Garzanti, 1967; Palermo: Sellerio, 1997; Turin: UTET, 2007; Turin: Einaudi, 2017).

—— *Il filo di mezzogiorno* (Milan: Garzanti, 1969; Milan: La Tartaruga, 2003).

—— *Destino coatto* (*Nuovi Argomenti*, 19, July–September 1970; Rome: Empiria, 2002; Turin: Einaudi, 2011).

—— *L'università di Rebibbia* (Milan: Rizzoli, 1983; 2006; Turin: Einaudi, 2012).

—— *Le certezze del dubbio* (Catania: Pellicanolibri, 1987; Milan: Rizzoli, 2007).

—— 'Vengo da lontano', in *Il cuore, la guerra e la parola* (Siracusa: Ombra editrice, 1991), 128–32.

—— *L'arte della gioia* (Rome: Stampa Alternativa, 1994, partial edition, 189 pages; Rome: Stampa Alternativa, 1998, with subtitle *Romanzo anticlericale*, 624 pages; Turin: Einaudi, 2008, 511 pages).

—— *Io, Jean Gabin* (Turin: Einaudi, 2010).

—— *Il vizio di parlare a me stessa. Taccuini 1976–1989* (Turin: Einaudi, 2011).

—— *Siciliane* (Catania: Il Girasole Edizioni, 2012).

—— *Ancestrale* (Milan: La Vita Felice, 2013).

—— *La mia parte di gioia. Taccuini 1989–1992* (Turin: Einaudi, 2013).

—— *Tre pièces e soggetti cinematografici* (Milan: La vita felice, 2014).

—— *Elogio del bar* (Rome: Elliot Edizioni, 2014).

—— *Appuntamento a Positano* (Turin: Einaudi, 2015).

—— *Cronistoria di alcuni rifiuti editoriali dell'*Arte della gioia, ed. Angelo Pellegrino (Rome: Edizioni Croce, 2016).

Foreign Editions of Goliarda Sapienza's Works

L'arte della gioia

Sapienza, Goliarda, *In den Himmel stürzen*, trans. (into German) Constanze Neumann (Berlin: Aufbau-Verlag, 2005).

—— *L'art de la joie*, trans. (into French) Nathalie Castagné (Paris: Viviane Hamy, 2005).

—— *L'art de viure*, trans. (into Catalan) Anna Casassas (Barcelona: La Campana, 2007).

—— *El arte del placer*, trans. (into Spanish) José Ramón Monreal (Barcelona: Lumen, 2007).

—— *A arte da alegria*, trans. (into Portuguese) Simonetta Neto (Alfragide: Dom Quixote, 2009).

—— *Η τέχνη της χαράς*, trans. (into Greek) Anna Papastavrou (Athens: Patakis, 2009).

—— *The Art of Joy*, trans. (into English) Anne Milano Appel (London: Penguin Books, 2013; New York: Farrar, Straus & Giroux, 2013).

—— *Elämän ilo*, trans. (into Finnish) Laura Lahdensuu (Helsinki: Gummerus, 2014).

—— *Mutluluk Sanatı*, trans. (into Turkish) Sinem Carnabuci (Istanbul: Kafka Kitap, 2017).

Lettera aperta; *Il filo di mezzogiorno*

—— *Le fil d'une vie: Lettre ouverte, Le fil de midi*, trans. (into French) Nathalie Castagné (Paris: Viviane Hamy, 2008).

Io, Jean Gabin:

—— *Moi, Jean Gabin*, trans. (into French) Nathalie Castagné (Paris: Attila-Le Tripode, 2012).

L'università di Rebibbia:

—— *L'Université de Rebibbia*, trans. (into French) Nathalie Castagné (Paris: Attila-Le Tripode, 2013).

Secondary Sources

Ahmed, Sarah, *The Cultural Politics of Emotions* (New York: Routledge, 2004).

Aleramo, Sibilla, *Una donna* [1906], 6th edn (Milan: Feltrinelli, 1977).

Alford, C. Fred, 'What Would It Matter If Everything Foucault Said About Prison Were Wrong? *Discipline and Punish* After Twenty Years', *Theory and Society*, 29 (2000), 125–46.

Amoia, Alba, ed., *20th Century Italian Women Writers. The Feminine Experience* (Carbondale: Southern Illinois University Press, 1996).

Anderson, Linda, *Autobiography* (London: Routledge, 2001).

Andrigo, Mariagiovanna, 'L'evoluzione autobiografica di Goliarda Sapienza. Stile e contenuti', in Giovanna Providenti, ed., *'Quel sogno d'essere' di Goliarda Sapienza* (Rome: Aracne, 2012), 117–30.

—— 'Goliarda Sapienza's Permanent Autobiography', in Bazzoni, Bond and Wehling-Giorgi, eds, *Goliarda Sapienza in Context* (Rutherford, NJ: Fairleigh Dickinson University Press, 2016), 17–31.

Antonello, Pierpaolo, and Giuseppe Fornari, *Identità e desiderio. La teoria mimetica e la letteratura italiana* (Massa Carrara: Transeuropa, 2009).

—— and Florian Mussgnug, eds, *Postmodern* Impegno: *Ethics and Commitment in Contemporary Italian Culture* (Oxford: Peter Lang, 2009).

Arena, Maria, '*Il filo di mezzogiorno*. Morte e rinascita attraverso la scrittura', in Giovanna Providenti, ed., *'Quel sogno d'essere' di Goliarda Sapienza* (Rome: Aracne, 2012), 149–56.

Arendt, Hannah, *The Human Condition* [1958], 2nd edn (London: The University of Chicago Press, 1998).

—— *The Origins of Totalitarianism*, 3rd edn (London: Allen & Unwin, 1967).

Asor Rosa, Alberto, 'I fondamenti epistemologici della letteratura italiana del Novecento', in Asor Rosa, ed., *Letteratura italiana del Novecento: bilancio di un secolo* (Turin: Einaudi, 2000), 5–33.

—— *Stile Calvino* (Turin: Einaudi, 2001).

Bakhtin, Mikhail, 'The *Bildungsroman* and its Significance in the History of Realism (Toward a Historical Typology of the Novel)', in *Speech Genres and Other Late Essays*, ed. Caryl Emerson and Michael Holquist, trans. Vern W. McGee (Austin: University of Texas Press, 1986), 10–59.

Barbarulli, Clotilde, 'Essere o avere il corpo', in Monica Farnetti, ed., *Appassionata Sapienza* (Milan: La Tartaruga, 2012), 132–47.

Barilli, Renato, *La linea Svevo-Pirandello* (Milan: Mondadori, 2003).

Bazzoni, Alberica, 'Agency and History in Sapienza's *L'arte della gioia* and Morante's *La storia*', in Bazzoni, Bond and Wehling-Giorgi, eds, *Goliarda Sapienza in Context* (Rutherford, NJ: Fairleigh Dickinson University Press, 2016), 147–61.

—— 'Gli anni e le stagioni: prospettive su femminismo, politica e storia ne *L'arte della gioia*', in Giovanna Providenti, ed., *'Quel sogno d'essere' di Goliarda Sapienza* (Rome: Aracne, 2012), 33–52.

—— 'Pirandello's Legacy in the Narrative Writings of Goliarda Sapienza', *Pirandello Studies*, 36 (2016), 111–26.

——, Emma Bond and Katrin Wehling-Giorgi, eds, *Goliarda Sapienza in Context. Intertextual Relationship with Italian and European Culture* (Rutherford, NJ: Fairleigh Dickinson University Press, 2016).

Bebel, August, *Woman in the Past, Present and Future*, introduced by Moira Donald, trans. H. B. Adams Walther (London: Swan, 1988).

Bella, Andrée, 'A Backbone Held Together by Joy', in Bazzoni, Bond and Wehling-Giorgi, eds, *Goliarda Sapienza in Context* (Rutherford, NJ: Fairleigh Dickinson University Press, 2016), 47–61.

Bicchietti, Giulia, 'Esperienze dal carcere', in Giovanna Providenti, ed., *'Quel sogno d'essere' di Goliarda Sapienza* (Rome: Aracne, 2012), 181–90.

Bonarrigo, Ornella, 'La città-casbah di Goliarda Sapienza', in Mario Barenghi, Giuseppe Langella and Gianni Turchetta, *La città e l'esperienza del moderno*, 3 vols (Pisa: ETS, 2012), II, 163–74.

Bond, Emma, '"A World without Men": Interaffectivity and the Function of Shame in the Prison Writings of Goliarda Sapienza and Joan Henry', in Bond, Bazzoni and Wehling-Giorgi, *Goliarda Sapienza in Context*, 101–14.

—— 'Zeno's Unstable Legacy: Case-Writing and the Logic of Transference in Giuseppe Berto and Goliarda Sapienza', in Giuseppe Stellardi and Emmanuela Tandello Cooper, eds, *Italo Svevo and his Legacy for the Third Millennium: Contexts and Influences* (Leicester: Troubador Publishing Ltd, 2014), 101–13.

Bono, Paola, and Laura Fortini, eds, *Il romanzo del divenire: un Bildungsroman delle donne?* (Rome: Iacobelli, 2007).

——, and Sandra Kemp, eds, *Italian Feminist Thought: A Reader* (Oxford: Blackwell, 1991).

Braidotti, Rosi, *Nomadic Subjects: Embodiment and Sexual Difference in Contemporary Feminist Theory* (New York: Columbia University Press, 1994).

—— *Nuovi soggetti nomadi* (Rome: Luca Sossella Editore, 2002).

—— *Patterns of Dissonance: A Study of Women in Contemporary Philosophy*, trans. Elizabeth Guild (Cambridge: Polity, 1991).

Brooks, Peter, *Reading for the Plot: Design and Intention in Narrative* (London: Harvard University Press, 1992).

Burns, Jennifer, *Fragments of* Impegno: *Interpretations of Commitment in Contemporary Italian Narrative, 1980–2000* (Leeds: Northern Universities Press, 2002).

Butler, Judith, *Gender Trouble: Feminism and the Subversion of Identity* (London: Routledge, 1990).

—— *Undoing Gender* (New York: Routledge, 2004).

Calapso, Jole, *Una donna intransigente. Vita di Maria Giudice* (Palermo: Sellerio, 1996).

Calvino, Italo, *Palomar* (Turin: Einaudi, 1983).

—— *Se una notte d'inverno un viaggiatore* (Turin: Einaudi, 1979).

Cambria, Adele: 'Dopo l'Orca arriva la Gattoparda', *Il Giorno*, 6 September 1979.

—— 'Goliarda. Ricordi di aristocrazia operaia', *L'Unità*, 16 November 2003.

—— 'Goliarda Sapienza, la terribile arte della gioia', *L'Unità*, 26 September 2006.

—— 'Non perdono un Paese che l'ha rifiutata come scrittrice', *Queer*, 8 June 2008.

Cannon, JoAnn, *Postmodern Italian Fiction: The Crisis of Reason in Calvino, Eco, Sciascia, Malerba* (Rutherford, NJ: Fairleigh Dickinson University Press, 1989).

Cardella, Lara, *Volevo i pantaloni* (Milan: Mondadori, 1989).

Carta, Anna, 'Finestre, porte, luoghi reali e spazi immaginari nell'opera di Goliarda Sapienza', in Giovanna Providenti, ed., *'Quel sogno d'essere' di Goliarda Sapienza* (Rome: Aracne, 2012), 261–76.

Castagné, Nathalie, 'Archeologia di Modesta', in Giovanna Providenti, ed., *'Quel sogno d'essere' di Goliarda Sapienza* (Rome: Aracne, 2012), 81–91.

Catalano, Maria Pia: 'Goliarda Sapienza e le libere donne di Rebibbia', in Giuseppe Traina and Nunzio Zago, eds, *Carceri vere e d'invenzione dal tardo Cinquecento al Novecento* (Acireale and Rome: Bonanno, 2009).

Cavarero, Adriana, *A più voci. Filosofia dell'espressione vocale* (Milan: Feltrinelli, 2003). Eng. tr. *For More Than One Voice: Toward a Philosophy of Vocal Expression*, trans. Paul A. Kottman (Stanford, CA: Stanford University Press, 2005).

—— 'Per una teoria della differenza sessuale', in Diotima, *Il pensiero della differenza sessuale* (Milan: La Tartaruga, 1987), 43–79.

—— *Tu che mi guardi, tu che mi racconti. Filosofia della narrazione* (Milan: Feltrinelli, 1997). Eng. tr. *Relating Narratives: Storytelling and Selfhood*, trans. Paul A. Kottman (Stanford, CA: Stanford University Press, 2000).

—— and Franco Restaino, *Le filosofie femministe* (Milan: Bruno Mondadori, 2002).

Cento Bull, Anna, and Adalgisa Giorgio, 'The 1970s through the Looking Glass', in Cento Bull and Giorgio, eds, *Speaking Out and Silencing. Culture, Society and Politics in Italy in the 1970s* (London: Legenda, 2006), 1–8.

Cervigni, Dino S., ed., 'Italy 1991: The Modern and the Postmodern', special issue of *Annali d'italianistica*, 9 (1991).

Ceserani, Remo, *Raccontare il postmoderno* (Turin: Bollati Boringhieri, 1997).

Chemotti, Saveria, *Lo specchio infranto. La relazione tra padre e figlia in alcune scrittrici contemporanee* (Padua: Il poligrafo, 2010).

Ciccone, Stefano, *Essere maschi. Tra potere e libertà* (Turin: Rosenberg&Sellier, 2009).

Cinquemani, Viviana Rosaria, 'Da *Lettera aperta* a *Le certezze del dubbio*: la voce autobiografica di Goliarda Sapienza', *Revista Internacional de Culturas & Literaturas*, 2015 <http://www.escritorasyescrituras.com/da-lettera-aperta-a-le-certezze-del-dubbio-la-voce-autobiografica-di-goliarda-sapienza/> [Accessed 11 August 2016].

Cisney, Vernon W., *Derrida's Voice and Phenomenon: An Edinburgh Philosophical Guide* (Edinburgh: Edinburgh University Press, 2014).

Cooke, Emily, 'Disobedience is a Virtue: on Goliarda Sapienza's "Art of joy"', *The New Yorker*, 24 January 2014 <http://www.newyorker.com/books/page-turner/disobedience-is-a-virtue-on-goliarda-sapienzas-the-art-of-joy> [Accessed 15 September 2016].

Coppola, Argia, '*La Rivolta dei Fratelli.* Un dramma di Goliarda Sapienza', in Giovanna Providenti, ed., '*Quel sogno d'essere' di Goliarda Sapienza* (Rome: Aracne, 2012), 205–19.

Coquet, Jean-Claude, *Le istanze enuncianti. Fenomenologia e semiotica*, ed. Paolo Fabbri, trans. Elena Nicolini (Milan: Bruno Mondadori, 2008).

Corleone, Franco, 'Postfazione. Quali garanzie e diritti nel carcere femminile', in Susanna Ronconi and Grazia Zuffa, eds, *Recluse. Lo sguardo della differenza femminile sul carcere* (Rome: Ediesse, 2014), 263–72.

Crispino, Anna Maria, ed., *Oltrecanone. Generi, genealogie, tradizioni* (Rome: Iacobelli, 2014).

—— and Marina Vitale, eds, *Dell'ambivalenza. Dinamiche della narrazione in Elena Ferrante, Julie Otsuka e Goliarda Sapienza* (Rome: Iacobelli, 2016).

Cutrufelli, Maria Rosa, *La briganta* (Palermo: La luna, 1990).

—— et al., eds, *Il pozzo segreto. Cinquanta scrittrici italiane* (Florence: Giunti, 1993).

D'Ambra, Maria, 'Goliarda Sapienza: manuale di libertà portatile', *Via delle belle donne* <http://viadellebelledonne.wordpress.com/2012/11/10/goliarda-sapienza-manuale-di-liberta-portatile/> [Accessed 4 September 2016].

Damasio, Antonio, *Descarte's Error: Emotion, Reason and the Human Brain* (New York: G. P. Putnam, 1994).

Darrieussecq, Marie, 'L'autofiction, un genre pas sérieux', *Poétique*, 107 (1996), 369–80.

Davies, Ioan, *Writers in Prison* (Oxford: Basil Blackwell, 1990).

de Ceccatty, René, 'Sapienza, principesse hérétique', *Le Monde Des Livres*, 16 September 2005.

de Céspedes, Alba, 'Lettera a Natalia Ginzburg', in Maria Rosa Cutrufelli et al., eds, *Il pozzo segreto. Cinquanta scrittrici italiane* (Florence: Giunti, 1993), 32–6.

de Lauretis, Teresa, 'Queer Theory: Lesbian and Gay Sexualities', *Differences*, 3, 2 (1991), iii–xviii.

De Roberto, Federico, *I Vicerè* [1894] (Milan: Garzanzi, 1957).

Debenedetti, Giacomo, *Personaggi e destino: la metamorfosi del romanzo contemporaneo* (Milan: Il Saggiatore, 1977).

Delmand, Rosalind, 'Autobiografiction. *The Art of Joy* by Goliarda Sapienza', *Women's Review of Books*, 31, 3 (May/June 2014), 29–31.

Derrida, Jacques, *Of Grammatology*, corrected edn, trans. Gayatri Chakravorty Spivak (Baltimore, MD: Johns Hopkins University Press, 1997).

—— *On Touching – Jean-Luc Nancy*, trans. Christine Irizarry (Stanford, CA: Stanford University Press, 2005).

—— *Speech and Phenomena, and Other Essays on Husserl's Theory of Signs*, trans. David B. Allison (Evanston, IL: Northwestern University Press, 1973).

Di Natale, Rosa Maria, 'La famiglia e la scrittura. Vita di Goliarda Sapienza', *La Repubblica*, 20 April 2011 <http://ricerca.repubblica.it/repubblica/archivio/repubblica/2011/04/20/la-famiglia-la-scrittura-vita-di-goliarda.html> [Accessed 10 September 2016].

Di Rollo, Aureliana, 'Reforging the Maternal Bond: Motherhood, Mother-Daughter Relationships, and Female Relationality in Goliarda Sapienza's *L'arte della gioia*', in Bazzoni, Bond and Wehling-Giorgi, eds, *Goliarda Sapienza in Context* (Rutherford, NJ: Fairleigh Dickinson University Press, 2016), 33–45.

Diamond, Lisa M., *Sexual Fluidity. Understanding Women's Love and Desire* (London: Harvard University Press, 2008).

Diotima, *Il pensiero della differenza sessuale* (Milan: La Tartaruga, 1987).

Donnicci, Rocco, *Intenzioni d'amore, di scienza e d'anarchia. L'idea husserliana di filosofia e le sue implicazioni etico-politiche* (Naples: Bibliopolis, 1996).

Dossi, Carlo, *L'altrieri: nero su bianco* [1868] (Turin: Einaudi, 1972).

—— *Vita di Alberto Pisani* [1870] (Turin: Einaudi, 1976).

Driver, F., 'Power, Space and the Body: A Critical Assessment of Foucault's *Discipline and Punish*', *Environment and Planning D: Society and Space*, 3 (1985), 425–46.

Dyson, Michael, *Pride* (Oxford: Oxford University Press, 2006).

Eco, Umberto, *Il nome della rosa* (Milan: Bombiani, 1980).

Elam, Diane, *Feminism and Deconstruction* (London: Routledge, 1994).

Epicuro, *Lettera sulla felicità* (Rome: Stampa Alternativa, 1990).

Erikson, Erik H., *Childhood and Society*, rev. edn (London: Vintage, 1995).

Evans, J. Claude, *Strategies of Deconstruction: Derrida and the Myth of the Voice* (Minneapolis: University of Minnesota Press, 1991).

Fabbri, Paolo, 'Tra *Physis* e *Logos*', in Jean-Claude Coquet, *Le istanze enuncianti. Fenomenologia e semiotica*, ed. Paolo Fabbri, trans. Elena Nicolini (Milan: Bruno Mondadori, 2008), vii–xx.

Farnetti, Monica, ed., *Appassionata Sapienza* (Milan: La Tartaruga, 2012).

——— '"L'arte della gioia" e il genio dell'omicidio', in Monica Farnetti, ed., *Appassionata Sapienza* (Milan: La Tartaruga, 2012), 89–100.

——— *Il centro della cattedrale. I ricordi d'infanzia nella scrittura femminile* (Mantova: Tre Lune Edizioni, 2002).

——— 'Goliarda Sapienza e l'arte della gioia', in Monica Farnetti, *Tutte signore di mio gusto. Profili di scrittrici contemporanee* (Milan: Baldini Castoldi Dalai, 2008), 231–8.

——— 'Introduzione', in Goliarda Sapienza, *Lettera aperta* (Turin: Einaudi, 2017), v–xv.

Ferrante, Elena, *L'amica geniale* (Rome: edizioni e/o, 2011).

——— *L'amore molesto* (Rome: edizioni e/o, 1995).

——— *Storia della bambina perduta. L'amica geniale, quarto e ultimo volume* (Rome: edizioni e/o, 2014).

——— *Storia di chi fugge e di chi resta. L'amica geniale volume terzo* (Rome: edizioni e/o, 2013).

——— *Storia del nuovo cognome. L'amica geniale volume secondo* (Rome: edizioni e/o, 2012).

Ferraris, Maurizio, *Introduzione a Derrida* (Bari: Laterza, 2008).

Ferro, Laura, 'Changing Recollections: Goliarda Sapienza and Fabrizia Ramondino Writing and Rewriting Childhood', in Bazzoni, Bond and Wehling-Giorgi, eds, *Goliarda Sapienza in Context* (Rutherford, NJ: Fairleigh Dickinson University Press, 2016), 181–98.

Fortini, Laura, '*L'arte della gioia* e il genio dell'omicidio mancato', in Monica Farnetti, ed., *Appassionata Sapienza* (Milan: La Tartaruga, 2012), 101–26.

——— 'Beyond the Canon: Goliarda Sapienza and Twentieth Century Italian Literary Tradition', in Bazzoni, Bond and Wehling-Giorgi, eds, *Goliarda Sapienza in Context* (Rutherford, NJ: Fairleigh Dickinson University Press, 2016), 131–46.

Fortney, James Michael, 'Con quel tipo lì: Homosexual Characters in Natalia Ginzburg's Narrative Families', *Italica*, 86 (December 2009).

Foscolo, Ugo, *Sesto tomo dell'io* [1799–1800] (Turin: Einaudi, 1991).

Foucault, Michel, *Discipline and Punish: The Birth of the Prison*, 2nd edn, trans. Alan Sheridan (New York: Vintage Books, 1995).

——— *The Will to Knowledge. Volume 1, The History of Sexuality*, trans. Robert Hurley (Harmondsworth: Penguin, 1990).

Fraire, Manuela, '*Il filo di mezzogiorno*. Goliarda paziente', in Monica Farnetti, ed., *Appassionata Sapienza* (Milan: La Tartaruga, 2012), 127–31.

Franzini, Elio, *L'altra ragione. Sensibilità, immaginazione e forma artistica* (Milan: Il Castoro, 2007).

Freud, Sigmund, 'The Aetiology of Hysteria' [1986], in *The Standard Edition of the Complete Psychological Works of Sigmund Freud*, 24 vols, trans. and ed. James Strachey (London: Hogarth Press, 1953–1974), III.

—— *The Ego and the Id*, trans. Joan Riviere (London: Hogarth Press, 1927).

—— 'Female Sexuality' [1931], in *The Standard Edition of the Complete Psychological Works of Sigmund Freud*, 24 vols, trans. and ed. James Strachey (London: Hogarth Press and the Institute of Psychoanalysis, 1953–74), XXI.

—— 'Femininity' [1933], *The Standard Edition of the Complete Psychological Works of Sigmund Freud*, 24 vols, trans. and ed. James Strachey (London: Hogarth Press and the Institute of Psychoanalysis, 1953–1974), XXII.

Gadda, Carlo Emilio, *L'Adalgisa. Disegni milanesi* [1944], 2nd edn (Florence: Le Monnier, 1945).

—— *La cognizione del dolore* [1963], ed. Emilio Manzotti (Turin: Einaudi, 1987).

Gasparini, Philippe, 'Autofiction *vs* autobiographie', *Tangence*, 97 (2011), 11–24.

Gianini Belotti, Elena, *Dalla parte delle bambine* (Milan: Feltrinelli, 1973).

Ginzburg, Natalia, 'Discorso sulle donne', in Maria Rosa Cutrufelli et al., eds, *Il pozzo segreto. Cinquanta scrittrici italiane* (Florence: Giunti, 1993), 27–32.

—— *Lessico famigliare* [1963] (Turin: Einaudi, 1992).

—— *Valentino* [1951], in *Cinque romanzi brevi*, 2nd edn (Turin: Einaudi, 1993).

—— *Le voci della sera* [1961], in *Cinque romanzi brevi*, 2nd edn (Turin: Einaudi, 1993).

Giorgio, Adalgisa, ed., *Writing Mothers and Daughters. Renegotiating the Mother in Western European Narratives by Women* (New York and Oxford: Berghann Books, 2002).

——, and Julia Waters, 'Introduction. Gender, Generation, Legacy', in Giorgio and Waters, eds, *Women's Writing in Western Europe: Gender, Generation and Legacy* (Newcastle: Cambridge Scholars, 2007), 1–19.

Gobbato, Emma, 'Goliarda Sapienza: The Unknown Scriptwriter', in Bazzoni, Bond and Wehling-Giorgi, *Goliarda Sapienza in Context*, 75–86.

—— 'Un primo piano di profilo', in Giovanna Providenti, ed., *'Quel sogno d'essere' di Goliarda Sapienza* (Rome: Aracne, 2012), 277–84.

Gramsci, Antonio, 'L'appello ai pargoli', in *Avanti!*, 31 July 1916.

—— 'Lettera a Teresina' (16 November 1931), in *Lettere dal carcere*, ed. Sergio Caprioglio and Elsa Fubini (Turin: Einaudi, 1968), 525–6.

—— 'Stregoneria', in *Avanti!*, 4 March 1916.

Gregg, Melissa, and Gregory J. Seigworth, eds, *The Affect Theory Reader* (Durham, NC and London: Duke University Press, 2010).

Guglielmi, Guido, 'Tradizione del romanzo e romanzo sperimentale', in Franco Brioschi and Costanzo Di Girolamo, eds, *Manuale di Letteratura italiana. Storia
per generi e problemi*, 4 vols (Turin: Bollati Boringhieri, 1999), IV, 556–615.

Halberstam, Judith, *Female Masculinity* (London: Duke University Press, 1998).

Heckert, Jamie, and Richard Cleminson, 'Ethics, Relationships and Power', in Heckert
and Cleminson, eds, *Anarchism and Sexuality: Ethics, Relationships and Power*
(Oxon: Routledge, 2011), 1–22.

Heffernan, Esther, 'Gendered Perceptions of Dangerous and Dependent Women:
"Gun Molls" and "Fallen Women"', in Barbara H. Zaitzow and Jim Thomas,
eds, *Women in Prison. Gender and Social Control* (Boulder, CO and London:
Lynne Rienner Publishers, 2003), 39–64.

Heidegger, Martin, *Being and Time*, trans. John Macquarrie and Edward Robinson
(Oxford: Blackwell, 1967).

Hernández, Maria Belén, 'La fortuna letteraria de *L'arte della gioia* in Europa', in
Giovanna Providenti, ed., *'Quel sogno d'essere' di Goliarda Sapienza* (Rome:
Aracne, 2012), 99–113.

—— 'La fortuna literaria de Goliarda Sapienza', *Arena Romanistica*, 5 (2009), 140–52.

—— 'Orlando and Modesta: Two Voices for the Freedom of Women', in Bazzoni,
Bond and Wehling-Giorgi, eds, *Goliarda Sapienza in Context* (Rutherford, NJ:
Fairleigh Dickinson University Press, 2016), 115–27.

Hildt, Moritz, 'Towards a Theory of Eccentricity', in *Off Centre. Eccentricity and
Gender*, 27 (2009) <http://www.genderforum.org/issues/off-centre/towards-
a-theory-of-eccentricity/> [Accessed 10 September 2016].

Holub, Renate, 'Weak Thought and Strong Ethics. The "Postmodern" and Feminist
Theory in Italy', in *Annali d'italianistica*, 9 (1991), 124–43.

Husserl, Edmund, *L'idea della fenomenologia: cinque lezioni*, ed. Carlo Sini (Rome
and Bari: Laterza, 1992).

Imberty, Claude, 'Gender e generi letterari: il caso di Goliarda Sapienza', in *Narrativa*,
30 (2008), 51–61.

Irigaray, Luce, *Speculum of the Other Woman*, trans. Gillian Gill (Ithaca, NY: Cornwell
University Press, 1985).

—— *This Sex Which is Not One*, trans. Catherine Porter (Ithaca, NY: Cornwell University Press, 1985).

Iser, Wolfgang, *The Act of Reading: A Theory of Aesthetic Response* (London: Routledge
& Kegan Paul, 1978).

Johnson, Mark, *The Body in the Mind. The Bodily Basis of Meaning, Imagination and
Reason* (Chicago: University of Chicago Press, 1987).

Kafka, Franz, *Racconti* (Milan: Mondadori, 1970).

Kerman, Piper, *Orange Is the New Black: My Time in a Women's Prison* (2010) (London: Abacus, 2013).

Kermode, Frank, *The Sense of an Ending: Studies in the Theory of Fiction: With a New Epilogue*, new edn (Oxford: Oxford University Press, 2000).

Kimmel, Michael, 'Men's and Women's Studies: Promise, Pitfall and Possibilities', in *About Gender*, 1, 1 (2012).

Kosofsky Sedgwick, Eve, *Epistemology of the Closet* (Berkeley: University of California Press, 1990).

—— *Touching Feeling: Affect, Pedagogy, Performativity* (Durham, NC: Duke University Press, 2003).

Lakoff, George, and Mark Johnson, *Metaphors We Live By* (Chicago and London: University of Chicago Press, 1980).

Landry, Donna, and Gerald MacLean, eds, *The Spivak Reader. Selected Works of Gayatri Chakravorty Spivak* (London: Routledge, 1996).

Langiano, Anna, '*Lettera aperta*: il dovere di tornare', in Giovanna Providenti, ed., '*Quel sogno d'essere' di Goliarda Sapienza* (Rome: Aracne, 2012), 131–47.

Lazzaro-Weis, Carol, 'Stranger than Life? Autobiography and Historical Fiction', in Maria Ornella Marotti and Gabriella Brooke, eds, *Gendering Italian Fiction* (Rutherford, NJ: Fairleigh Dickinson University Press; London: Associated University Presses, 1999), 31–48.

Le Piane, Fausta Genziana, *La meraviglia è nemica della prudenza. Invito alla lettura de 'L'arte della gioia' di Goliarda Sapienza* (Ragusa: Edizioni Eventualmente, 2013).

Lejeune, Philippe, *On Autobiography*, ed. Paul John Eakin, trans. Katherine Leary (Minneapolis: University of Minnesota Press, 1989).

Lessing, Doris, *The Good Terrorist* (London: J. Cape, 1985).

Levi, Carlo, *Cristo si è fermato a Eboli* [1947] (Turin: Einaudi, 1978).

Levi, Primo, *Se questo è un uomo* [1947] (Turin: Einaudi, 1986).

Lévi-Strauss, Claude, *The Elementary Structures of Kinship*, rev. edn, trans. James Harle Bell and John Richard von Sturmer (Boston, MA: Beacon Press, 1969).

Luperini, Romano, *Lezioni sul postmoderno: architettura, pittura, letteratura*, ed. Franco Marchese (Palermo: G. B. Palumbo, 1997).

—— *Pirandello* (Rome: GLF Editori Laterza, 1999).

McOmber, James B., 'Silencing the Patient: Freud, Sexual Abuse, and "The Etiology of Hysteria"', *Quarterly Journal of Speech*, 82, 4 (1996), 343–63.

Maenza, Maria Teresa, 'Fuori dall'ordine simbolico della madre: Goliarda Sapienza e Luce Irigaray', in Giovanna Providenti, ed., '*Quel sogno d'essere' di Goliarda Sapienza* (Rome: Aracne, 2012), 243–60.

Malatesta, Errico, *L'anarchia. Il nostro programma* (Rome: Datanews, 2001).

Manzoni, Alessandro, *I promessi sposi* [1840] (Milan: Garzanti, 1992).

Maraini, Dacia, *Bagheria* (Milan: Rizzoli, 1993).
—— *La lunga vita di Marianna Ucrìa* (Milan: Rizzoli, 1990).
—— *Memorie di una ladra* (Milan: Rizzoli, 1993).
—— 'Ricordo di Goliarda Sapienza', in Goliarda Sapienza, *Lettera aperta* (Palermo: Sellerio, 1997), 9–11.
—— *Voci* (Milan: Rizzoli, 1994).
Marotti, Maria Ornella, 'Autobiography', in Rinaldina Russell, ed., *The Feminist Encyclopedia of Italian Literature* (Westport, CT: Greenwood Press, 1997), 22–3.
——, and Gabriella Brooke, eds, *Gendering Italian Fiction* (Rutherford, NJ: Fairleigh Dickinson University Press; London: Associated University Presses, 1999).
Martín Clavijo, Milagro, 'I luoghi della formazione di Goliarda Sapienza: *Io, Jean Gabin*', in Giovanna Providenti, ed., *'Quel sogno d'essere' di Goliarda Sapienza* (Rome: Aracne, 2012), 157–74.
Mazza Galanti, Carlo, 'Autofinzioni', *minima&moralia*, 8 July 2010 <http://www.minimaetmoralia.it/wp/autofinzioni/> [Accessed 28 March 2016].
Michieli, Fabio, '"Ancestrale" di Goliarda Sapienza. Appunti di lettura, con una nota impropriamente filologica', *Poetarum Silva*, 7 November 2013 <http://poetarumsilva.com/2013/11/07/ancestrale-di-goliarda-sapienza-appunti-di-lettura-con-una-nota-impropriamente-filologica/> [Accessed 6 September 2016].
Miller, Alice, *The Drama of Being a Child: The Search for the True Self* (London: Virago, 1985).
Milletti, Nerina, and Luisa Passerini, eds, *Fuori della norma. Storie lesbiche nell'Italia della prima metà del Novecento* (Turin: Rosenberg&Seller, 2011).
Minsky, Rosalind, *Psychoanalysis and Gender: An Introductory Reader* (London: Routledge, 1996).
Morandini, Giuliana, *E allora mi hanno rinchiusa: testimonianze dal manicomio femminile* (Milan: Bompiani, 1977).
Morante, Elsa, *Aracoeli* (Turin: Einaudi, 1982).
—— *L'isola di Arturo* (Turin: Einaudi, 1957).
—— *La storia* (Turin: Einaudi, 1974).
Morelli, Maria, '"L'acqua in gabbia": The Heterotopic Space of the (Female) Prison in Goliarda Sapienza's and Dacia Maraini's Narratives', in Bazzoni, Bond and Wehling-Giorgi, *Goliarda Sapienza in Context*, 199–214.
Muraro, Luisa, 'Il pensiero dell'esperienza', in *Per amore del mondo* (2006) <http://www.diotimafilosofe.it/riv_wo.php?id=13> [Accessed 6 September 2016].
—— 'The Symbolic Independence from Power', *Cosmos and History*, 5, 1 (2009), 57–67.
Nozzoli, Anna, *Tabù e coscienza: La condizione femminile nella letteratura italiana del novecento* (Florence: La Nuova Italia, 1978).

Nussbaum, Martha, *Creating Capabilites. The Human Development Approach* (London: The Belknap Press of Harvard University Press, 2011).

Ortese, Anna Maria, *L'iguana* [1965] (Milan: Adelphi, 1986).

—— *Il porto di Toledo* [1975] (Milan: Adelphi, 1998).

Ortu, Giuliana, 'Cosa vedono gli occhi di quella bambina. *Lettera aperta*', in Monica Farnetti, ed., *Appassionata Sapienza* (Milan: La Tartaruga, 2012), 148–79.

—— 'Visi dischiusi ad ascoltare: Goliarda Sapienza narratrice di visioni', in Lucia Cardone and Sara Filippelli, eds, *Cinema e scritture femminili. Letterate italiane fra la pagina e lo schermo* (Rome: Iacobelli, 2011), 93–105.

Palieri, Maria Serena, 'La Sapienza e lo scrivere', *L'Unità*, 26 July 2003 <http://cerca.unita.it/ARCHIVE/xml/95000/91219.xml?key=PALIERI+MARIA+SERENA&first=20&orderby=0&f=fir> [Accessed 10 September 2016].

Panizza, Letizia, and Sharon Wood, eds, *A History of Women's Writing in Italy* (Cambridge: Cambridge University Press, 2000).

Parati, Graziella, *Public History, Private Stories: Italian Women's Autobiography* (Minneapolis: University of Minnesota Press, 1996).

Parisi, Luciano, 'Le adolescenti sole nella narrativa di Grazia Deledda', *Italian Studies*, 69, 2 (2014), 246–61.

—— *Uno specchio infranto. Adolescenti e abuso sessuale nell'opera di Alberto Moravia* (Alessandria: Edizioni dell'Orso, 2013).

Pasolini, Pier Paolo, *Lettere luterane. Il progresso come falso progresso* [1976] (Turin: Einaudi, 2003).

—— *Scritti corsari* [1975] (Milan: Garzanti, 2008).

Pellegrino, Angelo, 'Un'analisi selvaggia', in Goliarda Sapienza, *Il filo di mezzogiorno* (Milan: La Tartaruga, 2003), 5–12.

—— '*Ancestrale* ritrovato', in Goliarda Sapienza, *Ancestrale* (Milan: La Vita Felice, 2013), 5–16.

—— 'Goliarda e i suoi taccuini', in Goliarda Sapienza, *Il vizio di parlare a me stessa. Taccuini 1976–1989* (Turin: Einaudi, 2011), v–xi.

—— 'Introduzione', in Goliarda Sapienza, *Destino coatto* (Rome: Empiria, 2002), 5–7.

—— 'Introduzione', in Goliarda Sapienza, *Tre pièces e soggetti cinematografici* (Milan: La vita felice, 2014), 5–14.

—— 'Lunga marcia dell'*Arte della gioia*', in Goliarda Sapienza, *L'arte della gioia* (Turin: Einaudi, 2008), v–x.

—— 'I luoghi, la felicità, i personaggi', in Goliarda Sapienza, *Appuntamento a Positano* (Turin: Einaudi, 2015), 179–81.

—— 'Un personaggio singolare, un romanzo nuovo, una donna da amare per sempre', in Monica Farnetti, ed., *Appassionata Sapienza* (Milan: La Tartaruga, 2012), 69–88.

—— 'Postfazione', in Goliarda Sapienza, *Io, Jean Gabin* (Turin: Einaudi, 2010), 113–24.

—— 'Postfazione alla prima edizione', in Goliarda Sapienza, *Le certezze del dubbio* (Milan: Rizzoli, 2007), 187–9.

—— 'Ritratto di Goliarda Sapienza', in Goliarda Sapienza, *Lettera aperta* (Turin: Einaudi, 2017), 151–82.

Pincio, Tommaso, 'Il *what if* all'italiana. Un romanzo maestoso e misconosciuto', *Il manifesto*, 30 August 2008 <http://www.giugenna.com/interventi/tommaso_pincio_sul_new_italian.html> [Accessed 2 August 2014].

Pirandello, Luigi, *Il fu Mattia Pascal* [1904] (Milan: Mondadori, 1973).

—— *Maschere nude*, 2 vols [1958], 10th edn (Milan: Mondadori, 1986).

—— *Uno, nessuno, centomila* [1926] (Milan: Feltrinelli, 1993).

Polizzi, Goffredo, 'The Art of Change. Race and the Body in Goliarda Sapienza's *L'arte della gioia*', in Bazzoni, Bond and Wehling-Giorgi, eds, *Goliarda Sapienza in Context* (Rutherford, NJ: Fairleigh Dickinson University Press, 2016), 163–77.

Poma, Vittorio, *Una maestra tra i socialisti. L'itinerario politico di Maria Giudice* (Milan and Bari: Cariplo-Laterza, 1991).

Providenti, Giovanna, 'Funambola ai bordi del pozzo: Goliarda Sapienza', *Vita pensata*, 8 March 2011 <http://www.vitapensata.eu/2011/03/08/funambola-ai-bordi-del-pozzo-goliarda-sapienza/> [Accessed 10 July 2014].

—— 'Introduzione', in Giovanna Providenti, ed., *'Quel sogno d'essere' di Goliarda Sapienza* (Rome: Aracne, 2012), 13–30.

—— 'L'opera di Goliarda Sapienza tra ambivalenza e ambizione', in Giovanna Providenti, ed., *'Quel sogno d'essere' di Goliarda Sapienza* (Rome: Aracne, 2012), 289–302.

—— *La porta è aperta* (Catania: Villaggio Maori Edizioni, 2010).

——, ed., *'Quel sogno d'essere' di Goliarda Sapienza. Percorsi critici su una delle maggiori autrici del Novecento italiano* (Rome: Aracne, 2012).

Rame, Franca, *Stupro* (Archivio Franca Rame Dario Fo, 1975) <http://www.archivio.francarame.it > [Accessed 4 August 2015].

Ramondino, Fabrizia, *Althénopis* (Turin: Einaudi, 1981).

—— *Guerra di infanzia e di Spagna* (Turin: Einaudi, 2001).

Rauch, Sarah, '"The Art of Joy" by Goliarda Sapienza', *Lambda Literary*, 17 July 2013 <http://www.lambdaliterary.org/reviews/07/17/the-art-of-joy-by-goliarda-sapienza/> [Accessed 10 August 2015].

Rich, Adrienne, 'Compulsory Heterosexuality and Lesbian Existence', *Signs*, 4, 5, *Women: Sex and Sexuality* (Summer 1980), 631–60.

Rizzarelli, Maria, 'Schermo, schermo delle mie brame ... La formazione dello sguardo di Goliarda Sapienza', *Arabeschi*, 9 (2017), 32–47.

Rodigari, Tullia, 'Goliarda, Modesta e Machiavelli', in Giovanna Providenti, ed., *'Quel sogno d'essere' di Goliarda Sapienza* (Rome: Aracne, 2012), 93–8.

—— 'La personalità culturale e storica di Goliarda Sapienza' (Unpublished Doctoral Thesis, Università degli Studi di Milano Bicocca, 2011).

Ronchetti, Alessia, 'Postmodernismo e pensiero italiano della differenza sessuale', in Pierpaolo Antonello and Florian Mussgnug, eds, *Postmodern* Impegno: *Ethics and Commitment in Contemporary Italian Culture* (Oxford: Peter Lang, 2009), 99–119.

Ronconi, Susanna, and Grazia Zuffa, eds, *Recluse. Lo sguardo della differenza femminile sul carcere* (Rome: Ediesse, 2014).

Rosa, Giovanna, *Il patto narrativo* (Milan: Il Saggiatore, 2008).

Ross, Charlotte, 'Goliarda Sapienza's Eccentric Interruptions: Multiple Selves, Gender Ambiguities and Disrupted Desires', *altrelettere* (2012) <http://www.altrelettere. uzh.ch/article/view/al_uzh-2> [Accessed 19 July 2016].

—— 'Goliarda Sapienza's "French Connections"', in Bazzoni, Bond and Wehling-Giorgi, eds, *Goliarda Sapienza in Context* (Rutherford, NJ: Fairleigh Dickinson University Press, 2016), 87–100.

—— 'Identità di genere e sessualità nelle opere di Goliarda Sapienza: finzioni necessariamente *queer*', in Giovanna Providenti, ed., *'Quel sogno d'essere' di Goliarda Sapienza* (Rome: Aracne, 2012), 223–42.

Sackville-West, Vita, and Virginia Woolf, *The Letters of Vita Sackville-West to Virginia Woolf*, ed. Louise A. DeSalvo and Mitchell Alexander Leaska (London: Virago, 1992).

Sambuco, Patrizia, *Corporeal Bonds: The Daughter-Mother Relationship in Twentieth Century Italian Women's Writing* (Toronto: University of Toronto Press, 2012).

Sangars, Romaric, 'Goliarda Sapienza: l'art de la joie', *Chronicart.com*, 13 November 2005 <http://www.chronicart.com/livres/goliarda-sapienza-l-art-de-la-joie/> [Accessed 19 August 2016].

Santino, Umberto, 'Maria Giudice', *Enciclopedia delle donne* <http://www.enciclope diadelledonne.it/biografie/maria-giudice/> [Accessed 28 July 2014].

Sartre, Jean-Paul, *What is Literature?*, trans. Bernard Frechtman (New York: Harper and Row, 1965).

Scarpa, Domenico, 'Senza alterare niente', in G. Sapienza, *L'arte della gioia* (Turin: Einaudi, 2008), 515–38.

Scarparo, Susanna, and Aureliana Di Rollo, 'Mothers, Daughters and Family in Goliarda Sapienza's *L'arte della gioia*', *The Italianist*, 35, I (2015), 91–106.

—— and Rita Wilson, eds, *Across Genres, Generations and Borders: Italian Women Writing Lives* (Newark: University of Delaware Press, 2004).

Smith, Sidonie, *Subjectivity, Identity and the Body* (Bloomington: Indiana University Press, 1993).

Solinger, Rickie et al., eds, *Interrupted Life: Experiences of Incarcerated Women in the United States* (Berkley: University of California Press, 2010).

Somers, Margaret, 'The Narrative Constitution of Identity. A Relational and Network Approach', *Theory and Society*, 5, 23 (October 1994), 605–49.

Sovente, Michele, *La donna nella letteratura oggi* (Fossano: Esperienze, 1979).

Spierenburg, Pieter, 'The Origins of the Prison', in Clive Emsley, ed., *The Persistent Prison: Problems, Images and Alternatives* (London: Francis Boutle Publishers, 2005), 27–47.

Spinazzola, Vittorio, 'Le articolazioni del pubblico', in Alberto Asor Rosa, ed., *Letteratura italiana del Novecento: bilancio di un secolo* (Turin: Einaudi, 2000), 180–202.

—— *La modernità letteraria* (Milan: Il Saggiatore, 2001).

—— *L'offerta letteraria: narratori italiani del secondo Novecento* (Naples: Morano, 1990).

—— *Il romanzo antistorico* (Rome: Editori Riuniti, 1990).

Stalin, Joseph, 'Anarchism or Socialism?', in *Works, Vol. 1, December 1906–January 1907* (Moscow: Foreign Languages Publishing House, 1954), Marxist Internet Archive, 2008 <http://www.marxists.org/reference/archive/stalin/works/1906/12/x01. htm> [Accessed 22 August 2015].

Stellardi, Giuseppe, '*Pensiero debole*, Nihilism and Ethics, or How Strong is Weakness?', in Pierpaolo Antonello and Florian Mussgnug, eds, *Postmodern* Impegno: *Ethics and Commitment in Contemporary Italian Culture* (Oxford: Peter Lang, 2009), 83–98.

—— '"Il tempo degli atti possibili": qualche riflessione sulle dimensioni della temporalità in letteratura, a partire da *La cognizione del dolore*', in Maria Antonietta Terzoli, Alberto Asor Rosa and Giorgio Inglese, eds, *Letteratura e filologia fra Svizzera e Italia. Studi in onore di Guglielmo Gorni, Vol. 3* (Rome: Edizioni di storia e letteratura, 2010), 229–46.

—— 'Il "tempo ultimo": strutture della temporalità nell'opera di Italo Svevo', *Cuadernos de Filología Italiana*, 18 (2011), 115–39.

Sterne, Laurence, *The Life and Opinions of Tristram Shandy, Gentleman* [1760], ed. Tim Parnell (London: J. M. Dent, 2000).

Taglietti, Cristina, 'Goliarda Sapienza, dall'oblio a icona gauche', *Corriere della Sera*, 22 June 2006 <http://archiviostorico.corriere.it/2006/giugno/22/Goliarda _Sapienza_dall_oblio_icona_co_9_060622118.shtml> [Accessed 12 July 2014].

Tomasi di Lampedusa, Giuseppe, *Il Gattopardo* [1958] (Milan: Feltrinelli, 2004).

Tondelli, Pier Vittorio, *Altri libertini* [1980] (Milan: Feltrinelli, 1987).

Toscano, Anna, '*Ancestrale*, finalmente', in Goliarda Sapienza, *Ancestrale* (Milan: La Vita Felice, 2013), 181–93.

Trevisan, Alessandra, "'La gioia è più che ogni voluttà": sessualità e maternità ne *L'arte della gioia*', in Giovanna Providenti, ed., '*Quel sogno d'essere' di Goliarda Sapienza* (Rome: Aracne, 2012), 53–60.

—— 'Maria Giudice: nella storia e nella memoria di Goliarda Sapienza', *Poetarum Silva*, 26 February 2016 <https://poetarumsilva.com/2016/02/26/maria-giudice-nella-storia-e-nella-memoria-di-goliarda-sapienza/> [Accessed 4 October 2016].

Turner, Mark, *The Literary Mind* (Oxford: Oxford University Press, 1996).

Vattimo, Gianni, 'Nihilism as Emancipation', *Cosmos and History*, 5, 1 (2009), 20–3.

Venè, Gianfranco, *Il capitale e il poeta* (Milan: Sugar, 1972).

—— 'È l'alienazione che condanna gli uomini alla loro classe sociale', in Venè, *Pirandello fascista: la condizione borghese tra ribellione e rivoluzione* (Venice: Marsilio Editori, 1981), 103–12.

Verga, Giovanni, 'L'amante di Gramigna', in *Vita dei campi* [1880] (Milan: Longanesi, 1980).

—— *Mastro Don Gesualdo* [1889] (Milan: Feltrinelli, 1995).

—— 'La roba', in *Novelle rusticane* [1883], 2nd edn (Turin: F. Casanova, 1885).

Vigorita, Manuela, 'Omaggio a Goliarda Sapienza: se l'arte della gioia diventa libertà', *Buddismo e società*, 93 (July/August 2002).

Vittorini, Elio, 'Politica e cultura. Lettera a Togliatti', *Il Politecnico*, January–March 1947.

Wehling-Giorgi, Katrin, "'Ero separata da me": Memory, Selfhood and *Mother-Tongue* in Goliarda Sapienza and Elena Ferrante', in Bazzoni, Bond and Wehling-Giorgi, eds, *Goliarda Sapienza in Context* (New Rutherford, NJ: Fairleigh Dickinson University Press, 2016), 215–29.

—— "'Totetaco": The Mother-Child Dyad and the Pre-Conceptual Self in Elsa Morante's *La Storia* and *Aracoeli*', *Writing Childhood in Postwar Women's Writing*, special issue of *Forum for Modern Language Studies*, 49 (2013), 192–200.

Wilson, Rita, *Speculative Identities: Contemporary Italian Women's Narrative* (Leeds: Northern Universities Press, 2000).

Winnicott, Donald W., *Collected Papers: Through Paediatrics to Psychoanalysis* (New York: Basic Books, 1958).

—— *The Maturational Processes and the Facilitating Environment* (London: Hogarth Press and the Institute of Psychoanalysis, 1965).

Wittig, Monique, *The Straight Mind and Other Essays*, trans. Louise Turcotte (Boston, MA: Beacon Press, 2002).

Wolf, Arthur P., and William H. Durham, eds, *Inbreeding, Incest, and the Incest Taboo: The State of Knowledge at the Turn of the Century* (Stanford, CA: Stanford University Press, 2005).

Wood, Sharon, ed., *Italian Women's Writing* (Manchester: Manchester University Press, 1993).

—— *Italian Women's Writing 1860–1994* (London: Athlone Press, 1995).

Woolf, Virginia, *Moments of Being*, ed. Jeanne Schulkind (London: Chatto & Windus for Sussex University Press, 1986).

Zancan, Marina, *Il doppio itinerario della scrittura: la donna nella tradizione letteraria italiana* (Turin: Einaudi, 1998).

Zecchi, Barbara, 'Rape', in Rinaldina Russell, ed., *The Feminist Encyclopedia of Italian Literature* (Westport, CT: Greenwood Press, 1997), 280–3.

Audio-Visual Sources

Biagi, Enzo, *Film Story: la giustizia*, 1983. Part of the video is available on YouTube <https://www.youtube.com/watch?v=ojXxjHr6MUo> [Accessed 11 August 2016].

Carné, Marcel, dir., *Quai des brumes (Il porto delle nebbie)* (France, 1938).

Duvivier, Julien, dir., *Pépé le Moko (Il bandito della Casbah)* (France, 1937).

Maselli, Francesco, dir., *Lettera aperta a un giornale della sera* (Italy, 1970) <https://www.youtube.com/watch?v=GtCNFMh1gzM> [Accessed 5 June 2016].

Peirce, Kimberly, dir., *Boys Don't Cry* (US, 1999).

Pellegrino, Angelo, and Paola Pace, Excerpt of a reading of the letters of rejection of *L'arte della gioia* <https://www.youtube.com/watch?v=wsctDOZcrWU> [Accessed 5 August 2016].

Rotondo, Loredana, dir., *Processo per stupro* [A Trial for Rape] (RAI, Italy, 1979). <https://www.youtube.com/watch?v=Kj2qyo8xQ8w> [Accessed 31 July 2016].

Vigorita, Manuela, dir., *Goliarda Sapienza, l'arte di una vita* (RAI Educational: 'Vuoti di Memoria', Italy, 2002).

Other Online Sources

'L'arte della gioia', review by *Centro donna Lilith di Latina* <http://www.centro donnalilith.it/images/ L%27arte%20della%20Gioia%20-%20 G.Sapienza.pdf> [Accessed 10 September 2016].

'L'arte della gioia', *Reviews on Amazon* <http://www.amazon.it/Larte-della-gioia-Goliarda-Sapienza/dp/8806199609> [Accessed 10 September 2016].

'Inspired by', *Goliarda Sapienza in Context* <http://goliardasapienza2013.weebly. com/ inspired-by.html> [Accessed 6 September 2016].

Italian Ministry for Justice <https://www.giustizia.it> [Accessed 1 August 2016].

'Premio Letterario Goliarda Sapienza. Racconti dal Carcere' <http://www.raccon tidalcarcere.it/> [Accessed 6 September 2016].

Psychomedia, Ignazio Majore's website <http://www.psychomedia.it/neuro-snp/08-09/maiore.htm> [Accessed 6 September 2016].

Index

Studies in Contemporary Women's Writing

Series Editor

This book series supports the work of the Centre for the Study of Contemporary Women's Writing at the Institute of Modern Languages Research, University of London, by publishing high-quality critical studies of contemporary literature by women. The main focus of the series is literatures written in the languages covered by the Centre – French, German, Italian, Portuguese and the Hispanic languages – but studies of women's writing in English and other languages are also welcome. 'Contemporary' includes literature published after 1968, with a preference for studies of post-1990 texts in any literary genre.

Studies in Contemporary Women's Writing provides a forum for innovative research that explores new trends and issues, showcasing work that makes a stimulating case for studies of new or hitherto neglected authors and texts as well as established authors. Connections are encouraged between literature and the social and political contexts in which it is created and those which have an impact on women's lives and experiences. The goal of the series is to facilitate stimulating comparisons across authors and texts, theories and aesthetics, and cultural and geographical contexts, in this rich field of study.

Proposals are invited for either monographs or edited volumes. The series welcomes single-author studies, thematic analyses and cross-cultural discussions as well as a variety of approaches and theoretical frameworks. Manuscripts should be written in English.

VOL. 1   Gill Rye with Amaleena Damlé (eds)
         Experiment and Experience: Women's Writing in France 2000–2010
         2013. ISBN 978-3-0343-0885-4

VOL. 2   Katie Jones
         Representing Repulsion: The Aesthetics of Disgust in Contemporary
         Women's Writing in French and German
         2013. ISBN 978-3-0343-0862-5

VOL. 3   Natalie Edwards
         Voicing Voluntary Childlessness: Narratives of Non-Mothering in
         French
         2016. ISBN 978-3-0343-1809-9

VOL. 4   Elizabeth Anne Sercombe
         Strange Adventures: Women's Individuation in the Works of Pierrette
         Fleutiaux
         2016. ISBN 978-3-0343-0892-2

VOL. 5   Rosie MacLachlan
         Nina Bouraoui, Autofiction and the Search for Selfhood
         2016. ISBN 978-3-0343-1847-1

VOL. 6   Petra M. Bagley, Francesca Calamita and Kathryn Robson (eds)
         Starvation, Food Obsession and Identity: Eating Disorders in
         Contemporary Women's Writing
         2018. ISBN 978-3-0343-2200-3

VOL. 7   Alberica Bazzoni
         Writing for Freedom: Body, Identity and Power in Goliarda Sapienza's
         Narrative
         2018. ISBN 978-3-0343-2242-3